OCCUPATIONAL CLINICAL PSYCHOLOGY

OCCUPATIONAL CLINICAL PSYCHOLOGY

Edited by
James S.J. Manuso

PRAEGER

PRAEGER SPECIAL STUDIES • PRAEGER SCIENTIFIC

Library of Congress Cataloging in Publication Data

Main entry under title:

Occupational clinical psychology.

Includes bibliographies.
1. Psychology, Industrial—Addresses, essays, lectures. 2. Employee counseling—Addresses, essays, lectures. 3. Employee assistance programs—Addresses, essays, lectures. 4. Clinical psychology—Addresses, essays, lectures. I. Manuso, James S.J., 1948- . [DNLM: 1. Psychology, Industrial. 2. Psychology, Clinical. WA 495 014]
HF5548.025 1983 158.7 82-19065
ISBN 0-03-059006-X

Published in 1983 by Praeger Publishers
CBS Educational and Professional Publishing
a Division of CBS Inc.

3456789 052 9876543

Printed in the United States of America

DEDICATION

This book is dedicated to my parents: to my mother, Eleanor, whose human spirit and love of life prompted my professional interests in psychology, to my father, John, whose dedication and commitment to organizational life spurred my interests in the occupational arena, and to their love and lives together!

Preface

In 1975, I coined the term, "occupational clinical psychology," to designate the application of clinical psychological skills in organizational settings with the aim of facilitating individual and group change processes in order to enhance individual and organizational effectiveness and efficiency. Although there was a history in elements of what has come to be this field, I felt very much alone in my work. Hired as the clinical psychologist of the Equitable Life Assurance Society of the United States in 1974, I represented the genesis of nearly two decades of attention to occupational clinical psychological issues at the Equitable. In its earliest attention to the "troubled employee," the Equitable started an alcoholism program under the direction of Dr. Luther A. Cloud. The focus broadened to include substance abusers and, finally, to address all psychological concerns of employees in an in-house counseling program. This began the odyssey of novel clinical psychology work in corporations, which this volume will examine in part.

At the Equitable, my role was to enhance psychological functioning on the part of troubled employees. Dr. Leon Warshaw, the Corporate medical director, and the director of the health center, Dr. Robert S. Graham, were both committed to the ideal of offering comprehensive health services to employees, and they directed significant corporate resources to this end. In essence, a small community "hospital" was generated to meet the needs of corporate employee health. It was my privilege to offer the psychological component of this wide array of services.

Throughout the years, a significant learning process was permitted me. In particular, the importance of achieving a balance between straight clinical work and the enhancement of managerial and organizational effectiveness became paramount. There were early mistakes. I clearly remember the pride with which I presented a number of personnel managers the "stress barometer," which was guaranteed to pinpoint areas in the organization where stress levels, as measured through 17 variables, were abnormally high. Management cringed at the thought of yet another effectiveness criterion by which they would be judged. Perhaps this instrument's time is yet to come!

My early work at the Equitable involved direct clinical interventions. I was privy to a wide variety of organizational secrets and came to know the corporation through the eyes of a multitude of its citizens. The degrees of pathology encountered were vast: from the mild situational anxiety reaction to the full-blown schizophrenic episode. I worked hard to earn the trust of my new colleagues and to encourage their free use of this new resource, the occupational clinical psychologist.

My attempts to demonstrate the effectiveness of clinical psychology techniques in organizations were not in vain. In 1975, I was asked to address a number of managers on the topic of stress. Shortly thereafter, I was asked to examine what differentiates the "new employee" from his or her predecessors, in order to assist managers in managing this group better.

In addition, I was asked to train managers in working with job-abolished employees. I also worked with the employees whose jobs were abolished and came to learn more of the potential contributions of occupational clinical psychology. Over the years, the corporation has called upon me to address individual manager-employee relations questions, employee change issues, affirmative action enhancement through psychological approaches, and stress management workshops, along with providing advice on how to facilitate employee relocations. Indeed, as the corporation felt served, it expanded the roles it asked me to undertake.

Struggles for additional resources in an organization are continuous. The occupational clinical psychologist is another actor in the resource allocation process. For my own part, I was able to build an organization based on clinical psychology interns and, eventually, hired staff and consultants. Such a metamorphosis is addressed in my chapter in this book.

During the time when I was active in formulating the foundations for occupational clinical psychology, the field was advancing significantly. The concern for managing stress prompted my doctoral research at the Equitable and resolved into my founding the industry's first in-house biofeedback laboratory at the Equitable in 1975. Direct cost-benefit analyses pointed out the efficacy of this and related interventions. Support for other novel approaches grew. The Washington Business Group on Health, the New York Occupational Psychiatry Group, the Occupational Clinical Professions Group, and the Occupational Clinical Psychology Committee of the New York State Psychological Association reflected this growth and concern with occupational interventions.

The American Psychological Association, the American Psychiatric Association, the American Society for Personnel Administration, the American Society for Training Directors, and a variety of others began to actively promote occupational interventions on the parts of their memberships. Journals such as the *Kemps Journal of Occupational Medicine* stepped up its publication rate of articles by psychologists.

The primary credit for the early development of this field goes, of course, to Dr. Harry Levinson. It was Harry, along with people like Dr. Arthur Weider, one of the first employee counseling program directors, who were the loners in a field dominated by psychiatrists in corporations and social workers in unions. It was these pathfinders who helped those of us who came later to, first, find a place and, second, to shred out variations within the field.

Occupational clinical psychology is an embryonic field. It calls for the attention of clinical psychologists who are willing to expand their definition of "client." Because relatively little has been done, it is relatively easy to do something new and different in this field. And it is a field consistent with the health needs of our nation. Health systems costs in the United States, now approximately 10 percent of gross national product, are more costly than the benefits they are intended to generate. In part, this is due to the fact that Americans are dying from the degenerative diseases as never before in history. This health revolution presents the behavioral scientist with a rare opportunity. Because the majority of the degenerative diseases are behaviorally generated, the clinical psychologist is in the unique position of contributing to the amelioration of these conditions and, therefore, will be able to make major contributions to Western society, particularly through its large organizations, where increasing numbers of people live, work, and play.

Although occupational clinical psychology is not today a "Klondike," it is a growing field requiring appropriate attention. It is my hope that the reader will become stimulated by the vast array of practices and potentialities within occupational clinical psychology and will therefore dedicate himself or herself to this field. The rewards are significant. The calling is for the best, both clinically and organizationally. The impacts psychology may have can only be judged by the future. Let us build a sorely needed branch of psychology!

Contents

Introduction

Today, the majority of clinical psychologists engage in a fairly well defined set of professional behaviors. First, they are diagnosticians and treatment professionals. They also serve as educators, teachers, and trainers of those concerned with the management of the engagement with human behavior. Finally, they are testers and researchers, attempting to uncover elements of behavior in order to predict and control it. This latter role is that of theoretician.

Today, the interaction between the psychologist and the large corporation demands of the occupational clinical psychologist a variety of roles (e.g., public relations expert, employee behavior consultant, health policy maker, program developer, and manager), some of which differ from those inherent in the clinical psychologist's typical role. The occupational clinician lives in a different world. Yes, there is research, but the focus is very different. Behavioral medical interventions in employed, "captive" populations is different. Executives tend to use the occupational clinician as advisor for information on how to predict and control individual and group employee behavior. In this sense, the teacher role of the occupational clinician is to advise employees, managers, and executives alike in better self-management and departmental management strategies. As an employee in a large hierarchy, the occupational clinician is also subject to the political vicissitudes of organizational experience. Relationships with professional colleagues will be more extensive and go beyond the bounds of psychology. The occupational clinician is in a fortunate position to relate and coordinate with attorneys, physicians and other health professionals, middle to senior level executives, economists, sociologists engaged in organizational research, investment professionals concerned with the economic impact of health futures, actuaries devoted to the prediction of various health behaviors, and human resources professionals in the areas of benefits, employee relations, and hiring, to say nothing of the equal employment opportunity and social performance employees. Organizational life is professionally enhancing in a variety of ways for the occupational clinical psychologist.

Clinical psychologists can and do direct their attention to occupational clinical psychological issues. Their skills in testing and research, in teaching, and in diagnosis and treatment will continue to find need for their attention. The new roles of the psychologist in the occupational clinical area do relate closely to those aspects of clinical training that suit him or her to this work. The rewards are equal and superior in a variety of respects. The future of occupational clinical psychology will witness the massive application of behavioral medical principles in large populations, such as schools, worksites, and governmental organizations. Psychologists will be called upon to treat physical disorders using their unique skills. The psychologists will also be asked to function more as management consultants, as the behavioral aspects of jobs come to be better understood. As the science of organization management evolves, so too will this diversified role of the occupational clinical psychologist. Clinical skills will continue to be mandatory in order for the professional to best meet these complex, system-based organizational needs. The focus of work will continue to include both individuals and groups in complex behavioral interstices. The teaching role of the psychologist—in terms of the popular media, captive population, and professional colleagues—will need to be tapped in order to better train psychologists for this field.

Although much of the developmental work needs to be done by the universities, and perhaps the medical schools, large corporations should, in turn, like universities and the government, host advanced professional internships in all relevant disciplines. Thanks in part to the progressive management of the Equitable Life Assurance Society of the United States, the first internship in occupational clinical psychology began at the Equitable in 1976. This was followed, in 1979, by an experiment at the Wells Fargo Bank in San Francisco, California. At the time of this writing, there appears to be much demand for such internships, but relatively few sites are available. Major universities should extend the relationship between their clinical psychology professionals and local managements in such a way as to encourage this development.

SECTION ONE

History and Present Context

This history of occupational clinical psychology is quite short. Since World War II, clinical psychology has become more interested in the applied end of practice, while continuing its vital work in psychological testing and assessments, experimentation, and the development of theory. From this time, industrial/organizational psychology finds its beginning. Now there is growing an infusion of the clinical and industrial/organizational branches of psychology into occupational clinical psychology. Many of the early "industrial psychologists" were, in fact, clinicians. Through a variety of complex relationships between industry, government, and the array of clinical providers, there has developed the need for occupational clinical psychology. In addition, the personnel issues facing our nation's leaders in the 1980s will necessitate the assistance of occupational clinical psychology to a much greater degree than has ever been possible before.

Already established in large organizations are corporate medical departments and industrial/organizational psychologists. Occupational clinical psychologists may find themselves working in such departments or with professionals related to these disciplines. This section will examine the short history of occupational clinical psychology as seen, somewhat anecdotally, through the eyes of one of its founders, Harry Levinson. Dr. Levinson's chapter, "Clinical Psychology in Organizational Practice," charts the beginnings of occupational clinical psychology from a corporate focus on the behavioral antecedents and determinants of the "three A's": absenteeism, alcoholism, and accidents. Dr. Levinson discusses his concern regarding the clinical naiveté of proported experts in occupational settings. The famous Menninger Foundation seminars on the psychological aspects of leadership and management are reviewed. Dr. Levinson's organizational experience is hard-earned, and his extended immersion in the Kansas Power and Light Company in a "clinical anthropological vein" is highlighted. Issues pertaining to the application of clinical psychological methods in organizations, the need for an organizational diagnostic method and its development, and the intricacies of clinical consultations in business and industry grew out of this early experience. Issues of health enhancement, behavior-role fit, and increasing the effectiveness of organizations are cited by Dr. Levinson as the underpinnings of the calling for practitioners to the field of occupational clinical psychology.

In his chapter, "Personnel Policies for the 1980s," Jerome M. Rosow charts the labor force changes of the past decade, including the proliferation of white collar jobs, the decline in unionism, and the movement of women into the work force in the light of how these developments will influence the future.

In particular, the coming shortage of youth, the middle-age boom, the increasing role of women, and the resultant competition for desirable jobs, along with an increasing employment of older workers will require creative responses on the part of management. These trends will surely have a profound influence on the scope of practice of the occupational clinical psychologist, especially in the areas of health enhancement, new management work styles, and a variety of quality-of-work-life issues.

Finally, two already existing areas of "clinical" professional practice in corporations must be understood in order to develop further the field of occupational clinical psychology. These are the corporate medical department and the field of industrial/organizational psychology. Dr. Robert S. Graham, in his chapter, "The Corporate Medical Department," outlines the history of occupational health programs from the Civil War to the present. Interestingly, health professionals appear to experience periods of greatest growth during epochs of war and economic strife. Occupational medicine is no different in this regard. The increasing comprehensiveness of occupational medicine and its evolution from a sickness orientation to a wellness orientation provide significant opportunities for the occupational clinical psychologists for interaction and the development of new behavioral-medical programs for employees. Because occupational clinical psychologists often are housed within corporate medical departments, these organizations must be well understood. Health evaluation, health education, environmental health, rehabilitation, and a variety of preventive strategies being launched by the modern corporate medical department call for the attention of occupational clinical psychologists. The Equitable Wellness Program is examined, and new programs, such as those attending to the health needs of special populations and the development of new "personal concerns," are presented.

Another, closely allied, discipline is that of industrial/organizational psychology. Dr. Henry Morgan, in his chapter, "Clinical Aspects of Industrial/Organizational Psychology," reviews the history and development of industrial/organizational psychology, pointing out its current applications. Many of these are "ripe" for clinical attention. In addition, the opportunities for collaboration with industrial/organizational psychologists are significant. Because most clinicians do not have an appreciation for the needs of the organizational sector, the sophisticated industrial/organizational psychologist can be a meaningful ally. In addition, industrial organizational psychologists have long had a foothold in industry, thereby adding credibility to the embryonic role of the clinical psychologist. Because many industrial/organizational psychologists are interested in clinical interventions, coparticipation projects should be initiated.

This section will give the reader a suitable grounding in the historical antecedence of occupational clinical psychology and will review some of the contemporary problems giving rise to the need for a better-integrated occupational clinical psychology. The corporate medical department and industrial/organizational psychology, two allies for occupational clinical psychology, should certainly receive attention.

1 Clinical Psychology in Organizational Practice

Harry Levinson, Ph.D.

In 1954 when I joined the staff of the Menninger Foundation, I was asked by Dr. William C. Menninger to undertake a study of the extent and expression of emotional stress in business and industry. I undertook an 18-month, 60,000 mile traveling survey of policies, practices, methods, concerns, staffing, and foci in business and industrial organizations with respect to these issues. During that journey, I was dismayed that what we, as clinical psychologists, thought we had to know about the motivation of people for therapeutic effort was almost totally unknown in management. Here and there there were a few psychiatrists working in business organizations—Dr. Ralph Collins at Eastman Kodak, Dr. Fred Dersheimer at Du Pont, Dr. Walter Woodward at American Cyanamid, and Dr. Lydia Giberson at Metropolitan Life Insurance Company—and occasionally in one or another organization for a short period of time, but their contributions were limited to brief psychotherapy carried on as a function of the medical department.

During World War II psychiatrists had served Brooklyn Union Gas Company (Dr. Matthew Brody) and General Motors (Dr. Leonard Himler). No clinical psychologists were in evidence in such embryonic organizational mental health programs. At Caterpillar Tractor Company in Peoria, Illinois, Dr. Arthur Weider headed an in-house counseling unit, but his was the lone psychological voice in the organizational wilderness.

Earlier, beginning in 1938, Dr. Hyman Meltzer had become personnel director of the Orchard Paper Company in St. Louis and subsequently served as a consultant to that organization. However, few other clinical psychologists to my knowledge were involved in such roles. The single pioneering consulting firm was that of Rohrer, Hibler and Replogle.

True, during World War II clinical psychology had found its metier. The military services made extensive use of clinical psychologists, but few of them seemed to move into business and industry. While there was much formal testing for selection, and external psychological consultation grew, in particular the industrial/organizational kind, only a few consultants followed the Rohrer, Hibler and Replogle model. The embryonic work in management development was largely a function of industrial/organizational psychologists and remains so today with the addition of people trained in organization development. Some of the latter are psychologists, but few of them are clinically trained. While there is now a considerable amount of counseling in many organizations, much of this is carried on by people who also are not clinically trained.

The two pioneering counseling programs were at the Hawthorne plant of Western Electric in Chicago and at the Prudential Insurance Company in Newark. The Hawthorne counseling program followed on the classical study of Roethlisberger and Dickson (1940). It made use of nonprofessional counselors trained in the Rogerian method who were available to employees on the plant floor. The Prudential unit was headed by Dr. John Bromer and provided counseling services in a formally established counseling unit. Both of these programs later were phased out, the first because it could not demonstrate its usefulness statistically, being isolated from the rest of the organization by its canon of confidentiality. That rule was so strictly kept that the program had little to defend itself with when management raised questions. The Prudential program was terminated as a product of conflict between the counseling unit and the medical department when the latter wanted to exert its authority (Levinson, 1956).

In 1956 I established, and then for 14 years directed, the Division of Industrial Mental Health at the Menninger Foundation. Following on the original focus of that work, Dr. Menninger and I made a case for emotional first-aid stations in industry (Levinson and Menninger, 1954). Following my firsthand study of what was going on in industry, Dr. Menninger and I focused on the three A's—absenteeism, alcoholism, and accidents. We cited facts and figures to show that these were significantly a product of psychological stress and that companies would do well to have in-house services to help cope with such stresses, which in turn would reduce these symptoms. Subsequently, in reviewing alcoholism treatment programs it was apparent that most of these were carried on by Alcoholics Anonymous (AA), usually through industrial medical departments (Levinson, 1957). The then outstanding program at University Hospital in New York was a comprehensive clinical service, which served a number of companies in New York City (Levinson, 1955). However, clinical psychologists were not conspicious in any of those efforts.

I was dismayed by the discovery that organizations employing up to a million people were operating on assumptions about motivation that had little validity from a clinical point of view, and particularly from my own psychoanalytic point of view. As a result, I developed a series of week-long seminars for executives and for occupational physicians. In these seminars my intention was to educate executives from a psychoanalytic base about psychological aspects of leadership and management. Such an orientation would also help them to better understand what constituted stress and ways of managing in organizations that might alleviate, ameliorate, or even anticipate those events that precipitated stress.

The first of these seminars was undertaken in January 1956 in a conference room that actually was the attic of a former barn on the Menninger Foundation grounds. When the week was over, the janitor brought me the rolls of kraft paper that had covered the tables of the conference room. He thought I would be interested in translating the hieroglyphics the executives left behind.

The executive seminars grew in interest, popularity, and refinement. I now carry them on as a function of the Levinson Institute. We do 11 such public seminars each year, together with condensations and other variations in organizations.

The seminars for occupational physicians were directed to many of the same kinds of issues. Particularly, they were to help physicians understand the psychological aspects of illness and the kinds of pressures and stresses in organizations. These sessions included opportunities for the physician participants to interview patients in local mental health clinics under the supervision of the psychiatrists who were then in charge of those clinics.

The seminars took on another focus after I left Topeka, Kansas. When I moved to Cambridge, Massachusetts, I dropped the seminars for occupational physicians because of the limits of facilities and resources.

Meanwhile, I had begun to try to understand what was going on in organizations. Having had little organizational experience before I took on this task, it was necessary to become knowledgeable about business and industry. To do that, under a grant from the Rockefeller Brothers Fund, I established a team that included two other psychologists, a sociologist, and a psychiatrist. Three of us on that team spent the better part of the next two years becoming immersed in the Kansas Power and Light Company in a clinical anthropological way. We entered the organization without a formal research design to get familiar with the working lives of employees and managers. We interviewed some 850 people, accompanied them in their work, and attended their meetings. We made three extended trips over the company property, which covered two-thirds of the state of Kansas. Out of that came *Men, Management and Mental Health* (Levinson et al., 1962).

That study made apparent that there were many data in industrial/organizational research reports, but there was no information. By this I mean that there was no such concept in industrial/organizational psychology as an intervention of choice. There were generalizations, usually drawn from small samples with low correlations. Presumably, these generalizations could be applied to organizations. In fact, their authors advocated doing so, and they are the stuff of industrial/organizational textbooks. However, generalizations that apply to everybody in general apply to nobody in particular.

This limitation then raised the question of the clinical psychological method and its application in organizations. That is, if one were to intervene in an organization as one might have to intervene in an individual therapeutic relationship, then one would need to have sufficient theory to undertake a specific intervention, at a given point in time, for a defined problem, under a given set of circumstances. In short, the method or technique or principle had to be specifically appropriate to the problem at hand and logically defensible.

There was no such guided method in the industrial/organizational literature. That meant that as a clinician I had found myself in the position of having to integrate a significant body of industrial/organizational literature into a mode of understanding that would make sense to me. This created the need for a series of papers, many of them in the *Harvard Business Review,* in turn followed by a series of books. My article, "What Killed Bob Lyons?" (Levinson, 1963), an introduction to psychoanalytic theory, became one of the *Harvard Business Review* "classics," having sold more than 45,000 reprints.

There followed a series of papers on topics having to do with problems in business and industry that touched on issues that, for the most part, had not been discussed previously in that literature. Such concerns as problems in family businesses, management by guilt, psychological aspects of mergers, executive suicide, failures in the choice of chief executives and successors, and others brought clinical insights into managerial problems and tasks. As a consequence, they filled a need that could not be filled by traditional industrial/organizational psychology. Even today people without a clinical background write on performance appraisal without recognizing that most performance appraisal fails because it does not take into account unconscious guilt. By failing to take such phenomena into account, the recommended practices are doomed to repeated failure.

The second problem that I confronted as a product of the Kansas Power and Light Company study compelled a shift in my thinking. I had begun my work in organizations by looking at symptoms and recommending that there be internal facilities and services for coping with those symptoms and the strains that precipitated them. However, as experience in the Kansas Power and Light Company began to demonstrate, it became apparent that when an organization is managed well—that is, for its own perpetuation—then it is good for the people in it. To manage for perpetuation means that one must make the best use of available human resources and focus on the long-term. When, however, organizations are managed expediently, then that is not good either for the organization or for the people in it. To manage an organization expediently means to focus on the short-term, and that in turn means that people will be manipulated in whatever ways are necessary to attain short-term results. As a result, frequently they will be put under undue stress, exploited in the interest of the narrow goal, and otherwise be treated as instruments to be utilized by managers in their own self-interest. Working in expedient situations then will have a negative impact on the self-images of the people who are involved. This kind of experience would, consequently, arouse their hostility, which frequently, particularly among conscientious people, would be self-directed and result in accidents, absenteeism, and alcoholism.

Thus, it is clear that if one were to have a preventive and health-maintaining effect on an organization, one would need a method for studying, diagnosing, and intervening into organizations as systems of people and as work organizations. Therefore, the clinical psychologist, who would be an organizational consultant, required a diagnostic method akin to those methods he or she used in dealing with individual clients and patients. The clinician-consultant would need some way of focusing systematically on the problems of an organization that would take into account its history, its crises, its value system, its characteristic modes of responding to stresses, its demographics, its communication processes, and many other aspects of organizational functioning—all of which would have to be understood if one were to recognize the nature of the problems that the organization faced and systematically evolve a method for dealing with them. This need led to the writing of *Organizational Diagnosis* (Levinson, 1972).

This diagnostic method makes it possible for clinicians of whatever orientation to examine their own organizations or others in which they are consulting and to bring to bear inferences and interpretations drawn from their own frame of reference, which makes clinical sense of the facts they have gathered.

Subsequently, I evolved a seminar on that topic when I went to the Harvard Business School in 1968. I continue that seminar as a function of the Harvard Medical School and the Harvard Graduate School of Education.

The third activity that grew out of the first two from my Kansas Power and Light Company experience was consultation in business and industry. For the most part this has involved working with top managements, particularly of major corporations, in long-term relationships, usually about long-term organizational change problems, high level selection issues, group cohesion and conflict resolution efforts, and individual consultation with individual executives on personal and managerial problems. In addition, consultation also has involved organizational diagnosis and, from time to time, dealing with major organizational crises, such as staff production actions, relocations, etc.

One of the reoccurring contemporary consultation issues is the need on the part of organizations to try to understand why efforts at improving the quality of work life fail. Frequently, they fail because the consultants do not do a comprehensive diagnosis to pinpoint what kinds of interventions must be undertaken with groups and plants, as contrasted with addressing them all with the same set of techniques. Their orientations toward dealing with individuals and groups frequently fail to take into account the demographics and subcultures of the organization and the management of aggression. In short, they operate without either a theory of personality or a diagnostic method.

Meantime, beginning in the mid-1970s and antedated by my books *Emotional Health in the World of Work* (Levinson, 1964) and *Executive Stress* (Levinson, 1970), concern with stress in organizations began to arise. Suddenly, everybody was in the stress relief business. Much of this work was carried on by people who had no clinical training or experience. But many clinical psychologists began to be involved in stress relief programs in organizations, and, even more important, in employee assistance programs. The latter at last had begun to realize the position I had taken in 1954.

The new organization development movement became very much involved in team building and data-based interventions, survey research, and similar activities. Most of this work, however, was, and still is, devoid of a theory of personality and of clinical insights. In fact, clinicians who began to get involved in T-groups and organization development often seemed to lose their clinical identity and to act as if they had no clinical background, sometimes becoming divorced entirely from clinical orientation and practice.

These efforts have created a new atmosphere within which growing numbers of clinical psychologists are being drawn into business and industry as contributors to the well-being of people as employees, to the managerial understanding of motivation and behavior, to management development and training, and to the thinking of people at significant executive levels. While the numbers are yet relatively small, the range of activities as reflected in this volume is an indication of the degree to which clinical psychology has begun to find its role and contribution in the organizational setting. Here especially, its function is, as I had hoped a number of years ago, to keep well people functioning well, to prevent symptoms and illness, to provide immediate relief when these occur, and to contribute significantly to the management of organizations.

As organizations change ever more rapidly, it will become increasingly necessary to have clearer descriptions of the behavior required in various kinds of roles. That in turn will make it necessary to have a better grasp of the characteristic behavior of individuals, so that individuals in turn may be more accurately and adequately fitted to those roles. The rapidity with which behavior will change in a given role, with changes in the marketplace, will mean that managers, in particular, will be moving in and out of roles, just as football players are moved in and out of their specific positions. This demand for more accurate knowledge and understanding of individuals and groups of individuals, so that they may be better chosen to fit and carry out specific activities, will increase the demand for clinical psychological skills.

It is the last that will be the frontier for clinical psychologists working in organizations. The reason is very simple. If a clinical psychologist would make a significant contribution to his or her host organization and to the people in it, then the contribution will be most effective when it helps organizations function well. Under such circumstances, such a psychologist would truly be an agent of prevention and a promoter of well-being.

REFERENCES

Levinson, H. 1955. "Consultation Clinic for Alcoholism." *Menninger Quarterly* 9(1):14–20.

———. 1956. "Employee Counseling in Industry." *Bulletin of the Menninger Clinic* 20(2):76–84.

———. 1957. "Alcoholism in Industry." *Menninger Quarterly* 11(3A):1–20.

———. 1963. "What Killed Bob Lyons?" *Harvard Business Review* 41(1): 127–44.

———. 1964. *Emotional Health In the World of Work.* New York: Harper & Row.

———. 1970. *Executive Stress.* New York: Harper & Row.

———. 1972. *Organizational Diagnosis.* Cambridge, Mass.: Harvard University Press.

Levinson, H. and W.C. Menninger. 1954. "The Machine That Made Pop." *Menninger Quarterly* 8(2):20–26.

Levinson, H., Price, C.R., Munden, K.J., Mandl, H.J., and Solley, C.M. 1962. *Men, Management and Mental Health.* Cambridge, Mass.: Harvard University Press.

Menninger, W.C. and H. Levinson. 1954. "Industrial Mental Health: Observations and Perspectives." *Menninger Quarterly* 8(3):1–13.

Roethlisberger, F. and W.J. Dickson. 1940. *Management and the Worker.* Cambridge, Mass.: Harvard University Press.

2 Personnel Policies for the 1980s

Jerome M. Rosow

THE CHANGING NATURE OF THE WORK FORCE

During the decade of the 1970s, we witnessed significant changes in the U.S. labor force. Five of these changes were reasonably well predicted from the demographic material at hand, but three others presented surprises and changes that were grossly underestimated in nearly every responsible forecast.

Labor Force Changes In the Past Decade

Significant changes in the U.S. labor force were:

1. *A marked shift in employment from blue collar to white collar jobs,* particularly professional, technical and clerical positions. This shift was particularly marked among nonwhite workers.

2. *A near doubling in the governmental share of the labor force.* However, this rate of growth declined in the mid-1970s, and the outlook is clouded by Proposition 13 attitudes.

3. *Geographic shifts in the distribution of employment,* with a move away from eastern and midwestern industrial regions. The fastest growing regions were the South, Southwest, and to a lesser extent, the West Coast. New plants have sprung up in Texas, Louisiana, Florida, Arizona, and Colorado. The sunbelt outshone the snowbelt.

4. *A decline in private sector unionism,* offset in part by the growth of public sector unions. Twenty-five years ago, unions represented 34 percent of the nonagricultural labor force; now it hovers near 25 percent.

5. *An influx of "illegal aliens,"* primarily from Mexico and Latin America, representing a new force in the labor market. Experts claim there has been an influx of perhaps six million workers. These workers have been a major source of supply for low-skilled, low-wage jobs.

Three additional very important developments were grossly underestimated in nearly every forecast:

1. *The massive movement of women into the work force,* especially the dramatic rise in the participation of younger women.

2. *The growth in the number of younger workers.* This trend was underestimated despite its dependence on demographic factors. The reasons relate to the difficulties of forecasting the proportions of youngsters going to school, the entry of young women, and the influx of illegal young immigrants.

3. *The marked decline in the participation of older men.* Men in the prime age cohort 54 to 65 declined from 91 percent participation in 1947 to 75 percent in 1977—a drop of 16 percent.

Against this broad canvas of the changing U.S. labor force, what can we reasonably forecast for the decade ahead? Of course, this national panoramic view may not square with the "internal labor market" behavior of the individual firm. We foresee five major shifts.

The Coming Shortage of Youth

Because of the low birth rate of the 1960s, the absolute number of young workers is expected to fall sharply in the 1980s. The absolute decline will exceed one million persons between the ages of 16 to 24, a reduction of *six percentage* points. With relatively few workers, the age-earnings profile may twist in favor of the young. The problems of teen-age and youth unemployment will diminish but not in direct proportion with regard to black teen-age youth, where the birth rate has not declined as sharply. The only possible factor that could ameliorate the coming shortage of youth would be a marked increase in young immigrants, legal or illegal.

Although the 1980s will experience a decline in the overall youth population, it will be concentrated among white youth. Overall, the 16 to 24 year old group will drop by 2.8 million in the period 1980-85, whereas the nonwhite population will hold steady at 5.8 million. Thus the nonwhites as a percent of total 16 to 24 year olds will rise from 15.5 percent (1980) to 16.8 percent (1985) and 18.3 percent (1990). The same factors apply to the younger 16 to 19 year olds.

Middle Age Bulge or Talent Boom?

Perhaps one of the most remarkable factors in the decade ahead will be the demographic bunching of the prime-age work force in the 25 to 44 age bracket. In 1975, there were 39 million workers in this age bracket, and by 1990 there will be 60.5 million, an extraordinary jump of 55 percent. Their share of the total labor force will be 52 percent, an *increase of ten points* over 1975. These are the individuals who are typically competing for promotions, professional recognition, and supervisory responsibilities.

We can anticipate *intense competition* for promotions, severe disappointments, and increased pressure on the management/development training and pay policies in most work organizations. This age cohort suffered the same bottleneck problem when they were competing for a share of college admission. Now, in their mid-careers, this will translate into a bottleneck situation in the normal flow upward in the organization. Some of the major personnel and management problems of the 1980s will revolve around this critical group in the work force.

The Increasing Role of Women

The upward trend in the labor force participation of women is expected to continue, according to all forecasts. Those sectors of the economy that are more prone to favor women are most likely to grow, which in turn will create demand pressures. At the same time, the increased participation of women may well be accompanied by a greater diffusion across the work force and a rising female share in more occupations and industries. It is predicted that by 1990, 61 percent of all women in the United States will be working, matching the present level of participation in Sweden.

Competition for Desirable Jobs

The competition for the better jobs will be intensified by the growing role of women in traditional male occupations and by continued equal opportunity pressures. The rise in qualified black and women workers, some of whom may enjoy favored treatment, will create new competitive forces. Thus, the force of a sharp rise in the absolute numbers of middle-aged, talented workers combined with the entry of women and minorities could lead to a doubling of the competition for the better jobs.

Increased Employment of Older Workers

Although this is a speculative shift, the indications are that it will certainly occur by 1990. In fact, the raising of the mandatory retirement age to 70 is producing shifts in the labor force trends. By the end of the next decade, employers will be more motivated to attract and retain older workers than ever before. This will necessitate a loosening of social security restrictions, more flexible working arrangements for older people (hours, weeks, and months), phased/gradual or tapered retirements, job redesign to accommodate physical and psychological abilities and needs, and a general set of personnel policies that are more responsive to the older character of the labor force. This also represents a great area for personnel management experiments and change, in anticipation of the coming age shift.

3 The Corporate Medical Department: History of the Development of Occupational Health Programs and an Overview of the Future

Robert S. Graham, M.D.

Most of the earliest occupational medical activities in the United States began during time of war. The Civil War required increased productivity not previously demanded. Safety precautions were almost unknown, and disabling accidents occurred to the degree that production was threatened. Workplaces were frequently unsanitary and hazardous to health, contributing to a high incidence of employee absence for illness.

The first real occupational health efforts occurred in the United States as business and industry expanded dramatically early in the twentieth century, when it worked to arm the world just prior to World War I. Occupational medicine during that period began to be recognized as a means of keeping people well and on the job. Preventive medicine and periodic health examinations became a part of the new health effort. The growth of occupational programs after World War I was modest. Programs were largely oriented toward accident prevention and first-aid treatment of on-the-job accidents.

The next period of marked expansion was during World War II. Occupational medical departments began to develop both clinical and occupational medicine programs with strong emphasis on accident and illness prevention, early detection of disease and referral for intervention, toxicology, epidemiology, and industrial hygiene. The primary objective throughout the period from the Civil War through World War II was conservation of manpower—just as it is today.

During the 1950s, occupational medicine became a symbol of the concern and worth with which a company regarded its employees. To the employee it became still another benefit provided by a good employer. Periodic health evaluations, alcoholism programs, health education, emotional health counseling at the worksite were developed, and a marked increase in clinical services offered at work occurred.

Further expansion was experienced in the 1960s. Many people now began to regard medical services on the job as a "right." It was believed by some that a good medical department helped attract and retain employees. Inner-city people, minorities, women, and others perceived to have special health needs were now entering the work force. A few companies expanded their medical department functions to include a wide range of clinical services. Very few began to provide primary care. Preemployment (by now called "preplacement") examinations tended to become more extensive, including such things as urine testing for drugs, sickle cell testing, serology, etc. Very few of these expensive and time-consuming procedures resulted in better placement of employees or in a healthier work population. And no significant conservation of benefits funds occurred. But it did give some occupational physicians and managers the self-assurance that they were "doing something" necessitated by the times. Probably the most dramatic changes of the 1960s and early 1970s were prompted by legislation that had as its purpose safe and healthful workplaces and an end to discrimination in employment because of perceived or actual handicaps. The Occupational Safety and Health Act, the Toxic Substances Control Act, and the Employment of the Handicapped Act (Section 503) have gone far to stimulate business and industry to make the changes needed to accomplish the goals of legislation. Environmental health services arising from concern over the chronic health effects of long-term exposures to low levels of chemical, radiation, and physical agents continued to develop and expand.

The 1970s saw a marked increase in interest in the emotional condition of employees and the effects of change and stress on health and productivity. Employee assistance programs providing alcoholism and other substance abuse programs, counseling services, and stress management began to be a major focus in some employee health programs.

Another concern of the 1970s was the dramatically escalating costs of health care and health-related benefits. This problem remains in the 1980s. During the 1970s, it caused companies to turn to their medical departments for advice when health benefits for employees were being developed, evaluated, or changed. Departments were asked to monitor the costs and results of health benefits. At the same time, the increasing cost of operating an occupational medical service focused attention on the department itself. What was actually being accomplished having these expensive services? Some progressive occupational medical departments began to question what they were doing and how they were doing it. For instance, the long-term disability roles of a large non-manufacturing company revealed that from 84 to 92 percent of the disabling conditions were chronic degenerative diseases such as heart disease, cancer, stroke, arthritis, depression, and emotional problems related to stress.

Yet most occupational programs were not addressing these problems from a standpoint of prevention. Since the early 1960s, the U.S. Public Health Service has emphasized that infectious and communicable diseases no longer constitute the major health threat to people of the United States. Seventy-five percent of all deaths in the country are due to heart disease, stroke, cancer, accidents and environmental hazards. All of these can be decreased by modification of behavior. They are essentially preventable problems.

However, in spite of the efforts of the Public Health Service and a few others, the major expenditures for health care and research in this country continue to be for other than prevention. Only as the 1970s were drawing to an end did some medical schools and a few major health institutions begin to take note that a major health development was occurring in this country—and largely without them. The era of prevention had arrived. More and more, people demonstrated an interest in their own health and in the management of it. The proliferation of health education materials, the media focus on health subjects, the dramatic growth of exercise programs and of interest in nutrition and behavior modification clearly showed that many people were well ahead of their health professionals in prevention concepts. Yet occupational medical departments with rare exceptions still have not taken a lead in providing services to promote health.

In 1979, the Surgeon General published a report on health promotion and disease prevention called *Healthy People.* This report is a valuable resource in learning of the general state of health of our people today and of its cost. It provides a "blueprint" of planning for effective health care in the future. It is considered one of the most essential documents for study by persons interested in the health of the people of this nation. It is especially important to those concerned with occupational health programs. *Health promotion in the workplace is clearly one of the most effective means of improving the general health of the people of this nation.* It is becoming an essential part of strategy to improve the competitive position of this country in world markets. Increasingly, it is recognized that conservation of manpower through maintaining a healthy work force is a major factor in improving productivity and, therefore, our competitive effort.

Alvin Toffler, the futurist, and others tell us that the industrial revolution is at an end and that industry as we know it will slowly fade away. Certainly, trends in business and industry in the early 1980s appear consistent with that theory. Technology is progressing rapidly. This is particularly true with telecommunications. Telecommunications will allow much of business to be conducted from the home. Corporations will tend to consist of smaller and smaller functioning units, efficiently located and managed through telecommunications, with the repetitive and nonchallenging functions being carried out by computers and robots. Potentially, it could result in more healthy, meaningful, productive, and less stressful lives for many. However, the threatening economic and social climate accompanying the change is creating great stress. As the new era of technology emerges, stress and adjustment problems will continue to increase. This trend provides a principal threat to the public health and state of well-being, and, if not properly managed, it may threaten the continued viability of the United States as a competitive nation in world markets.

OCCUPATIONAL HEALTH PROGRAMS TODAY

In 1979, a report was made by the Occupational Medical Practice Committee of the American Occupational Medical Association entitled, "Scope of Occupational Health Programs and Occupational Medical Practice." It provides a description of recent changes in occupational medicine and clearly outlines the obligations, purposes, goals, and components of occupational health programs. This excellent report indicates the components of the best of occupational health programs at that time. This document lists some 13 components of occupational health programs as essential. They are:

1. Health Evaluation of Employees with a major emphasis on informing the employee of results and when abnormalities are found or referring the employee to the personal physician for further diagnostic procedures and/or treatment. Health evaluations are generally carried out as follows:

   a. Preassignment—to assure that the person can perform the job safely and efficiently without endangering the person's own safety or that of others. This examination should include an emotional assessment as physical evaluation and include:
      - medical history
      - occupational history
      - assessment of organ systems likely to be affected by the assignment, including emotional health
      - evaluation of the description and demands of the job to which assignment is being considered.

   b. Periodic—to review the health status of employees on a regular basis. The current trend is for the frequency and content of the examination to be related to the age, past medical history, family history, and workplace exposure or activities that could affect health.

   c. Postillness or injury—to assure that the employee has recovered sufficiently and is not on a medication that may make the performance of the job a danger to the individual or others.

   d. Termination and retirement—an evaluation to provide the employee with a report of his or her health status and to advise the individual regarding any health problems resulting from the job.

2. Diagnosis and treatment of occupational injuries or illness, including rehabilitiation, depending on the medical facilities available at the workplace.

3. Emergency treatment of nonoccupational injuries or illnesses, including emotional crises occurring while at work within the capacity of the medical department to provide these services. In general, treatment is only palliative, to avoid increased disability or death.

4. Education of employees regarding actual or potential hazards associated with their job or workplace, methods of prevention and early recognition of possible adverse health effects.

5. Evaluation of job activities for use of indicated protective devices such as helmets, earplugs, safety spectacles, respirators, etc.

6. Assistance to management in providing a safe and healthful work environment.

7. Toxicological studies on the short-term and long-term effects of chemical substances used in the workplace on which adequate testing has not been accomplished.

8. Biostatistics and epidemiology where persons at work are experiencing a possible risk to health.

9. Maintenance of occupational medicine records. Privacy and confidentiality is essential.

10. Immunization against possible occupational infection where the employee has a potential hazard and immunization procedures exist.

11. Assistance to management in planning, providing, and evaluating the quality and cost of employee health benefits.

12. Assistance in interpretation and implementation of governmental health and safety regulations.

13. Periodic evaluation of the occupational health program for validity and effectiveness.

Elective components of occupational health programs are as follows:

1. Palliative treatment of disorders to allow completion of the work shift or of disorders for which an employee may not ordinarily consult a physician.
2. Repetitive treatment of nonoccupational conditions prescribed and monitored by the employee's personal physician (physiotherapy, routine injections, etc.).

3. Assistance in rehabilitation of alcohol or drug dependent employees or those with emotional disorders.
4. Health education and counseling (emotional health, hypertension control, diabetes control, obesity, exercise, etc.)
5. Assistance to management in control of illness-related absence from the job.
6. Disaster preparedness planning for the workplace and, where appropriate, the community.
7. Immunization against nonoccupational infectious diseases.

In the report's summary, the committee indicated that "the goal of an occupational health program is to insure a safe and healthful workplace." The committee described its efforts as a compilation of the necessary and important parts of an occupational health program, with the details regarding structure or how each component will function not provided. Individual program structures and functions will, of course, differ, depending on the type of business or industry the occupational health program serves, on the specific needs of the employees, and the medical and health resources of the communities from which the employees come. Most importantly, the structure, content, and detail will vary as technology advances, demographics change, and as industry reorganizes for greater productivity. These elements will also be affected as changes at home and at work become a principal hazard to the health of the worker.

NEW CHALLENGE

Occupational health programs and medicine are expensive today and are rapidly increasing in cost. Such programs and occupational health as a medical specialty can only hope to survive if they are responsive to the needs of management—which are essentially the same as the needs of employees. The search for better and yet cost-containing ways of accomplishing essential health care functions must be ongoing. In some cases, this will mean the contracting out of some services to health organizations that have as their primary business the providing of health and/or environmental services. For certain types of services and programs, the use of community resources may be a more effective way of providing a program. Certainly, use of new technology will be essential. *Awareness of emerging potential health problems, identification of the most effective means of preventing them, and maintenance of a high degree of flexibility are the keys to meeting the challenges to occupational health programs, today and tomorrow.* Adapting to change is just as important to the health professional as to any other member of society. Therefore, the progressive occupational health department must provide the environment and the resources that can help staff members manage themselves effectively as they deal with new problems, concepts, technologies, delivery systems, and populations. Among the new challenges, the following are of particular interest.

The Need for Appropriate Health Services for the "Well"

A health delivery system that provides for the enhancement of health and well-being of clients while stabilizing the demand for medical services, the costs of health care, and the availability of services is the ideal. However, the ideal must be brought to reality if the health of the nation is to improve and the cost of health care is to be stabilized. Dr. Sidney R. Garfield, the "father" of the Kaiser Permanent Health Plan, has proposed a new concept of health care delivery that can accomplish this goal. It is explained in chapter 12 of Chadro's *Health Handbook* (Garfield, 1979). In my opinion this book is a "must" for those interested in health care. Dr. Garfield's chapter provides insight into our present chaotic health care system and the runaway costs it generates.

Before the development of prepaid and health insurance plans and the provision of health services at no cost or minimal cost to the user, only the sick entered the health care system. The well people had other uses for their resources. However, many times those who were sick did not have the means to obtain medical services. Therefore, society demanded that medical services be available to all. This is good. It was accomplished by prepaid and other health insurance plans including medicaid and medicare and provided for medical services at no charge or minimal charge to most all Americans. However, what has occurred is a flood of demand for physician services, much of which is from the well, the "worried well," or the early sick. The demand by this group of clients violates the basic criteria of insurability and floods the system. This results in:

1. The sick having to compete with the well for services and the attention of physicians.

2. Physicians being confronted with a large part of their practice consisting of the well, "worried well," or early sick. Physicians by training deal with specific signs, symptoms, and laboratory findings. The well have only nonspecific complaints and do not fit the pattern. This then requires extensive diagnostic procedures involving all systems of the body. Finally, no specific problem is found, and the patient may be turned away labeled as a neurotic or be given a tranquilizer or some other medication. The result is a dissatisfied patient who will then go to another physician and repeat the process again and again. This results in enormous expenditures for health care (about 10 percent of the gross national product), does nothing to improve the health of the people, and consumes the valuable time of physicians that should be dedicated to care for the sick.

Occupational health departments that provide diagnostic and treatment services for nonoccupation related conditions independent of the employees' personal physicians have had much the same experience as the medical system outside of the occupational field in recent years. As a consequence, where such services are provided, availability of physician time for health services related to occupational needs has been severely limited and the expense of operating these programs has soared without producing much for the company (not even goodwill) or the employees.

As Dr. Garfield points out, what is needed is a new entry into the medical care system. He suggests appropriate "health testing," which will identify the well, the "worried well," the early sick, the acutely sick, and the chronically sick, so that they may be guided into programs that have the potential for their specific health needs. This will have a profound impact on costs. Physician time will be devoted primarily to the acutely ill and, to some extent, to the early ill and chronically ill. Programs for the well and the "worried well," as well as the early sick and chronically sick, are primarily carried out by allied health personnel. Health testing required for this "systemization" of demand is an allied health function and is far more productive and dramatically less costly than the elaborate, costly, nonproductive diagnostic testing that must now frequently be carried out to assure the absence of sickness. This is of significance to occupational health departments or programs. They provide for the employed who essentially are well or "worried well." In order to improve and maintain the health of the work force as well as, in the long term, to reduce the cost of health care benefits, companies are beginning to look at "wellness" programs. This is a new challenge to occupational health programs.

The medical and personal concerns department of the Equitable Life in response to that challenge developed a model for a wellness program that would best suit their needs. This program has now been successfully piloted and is about to be expanded for the Equitable people into some of the sections of the country in which the Equitable has major operating units. The elements of that model are described below.

1. *Objectives:*

   Primary. To provide to working people a program designed for the 1980s, consistent with national health priorities, with a goal of reducing mortality and health benefits costs.

   Secondary.

   a. To enhance the image of the company as an organization of people with mutual interest in individual employee well-being.
   b. To provide a self-managed wellness program that potentially may improve wellness, heighten feelings of well-being, and increase enjoyment of work and leisure time.
   c. To contribute to maintenance of productivity.
   d. To develop a working model of a wellness program that can be reproduced in most any location at modest cost by management.

e. To participate as a socially responsible corporation in an effort by the federal government to encourage the development of wellness programs in the workplace nationally.

2. *Specific Aims:*
   a. To provide each eligible individual with enough information regarding wellness enhancement and its potential rewards to motivate him or her to take the initial step toward self-health management. Each would maintain his or her own medical records.
   b. To make available the means for all eligible individuals to obtain an assessment of their own health hazards and proper counsel. Referral will be made to their own physicians if they are ill or to the appropriate intervention expert if they are "well" but have hazards to health.
   c. To motivate those who have health risk behaviors to modify them successfully and thereby reduce or eliminate the risk.
   d. To provide a program that can be managed by most company units with a minimum amount of time, effort, expense, and corporate assistance.
   e. To utilize good local community resources, which have flexible schedules, effective motivation methods, and programs that can be used by other members of the family, at the member's own expense.
3. *Program Content* (See Figure 3.1):
   a. Screening exam—a biometric examination by paramedical people that provides to the participant needed information with which to complete an automated personal risk questionnaire. This consists of height, weight, blood pressure, and blood chemistry determinations.
   b. Completion of the health hazard appraisal questionnaire plus two additional forms (a personality type profile and a symptom checklist). Throughout, it will be emphasized that this is a wellness program and that it in no way replaces sickness care. All will be encouraged to start or to continue periodic health examinations by their own physicians. The educational program will emphasize that a physician should be consulted if sickness or unexplained symptoms occur.
   c. The health hazard appraisal forms will be sent for computer processing and determination of individual risks.
   d. Each eligible individual will receive a confidential appraisal. Participants will make an appointment with the health educator if there are questions regarding the findings.
   e. The appraisal, the profile, and the symptom checklist will be interpreted by the health educator for the participant (with the spouse

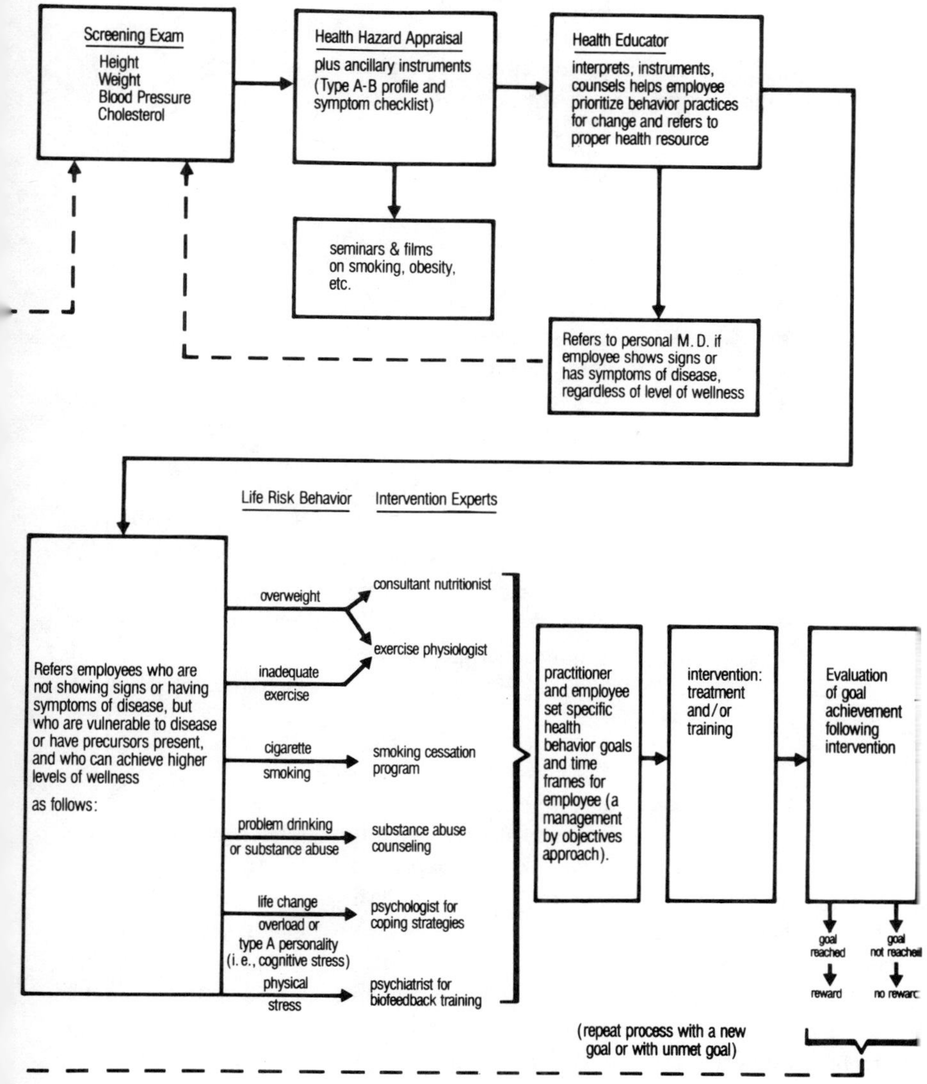

igure 3.1. Flow Chart of The Health Management Program

present when desired). Counseling will be given and indicated referrals made. If there is evidence of sickness, or if the individual is already under treatment for a significant sickness, the patient will be referred to his or her attending physician. If there is no evidence of sickness but a life risk behavior is present, the patient will be referred to the appropriate intervention expert. Life risk behaviors can include any of the following:

- Poor eating habits,
- Inadequate exercise,
- Cigarette smoking,
- Problem drinking and/or substance abuse,
- Carelessness leading to accidents,
- Life change overloads,
- Personality factors creating stress,
- Poor stress management.

f. The participant will obtain an appointment with the intervention expert. At the end of the consultation, specific goals will be agreed on and time frames established. Indicated lifestyle changes will be started.

g. Evaluation of goal achievement will be made by the participant and his practitioner at planned time intervals. If the goal is reached, a reward is given and the process may be repeated with a new goal. If the goal is not achieved, no reward is given and the process is repeated with the unattained goal as the objective. The reward will depend on local management and on the type of fee payment option in effect.

Life Change Overload Problems

The occupational health program dedicated to the enhancement and maintenance of the health of the work force must expand from the traditional services to include coping strategies for employees who appear to be suffering life change overload problems. Whether or not these services are provided in-house by a consultant or a professional employee or off the premises by a professional under contract depends on the size and facilities available to the program. Some employee health benefits may cover these services. Details regarding the contents and techniques of this program component are covered elsewhere in this book.

New Internal Environmental Health Problems

Increasingly, new technology is a source of internal environmental health problems, perceived and real. The explosive expansion of the use of visual display terminals and the equally explosive volume of complaints from those using them is an example. Anticipating problems *before* new technology is put into operation will be a major challenge for occupational health programs of the future. Manufacturers of equipment are much too hard put keeping up with technical breakthroughs, which may change their share of the market if not incorporated into their product, and with marketing and training users to spend time and money exploring what operators' complaints may be and how to prevent them. Serious hazards to health such as radiation, thermal, and chemical agents are ordinarily taken into account by manufacturers and are not the problem. It is the human factor that becomes the problem. This generally involves ergonomics, perception of (nonexistent) hazards, stress produced by too long a time spent in operating the equipment, etc., which becomes the problem.

Health Surveillance of the Health of Employees

Because of the importance of health to productivity, some occupational health programs have created health management units. Each employee is assigned to a health management unit. The unit head is responsible for maintaining health surveillance of each employee in the unit. This is done by monitoring all significant health transactions involving employees in the unit. The charge to the unit head is to make each individual more health aware and to motivate the person to cultivate a "wellness lifestyle," as well as to refer the individual for any necessary behavior modification intervention actions needed. Those employees who are sick are referred to their personal physicians or some other community health resource for diagnosis and treatment.

Maintaining Awareness of New Developments in the Health Care System

As stated earlier, marked changes are going on in the health care system. In order to maintain an efficient, effective, relevant, responsive occupational health program during a period of rapid changes in concepts, in technology, and in the social, economic, and work environments, it is essential to provide for an ongoing examination of various health systems. Larger occupational health programs and departments are making this important function a new part of the organization's planning and development.

Health Needs of Special Populations

During the next decade and beyond, there will be a marked change in the U.S. work force. The products of the baby boom are aging. The markedly decreasing birthrate will shrink the pool of the traditional populations from which employees are taken. In some states, the decrease may amount to 35 percent and more. Therefore, in order to continue to function, business and industry must look to special populations that were not previously a significant source of workers. This will include older people who at this time may be considered retired, more housewives, the physically and/or mentally disabled, and the socially, economically, and educationally handicapped. For many of this group of people, the need for health services offered at the worksite or through the company will be greater than for the traditional employee population. Some special services may be required, and other regular services may need to be modified. Geriatric needs must be met. Health education needs will increase. Techniques for coping with change and stress will be important.

Personal Concerns

In the past few years, some companies have recognized that employees have many health related problems not provided for through traditional occupational health programs. Among these are individual problems for which appropriate help has not been found in the community. However, equally destructive to productivity are family problems. Whether or not these are related to health, finances, security, housing, etc. and concern children, parents, mates, friends, or others, the distress is there. It may constitute a hazard to the individual's health and/or markedly reduce the person's productivity. The following is a description of the Equitable's program.

The personal concerns program is a corporate resource to be used by people in times of personal crisis. It supplements and extends the personal concerns program of each agency, division, department, and operations complex. The objectives of the program are to assist other company activities in conserving manpower, maintaining productivity, and contributing to good company/people relationships and a cohesive loyalty. Assistance provided is primarily medical or medically related. It includes:

1. *Information.* Qualifications and professional appointments of specific physicians, accreditations and facilities of specific hospitals and other medical facilities may be obtained. Explanation is offered regarding medical conditions, diagnostic tests, treatment, and prognosis. People are assisted in communicating effectively with physicians, staffs of hospitals, and other medical facilities. Names of qualified physicians, properly accredited hospitals, and other needed medical resources in any community or region are given.

2. *Direct involvement in patient care.* Generally, this occurs only when there is a complex disabling or life-threatening illness or injury. It includes documentation of medical history, test results, treatment received, and consultations with attending physicians. This information is evaluated to determine the appropriateness, quality, and adequacy of care being received. When needed, specialist consultants are used. Referrals may be made to local or regional specialists. Transfer of a patient may be made to a hospital better equipped to provide needed services. In extraordinary circumstances regardless of where in the country the patient may be located, a personal visit may be made to examine the patient and assist in obtaining needed

help. When no known adequate resources exist locally or regionally, provision may be made for the patient to be cared for in New York or some other national medical center. Monitoring of medical care being received and of the patient's progress is carried out on an ongoing basis through continued communications with attending physicians and with the patient and/or family. Maintaining patient and family morale is given high priority.

Nonmedical assistance ordinarily consists of referral to other company resources for help in such areas as legal problems, financial advice, benefits available, etc. or to community resources. Confidentiality is maintained to the degree specified by the person or by the family of the patient.

Patient care costs are ordinarily provided for in the usual manner through agent/employee benefits. Travel costs are the responsibility of the individuals involved or may, at times, be provided by the company.

Alcoholism and Substance Abuse

An essential part of a good occupational health service is an effective alcoholism program. Some companies have had programs for years. However, most need a periodic review to evaluate how well the program facilitates detection, referral for treatment, and rehabilitation and return to the job. The "bottom line" is the success rate over the long term. If it is less than 70 percent, a problem exists. New trends and research findings should be evaluated and incorporated into the program if found to be helpful. Substances abuse other than alcohol has largely been ignored by occupational health programs, although it is a significant problem for many working people. Occupational health programs need to include services similar to those provided through alcoholism programs to effectively detect employees whose work has been affected by drug problems. Appropriate community resources should then be identified to whom employed people may be referred for treatment, rehabilitation, and follow-up after return to work.

THE FUTURE

Never before in history have occupational health programs and medicine had a greater challenge. Never before has the nation depended so much on enhancement of the health of employees in the workplace to improve the public health and to help maintain the United States as a productive, competitive nation in world markets. How this challenge is met will affect not only the survival of occupational health programs and medicine, but also—possibly—the future of this country.

REFERENCES

Brennan, Andrew J.J. 1981. "Health Promotion in Business: Caveats for Success." *Journal of Occupational Medicine* 23 (September).

Garfield, Sidney, R. 1979. "Health Testing–A New Concept of Health Care Delivery." In *Health Handbook,* edited by George Chadro, pp. 179–89. North-Holland Publishing.

Healthy People. 1979. The Surgeon General's report on health promotion and disease prevention. Publication No. 79-55071. U.S. Government Printing Office, Washington, D.C.

McDonogh, Thomas J. 1982. "The Physician as a Manager." *Journal of Occupational Medicine* 24 (February).

Woodsides, Kenneth T. 1980. "Yes, Management, Your Medical Department Can Affect the 'Bottom Line.'" *Journal of Occupational Medicine* 22 (April): 232–34.

4 Clinical Aspects of Industrial/ Organizational Psychology

Henry Morgan, Ph.D.

INTRODUCTION

Each generation of psychologists develops new terminology to define areas of practice and important concepts. What was once called personnel psychology is now referred to as industrial/organizational psychology. This new terminology reflects the concern of today's psychologists with the active management and development of human resources through a broad range of psychological procedures and interventions.

The traditional disciplines and concerns of industrial psychology have in recent years been broadened, with the development of new methods and techniques for studying people in organizations and with the development of theories that help to explain human behavior in the industrial context (McCormick & Ilgen, 1980). The field of industrial/organizational (I/O) psychology includes both the "science" of psychology, as rooted in research, and the "profession" or "practice" of psychology. The latter deals specifically with the application of the knowledge from the theories and methods of psychology to the practical human problems in organizations.

The practice of "occupational clinical psychology" (O/C) and the practice of I/O psychology overlap, as might two circles that we might imagine as representing the domain of each of these practices. Within the domain of I/C psychology, lying outside that of O/C psychology, are many traditional personnel topics such as job analysis, personnel rating systems, general selection procedures test construction, equal employment opportunity, personnel training, job satisfaction studies, human factors in job design, and studies of working conditions.

Areas of O/C psychology lying outside the domain of I/O psychology would be those practices that emphasize therapeutic procedures that are not closely job-related or job-oriented. Thus, for example, long-term psychotherapy as contrasted to short-term counseling, or sensitivity training, "T-groups," as contrasted with more structured training experiences, would lie outside the domain of I/O psychology.

The overlap between O/C and I/O is in the domain of interpersonal psychology where psychologists are dealing directly with individuals or groups of people in the context of their working environment. The psychologist's intervention is usually concerned with the assessment or development of either individuals or groups with the purpose of predicting or changing job-related behaviors. In a number of specific services rendered by I/O psychologists, the clinical aspects are sufficiently important to include them in the area of overlap between I/O and OC/ psychology:

- Psychological evaluations or assessments.
- Developmental counseling.
- Group counseling.
- Interview training.
- Outplacement counseling.
- Retirement planning.
- Life skills programs.
- Management and supervisory training.
- Psychological consulting.

PSYCHOLOGICAL EVALUATIONS OR ASSESSMENTS

Since World War II, personnel and industrial psychologists, many with clinical backgrounds, have provided to employers evaluations of job applicants or current employees. These evaluations are designed to enrich the information available to employers to help them make wise decisions in regard to staffing their organization and developing their human resources.

In psychological assessments, a battery of appropriate tests and questionnaires, as well as other procedures, provides information that is subsequently interpreted in the light of a comprehensive interview that encompasses work experience, educational background, and other job-related aspects of the individual's experience. The evaluation is usually related to the scope and requirements of a specific job or career opportunity, but assessments also are made for general potential, particularly in regard to managerial or leadership capabilities.

Such assessments are carried out by psychologists who are in private consulting practice or by groups of I/O psychologists who are employees or partners offering human resources consulting to management. Occasionally, assessments are done by individuals working within the organization itself. The work is primarily diagnostic, employing clinical insights and sensitivity, but the reports are job- and career-related and written in laymen's language. These reports and the relationships established through the evaluation procedure sometimes lay the groundwork for developmental counseling or coaching, particularly among current employees of an organization with whom the consulting psychologist may have a continuing relationship.

DEVELOPMENTAL COUNSELING

I/O psychologists almost inevitably become involved in counseling or coaching, focusing their attention on situations and behavior that are job-related, rather than purely personal or private. Since job behavior is only part of the individual's repertoire of behavior and is strongly influenced by outside circumstances and historical events, the developmental counseling does not deal exclusively with job-related behavior, but the goals of the psychologist in the counseling relationship are usually limited to helping individuals perform more effectively in their jobs, develop appropriate career plans, or change specific behavior that is counterproductive within the organizational context. For troubled employees who need longer-term psychotherapy, the I/O psychologist is likely to refer to professionals in private practice or to clinics offering appropriate services.

In today's stressful work environment, individuals can often benefit from a brief series of conferences to learn how to cope with their anxieties. Alcohol and drug abuse are common symptoms of maladaptive behavior where early intervention may prevent major abuse.

GROUP COUNSELING

Some of the developmental experiences that are planned for individuals and groups of people, involving both assessment and counseling sessions, may evolve into group counseling or coaching sessions that, in another context, might be considered group therapy. However, the focus is maintained on job-related matters, as contrasted to a similar procedure outside of the occupational setting where concerns might range over the whole spectrum of human behavior.

The industrial/organizational psychologist is likely to use a structured rather than an unstructured approach in group counseling, and the type of sensitivity training offered by the National Training Laboratory, although valuable to many participants, would probably not be classified as industrial/organizational psychology. Likewise, encounter groups and Gestalt therapy sessions are more clearly "clinical" and are usually best accomplished privately away from the working environment.

INTERVIEW TRAINING

Psychologists have used their insights, from the evaluation interview, to develop effective interview skills training for personnel specialists and line managers (Fear, 1980; Morgan & Cogger, 1980). Some of these training sessions or workshops are perceived by human resources managers as offering participants the equivalent of a short course in "occupational clinical psychology" while developing insights into the dynamics of interpersonal relationships and career development. For example, a five-day intensive interview training program, developed at the Psychological Corporation over 30 years ago, is still conducted by a number of psychologists familiar with the procedures. In this intensive program, five individuals study textbooks and prepare carefully for five days of practice in which their interviews with volunteer interviewees are monitored and critiqued, using videotape to allow full feedback and discussion. The participants learn not only how to interview skillfully and evaluate the information they have gathered; they gain important insights into their own lives, with particular reference to their own communication skills, social behavior, and career development.

This intensive experience is similar to graduate practicum courses offered in clinical or counseling psychology. Although participants see it as an intensely personal experience, they also see it as primarily job-related. They become more effective evaluators who can make wiser staffing decisions, using some of the insights of psychology but not considering themselves to be psychologists.

Even shorter versions of interview training workshops, enrolling larger numbers of participants, may prove to be enlightening, in terms of interpersonal skills and understanding people, including one's self. In some instances, individuals experience these workshops so intensely and gain such surprising insights that the programs might be perceived as "occupational clinical psychology" sessions.

OUTPLACEMENT COUNSELING

In recent years, a burgeoning field of consulting for I/O psychologists and other personnel specialists has been outplacement counseling (Morin, 1981). Consultants can provide an organization with individualized or group programs that facilitate the termination of employees prior to a company's geographical relocation, reorganization, reduction in force, or elimination of certain job categories or departments.

Historically, outplacement counseling has been offered on a one-to-one basis for specific individuals who may face termination, usually persons who have been employed for some years with the company. However, the more dramatic engagements of outplacement counselors are with organizations where several hundred individuals may be terminated at a given instant. Careful planning with executives and with the community are necessary for massive terminations to be accomplished smoothly with the least amount of disruption to the organization and the least trauma to the individuals concerned.

The work of the outplacement counselor is, in a sense, "clinical." The counselor, as well as the outplacement services manager, must be extremely sensitive to the human factors in such situations, working to defuse potentially explosive conditions that would adversely affect morale and operations.

For the terminated persons, group sessions for as many as 15 or 20 people may be held. During these sessions, feelings of frustration and anger may be voiced and dealt with openly. Employees can be provided with the rationale for the terminations and with tailored services that help them either toward early retirement or toward new career opportunities. Thus, many of the employees will enter into group and individual counseling sessions where they are able to assess their talents and interests, obtain new job and career information, and practice their job interviews using videotape procedures. They can then develop their job campaign strategies and tactics and receive coaching on their job search behavior.

Also important is the help given in building a network of people through whom terminated employees may find new opportunities. In all of this, a sensitive, psychologically trained counselor is likely to be more effective than someone who is untrained in such matters. However, many of the outplacement counselors are not psychologists. Former personnel specialists, ministers, college professors, and others who are oriented toward helping or teaching may function well in this counseling role, particularly if they have some psychological training. The more highly regarded firms tend to employ at least some psychologists to help in diagnostic and therapeutic work, particularly for individuals who may need special attention and sensitive counseling. Thus, outplacement counseling can be considered a form of "occupational clinical psychology."

RETIREMENT PLANNING

I/O psychologists may become involved in retirement planning sessions in organizations that are concerned about older employees who need to make appropriate plans before their imminent retirement. Such sessions are often concerned with many practical matters for which a psychologist is not necessary: legal advice, real estate, tax, and accounting considerations, and pension benefits. However, a central concern in most well designed retirement planning programs is psychological.

An experienced psychologist can be an effective group leader among individuals who are concerned with working through the various factors that are going to be important in planning their retirement, not only those mentioned above, but also such things as social setting, alternative work activities, spouse relationships, potential changes in self-concept, and a range of other psychological issues.

Frequently, organizations develop their own package of materials or utilize those of one of the national organizations, such as the Association for Independent Maturity (AIM) of the American Association of Retired Persons (AARP). To supplement or enhance such programs, the sponsor may engage the services of an I/O or clinical psychologist to serve as catalyst for group discussion or as a resource person to provide insights through group discussions or individual counseling. In these programs, individuals are encouraged to develop realistic and appropriate retirement goals, and the psychologist can play a key role in the process.

LIFE SKILLS PROGRAMS

Still another application of psychology in the occupational setting, as well as in the community, is a programmatic approach to preparing people for jobs for which they may be inadequately prepared by background and experience. A dramatic example of this is the success of the Adkins Life Skills Programs developed at Teacher's College, Columbia University, and at the Psychological Corporation (Adkins, 1974). Dr. Winthrop Adkins has developed a systematic program that enrolls participants from minority groups who need group and individual sessions in order to abandon certain behaviors and attitudes and to develop new and appropriate ones that would ensure their success not only in finding jobs but in keeping them. Programs of this sort may be psychologically sophisticated in their design and provide practical assistance through skilled trainers, most of whom will have had some psychological training but who have not necessarily been psychologists.

Variations on this type of program have also been developed for women in terms of assertiveness training or training for other social and supervisory skills that may not be sufficiently developed for their success in the industrial setting.

Through the theoretical and practical contributions of a psychologist, programs can be designed to produce insights and behavior changes in individuals that vastly increase the chances of their leading productive lives that benefit them and society. The design and implementation of such a program might be seen as an example of "occupational clinical psychology."

MANAGEMENT AND SUPERVISORY TRAINING

Psychologists or trainers with psychological background offer programs that enhance supervisory or managerial effectiveness of participants. Some of these programs utilize "clinical" methods of individual conferences or group counseling sessions at which individuals may review and analyze their job-related behavior in terms of its effectiveness. Appropriate modeling by the instructor, either in person or through videotape presentations, can demonstrate appropriate interpersonal relationships and interactions that may not have been in the participants' repertoire heretofore.

PSYCHOLOGICAL CONSULTING

Through the use of "clinical" interviews, an I/O psychologist may undertake a wide range of consulting work that relates him or her to key people in a client organization. The use of clinical procedures and concepts helps the consultant deal effectively with client problems, although the I/O psychologist is not likely to label his or her methodology as "clinical."

One example of clinical interviewing is a management climate survey where psychologists interview a substantial number of top management people in wide ranging conversations to ascertain the "climatic" conditions or problems that may need attention in order for the organization to function effectively. These conversations are frequently emotionally laden with strong feelings and strongly held opinions that must be sorted out and evaluated for eventual feedback to the participants and to top management. After such a survey, constructive action needs to be undertaken with the guidance and advice of the psychologist but at the initiative and under the management of the company's own personnel. The process can be therapeutic not only for the individuals but for the organization, provided the psychologist is professionally competent and broadly experienced and feels comfortable in a role that might be labeled "occupational clinical" psychologist.

In the context of general consulting with a client organization, I/O psychologists are likely to do a variety of "clinical" activities without ever referring to them as such. Helping executives cope with stress, facilitating decision making, improving staffing, and clarifying executive thought processes—all of these and more make up the clinical practice of an I/O psychologist in an occupational setting.

OVERVIEW OF I/O PSYCHOLOGY

For readers interested in examining the field of industrial/organizational psychology, an overview is presented in *Professional Psychology,* published by the American Psychological Association (*Professional Psychology,* 1980) under guest editors Hyman Meltzer and Ross Stagner. The various specific articles are organized under four major headings: (1) contemporary personnel psychology,

(2) the individual in the work environment, (3) understanding organizational behavior, and (4) organizational development and change. An epilogue by the editor includes this comprehensive coverage.

A review of the traditional areas of industrial psychology is offered by McCormick and Ilgen in the seventh edition of a textbook *Industrial Psychology* (McCormick & Elgen, 1980) and by DuBrin in *The Practice of Managerial Psychology* (DuBrin, 1972).

INDUSTRIAL ORGANIZATIONAL PSYCHOLOGIST: JOB SCOPE AND REQUIREMENTS

The qualifications for I/O psychology are so varied as to negate any highly specific recommendation in terms of education or work experience. Certainly, the person seeking to practice as an I/O psychologist should have a rigorous program in psychology at the graduate level. Ideally, the person would also have had specific I/O courses, traditional personnel psychology, test and measurements, and some clinical course work. The person would also have had sufficiently broad experience in psychology and in the business or industrial setting to be generally knowledgeable about the world of work and the functioning of large organizations. Successful I/O psychologists are probably characterized by an eclectic or pragmatic approach to problems and by flexibility in dealing with a wide variety of individuals and circumstances.

The clinical aspects of industrial/organizational psychology may make it an attractive area for psychologists whose background has been primarily clinical practice with private clients or hospital patients. Such persons can prepare for transition to I/O in several ways. Appropriate reading and course work in I/O psychology is recommended. Additionally, some experience in industrial or business organizations is advisable. Personal consultation with an I/O psychologist and a period of supervision under an experienced practitioner might ease the transition and assure professional quality for a psychologist moving into a new area of practice.

Psychologists share the same quandry experienced by other professions. On the one hand, all psychologists are equivalent in terms of their sharing a common core of knowledge, skills, and attitudes. On the other hand, psychologists vary greatly in terms of their education, work experience, talents, interests, and personalities to the degree that they are hard to categorize in any standard taxonomy. In this chapter, we have reviewed a number of services that utilize clinical knowledge, skills, and methods in an area or setting that can be labeled occupational or industrial/organizational. For psychologists, the core of common training is the primary reality of their professional life and the context of practice is secondary.

REFERENCES

Adkins, Winthrop R. 1974. "Life Coping Skills: A Fifth Curriculum." *Teachers College Record* 75 (May) 507–26.

Association for Independent Maturity, American Association of Retired Persons, 1909 K Street, N.W., Washington, D.C. 20049.

DuBrin, Andrew J. 1972. *The Practice of Managerial Psychology.* New York: Pergamon Press.

Fear, Richard A. 1980. *The Evaluation Interview.* New York: McGraw-Hill.

Figler, Homer R. 1978. *Overcoming Executive Mid-Life Crisis.* New York: John Wiley.

McCormick, Ernest J. and Daniel R. Ilgen. 1980. *Industrial Psychology,* seventh edition. Englewood Cliffs, N.J.: Prentice-Hall.

Morgan, Henry H. and John C. Cogger, 1980. *The Interviewer's Manual.* New York: Drake Beam Morin.

Morin, William J. 1981. *Successful Termination.* New York: Drake Beam Morin.

"Special Issue: Industrial/Organizational Psychology: 1980 Overview." *Professional Psychology* 11 (June 1980).

SECTION TWO

Worksite Alcoholism Treatment: The Precursor to the Employee Counseling Program

Since the 1950s, many corporations and unions have developed alcoholism programs for their employees because of the high health impacts and costs associated with this disorder. This provided an easy entry for clinical psychologists into the field of occupational psychology. Today, alcoholism or employee assistance programs are growing in number and are becoming more significant in their host organizations. And once an organization admits that its employees suffer such disorders, and when the employees understand the value of appropriate services, these programs evolve into "broad brush" employee counseling programs that address a vast number of issues. Alcoholism will remain one of the major problems to be addressed by occupational clinical psychologists and must be understood by any practitioner desiring of becoming an occupational clinician. This section will review the strains of alcoholism programs in industry and will present some current issues, research, and working models.

Because occupational clinical psychology is so young, occupational clinical psychologists hail from a number of backgrounds. Dr. Paul Sherman, trained as an industrial/organizational psychologist, is today one of the foremost alcoholism practitioners in industry. Dr. Sherman's chapter, "The Alcoholic Executive," examines the history of alcoholism since the 1930s, when alcoholism was poorly understood. The need for Alcoholics Anonymous is highlighted. Early prototypes of contemporary employee assistance programs are examined, and the slow, painful history of development of the field is reviewed. Dr. Sherman chooses as his focus the alcoholic executive and the unique diagnostic and treatment problems thereby presented. A brief case study is offered in his chapter.

Finally, Drs. Ovide Pomerleau and Ronald Kadden, in their chapter, "Behavioral Treatment Strategies for Employed Alcohol Abusers: Techniques for Moderation and Abstinence," differentiate the alcohol abuser from the alcoholic. Variable treatment programs for each are reviewed, along with relevant research. The use of behavioral methods in treating the employed alcohol abuser will continue to receive attention in the future. It must be recognized, however, that the Alcoholics Anonymous approach remains the single most effective treatment modality for treating alcoholics to date.

The importance of training in alcoholism treatment for the aspiring occupational clinical psychologist cannot be understated. Because most corporations begin their foray into the field of employee counseling via the alcoholism treatment route, the clinical psychologist would do well to supplement his or her training in order to acquire these important skills.

5 The Alcoholic Executive

Paul A. Sherman, Ph.D.

Effectively reaching and helping the executive with a drinking problem poses some special and difficult problems. Employee assistance and employee alcoholism programs usually do not reach the person at this level. The approaches to the problem utilized by the employee assistance model can be modified and used with executives. That model will be described in this chapter.

INTRODUCTION

Alcoholism in the workplace has been an acknowledged problem for many years. As far back as the 1940s there were industrial programs created to deal with alcoholism. Over the years these have become increasingly sophisticated and effective.

There is nothing at present to compare with an effective employee assistance (EAP) or employee alcoholism program in reaching the employed alcoholic and motivating him or her to accept help. However, most programs do not effectively reach the executive with a problem, primarily because of the organizational level of the person and the subtle ways executive performance is affected. Once these differences are acknowledged, it then becomes possible to reach and help the executive with a drinking problem. The EAP model is used, but in a very different way and form.

Therefore, as background to a discussion of executive alcoholism, the following will first be covered: (1) a brief history of occupational programs, (2) a definition of a program, and (3) an analysis of why programs have not worked with executives. Finally, the topic of executive alcoholism will be covered in depth.

HISTORY OF OCCUPATIONAL PROGRAMS

The 1930s

Prior to 1935, the alcoholic was by and large regarded as a "hopeless drunk." There was no proven method of treating the alcoholic. The most common methods were persuasion, urging, and attempts to convince the alcoholic that he needed to adopt a better and more moral way of life. In short, alcoholism was regarded as a moral problem and those who managed to recover were referred to as "reformed" alcoholics, a term unfortunately still heard and carrying the moral connotations of many years ago.

It is not surprising that the typical procedure in those days was to terminate the alcoholic when he did not get better. The purpose was to warn every alcoholic that his affliction (considered self-afflicted) would not be tolerated. Today, we know that alcoholism is a progressive disease; however, in earlier years it was considered moral weakness. Therefore, when an employee could no longer conceal his problem, he would be terminated. Again, the warning was given to others that they had to manage and conceal their alcoholism. It is not surprising that very little was accomplished with this approach.

Alcoholics Anonymous

Perhaps the key historical point in the treatment of alcoholism was the creation of Alcoholics Anonymous (AA) in 1935. AA was started by a stockbroker and a physician, neither of whom could stay sober. They found that by helping each other they *were* able to stay sober. This discovery led them to seek other alcoholics to help, and thus began the movement that was to become the fellowship of Alcoholics Anonymous. The movement grew rapidly, and today there are over a million members internationally.

Over the years, AA was a prime force in leading to the acceptance of the disease concept of alcoholism and the present treatment and recovery programs. Today, AA is regarded as the most effective long-term treatment for the disease of alcoholism. The key significance of AA is that it introduced the notion that alcoholics *could get well,* bringing hope to those with the disease.

The 1940s

The 1940s brought the early prototypes of the modern occupational alcoholism program. Examples of the early programs are those established by Eastman Kodak and by Du Pont. Programs in those days were often started by either recovered alcoholics or by physicians who had become quite interested in alcoholism as a result of seeing some of the early recoveries.

The early programs dealt only with alcoholism and taught supervisors how to spot alcoholism in the workplace. Supervisors were trained to look for symptoms of alcoholism, such as bloodshot eyes, tremors, drunkenness on the job and the odor of alcohol. For the supervisor this was very difficult: it put him in the role of diagnostician and into a position where he had to inform on a person who may have been a friend as well as a subordinate. Further, it often became a "witch-hunt."

The end result of such programs was highly predictable. Supervisors made absolutely sure there was a problem before making a referral. Thus, the referrals tended to be in the late stages of the disease, where the alcoholism had been rampant for a number of years. Since the employee was being referred at such a late stage, recovery was more difficult to achieve.

However, despite the crudeness of the early programs, people did begin to recover. Alcoholics Anonymous was a prime resource in these early programs. This type of program continued through the 1950s and into the 1960s. A number of new programs were started, but progress was very slow.

The 1960s

The work of Von Wiegand and Presnall in the early 1960s demonstrated that one did not have to look for alcoholism in order to reach the alcoholic and that one could do so much earlier by focusing on job performance and the deterioration that accompanies alcoholism cases. Von Wiegand and Presnall documented their ability to go through corporation records on absenteeism and identify problems in this way.

In the early stages of alcoholism, performance becomes erratic. However, other problems can also lead to erratic performance. Therefore, programs began to broaden from concerns only with alcoholism to employee assistance or employee counseling models that focused on a number of problems but that kept an emphasis on alcoholism *and* looked at job performance. The end result of this effort was that alcoholism cases began to be reached earlier. The recovery rates began to climb. Organizations with programs began reporting recovery rates of 50 percent or better.

The 1970s

The Hughes Act created the National Institute on Alcohol Abuse and Alcoholism (NIAAA). NIAAA became a moving force to reach and help the alcoholic in this country. Along with the National Council on Alcoholism, the leading voluntary agency dealing with alcoholism, a priority for this area was created that greatly increased the focus and effort devoted to it.

With the creation of an occupational branch in NIAAA, a focus on programming was established and dollars were made available to each state to hire two occupational program consultants to market occupational programs. Many of the states very quickly expanded the number of occupational program consultants and began to focus on increasing program activity within the estate because of the effectiveness of this area.

The 1970s brought a greater shift to performance-based programs of a broadened type. The focus of the programs was broadened further.

ALMACA

A major reason for the significant growth of the occupational field was the creation of the Association of Labor-Management Administrators and Consultants on Alcoholism, Inc. (ALMACA). Created in 1972 to focus on alcoholism in the workplace and to provide a means of identification and sharing for people who worked in the field of occupational alcoholism, ALMACA grew from 24 original members to 250 by 1974, to 1,600 by 1978, and to 2,700 by 1981. ALMACA became the voice for occupational alcoholism programs and began to exert an influence on business, industry, organized labor, and the federal government to stimulate growth and development of these programs. ALMACA continues to play the major role in the promulgation of these programs, even more so into the 1980s with the decline of the role of the NIAAA. The number of programs increased in the 1970s from the 300 that were reported to exist in 1970 to over 5,000 that were reported at the end of 1979.

WHAT IS AN OCCUPATIONAL PROGRAM?

In its simplest form, an occupational program is a system that focuses on job performance and affirms that when performance has been adversely affected and has not responded to normal corrective action, that a behavioral-medical problem may be involved. Alcoholism accounts for between 30 to 60 percent of the problems in most programs. Programs can vary from "alcoholism only" to broad "troubled employee" programs. However, the essence of all current occupational programs is that they create a system of intervention that uses job performance to create a crisis that motivates the problem employee to accept help.

Elements of a Program

In many instances, implementation of a program begins with the development of a policy statement by the company, describing the company's position regarding problems and a program to deal with them. The next step is to establish a set of procedures for implementing the policy and for describing what is expected of supervisors at all levels and of employees with a problem. In order to facilitate this development, many organizations bring supervisors and employees together for a series of meetings. Questions about confidentiality and record keeping must be spelled out. The involvement of unions in organizations with collective bargaining agreements is defined. Benefits are reviewed to see if they are in line with needs. Equal employment opportunity issues and legal requirements are addressed. Every attempt is made to tie in the new program with the existing performance appraisal program or process.

How Performance is Affected at Different Organizational Levels

The cornerstone of an effective EAP will be its connection with the monitoring of performance. Whereas many personal problems can affect performance adversely, the experience of EAPs has been that alcoholism affects performance in a consistent and predictable fashion. At lower levels in a company, alcoholism will affect performance in clearly observable ways: lateness and absenteeism, decreased output, and increased number of grievances and altercations. The performance difficulties of employees functioning at middle management levels are somewhat more difficult to observe. There is a decrease in the quality of work; there are also interpersonal difficulties and missed schedules. At both lower and middle management levels, there is a drop in performance that can be observed and measured. As will be seen in the remainder of this chapter, executive performance is affected very differently.

EXECUTIVE ALCOHOLISM

Alcoholism and problem drinking on the executive level are of increasing concern to business and industry. This represents a substantial shift over years ago, when there was much greater denial about the existence of such problems at top corporate levels.

Dimensions of the Problem

There are two recent studies that suggest that the problem of alcoholism and alcohol abuse may be serious and fairly widespread. In the first study (Opinion Research Corporation, 1979), 18 percent of Fortune 500 executives interviewed admitted concern over their own drinking. There is an increasing awareness at top levels that a person's drinking *can* get out of hand.

In another study (Shirley, 1981), recovered alcoholic executives recalled that their drinking had increased steadily and that business associates had tried to intervene, but unsuccessfully. Yet these executives state that they were open to receiving help a number of years before they eventually got the help.

As one rises to upper executive levels, stress and isolation increase. For those with a propensity or predisposition to alcoholism, the stress and isolation may accelerate a drinking problem.

While it is hard to state just how widespread it is, one can safely say that the problem probably exists at least to the same degree at the upper levels as it does at the middle and lower levels. However, its effect on performance is quite different.

How Executive Performance is Affected

The key to identifying the alcoholic executive *early* in the progression of the disease is to carefully review the executive's performance. As previously stated, at lower levels there is a noticeable drop in performance with whatever indicators are used (i.e., absenteeism, lateness, grievances, missed schedules or deadlines, interpersonal conflict). Performance at the executive level remains high for a number of years. What the executive does, he does well. However, the job begins to shrink, because he does fewer and fewer things.

The immediate superior of the executive will sense that something is different but be unable to articulate what the difference is or to observe the implications of this difference. Yet, intuitively, the immediate superior will sense that something is wrong and begin to hear comments such as, "Joe's performance is excellent, but he's just not the person he used to be." The alcoholic executive may have appeared on promotion lists and now no longer does. When a critical problem arises, and the executive's immediate superior has to give it to an underling, he or she will give the problem to the alcoholic executive much less frequently than in the past, and this accelerates the job shrinkage that is already occurring.

A key component of executive performance is trust. At upper executive levels of an organization, it is important that one executive be able to trust another executive to perform a certain task, be at a certain place, or react as part of the team in a clear and predictable manner. In executive alcoholism, trust breaks down.

Denial, Progression, and Continuing Job Shrinkage

A mechanism used by the alcoholic is denial. The alcoholic minimizes the extent of the trouble and denies there is a problem. For many years, the spouse does the same—and so does the immediate superior.

In the early and into the middle stages, the executive will not be thought of as an alcoholic because he or she does not look like a "falling down drunk." If one waits until the alcoholic does fit this stereotype, years will pass, and in all likelihood the executive will be an executive in name only, although there are exceptions to this rule.

As the alcoholism progresses and the job continues to shrink, events follow a typical pattern. First, the executive's secretary begins to assume more and more of a protective stance, often handling large amounts of responsibility and making critical decisions. The secretary covers up when the executive is not there. Second, after initially denying that any problem exists, the immediate superior may after a time sense that alcoholism is the problem and will talk to the executive about his or her drinking. After a number of futile talks, some of which work for a short period of time, the immediate superior may then get frustrated and angry and change from wanting to help to wanting to terminate the alcoholic executive. Third, coworkers, for a variety of reasons, also cover.

In many cases, the alcoholic executive is not a threat to them. Fourth, subordinates' reactions vary, but they include a lot of cover and handling of responsibilities that the alcoholic should handle.

All of the above forges what has been termed a "conspiracy of silence" which enables the alcoholic executive to go on drinking and not face the problem.

SUCCESSFUL INTERVENTION

By assessing how executive performance has changed, and using this to confront the alcoholic executive, intervention can take place years earlier than would otherwise occur (Sherman, 1981). Executive case management is an approach that uses a consultant specializing in executive alcoholism to intervene in such a way as to create a crisis that motivates the executive to accept treatment.

The alcoholic executive is talented and has likely had a number of promotions to reach his or her current level in the organization. Many are long service people who have been privy to the secrets and strategies of the organization and whose contribution over the years has been significant.

To assess the impact on performance and to separate present performance from past accomplishment is an important first step in planning an intervention. The ideal is to be willing to terminate the individual, if need be, for performance. Paradoxically, the *willingness* to do this increases the chances for a successful intervention and decreases the chances that termination will occur. A case history is revealing:

> Tom G. was a successful marketing executive. His scope was national and his contribution to the company had been significant over the years. His alcoholism had progressed, however. When one looked at this performance, he was always at work and handled his assignments beautifully, except on several occasions. These occasions had become somewhat more numerous in the last year. Often when visiting one of his operations, he would be fine during the day and get drunk at night, still managing to make it into the office the next morning.
>
> The issue arose in discussing the case with his immediate superior as to whether getting drunk at night constituted an effect on performance, for essentially he represented the company whenever he went to one of his locations. Combined with the issue of the increasing, though still small, number of lapses, his immediate superior decided to confront. Where his previous reaction to help had been negative, his supervisor now called him in and stated, "I'm going to give you a choice: either cooperate with the program that has been described to you, or you will be terminated for performance."

After no more than a matter of several minutes, the individual decided to cooperate and today remains an outstanding executive with the corporation.

The job, to an executive, has almost a mystique. For a number of years, people have in all likelihood been commenting on his drinking. The executive has usually denied there is a problem and told himself that he would not be able to do the important work that he does if drinking were indeed a problem. Over a period of time, the job becomes the foundation of the alcoholic's denial. Thus, this type of confrontation gets to the very heart of the denial system and creates an immediate crisis. To be terminated for performance means that he never again can use his work as part of his denial. For the executive to be able to handle what is being asked means that he must do something about his drinking.

The closer one can come to this kind of intervention, the better the results. However, it is extremely sensitive. Performance must be carefully documented and the person doing this kind of intervention must be extremely knowledgeable, not only about alcoholism, but about executive alcoholism.

TREATMENT OF THE EXECUTIVE ALCOHOLIC

Once an executive has agreed to accept help, the issue becomes the type of treatment. The first assessment involves whether it is safe for him to stop drinking by himself, and medical inputs are necessary. If the alcoholic is being reached early enough, in many if not most cases it will be sufficiently safe. There is an advantage to out-patient treatment for executive alcoholics in that they don't have to explain to others why they were away from the office for an extended period (up to 28 days, the period involved in most rehabilitation programs).

However, if self-help is not possible on an out-patient basis, then some form of in-patient treatment is required. Many organizations try to match the executive to the specific outlook and philosophy of a treatment center.

Any rehabilitation effort is but a first step, for what is involved is that the executive has to stop drinking—and stay stopped. There is at present no safe and predictable way that an alcoholic can return to controlled drinking. A small percentage of cases have been able to do it, but most have not.

The most successful long-term therapy for alcoholism at the executive level remains Alcoholics Anonymous. By sharing experiences with other people who have had similar problems, executive alcoholics are able to draw on the resources of AA in a way that assists in a program of long-term recovery.

Executives are a vital resource to a corporation. Programs of intervention at an executive level can be very helpful in saving a person who would otherwise be lost. The financial benefits to the corporation are outstanding.

It is apparent from the above discussion that there is a need for continuing research into executive alcoholism. While the effects of alcoholism on any employed population can be very complex, at the executive level they are even more so. Today, many questions about executive alcoholism are being raised, and research over the next few years should yield considerable information about how alcoholism affects executives and how the intervention processes can be refined.

REFERENCES

Alcoholics Anonymous World Services. 1957. *Alcoholics Anonymous Comes of Age.* New York.

Follmann, J.F. 1976. *Alcoholics and Business: Problems, Costs, Solutions.* New York: AMACOM.

———. 1978. *Helping the Troubled Employee.* New York: AMACOM.

Foote, A. and J.C. Erfurt. 1977. "Occupational Employee Assistance Programs for Substance Abuse and Mental Health Problems." Ann Arbor: Institute of Labor and Industrial Relations, University of Michigan.

Foote, A., J.C. Erfurt, P.A. Strauch, and T.L. Guzzardo. 1978. "Cost-Effectiveness of Occupational Employee Assistance Programs: Test of an Evaluation Method." Ann Arbor: Institute of Labor and Industrial Relations, University of Michigan.

Godwin, D.F., J.A. Baxter, and G.M. Rooney. 1978. "Future Directions in Occupational Programming." *Labor-Management Alcoholism Journal* 8 (2): 64–71.

Isenberg, Susan. 1979. "The Evaluation of Occupational Drug and Alcohol Programs." Occupational Drug and Alcohol Programs Conference, Australian Foundation on Alcoholism and Drug Dependence, Melbourne, Australia.

Mann, Marty. 1958. *New Primer on Alcoholism.* New York: Holt, Rinehart and Winston.

Masi, D. 1979. "Combatting Alcoholism in the Workplace." *Health & Social Work* 4 (4):41–59.

Opinion Research Corporation. 1979. "Executives' Knowledge, Attitudes, and Behavior Regarding Alcoholism and Alcohol Abuse." Study IV, a report of executive caravan findings, prepared for National Institute on Alcohol Abuse and Alcoholism.

Phillips, Donald A. and Harry J. Older. 1981. "Models of Service Delivery." *E.A.P. Digest* (May/June).

Roth, Richard and William Dunkin. 1981. "The E.A.P. Works: An Overview." *Alcoholism, The National Magazine* 1 (March/April): 23–27.

Shain, Martin and Judith Groeneveld. 1980. *Employee-Assistance Programs.* Toronto: Lexington Books.

Sherman, Paul A. "Cost-Benefit Analysis of I.T.T. Alcohol and Behavioral/Medical Programs." Unpublished study.

———. 1980. "The Executive Alcoholic–Strategies of Intervention." Silver Hill Foundation Conference.

———. 1981. "Executive Case Management." Unpublished proposal.

Sherman, Paul A., L. Perlis, D.A. Masi, D. Phillips, and M.H. Cahill. 1980. "Perspectives: An Interview Feature on Occupational Alcoholism Programs." *Alcohol Health and Research World* 4 (3): 32–38.

Shirley, Charles. 1981. "Hitting Bottom in High Places." Topex Study.

Small, Edward J. 1981. "E.A.P.'s for White Collar Workers." *Alcoholism, The National Magazine* 1 (March/April).

Trice, Harrison M. 1980. "Job-Based Alcoholism and Employee Assistance Programs." *Alcohol Health and Research World* 4 (Spring).

Trice, H.M. and J.M. Beyer. 1981. "A Performance-Based Evaluation of the Constructive Confrontation Strategies in a Long-Standing Alcoholism EAP Program." Annual Meeting of the American Sociological Association, Toronto.

Trice, H.M. and P.M. Roman. 1972. *Spirits and Demons at Work: Alcohol and Other Drugs on the Job.* Cornell University Press.

Trice, H.M. and M. Schonbronn. 1981. "A History of Job-Based Alcoholism Programs: 1900–1955." *Journal of Drug Issues* (Winter).

Von Wiegand, Ross A. 1972. "Main Objective: Alcoholics or 'Troubled Employees'?" *Labor-Management Alcoholism Journal* 2 (November-December).

Wolfe, I., M.E. Chafetz, H.T. Blane, M.J. Hill. 1965. "Social Factors in the Diagnosis of Alcoholism, Part II: Attitudes of Physicians." *Quarterly Journal of Studies on Alcohol.* 26: 72–79.

Wrich, James T. 1980. "The Employee Assistance Program, Upgraded for the 1980's." New York: Hazelden Press.

6 Behavioral Treatment Strategies for Employed Alcohol Abusers: Techniques for Moderation and Abstinence

Ovide F. Pomerleau, Ph.D., and Ronald M. Kadden, Ph.D.

INTRODUCTION

In keeping with public recognition of the serious medical, social, and economic consequences of alcohol abuse, numerous programs for prevention, detection, and rehabilitation have been organized in business and industry. These programs have included alcohol education campaigns, troubled employee counseling, crisis intervention centers and hotlines, referral systems for detoxification and rehabilitation, as well as the encouragement of sobriety through participation in Alcoholics Anonymous. While most research on behavioral treatment of alcohol problems has been conducted in academic and medical settings, the techniques and programs developed have implications for the management of alcohol abuse in the workplace. The present chapter is an overview of behavioral approaches to assessment, the inculcation of moderation and abstinence, and the prevention of relapse. By way of introduction, some general comments on alcohol abuse and on the background of behavioral approaches to alcohol problems are in order.

There is growing recognition that alcohol abuse exists on a continuum of severity, ranging from occasional drunkenness with relatively few side effects to drinking that is part of an addictive cycle with tolerance and withdrawal symptoms (Miller & Caddy, 1977; Pomerleau, Pertschuk, & Stinnett, 1976). Less severe difficulties can be described as problem drinking and can be differentiated from the more severe disorders that constitute alcoholism (gamma or delta in the classification system of Jellinek, 1952). In the present context, milder alcohol problems will be distinguished from more severe disorders in accordance with the above usage.

Behavioral treatment of problem drinking and alcoholism is based on social learning, Pavlovian conditioning, and operant conditioning concepts (Bandura, 1969; Pavlov, 1927; Skinner, 1953). Within this broad learning theory framework, maladaptive behavior, including abusive drinking, is viewed as under the control of both antecedent stimuli and consequent events (reinforcers); the task of remediation and therapy is thus one of changing behavior and environmental conditions to minimize problem drinking, engender sobriety, and improve social functioning. The techniques described below are derived from behavior modification therapy (Leitenberg, 1976), and, more recently, from behavioral medicine (Pomerleau & Brady, 1979).

BEHAVIORAL ASSESSMENT

Most occupational programs for referral and treatment of troubled employees focus on deteriorating job performance (e.g., absenteeism, lateness, reduced quantity or quality of output, missed deadlines, etc.) as the principal basis for intervention (Roman & Trice, 1976). Both union and management have agreed that their authority and interest should not extend beyond work performance. This attitude has fostered the development of broadly based occupational programs that deal with any of a number of employee problems that have an impact on job performance. A feature of the approach is that it relieves the supervisor of the responsibility of diagnosis or counseling employees with personal problems and, in the case of alcoholic employees, of having to confront them in the face of massive denial. Roman (1981) has questioned the value of this approach as an exclusive strategy, because the powerful contingencies of the workplace are not effectively utilized as part of the treatment intervention. Regardless of how this issue is handled, it is essential that supervisors document interference with job performance as objectively as possible and make explicit the consequences of continued deterioration of performance.

Once the employee has entered the assistance system, the next task is an accurate assessment of drinking behavior and its environmental precursors and consequences. Assessment is important for appropriate referral to treatment as well as for the designation of meaningful treatment goals and the development of an effective plan for remediation. A useful by-product of the assessment process is often an increase in the employee's awareness of the seriousness of the problem.

Drinking behavior can be assessed either retrospectively or on an ongoing basis. Marlatt (1976) has developed a comprehensive inventory to provide basic information, on a retrospective basis, for analyzing drinking patterns as well as the events that typically precede drinking and the events that follow as a consequence of drinking. Pomerleau and Adkins (1980) have published a brief, one-page variation of Marlatt's questionnaire, focusing on the quantification of recent drinking and on the antecedents and consequences of drinking.

Various inventories for obtaining an ongoing stimulus-control analysis of drinking have been devised: Sobell and Sobell (1973) developed a form for self-monitoring and recording each day's drinking behavior; as revised by Miller and Mastria (1977), this form requires the problem drinker to record, for each drinking episode, the situation, the time of day, the number and kind of drinks, the events that preceded and followed drinking, as well as thoughts and mood at that time. Pomerleau and Adkins (1980) used a similar approach and, in addition, gave detailed instructions for calculating ethanol consumed, to provide a drink-by-drink analysis. Self-report is typically validated by querying spouse and friends (with consent of the participant), by using breath-alcohol testing devices, and by using sensitive indicators of liver function (e.g., the gamma glutamyl transpeptidase test, described by Rosalki & Rau, 1972).

The treatment goal of sobriety, whether achieved through moderation or abstinence, requires an evaluation of functioning in a number of areas of daily living. Among the different measures in common use are assessments of social interaction (Watson & Friend, 1969), assertiveness (Rathus, 1973; Gambrill & Richey, 1975), marital problems (Azrin, Naster, & Jones, 1973), and psychological functioning such as anxiety (Spielberger, Gorsuch, & Lushene, 1970), fear (Wolpe, 1973), and depression (Beck, et al., 1961). A number of handbooks have been published recently on the subject of behavioral assessment (e.g., Ciminero, Calhoun, & Adams, 1977; Hersen & Bellack, 1976). Utilizing these various methods, an individual profile can be developed in which behavioral deficits and excesses, as well as areas of adequate functioning, are taken into account.

TECHNIQUES FOR MODERATION

Abstinence from all alcoholic beverages is the most conservative approach to managing drinking problems. However, the established tradition of treating alcohol problems as a unitary disorder or disease, and the designation of abstinence as the only acceptable outcome of treatment, has certain disadvantages: Of the millions of problem drinkers in the United States, only a small fraction (perhaps less than 10 percent) is currently receiving help. Most alcohol abusers are still functioning in society and may not yet have experienced the full negative impact of sustained excessive drinking, such as loss of health or loss of social and economic support. The traditional approach has been to assume that those who enter treatment have "hit bottom" and are now willing to "surrender to therapy" (Tiebout, 1949). Consequently, the difficulty of getting many problem drinkers into therapy while they still have something to lose by continued excessive drinking may come from the fact that they have not "hit bottom" and are reluctant to enter a treatment modality that insists on unconditional commitment to abstinence.

This section reviews research on behavioral techniques to inculcate a pattern of moderation. The intent of the programs described below was to devise procedures that might attract people with drinking problems into therapy while they were still in the early stages of alcohol abuse. In business and industry, the approach can serve as a first line of defense for dealing with employees who admit to having a problem with drinking but may as yet be unwilling to abstain. It should be emphasized that the goal of treatment–controlled drinking–differs from ordinary social drinking in several key respects: The prescribed pattern of moderation, for example, the "3-3-10 rule" (Pomerleau, et al., 1978), is one in which drinking is restricted to designated situations; in this case, consumption is limited to 3 days out of 7, to no more than 3 ounces of absolute ethanol per day, and is not to exceed 10 ounces in 7 consecutive days. A feature of the approach is that once the problem drinker is in therapy, alcohol consumption is monitored on an ongoing basis; should drinking continue to exceed designated quotas, the goal of therapy can be shifted to abstinence.

Pomerleau and colleagues developed an integrated treatment sequence using self-management techniques for employed problem drinkers (Pomerleau, et al., 1978). Therapy was provided on an out-patient basis, with weekly treatment sessions over three months and five follow-up sessions at increasing intervals over nine months. In addition to paying a fee for service on a sliding scale based on income, participants were asked for a "commitment fee" of up to $300. The fee was prepaid and could be earned back to its entirety by (1) keeping daily records of alcohol consumed or craved, with refunds based on completeness of records, not content, (2) coming to treatment with no detectable breath alcohol, (3) carrying out selected nondrinking activities as corroborated by a monitor, and (4) attending subsequent follow-up sessions. If the participant dropped out of therapy, all fees were forfeited. Participants were required to set daily quotas for alcohol consumption; quotas were stated publicly each week in a small group setting, and social reinforcement for success in meeting the quotas was provided by both therapists and participants. In keeping with the operant conditioning principle of response shaping, the emphasis in the early sessions was on gradual, steady improvement, requiring fulfillment of the "3-3-10 rule" after four to six weeks, rather than demanding abrupt change. If further use of ethanol was contraindicated, however, subgoals were set more stringently, so that abstinence could be reached within a fortnight. Participants were taught various stimulus control techniques: for example, they designated appropriate and inappropriate times and places for drinking; they learned to keep glasses filled with nonalcoholic beverages at social occasions; they were instructed to write down a specific drinking plan prior to known problem situations (preplanning); they practiced sipping drinks rather than gulping; and they were told not to stockpile liquor in the home. Desire to drink was handled in part through covert conditioning—pairing craving with the imagined consequences of excessive drinking, (e.g., a desire for a morning drink paired with imagined loss of job as a result). Behavior therapy for depression, tension, or nonassertiveness was also available, as needed.

In a test of the procedure, 32 participants were assigned randomly to either the behavioral treatment just described or "traditional" treatment groups led by experienced therapists. The traditional treatment was conducted over the same number of sessions as the behavioral treatment, but abstinence was emphasized rather than moderation. This comparison therapy consisted of confronting denial of problem drinking, social support for nondrinking, and psychotherapy for depression, anxiety, or inadequate socialization. Fees, set on a sliding scale, were paid before each session. The results were as follows: Participants reduced their alcohol consumption significantly in both treatment programs. Behavioral participants reduced alcohol consumption significantly *during* therapy, whereas traditional participants reduced significantly *prior* to therapy. Significantly more traditional participants (43 percent) dropped out of therapy than did behavioral (11 percent). At the first anniversary point, 72 percent of behavioral participants were classified as improved (6 percent abstinent, 66 percent drinking a median of 35 percent of baseline rate) compared with 50 percent of traditional participants (14 percent abstinent, 36 percent drinking a median of 40 percent of baseline rate). These data suggest that the effects of traditional therapy were mixed, helping those participants who were receptive, driving out those who were not; moreover, reduced consumption seemed to be more the result of compliance with initial therapist demands (made during the screening period) than the effect of confronting the patient's denial in subsequent therapy. The favorable effects of behavioral treatment occurred during therapy, consistent with other reports on contingency management in the literature (Mahoney & Thoresen, 1974).

These findings for middle-income problem drinkers are corroborated by a study of a similar population by Miller (1978): 78 percent of subjects taught to use self-control techniques to inculcate moderation were found improved at a one-year follow-up, compared with 70 percent of subjects treated using aversive conditioning and 54 percent of subjects treated with a composite of the two procedures. Posttreatment drinking by self-control subjects was approximately one-third of pretreatment levels, the same as in Pomerleau's study. A recent report on 70 socially stable problem drinkers by Sanchez-Craig (1980) provides an important replication and extension of the findings for controlled drinking, as it is the first study in which the only difference in therapy for randomly assigned subjects was the *goal* of treatment—abstinence or moderation. Preliminary results indicate that patients assigned to controlled drinking consumed significantly less alcohol than those assigned to abstinence during the first three weeks of treatment (a time during which both groups were expected to abstain); moreover, patients assigned to controlled drinking continued to be more successful than those assigned to abstinence during the remainder of therapy. Sanchez-

Craig suggested that more frequent drinking in the abstinence group may reflect the unacceptability of such a goal for this particular population, and it may also represent a difficulty inherent to an either/or rule, in which a slip from abstinence is not clearly differentiated from total relapse.

The development of behavioral techniques to inculcate moderate drinking is consistent with recent efforts to match therapy to the alcohol abuser's particular strengths and weaknesses. The crucial issue is to differentiate those problem drinkers for whom controlled drinking would be appropriate and helpful from those for whom it may be harmful or ineffective. Current experience suggests that controlled drinking should be restricted to those problem drinkers who refuse more traditional, abstinence-oriented approaches and who can substantiate periods of moderate drinking in the past; moderation programs are certainly contraindicated for those who have medical conditions that preclude consumption of alcohol (Miller & Caddy, 1977; Pomerleau, Pertschuk & Stinnett, 1976). While there is evidence suggesting that addicted, gamma alcoholics can be taught social drinking (Sobell and Sobell, 1976), the treatment procedures involved are complex and intensive. As a practical guideline, addicted drinkers, or problem drinkers who exhibit bizarre or uncontrolled behaviors while drinking, should enter treatments that have abstinence as the goal.

TECHNIQUES FOR ABSTINENCE

A common objective of most behavioral treatments of alcohol abuse, and one that is especially emphasized in abstinence-oriented programs, is to train and strengthen behaviors that are incompatible with drinking (Miller, 1976). Recognizing that alcohol abuse involves many aspects of a person's life, effective treatment must deal not only with drinking behavior per se, but also with behavioral problems that precede or maintain bouts of abusive drinking. Thus, behavioral treatment programs typically use multiple techniques to deal with the various problems that are identified in the assessment phase. These problems may include anxiety, for which relaxation training may be provided, or inability to handle interpersonal relationships and social pressure, which may call for social skills training or assertiveness training. Marital, sexual, and vocational problems are also often associated with abusive drinking patterns; counseling in areas that are troublesome will be necessary to provide a stable basis for a sober lifestyle. A variety of behavioral approaches have been developed to treat these problems, and a number of clinical handbooks are available for treatment details (e.g., Miller & Mastria, 1977; Turner, Calhoun, & Adams, 1981).

Drinking behavior itself has been treated using a wide variety of behavioral procedures. Punishment of drinking behavior and the pairing of drinking sights, smells, and tastes with aversive stimuli in Pavlovian conditioning are among the oldest behavioral techniques for treating alcohol abuse. Despite current de-emphasis of aversive procedures, the association between aversion therapy and behavior modification lingers among nonbehaviorists.

While initial reports on the use of electrical aversive conditioning with alcohol abusers were quite encouraging, recent, better controlled studies have failed to support the early claims (Hedberg & Campbell, 1974; Miller, et al., 1973). Moreover, theoretically oriented research has not supported the widely held belief that dermal shock establishes a conditioned aversion to ethanol: in a laboratory test where consumption was neither encouraged nor discouraged, *ad libitum* drinking remained unchanged following application of aversive conditioning procedures (Wilson, Leaf, and Nathan, 1975).

The current status of chemical aversion therapy using nausea-inducing substances, such as emetine, is more ambiguous. The procedure first developed by Voegtlin in 1940 continues to be used: an emetine-pilocarpine-ephedrine solution is administered intravenously; at the earliest sign of nausea, the patient is given a drink of his or her preferred beverage to smell and to taste, with additional drinks given over a 30-minute to one-hour period as nausea and vomiting persist. Subsequently, booster sessions are given to patients whenever they feel a return of the urge to drink. Of over 4,000 patients treated in 13 years at Shadel Hospital, a private institution, 44 percent were reported to be abstinent from two to 13 years (Lemere & Voegtlin, 1950). Similar results were obtained at Raleigh Hills Hospital (Wiens, et al., 1976), with 63 percent of 261 alcoholic patients remaining abstinent at a one-year follow-up. In an attempt to explain why these techniques are not more widely used, given their apparent efficacy, Nathan and Goldman (1979) pointed out that alcohol abusers who choose such treatment have to be highly motivated to subject themselves to these unpleasant procedures and, given the nature of the private hospital settings in which these techniques were employed, the patients may have more favorable prognoses because they come from a higher socioeconomic background. Nathan and Goldman also observed that chemical aversion is but one facet of treatment in the Shadel and Raleigh Hills hospitals: the contribution of rehabilitation, personal counseling, family therapy, Alcoholics Anonymous, and a supportive milieu should not be minimized.

A variety of therapeutic interventions using positive reinforcement contingencies have been developed over the past ten years. Nonaversive, contingency management interventions are more consistent with current behavioral theory and more representative of current behavioral practice. Some of these techniques have been described briefly in the section on controlled drinking.

The value of straightforward application of simple contingencies has been tested at Baltimore City Hospital. Hospital employees were referred to treatment on the basis of observed decrements in work and increased absenteeism resulting from excessive drinking. Treatment consisted of being given the opportunity to continue to work, *contingent* on taking Antabuse; failure to report to the hospital's alcoholism clinic on a given day resulted in no work for that day, and thus no pay. For 21 employees treated in this program, absenteeism dropped significantly, from 9.8 percent prior to treatment to 1.7 percent during treatment (Robichaud, et al., 1979). When the Antabuse requirement was eliminated, absenteeism went back up to 6.7 percent, suggesting that the contingency, rather than the identification of the employee as alcoholic or the threat by the employer, was the effective component of therapy. The study also illustrates that the maintenance of treatment benefits cannot simply be left to chance; rather, it requires long-term contingencies and management.

In a similar approach with 20 alcohol abusers, monetary deposits were returned, contingent on taking Antabuse at a clinic over a prescribed period of time (a minimum of three months); two months of complete abstinence was obtained in 95 percent of the patients and six months of abstinence in 40 percent (Bigelow, et al., 1976). In related work, the same group of investigators demonstrated that chronic alcoholic inpatients will voluntarily moderate their alcohol intake when positive reinforcement is contingent on doing so and punishment or loss of reinforcement is contingent on not doing so. Among the reinforcers and punishers used were enriched versus impoverished living environments, weekend passes and special ward privileges versus no passes and limited privileges, and usual socialization privileges versus brief interpersonal isolation. As a whole, the work of these investigators demonstrates that the behavior of even "hard core" addicts can be modified if appropriate contingencies are provided in such a way that reinforcement for continued sobriety is greater than that for alcohol consumption.

The use of simple contingencies leads logically to more complex procedures in which positive reinforcement is used more extensively, not just in the workplace or hospital. The community reinforcement procedure developed by Hunt and Azrin (1973) at Anna State Hospital consists of four components designed to strengthen behaviors that interfere with drinking: (1) placement in steady and remunerative employment, (2) marital and family counseling to increase involvement and pleasure in family activity, (3) social clubs to provide support for nondrinking during free time, and (4) enhancement of activities, such as hobbies and formal recreation, to provide alternatives to drinking. Results from the program were favorable, with the treated group significantly improved on such indicators as time spent drinking, time unemployed, time away from home, and time institutionalized, when compared with a matched control group.

A recent revision of the program (Azrin, 1976) attempted to overcome some of the limitations of the original procedure: temporary lapses (slips) into problem drinking in response to job loss or to some short-term impulse were handled by incorporating Antabuse into the treatment program. The program was also modified to include procedures that taught the patient to identify and to deal with situations that were known to lead to excessive drinking, or with feelings that constituted danger signals. To make therapy more efficient, demands on the counselor to provide help with numerous non-alcohol-related problems were shifted to nonprofessional "buddies" in the patient's neighborhood. Results for two matched groups of 20 alcoholics indicated that control patients given the standard hospital treatment drank 27 times more often than community reinforcement patients, were institutionalized 100 times as much, and were absent from their homes nine times as much. Benefits of community reinforcement treatment were sustained over a two-year follow-up. Additional evidence for the helpfulness of procedures that increase social support for nondrinking is provided by Hedberg and Campbell (1974) using behavioral family counseling and by McCrady, et al., (1979) using joint hospitalization followed by out-patient couples therapy.

RELAPSE PREVENTION

Relapse to uncontrolled drinking is a significant problem for all treatment programs, whether the goal of treatment is moderation or abstinence. To obtain a better understanding of the phenomena that comprise relapse to drinking, Marlatt and Gordon (1980) collected information from a large number of alcohol abusers about events, feelings, physical settings, time, social situations, etc. that immediately preceded their previous relapses. Although 13 factors related to relapse were identified, nearly 75 percent of all cases fell into three categories: dysphoric (negative) emotional states (38 percent), interpersonal conflicts (18 percent), and social pressure to resume drinking (18 percent). One of the implications of this research is that providing patients still in therapy with a behavioral repertoire to enable them to cope with these "high risk" situations might prevent or minimize relapse.

Marlatt and his associates have developed a cognitive-behavioral model of relapse and have indicated interventions that may be appropriate at critical points (Cummings, Gordon, & Marlatt, 1980). For example, they suggest that setting abstinence as an all-or-nothing goal at the onset of therapy may contribute to subsequent relapse: if the requirement of abstinence is conceptualized in absolutistic terms, then, should a drink be taken later on, the therapeutic rule, "don't drink again," is broken and all control is surrendered. This is known as the "abstinence violation effect." A preferable cognitive strategy is, therefore, to define the object of therapy as sobriety rather than perfect abstinence; that way, one drink does not provide an excuse for a binge. Marlatt's model also attempts to increase awareness of various other cognitions that lead to trouble. Otherwise, when the patient expects that the consumption of alcohol will provide certain benefits (e.g., "I won't feel so nervous" or "I'll stop trembling and feel better"), the stage is set for a relapse. As a way of countering these self-defeating rationalizations, patients are taught alternative responses, such as deep muscle relaxation, to provide a substitute for the presumed benefits of ethanol consumption. Among other suggested intervention strategies are (1) behavioral assessment to identify potential high-risk situations, (2) review of decision making to foster recognition of minidecisions (AIDs—"apparently irrelevant decisions") that precede a relapse, (3) coping-skills training, including modeling, role playing, etc., (4) cognitive restructuring concerning positive expectations about alcohol, and (5) in some cases, actually staging a "programmed relapse," in which the therapist controls settings and events associated with resumption of drinking and allows the patient to learn that he or she determines the outcome, not the alcohol.

Treatment research based on this model has been carried out: Chaney, O'Leary, and Marlatt (1978) provided relapse prevention therapy, focusing on how *not* to drink. Forty inpatient alcoholics were assigned to a relapse prevention skill training group, to a discussion group, or to standard hospital treatment. On a verbal role-playing measure of responses to situations associated with drinking and relapse, the patients receiving skill training demonstrated a significant performance improvement over the control groups. Follow-up one year after treatment validated the analog (role-playing) test: skill training decreased the duration and severity (though not the frequency) of relapse episodes. While it remains to be demonstrated definitively that self-reported reasons (attributions) for drinking and relapse actually do cause the behaviors in question, the fact that alcoholics given skill training drank less, were employed more, and attended after-care more regularly is of considerable practical benefit.

CONCLUSION

The behavioral point of view has led to a critical examination of current assumptions and practices in the treatment of drinking problems. Among the concepts that have been brought into question, mainly because of lack of scientific support, have been the disease model (when applied indiscriminately over the *entire* spectrum of alcohol abuse) and abstinence as the sole legitimate goal of treatment (Lloyd & Salzberg, 1975; Pomerleau, Pertschuk, & Stinnett, 1976). The behavioral perspective has fostered such treatment innovations as contingency management and relapse prevention and has contributed to the recent trend toward matching therapies to patient characteristics (Skinner, 1981).

The behavioral approach has also raised standards for treatment research. In a recent book by the Sobells (Sobell, Sobell, & Ward, 1980), key elements for clinical and program evaluation were identified: among the recommendations were the assessment of functioning in multiple life areas, the determination of pretreatment baseline measures, the use of extended follow-up intervals, and the validation of self-report using both social and biological measures. An emphasis on empirical documentation of treatment process and outcome is an important step in the development of new and better treatments.

Prospects for the future are encouraging. Relapse prevention is being replicated and extended by numerous investigators, and comparison of relapse prevention with more commonly used treatments, such as Antabuse, is being undertaken. Contingency management procedures are being used to increase the effectiveness of traditional therapies, for example, to enhance adherance to prescribed Antabuse or even to facilitate compliance with the Alcoholics Anonymous program. In the work setting, comparable strategies could be used to improve the performance of supervisors by providing contingent reward for effective monitoring and timely referral of troubled employees.

While the new developments are promising, and therapeutic practice continues to change, there is still no treatment that can provide sustained sobriety for a majority of unselected alcohol abusers, and there is no assessment system that can reliably match patients to the most appropriate treatment modality. Thus, research will press for better treatment methods and for a better understanding of patient characteristics to permit more efficient assignment to treatment. We anticipate that behavioral methods will continue to be productive in improving the management of alcohol problems in the clinic, as well as in business and industry.

REFERENCES

Azrin, N.H. 1976. "Improvements in the Community-reinforcement Approach to Alcoholism." *Behavior Research and Therapy* 14: 339–48.

Azrin, N.H., B.J. Naster, and R. Jones. 1973. "Reciprocity Counseling: A Rapid Learning-based Procedure for Marital Counseling." *Behavior Research and Therapy* 11: 365–82.

Bandura, A. 1969. *Principles of Behavior Modification.* New York: Holt, Rinehart and Winston.

Beck, A.T., C.H. Ward, M. Mendelson, J. Mock, and J. Erbaugh. 1961. "An Inventory for Measuring Depression." *Archives of General Psychiatry* 4: 561–71.

Bigelow, G., D. Strickler, I. Liebson, and R. Griffiths. 1976. "Maintaining Disulfiram Ingestion among Outpatient Alcoholics: A Security-deposit Contingency Contracting Procedure." *Behaviour Research and Therapy* 14: 378–81.

Chaney, E.F., M.R. O'Leary, and G.A. Marlatt. 1978. "Skill Training with Alcoholics." *Journal of Consulting and Clinical Psychology* 46: 1092–104.

Ciminero, A.R., K.S. Calhoun, and H.E. Adams. 1977. *Handbook of Behavioral Assessment.* New York: John Wiley.

Cummings, C., J.R. Gordon, and G.A. Marlatt, 1980. "Relapse: Prevention and Prediction." In *The Addictive Behaviors*, edited by W.R. Miller, pp. 291–321. Oxford, England: Pergamon.

Gambrill, E.D. and C.A. Richey. 1975. "An Assertion Inventory for Use in Assessment and Research." *Behavior Therapy* 6: 550–61.

Hedberg, A. and L. Campbell. 1974. "A Comparison of Four Behavioral Treatments of Alcoholism." *Journal of Behavior Therapy and Experimental Psychiatry* 5: 251–56.

Hersen, M. and A.S. Bellack, Eds. 1976. *Behavioral Assessment: A Practical Handbook.* Oxford, England: Pergamon.

Hunt, G.M. and N.H. Azrin. 1973. "A Community-reinforcement Approach to Alcoholism." *Behaviour Research and Therapy* 11: 91–104.

Jellinek, E.M. 1952. "Phases of Alcohol Addiction." *Quarterly Journal of Studies on Alcohol* 13: 673–84.

Leitenberg, H., Ed. 1976. *Handbook of Behavior Modification and Behavior Therapy.* Englewood Cliffs, N.J.: Prentice-Hall.

Lemere, F. and W. Voegtlin. 1950. "An Evaluation of the Aversive Treatment of Alcoholism." *Quarterly Journal on Studies on Alcohol* 11: 199–204.

Lloyd, R.W. and S.C. Salzberg. 1975. "Controlled Social Drinking: An Alternative to Abstinence as a Treatment Goal for Some Alcohol Abusers." *Psychological Bulletin* 82: 815–42.

Mahoney, M.J. and C.E. Thoresen. 1974. *Self-control: Power to the Person.* Monterey, Calif.: Brooks/Cole.

Marlatt, G.A. 1976. "The Drinking Profile: A Questionnaire for the Behavioral Assessment of Alcoholism." In *Behavior-Therapy Assessment: Diagnosis and Evaluation,* edited by E.J. Mash and L.G. Terdal, pp. 121–37. New York: Springer.

Marlatt, G.A. and J.R. Gordon. 1980. "Determinants of Relapse: Implications for the Maintenance of Behavior Change." In *Behavioral Medicine: Changing Health Lifestyles.* Edited by P. Davidson and S.M. Davidson, pp. 410–452. New York: Brunner/Mazel.

McCrady, B., T. Paolino, R. Longabough, and J. Rossi. 1979. "Effect of Joint Hospital Admission and Couples Treatment for Hospitalized Alcoholics: A Pilot Study." *Addictive Behaviors* 4: 155–65.

Miller, P.M. 1976. *Behavioral Treatment of Alcoholism.* Oxford, England: Pergamon.

Miller, P.M., M. Hersen, R. Eisler, and D. Hemphill. 1973. "Electrical Aversion Therapy with Alcoholics: An Analogue Study." *Behaviour Research and Therapy* 11: 491–97.

Miller, P.M. and M.A. Mastria. 1977. *Alternatives to Alcohol Abuse: A Social Learning Model.* Champaign, Ill.: Research Press.

Miller, W.R. 1978. "Behavioral Treatment of Problem Drinkers: A Comparative Outcome Study of Three Controlled Drinking Therapies." *Journal of Consulting and Clinical Psychology* 46: 74–86.

Miller, W.R. and G.R. Caddy. 1977. "Abstinence and Controlled Drinking in the Treatment of Problem Drinkers." *Journal of Studies on Alcohol* 38: 986–1003.

Nathan, P.E. and M.S. Goldman. 1979. "Problem Drinking and Alcoholism." In *Behavioral Medicine: Theory and Practice,* edited by O.F. Pomerleau, and J.P. Brady, pp. 255–78. Baltimore: Williams and Wilkins.

Pavlov, I.P. 1927. *Conditioned Reflexes,* translated by G.V. Anrep. London: Oxford University Press.

Pomerleau, O.F. and D. Adkins. 1980. "Evaluating Behavioral and Traditional Treatment for Problem Drinkers." In *Evaluating Alcohol and Drug Abuse Treatment Effectiveness: Recent Advances*, edited by L. Sobell, M. Sobell, and E. Ward, pp. 93–108. New York: Pergamon Press.

Pomerleau, O.F. and J.P. Brady, Eds. 1979. *Behavioral Medicine: Theory and Practice*. Baltimore: Williams and Wilkins.

Pomerleau, O.F., M. Pertschuk, D. Adkins, and J.P. Brady. 1978. "A Comparison of Behavioral and Traditional Treatment for Middle-income Problem Drinkers." *Journal of Behavioral Medicine* 1: 187–99.

Pomerleau, O.F., M. Pertschuk, and J.A. Stinnett. 1976. "A Critical Examination of Some Current Assumptions in the Treatment of Alcoholism." *Journal of Studies on Alcohol* 37: 849–67.

Rathus, S.A. 1973. "A 30-item Schedule for Assessing Assertive Behavior." *Behavior Therapy* 4: 398–406.

Robichaud, C., D. Stickler, G. Bigelow, and I. Liebson. 1979. "Disulfiram Maintenance Employee Alcoholism Treatment: A Three-phase Evaluation." *Behaviour Research and Therapy* 17: 618–21.

Roman, P.M. 1981. "From Employee Alcoholism to Employee Assistance." *Journal of Studies on Alcohol* 42: 244–72.

Roman, P.M. and H.M. Trice. 1976. "Alcohol Abuse and Work Organizations." In *The Biology of Alcoholism: Social Aspects of Alcoholism*, vol. 4. edited by B. Kissin and H. Begleiter, pp. 445–517. New York: Plenum.

Rosalki, S.B. and D. Rau. 1972. "Serum Gamma-glutamyl Transpeptidase Activity in Alcoholism." *Clinical Chimica Acta* 39: 41–47.

Sanchez-Craig, M. 1980. "Random Assignment to Abstinence or Controlled Drinking in a Cognitive-behavioral Program: Short Term Effects on Drinking Behavior." *Addictive Behaviors* 5: 35–39.

Skinner, B.F. 1953. *Science and Human Behavior*. New York: MacMillan.

Skinner, H.A. 1981. "Different Strokes for Different Folks: Differential Treatment for Alcohol Abuse." In *Evaluation of the Alcoholic: Implications for Research, Theory, and Treatment*, edited by R.E. Meyer, et al. DHHS Publication No. (ADM) 81–1033. Rockville, Md.: National Institute on Alcohol Abuse and Alcoholism.

Sobell, L.C. and M.B. Sobell. 1973. "A Self-feedback Technique to Monitor Drinking Behavior in Alcoholics." *Behaviour Research and Therapy* 11: 237–38.

Sobell, L.C., M.B. Sobell, and E. Ward, Eds. 1980. *Evaluating Alcohol and Drug Abuse Treatment Effectiveness: Recent Advances*. New York: Pergamon.

Sobell, M.B. and L.C. Sobell. 1976. "Second-year Treatment Outcome of Alcoholics Treated by Individualized Behavior Therapy: Results." *Behaviour Research and Therapy* 14: 195–215.

Spielberger, C.D., R.L. Gorsuch, and R.E. Lushene. 1970. *Manual for the State-trait Anxiety Inventory*. Palo Alto, Calif.: Consulting Psychologists Press.

Tiebout, H.M. 1949. "The Act of Surrender in the Therapeutic Process with Special Reference to Alcoholism." *Quarterly Journal of Studies on Alcohol* 10: 48–58.

Turner, S.M., K.S. Calhoun, and H.E. Adams. 1981. *Handbook of Clinical Behavior Therapy*. New York: John Wiley.

Watson, D. and R. Friend. 1969. "Measurement of Social-evaluative Anxiety." *Journal of Consulting and Clinical Psychology* 33: 448–57.

Wiens, A., J. Montague, T. Manaugh, and C. English. 1976. "Pharmacological Aversive Counterconditioning to Alcohol in a Private Hospital: One Year

Follow-up." *Journal of Studies on Alcohol* 37: 1320–324.

Wilson, G.T., R.C. Leaf, and P.E. Nathan. 1975. "The Aversive Control of Excessive Alcohol Consumption by Chronic Alcoholics in the Laboratory Setting." *Journal of Applied Behavior Analysis* 8: 13–26.

Wolpe, J. 1973. *The Practice of Behavior Therapy,* 2nd edition. New York: Pergamon.

SECTION THREE

Employee Counseling Programs

Second to alcoholism programs, the employee assistance or employee counseling program is one of the oldest and most common type of program instituted by the occupational clinical psychologist. They have been variously instituted at all types of organizations over the past four decades. Recently, there has been considerable interest in the employee counseling program as a potential vehicle for employee health care cost containment, as a method for enhancing productivity, and as an expression of management's genuine concern for their employees.

Because of a wide variety of circumstances and contingencies, different organizations institute different programs with different emphases. This section will examine a number of counseling models, settings, specific foci, and issues related to their development and success.

In his chapter, "Executive and Employee Counseling Program Models and their Uses," Dr. Harold Schmitz proposes a definition of employee counseling programs as developed by the New York Occupational Clinical Professions Group. The chapter discusses the rationale for the development of an employee counseling program and looks at a variety of program models: the alcoholism and/or substance abuse program, the information and referral program, the executive and employee counseling program, and the comprehensive employee counseling program. Dr. Schmitz is careful to consider the variety of models used as vehicles for providing employee counseling program services (such as the internal or external program), the need for an organization-specific program, the access to programs, special populations requiring particular types of attention, program sponsorship and location, the orientation of the program, and program accountability. Dr. Schmitz ends with a comment on program evaluation and his list of predictors for program success.

Whereas Dr. Schmitz's chapter focuses on general employee counseling program models and issues, it is primarily aimed at discussing private corporation-based programs. Dr. Lawrence Fisher, in his chapter, "Employee Counseling Programs and Related Services in the Public Sector," devotes his attention to the employee counseling program in the federal government. Dr. Fisher outlines the primary characteristics of government-sponsored counseling programs and walks the reader through a "typical" federal counseling program. Although there are many similarities between the corporation-based program and the government-based one, there are numerous subtle but important differences. In particular, the legal and administrative structure of the government requires specific differences. In his overview on the assistance process, Dr. Fisher reviews the mechanics of counselor-management interactions, the initial assessment of the problem and the course of action it requires, and the importance and nature of training supervisors to attend to performance problems with an eye toward a referral to the counseling program. The importance of confidentiality within the context of federal regulations is also discussed. Dr. Fisher then covers the various program models within the federal government, winding up with his thoughts regarding the effectiveness of a program, concentrating on the need for more attention to the dilemmas of federal managers and supervisors and the need for a more general upgrading of services.

An appropriately recurring concern on the part of any employee counseling program is that regarding program credibility, confidentiality, and related ethical issues. In her chapter, "Credibility, Confidentiality, and Ethical Issues in Employee Counseling Programming," Dr. Marilyn Puder reviews the importance and complexity of these issues in establishing and maintaining a viable employee counseling program, regardless of where it may be located or what its intentions may be. The subtleties and difficulties involved in serving the host corporation and the client require an astute concern for maintaining the highest of ethical standards. Dr. Puder's notion of the therapeutic alliance, as cultivated by the occupational clinical psychologist, serves as a springboard for her discussion regarding ethical issues, the limits and nature of confidentiality in the occupational setting, the duty to warn clients regarding those limits, and the need for developing a specific set of ethical principles that must be communicated to all actors in the organizational setting.

Although the development and maintenance of credibility, confidentiality, and the highest standards of ethics are critical factors in running a successful program, there are other issues requiring attention if the employee counseling program is to survive in the host corporation. All too often, in both clinical case studies and descriptions of programs, we are plied with "successes." We know from experience that not all interventions are successful. Dr. Steven Nahrwold, in his chapter, "Why Programs Fail," reviews the primary reasons for the failure of an employee counseling program. In addition to the breech of ethics as a factor in program failure, Dr. Nahrwold discusses the absence of senior management support, incompetent or inappropriate staff, crusading and "brush beating," excessive advocacy, antibusiness attitudes, unrealistic promises regarding possible results, and political factors.

Finally, Dr. James Manuso, in his chapter, "The Metamorphosis of a Corporate Emotional Health Program," reviews the reasons for the development of employee counseling programs at this time in the history of the United States and focuses on the gradual development of the Emotional Health Program at the Equitable Life Assurance Society of the United States from its founding in 1956 to the present. Program services, users, and utilization patterns are evaluated, and guidelines for program staffing patterns are generated. This chapter ends with an appreciation for the metamorphoses a program may experience over the course of its existence.

The reader will leave this section with a good sense of the multifaceted issues regarding a relatively simple matter—a counseling program intended for employees. The major and subtle differences between an employee counseling program and any other counseling program will be better understood following this section.

7 Executive and Employee Counseling Program Models and their Uses

Harold V. Schmitz, Ph.D.

Executive and employee counseling programs, in one form or another, go back over 40 years. They began as occupational alcoholism programs in the 1930s and 1940s and gradually increased their scope until, in the 1970s, they began to deal with other emotional problems affecting job performance. From 300 company-sponsored programs in 1972, they have grown to around 5,500 today and are found in many major corporations (Schmitz, 1977, 1981).

The reasons for industry's interest in establishing executive and employee counseling programs (ECPs) are twofold: a humanitarian concern and a concern for productivity. The humanitarian reasons for helping someone with personal difficulties are obvious. But industry is becoming most sensitive to the impact of personal problems on productivity as well. Reductions in absenteeism and wage garnishments, costs of replacing trained employees and valued executives, increases in productivity, savings on medical benefits, reductions in employee turnover rates, especially among minorities and women, have all been established as direct results of ECPs (Schmitz, 1979, 1980). Dolan (1978) has reported on the risks reduced through employee counseling programs.

Basically, corporations have established occupational mental health programs because they make good business sense. Such programs protect and develop human resources. When the climate is right management supports these programs, emotional problems are less stigmatized, and employees, including traditional nonutilizers of such services, seek psychotherapy when available (Cummings, 1977).

WHAT ARE EXECUTIVE EMPLOYEE COUNSELING PROGRAMS?

ECPs have been described by the Occupational Clinical Professions Group, a New York based professional association (Bailey, et al., 1978). Executive and employee counseling programs are defined as professional counseling, consultative, and/or supportive services provided to executives, employees, and organizations within the context of their work community.

Counseling programs in industry have two main goals: the prevention or early detection of problems that might affect work performance and the maintenance or restoration of valuable human resources to full productivity. Counseling and supportive services address the major personal problem areas that affect an individual's functioning in work or other life settings: emotional, financial, legal, marital, family, job, and substance abuse concerns. The counseling services are tailored to the needs of the employees. They include: assessment and evaluation, information, professional counseling, rehabilitation, referral, and follow-up.

Those services can be structured to accept individuals on a voluntary basis or through referrals for job jeopardy, or both. Services may be provided to family members or retirees, as well as to active employees. An ECP can provide some or all of these services.

Programs may also provide consultation and education services. Supervisors can be instructed on how the program works to encourage employees in need of help to use the service. Managers can be trained to identify and refer individuals whose work performance is suffering. Educational seminars can be held for employees on problems known to cause stress and impair performance. And consultation can be made available to individual supervisors concerning specific problems.

To satisfy professional codes of ethics and standards and meet insurability requirements, all ECPs should be under the direction of a licensed mental health professional. Moreover, programs must adhere to all standards that govern privacy and confidentiality.

WHY AN ECP?

It is an accepted fact in industrial psychology that many corporate problems—high turnover rates, chronic absenteeism and lateness, work-related "accidents," premature death, and high utilization of medical insurance coverage—are based in large part on the personal and interpersonal difficulties experienced by employees. These difficulties include (1) job changes that produce stress, such as coping with transfers, demotions, or job abolishment (Manuso, 1977, 1979b), (2) family problems, (3) divorce, (4) financial problems, and (5) interpersonal difficulties.

Research by Holmes and Rahe (1976) has shown that more than 75 percent of important stress reactions experienced by individuals originate in their private lives. These stress reactions are transferred to the work setting, where performance suffers because of outside preoccupations. Management as well as union employees are affected by these problems, and an impressive number of studies, including those of Levinson (1981), Selye (1980), Manuso (1979a), and McLean (1974), describe the effects of stress and anxiety on executives.

ECPs aim to help executives and employees cope more effectively with these difficulties through a program of active, brief counseling. Individuals are helped in identifying issues in their lives that interfere with their functioning and sense of well-being and to clarify possible solutions. ECPs, as one aspect of wellness programs in business and industry (Schmitz, 1981; Egdahl, Walsh and Goldbeck, 1980; Matarazzo, 1980; Manuso, 1979b, Kiefhaber & Goldbeck, 1979; Sehnert & Tillotson, 1978; Cohen, 1969), emphasize prevention and health promotion through the service of psychologists and other mental health professionals. ECPs aim at lifestyle modification and at maintenance and enhancement of healthy, or healthier, levels of well-being and functioning. As mental wellness programs, ECPs are currently gaining an increasingly interested, if sometimes skeptical, audience in industry at a time when employer costs for insurance coverage of medical and psychological treatment have sharply risen.

PROGRAM MODELS

Beginning an executive and employee counseling program requires, first of all, a clear concept of the type of service needed by a given corporation. The range of human problems is practically infinite, and no program can supply help for them all. Realistic decisions, based on an accurate needs assessment, are made for one or another of many clinical services this type of program can offer.

This chapter presents the wide range of options open to a company in need of executive and employee counseling services. The best program is the model that best fits the company's assessed needs (Schmitz, 1981).

There are four basic models of executive/employee assistance and counseling: (1) alcohol/substance abuse, (2) information and referral, (3) executive and employee counseling, and (4) comprehensive ECPs.

Alcohol/Substance Abuse

Alcoholism counseling programs have a long and successful history in industry. The third Conference Board study (Weiss, 1980) on occupational alcoholism indicates that the number of actively concerned companies has increased significantly. Of the 346 programs described in this report, only 61 were in existence in 1970.

Much evidence supports the fact that these programs continue to have significant impact on the recovery of alcoholic executives and employees (Dolan, 1978; Follmann, 1978; Herzlin, 1976). Business is impressed with this evidence, especially since alcoholism ranks among the top three or four of America's health problems (Weiss, 1980).

These programs emphasize that alcoholism is a disease. Since one of the first symptoms is deteriorating job performance, the workplace is an appropriate alcoholism treatment setting. The supervisor typically assumes program referral responsibilities. Programs are located in corporate medical or employee relations departments. The latter departments are particularly interested because of the focus on job performance.

Many occupational alcoholism programs–properly labeled "employee assistance programs," "EAPs," or "troubled employee programs"–rely on staff comprised of recovered alcoholics. Currently there is a definite shift to expanding the program to address all substance abuse and to professionalizing these programs through the addition of licensed mental health staff (Manuso, 1979b; Puder, 1979; Schmitz, 1979).

Prescribed treatment is frequently in accord with the principles of Alcoholics Anonymous (Poley, Lea, & Vibe, 1979; Mendelson & Mello, 1979; Follmann, 1978). Most recently, there has been a greater reliance on treatments based on detoxification and rehabilitation at residential alcoholism treatment facilities. While costly, detoxification insurance coverage is currently available. Many occupational alcoholism programs provide assistance to family members as well.

Information and Referral

Internal information and referral services, when nonprofessionally based, address a variety of employee concerns: legal, consumer, financial, child-care, housing, and education matters to name just a few. In addition, staff provide referral to appropriate outside or internal helping resources or agencies. Staff are not expected to provide direct, brief, or long-term counseling regarding matters of personal concern, such as emotional problems, interpersonal relations, marital and family relations, and substance abuse difficulties. Services are usually provided at convenient company locations and through telephone hotlines by part-time or full-time staffs within the personnel or employee services function.

Referral services, when professionally based, exclude direct counseling and psychotherapy, while providing diagnostic intake and referral to an appropriate treatment resource for presenting executive/employee problems. Professional referral services are frequently provided by ECP consulting firms. Often times, and certainly for larger companies, the differences in cost between "referral only" services and brief counseling services is slight.

Executive and Employee Counseling

ECPs address executive and/or employee concerns through diagnostic intake, counseling, information, and referral services. Counseling when provided is brief: employees are informed at the outset that there is a fixed time limit for services, thereby encouraging rapid identification of issues and a focused approach to problems. This model recognizes the psychotherapeutic advantages (Budman, 1981) and cost benefits (Cummings, 1977) of brief therapy. Counseling is provided by mental health professionals and specialized counselors.

All personal problem areas are addressed, including, but not limited to, marital and family relations, interpersonal relations, emotional difficulties, and career concerns. Substance abusing executives and employees receive diagnosis and referral treatment. Services are provided on-site or off-site, through medical or personnel department sponsorship, and by in-house staff or external consultants.

Comprehensive ECPs

The comprehensive model provides broadly based, integrated professional services that emphasize prevention and rehabilitation rather than treatment and wellness rather than illness. Comprehensive ECPs, while recognizing the need to treat one problem area so as to improve executive and employee performance, also recognize the need for broadening ECP services. Rather than provide a fragmented resource for any one personal problem—alcoholism, interpersonal difficulties, stress—comprehensive ECPs address the whole person. Comprehensive ECP staffs can provide a treatment approach that recognizes multiple problems as well as their interelationship. Employees abusing alcohol or drugs will have additional emotional and family difficulties needing treatment. Comprehensive ECPs are sufficiently staffed to respond to multiple problems.

Comprehensive ECPs emphasize prevention through sponsorship of special issues programs. These programs are educational, informative, and wellness facilitating. Special programs such as parenting, caring for aged relatives, budgeting, career development, preretirement and retirement planning can make significant contributions to helping executives and employees prevent and cope with stress.

SERVICE MODELS

ECP services are provided by internal or external staff comprised of professionals, paraprofessionals, and nonprofessionals. At least one mental health professional licensed or certified to practice psychology, social work, or psychiatry should be on staff and have program responsibility. Whatever the program model,

ECP professional services should not be entrusted to persons without extensive training, relevant corporate experience, and statutory protection regarding confidentiality. Unlicensed staff should be under the supervision of licensed staff. Criteria for psychologists rendering occupational clinical services as well as for other occupational mental health practitioners has been addressed (Schmitz, 1981).

Internal ECPs provide executives and employees with in-house professional services by staff who are on the company payroll or by independent practitioners under company contract. External ECPs provide executives and employees with professional services provided by ECP consulting firms. These services indicate that external ECPs typically provide assistance at an off-company site. Many variations exist on internal/external ECP models reflecting a combination of some internal and some external services. In some companies, employees have a choice between external or internal services.

Few companies provide "pure" internal or external programs. In a survey of companies with employee assistance programs, Ford and McLaugin (1981) found that approximately two-thirds of the companies reported alcohol, drug, and legal counseling to be available through outside services. Nearly all internal ECPs of companies surveyed by Schmitz (1977) were found to rely on referral to outside assistance for long-term counseling psychotherapy and for marital, family, legal, and financial matters. Most of these companies used outside resources for treating chemical dependency.

PROGRAM COMPONENTS

The program model once selected, must be fine tuned to a specific corporation. Consideration of the advantages and disadvantages of each model (Schmitz, 1981) and consideration of a number of program options leads to the selection of model components that best fit corporate needs. The major program components describe: referral access, special populations, sponsorship, location of services, orientation, accountability, and evaluation.

Referral Access

ECPs are accessed through voluntary and/or supervisory referral. In voluntary access, the option to seek help and the decision to call for an appointment rests solely with the executive or employee. No one should make an appointment for the executive or employee other than himself or herself. It does not mean that supervisors who observe personal difficulties that are obviously affecting work or personal functioning cannot speak to the employee about the availability of ECP services and their potential usefulness.

In supervisory referral, the decision to call for an ECP appointment rests either with the supervisor or with the employee wishing to prevent pending job discipline. Under no circumstances are employees forced to accept treatment, because a punitive approach is harmful in many ways. Assuming confidentiality is completely protected (Puder, 1979), supervisory referrals have certain disadvantages (Schmitz, 1981), especially if ECP training for supervisors is not properly presented at appropriate intervals.

Some ECPs specify both access models through a corporate policy that outlines the circumstances for supervisor referral and self-referral. Depending on organizational climate, a clear procedural separation of these two access tracks within the same program can encourage proper utilization.

Special Populations

While ECP benefits are available to company executives and employees, program availability for other populations may be considered. These populations include spouses and/or children of executives and employees, retired employees and their dependents, part-time employees, and terminated employees.

While all companies surveyed by Schmitz (1977) excluded terminated employees from ECP services, the current practice for the remaining groups vary. Most companies report that while few retirees actually visit the counseling office, many make telephone inquiries regarding needed referral services. The goodwill created more than offsets minor additional costs. Providing ECP services to dependents is related to company policy, additional costs, and staff availability. The availability of ECP services to part-time employees usually conforms to the availability of other company benefits to this group.

Sponsorship

Generally, ECPs are located in or sponsored by personnel or medical departments. Placement of program responsibility in any one of the departments does not eliminate the need for the cooperation and support of other departments. However, wherever it is placed organizationally, it is important that ECPs function ethically and at an organizational level that obtains desired utilization of a company's executive and employee population.

Location of Services

ECP services can be provided at one or several on-site or off-site locations. The use of multiple ECP centers is dependent upon considerations of company size, geographic region served, availability of staff, travel time to ECP centers, and program costs.

Information and referral can also be provided by telephone services. Providing such services during business hours or through emergency 24-hour hotlines is dependent upon existing mental health and social resources within each corporation's community.

Orientation

An ECP is utilized to the extent it is properly and clearly communicated through multiply based orientation training programs. Program orientation clearly communicates the company's ECP and encourages proper referral, access, and utilization.

Self-referral is enhanced when ECP staff communicate the program at all new-employee orientations, executive development programs, and other special employee relations programs. Supervisory referral is enhanced when supervisors learn, through formalized ECP training programs, how executive and employee counseling addresses supervisory needs. The frequency and type of program communication is finely tuned through a monitoring of program referral by supervisors within various organizational groups and utilizations.

Program Accountability

ECPs are accountable to senior management according to ethical standards and national and local law regarding privacy, privilege, and confidentiality (Gibbons, 1980; Everstine et al., 1980; Puder, 1979; American Psychological Association, 1977; Shah, 1969-70). Program accountability is enhanced by professionally based record keeping and management feedback reports, which rely on an analysis of anonymous aggregate data. Such data describe program utilization according to a specified demographic breakdown and relate cost benefits according to measurable program outcomes. The type of aggregate data collected, analyzed, and reported and the frequency of such reports to senior management addresses accountability areas specified in the proposal.

Program Evaluation

When designing program evaluation models, keep in mind that many companies with ECPs do not use traditional cost-benefit analysis to justify their programs. The collective experiences of these companies underscore the need for caution when proposing methods to obtain difficult-to-determine ECP benefits. Except for ECP components responding to alcohol or drug abuse problems within a supervisory referral framework, cost-benefit data become most difficult to obtain validly and reliably. Obtaining personnel data from personnel files for program evaluation must not be done without informed release from the executive or employee (Schmitz, 1981; Nahrwold, 1980).

PREDICTORS OF PROGRAM SUCCESS

There are a variety of interdependent predictors of successful ECP models. A significant reduction in the input of any of these can hamper program success and the quality of care from the outset. Basically, executive and employee counseling programs prosper to the extent that:

- Senior management provides support.
- Union support is provided when employees are organized.

- The program is confidential.
- The program is placed at an appropriate organizational level in the company.
- Medical, personnel, and labor relations departments cooperate.
- The staff has professional expertise and skills.
- The professional staff has full knowledge and experience with eclectic and brief goal-oriented counseling models.
- A full-time program director is assigned for in-house programs.
- An in-house coordinator is assigned for external programs.
- Clear corporate policy is communicated.
- Suitable external resources are cooperative.
- Program communication is targeted in a timely fashion.
- The program is nonpunitive.
- The program is accepted by the company's executives and employees.

A clear focus on these criteria is required throughout the design phase of the program. Periodic monitoring of these criteria, once the program is running, will help determine program areas in need of adjustment.

REFERENCES

American Psychological Association. 1977. *Ethical Standards of Psychologists.* Washington, D.C.

———. 1979. *Psychology as a Health Care Profession.* Washington, D.C.

Bailey, M., J.S.J. Manuso, M. Puder, and H.V. Schmitz. 1978. *Executive and Employee Counseling Programs.* Unpublished manuscript. (Available from authors).

Budman, S.H., Ed. 1981. *Forms of Brief Therapy.* New York: Guilford Press.

Cohen, W.J. 1969. "Revolution in Mental Health." *Personnel Administration* 32: 4–8.

Cummings, N.A. 1977. "The Anatomy of Psychotherapy under National Health Insurance." *American Psychologist* 32: 711–18.

Dolan, J. 1978. "Reducing Risks through Employee Assistance Programs." *Risk Management* (October): 1–5.

Egdahl, R.H., D.C. Walsh, and W. Goldbeck, Ed. 1980. *Mental Wellness Programs for Employees.* New York: Springer-Verlag.

Everstine, L., D.S. Everstine, G.M. Heyman, R.H. True, D.H. Frey, H.G.J. Johnson, R.W. Seiden. 1980. "Privacy & Confidentiality in Psychotherapy." *American Psychologist* 35 (9): 838.

Follmann, J.F., Jr. 1978. *Helping the troubled employee.* New York: AMACOM.

Ford, R.C. and F.S. McLaughlin. 1981. "Employee Assistance Programs: A Descriptive Survey of ASPA Members." *Personnel Administrator* 26 (9): 29–35.

Gibbons, J.A. 1980. *Privacy, Protection and Personnel Administration.* New York: New York Chamber of Commerce & Industry.

Herzlin, D.O. 1976. "A Psychiatrist's Concept on Treatment of Employed Alcoholic People." *NCA Labor-Management Alcoholism Journal* 5(6): 1–5.

Holmes, T.H. and R.H. Rahe. 1976. "The Social Adjustment Rating Scale." *Journal of Psychosomatic Research* 11: 213–18.

Kiefhaber, A. and W.B. Goldbeck. 1979. *Employee Mental Wellness Programs: A WBGH Survey.* Washington Business Group on Health, Washington, D.C.

Levinson, H. 1981. "When Executives Burnout." *Harvard Business Review* 59 (3): 72–81.

Manuso, J.S.J. 1977. "Coping with Job Abolishment." *Journal of Occupational Medicine* 19 (9): 590–602.

———. 1979a. "Executive Stress Management." *The Personnel Administrator* (November).

———. 1979b. "The Metamorphosis of a Corporate Emotional Health Program. Presented at the convention of the American Psychological Association, New York, September.

Matarazzo, J.D. 1980. "Behavioral Health and Behavioral Medicine: Frontiers for a New Health Psychology." *American Psychologist* 35 (9): 828–40.

McLean, A.A. 1974. "Mental Health Programs in Industry." In *American Handbook of Psychiatry,* vol. 2, edited by S. Arieti, pp. 786–99. New York: Basic Books.

Mendelson, J.H. and N.K. Mello, Eds. 1979. *The Diagnosis and Treatment of Alcoholism.* New York. McGraw-Hill.

Nahrwold, S.C. 1980. "Ethics in Industrial Mental Health." In *Mental Wellness Programs for Employees,* edited by E.H. Egdahl, D.C. Walsh & W. Goldbeck, pp. 112–21. New York: Springer-Verlag.

Poley, W., G. Lea, and G. Vibe. 1979. *Alcoholism: A Treatment Manual.* New York: Gardner Press.

Puder, M. 1979. "A Professional Employee Counseling Program: Credibility Issues." Presented at the convention of the American Psychological Association, New York, September.

Schmitz, H.V. 1977. *ECP Survey of Business and Industry.* New York: Author.

———. 1979. *"Occupational Clinical Psychology: A New Field for Psychologists."* Symposium chaired at the convention of the American Psychological Association, New York.

———. 1980. "Costs and Benefits of Employee Counseling." Presented at the convention of the American Psychological Association, Montreal, September.

———. 1981. *Executive and Employee Counseling: A Handbook.* New York: The New York Business Group on Health.

Sehnert, K.W. and J.K. Tillotson. 1978. *A National Health Care Strategy: How Business Can Promote Good Health for Employees and their Families.* Washington, D.C.: National Chamber Foundation.

Selye, H. 1980. "The Stress Concept Today." In *Handbook on Stress & Anxiety,* edited by L.B. Kutash and Schlesinger & Associates, San Francisco: Jossey Bass, 127–43.

Shah, S.A. 1969–70. "Privileged Communications, Confidentiality and Privacy." *Professional Psychology* 1 (56–69): 159–64, 243–51.

Stanford Research Institute. 1976. *Occupational Alcoholism Programs in U.S. Companies.* LRPS Report No. 572. Meno Park, Calif.: Stanford Research Institute.

Weiss, R.W. 1980. *Dealing with Alcoholism in the Workplace.* Report. No. 784. New York: The Conference Board.

8 Employee Counseling Programs and Related Services in the Public Sector

G. Lawrence Fisher, Ph.D.

CHARACTERISTICS OF EMPLOYEE ASSISTANCE PROGRAMS IN THE FEDERAL GOVERNMENT

The EAP* in government was conceived in legislation (Public Laws 91-616, 92-255, and 93-282) and regulations (U.S. Office of Personnel Management). The EAP in industry was developed partially in response to the humanism of the 1960s and largely to reduce employee costs. Both governmental and industrial programs will continue to evolve, and their paths are predictably different. Governmental EAPs will continue to conform with the stream of legislation that deals with government employees. Private EAPs may be expected to respond to employee, managerial, and industrial needs. Further, ineffective and costly practices may be expected to be dropped by private industry relatively quickly. Governmental EAP practices will continue for as long as legislation and regulations dictate.

EAPs are expected to serve the interests of individual employees, supervisors, and management simultaneously. Sophisticated EAP staff tend to maintain distance perspective lest they feel the short-term pangs of conflict of interest. For instance, the agenda of a federal personnel office is to ensure adherence to

*The acronym EAP (employee assistance program) is used to refer to: troubled employee, health service, employee alcoholism and drug abuse, and employee counseling service programs. Similarly TE is used to refer to all manner of *troubled employee.*

Office of Personnel Management (OPM) regulations. Management wants productivity that is apparent in reports sent on to the cabinet member who is ultimately responsible for the mission of the agency. Employee and first-line supervisory requirements, in contrast, tend to be turgid. The TE who is self-referred often does not know what he wants, although relief from some pressure in his life or "regaining control" is usually the stated objective. From the EAP point of view the primary objective is to alleviate the TE's problem sufficiently to improve his performance *on the job.* However, as Rouseau (1978) points out, nonwork factors are more highly related to job stress than are work factors. Further, work factors are more highly related to job satisfaction. Thus, EAP personnel often find themselves addressing a high proportion of problems derived from relationships with spouses, children, and personal financial problems. Determining the individual-case boundary constraints is often difficult. EAP coordinators and counselors may follow many paths to reach their ultimate objectives.

EAP staff serves importantly during their transactions with supervisors. Most supervisors identify with the organization, the employees, and, to some degree, with senior management. They are most vulnerable when they deviate from Office of Personnel Management (OPM)-stipulated procedures and equal employment opportunity (EEO)-related issues. EAP objectives when dealing with supervisors include personal counseling to relieve the supervisor's stress, training supervisors to perform early recognition and referral of TEs, assisting them with their documentation requirements (e.g., encouraging daily logging of poor work performance, which many supervisors are loathe to do). The EAP staff must perform these functions without violating the rights and privacy (confidentiality) of the TE. Further, when TEs are referred to an EAP by the supervisor the referral is treated as a *personnel action.* The supervisor must always act consistently with local personnel policy and the *Federal Personnel Manual.* In summary, a major objective of EAP coordinators, counselors, and consultants is to be legalistically astute and extremely flexible at all times. Ultimately the EAP must answer to everyone.

A TYPICAL FEDERAL EAP

The EAP presented below is a composite from a model proposed by the United States Office of Personnel Management, material drawn from reports of Greater Boston federal agency EAPs, discussions with EAP coordinators and counselors, and the author's personal experiences.

The government EAP is usually managed by a *coordinator,* who is either a federal employee or a private contractor. The hierarchical level of the coordinator varies among EAPs and is largely dependent upon organizational characteristics. In some instances he is a doctoral-level individual with extensive experience in psychology, industry, government, and academia. At the other end of the continuum he may be a lower or middle grade employee from the personnel office who was assigned to the job in order that the organization comply with the law. Licensed clinical social workers, nurses, clinical psychologists, and ex-ministers have all been co-opted into the role. The specific skills required, of course, vary with the demands and characteristics of the organization and the population to be served. In some instances the coordinator reports to an advisory committee, or to organizational administrators responsible for health and safety of their employees.

Many coordinators develop a referral directory of in-house resources and community resources. These are exceedingly important because of limitations on the extent to which therapy can be offered on the premises and the varieties of presenting problems. The in-house directory will contain such information as names, telephone numbers, and locations of staff who could be available to assist an employee seeking assistance. Typically, the health unit, personnel office, credit union, equal employment opportunity council, recreation association, Alcoholics Anonymous (in-house), federal women's program and other service units are included. These directories may be annotated with the specific services offered. The community resource directory will include all likely service agencies, AA, Al-Anon, Alateen, Mental Health Association, legal aid clinics, hotlines, and many more. The better directories provide information regarding services the resources offer, populations served, fees, orientation, and other salient information. Another important component of a community resource directory provides annotated lists of mental health services available, including groups and individuals in private practice.

A few EAPs provide stress management training both on an individual and group basis. These are presented either by staff members or contractors. The training may consist of a seminar lasting a few days or an extended series of meetings lasting several months.

All EAPs appear to provide some form of counseling services. These may be limited to a few sessions prior to referral out, or crisis intervention, or even extended counseling if referral out is not feasible and qualified counselors are available. Successful counseling requires that the duration and style be appropriate to the TE, the problem at hand, and organizational realities.

Those EAPs that are connected with health units tend to integrate their services with those provided by the medical staff. The nursing staff also functions as an important source of in-house referrals. This is especially true of alcohol abusers and persons who are at risk for cardiac disorders. Many individuals appear at health units regularly and frequently for blood pressure checks, allergy shots, and other repeatable medical procedures. These people can often be persuaded to have a brief interview with an EAP counselor to determine if there are problems amenable to EAP services.

Biofeedback and relaxation training clinics seem to be on the upswing. These seem to have been developed in larger organizations.

EAPs have record maintenance and reporting systems that conform to strict confidentiality requirements of federal regulations. It is notable that under current legislation EAP coordinators may be fined up to $5,000 for violating the confidentiality of an employee's referral/treatment.

A REPRESENTATIVE ASSISTANCE PROCESS

A troubled employee arrives at the EAP office either at his own initiative or that of his supervisor. The receptionist or appropriately assigned EAP staff obtains preliminary information. If the employee has been referred by a supervisor, a formal procedure is required. In either case, background information about the employee is obtained, so material can be mailed to his home address and a significant person can be reached by telephone if that becomes advisable. Personal data that can influence the management of the problem and/or safety of the individual is obtained.

Assuming that the supervisor makes the initial contact with the EAP to seek advice, he is invited to discuss details of the problem within the confidentiality of the EAP environment. The counselor attempts to elicit complete job-related details of the situation. Both the supervisor and counselor clarify their respective positions. They also decide if there will be a meeting of the counselor, employee, and supervisor. No information provided by the employee may be given to a supervisor without written consent by the employee. If disciplinary action is being contemplated the employee must sign a consent form allowing the counselor to disclose private information for use in a disciplinary situation. However, this information, if disclosed, must not be harmful to the patient, the program, or the patient-counselor relationship. Management must presume that where an employee does not provide consent for disclosure in a disciplinary situation, the information will not be forthcoming. Disciplinary actions are always based on job performance not progress in a rehabilitative program. In the instance of self-referral, management is not entitled to any information from the counselor and the agency is not involved except at the TE's request. In either case, the TE must participate voluntarily to achieve benefit, even if the supervisor provides the motivation.

Assessment of the Problem

The counselor usually determines the parameters of the problem in a few sessions. If supervisors or management are involved EAP staff may request signed consent to obtain additional information. The purpose is to avoid misinterpretation by any of the parties involved. Strict confidentiality is maintained, except to authorized persons who are provided information with prior consent of the TE. The counselor, after assessment, shares observations with the TE and may suggest a means by which the presenting problem may be remedied. If accepted by the TE, the next phase begins.

Course of Action

The counselor prepares a plan of action and presents it to the TE for his consideration. The plan has the status of a *suggestion* by the counselor. It is discussed by the TE and counselor, and implications and responsibilities of all parties are clearly stated. The plan can be presented in the form of options, with the TE selecting the one he feels is most appropriate and acceptable. The options may include referral to a community resource (AA or other appropriate group), referral to a community mental health professional, or short-term counseling by the EAP staff if they are qualified. Long-term therapy is not provided by the EAP staff. Because the costs of extended therapy could exacerbate an already difficult situation, crisis intervention in the form of stress management training, advisement, and discussion may be appropriate approaches if they are likely to prevent a drastic behavioral act. The decision is the responsibility of the counselor or coordinator. An action plan is agreed upon and written as an agreement. It is later reviewed during the course of intervention. If short-term intervention opens up new issues or if, for any reason, long-term therapy is advisable, the TE is referred to the most appropriate community mental health organization or other resource. The referral file is a most valuable asset at this stage in the transaction. The counselor also acts as an advisor to the TE by discussing health insurance benefits, transportation problems and remedies; the counselor even acts as a negotiator with the agency to ensure that everyone concerned is aware of the problems, proposed solutions, and planned outcomes. The TE moves into the last phase, monitoring and follow-up.

If the TE is referred out, the EAP staff seeks permission from the TE to discuss progress with the therapist. The TE is encouraged to return to the EAP at suitable intervals and provide progress reports to the responsible EAP staff. If an employee does not fulfill the treatment plan, or does not show demonstrable improvement in job performance, the supervisor decides whether or not to pursue an alternative personnel action. Thus, it is important to train supervisors to judge job performance in a reliable and communicative fashion.

Training Supervisors in a Federal Setting

Training supervisors in a federal government setting is difficult. Many supervisors have been promoted into their positions on the basis of skills other than supervisory. Many newcomers are insecure and overburdened in the role. Thus, as suggested by Phillips, Purvis, and Older (1980), supervisors who deal with troubled and alcoholic subordinates themselves require counseling. Typically, supervisors attend relatively short training seminars into which a great deal of material has been compressed. They are presented federal policies and procedures regarding employees who are either acting out or drinking excessively. They are taught how to use these procedures in their own organizational setting. They are presented with the warning signs of alcohol abuse, primarily on the basis of employee behavior. They are encouraged to refer troubled subordinates to the

EAP. Regardless of how well this material is covered, if the supervisor is hesitant to use the information meaningfully, there is little point to the training. Unfortunately, many governmental organizations often reward supervisory inaction, preferring instead to cover a problem. This has been justified (during the author's personal conversations with supervisors) on the basis that they (supervisors) would have to spend more time dealing with personnel regulations than would be justified by protracted supervisory actions. Bayer and Trice (1978) found in research on the Federal Civilian Alcoholism program that when supervisors were first taught, and then accepted, the medical model of alcoholism, they were cautious in dealing with the EAP.

An approach that incorporates supervisory needs has been offered by Phillips, Purvis, and Older (1980) and should be considered. They developed a supervisory training seminar that includes the following topics among others:

- Federal and organizational policies and procedures.
- Behavioral indices that signal excess alcohol intake or existence of other problem.
- Techniques for confronting the subordinate.
- Procedures for referring the subordinate to the EAP or other service unit.

Usually the supervisor is rendered uncomfortable by this information when he realizes that he is supposed to use it to do something to or with someone else who may not like the idea! Supervisors are encouraged to present themselves before an EAP counselor to deal with their own emotional conflicts first; then they fulfill the procedures that are required and/or advisable in dealing with the TE. The supervisor is made aware that it is not a "cop-out" to ask EAP staff to assist him. He is helped to understand that seeking advice and receiving it does not obligate him to use it and that what he has discussed in confidence will remain confidential. Regular attempts are made to establish and maintain trust between supervisors and EAP staff.

The supervisor is often his own measuring instrument when determining the severity of the problem. The extent to which he feels uncomfortable is itself a useful measure of the severity of the disturbance of the routine activities of the organization. The EAP staff counselor is presented as a supporter, colleague, and competent aide for the supervisor. The intent is that referrals will be made sufficiently early to preclude reaching crisis levels.

CONFIDENTIALITY

The prudent EAP coordinator and his staff are knowledgeable about all aspects of privacy and confidentiality legislation.

The Privacy Act of 1974 requires that a person being asked for personal information be given certain facts before acting on the request. The EAP can only request the TE's social security number. In addition, legislation provides for the confidentiality of alcohol and drug abuse records. The individual is not required to provide any personal information under the program. Participation is voluntary. Information provided by a participant will not be disclosed without the participant's written consent. Evaluations are performed on records that do not allow identification of an individual. However, EAP counselors do have access to the participant's file, as do the participants. In no case is the individual's file or data allowed to be released to a supervisor. The files are usually physically located in the offices of the EAP; individual files seldom leave the counseling facility.

This and similar legislation specifies that there is a distinction between supervisors and EAP staff; the EAP staff is discouraged from discussing confidential material with persons without a "need to know." Further, the supervisor is not entitled to information about a subordinate he has referred to EAP staff. Alcohol or drug-related information developed during preemployment and fitness for duty examinations are accorded confidentiality. Information regarding alcohol and drug abuse may be released for determining eligibility for disability retirement, or for a prospective employer only with written permission by the individual. EAP staff may disclose information obtained during a counseling interview regarding alcohol and drug abuse and relating to criminal activity if "patient identifying information" is excluded. Disclosure of "patient identifying information" is permitted with a court order and if a crime involves bodily harm or may be committed on program premises. This legislation also specifies procedures for obtaining authorizing court orders.

Because the coordinator does perform an alcohol or drug abuse prevention function, as defined in Section 2.11 k of Public Law 93-282, he is liable under Section 2.14 for fines up to $5,000 for violation of the confidentiality of an employee's referral treatment.

Thus, governmental EAP coordinators are, or should be, circumspect and prone to documentation. Further, they are always well-advised to inform the TE of his rights under pertinent legislation.

Federal Personnel Manual Regulations

All EAP coordinators who do not relate directly to a personnel office are advised to do so, even if informally. Federal personnel regulations fill volumes, and many of the activities of EAP staff touch these regulations. These include unsatisfactory job performance reports, other adverse actions, reductions-in-force, EEO actions, disabilities, retirement, and many more. The prudent EAP coordinator checks with a personnel "mentor" when any sensitive issue comes up in counseling or during preliminary interviews. It is also important that no "person identifying information" be provided during these inquiries. The EAP counselor is especially "at risk" when a troubled employee is referred by a supervisor because of job performance deterioration and/or "poor interpersonal relationships." The EAP counselor is always attentive to both regulations and confidentiality issues during his dealings with both the TE and the supervisor.

EAP MODELS IN THE FEDERAL GOVERNMENT

Agencies may operate an EAP using a variety of alternatives. In fact, the same functions are served by all models; what varies is how and by whom shall the TEs be served. An agency may have its own EAP with services performed by in-house staff or qualified individuals brought in under contract. An alternative is to use another federal agency's in-house program or contract, with another agency assuming contract leadership. The responsibility for the maintenance of an effective program always rests with the agency served, and they decide if it is to be maintained in its current form and/or with the current staff.

Single Federal Agency Program

Selection of this model is determined by the characteristics of the work population and their families. For instance, a large, geographically isolated installation is best served by an on-site, in-house program. Conversely, a large, widely dispersed and mobile population suggests that more effective service could be delivered by a set of counseling sites scattered throughout areas where employees normally work, or by regional telephone networks staffed by counselors skilled in telephone interviewing and knowledgeable about resources available in the employee area. Where a work force is relatively small the agency may hire a part-time counselor, or retain a consultant on a limited basis, or contract with a nearby community resource to provide services on a per capita basis.

Multiple Federal Agency Programs

Small federal installations may use another's in-house capability. Usually the smaller agency will appoint its own program coordinator. A "tenant committee" is established to assist the host agency providing the service with the administration of the facility.

When no single federal agency program can function as a provider and combined employee populations of several local installations may be sufficiently large to support a contract for a cooperative program, such a contract may be awarded. One agency serves as the principal contracting agent for all participants. The participating agencies are bound to the contract with the service provider through a memorandum of agreement with the contracting agent.

Fortunately, federal regulations are often sufficiently flexible to allow any appropriate model EAP, as long as it serves well. One is constrained only by the limits of imagination and sophistication of management.

EFFECTIVENESS OF EAPS

Confidentiality legislation renders a meaningful evaluation of EAPs nearly impossible. The true worth of a program is the change in employee performance influenced by EAP efforts. However, change in a person is difficult to measure and illegal to publish. Performance measures commonly used because they are more easily metricized are often influenced by non-EAP factors, the vested self-interest of EAP staff in maintaining their program, and the career investment of sponsoring managers who, once having made the decision to fund a program, are committed to its apparent success.

Most federal programs use input measures, that is, counts of people using the services and tallies of how many users improved, did not improve, or terminated (retirement, adverse actions, disability, etc.). While these measures are useful for determining program utility in identifying problems and providing supervisors with a useful tool, they provide little guidance for improving the quality of services.

The political nature of EAPs is documented in an excellent survey volume by Shain and Groeneveld (1980). They summarize a study of the Baltimore Employee Health Program that existed from 1973 through 1976. The program was phased out for lack of funding. It was an outpatient service for 12 employing organizations contracted by the U.S. Department of Labor to be managed by the Johns Hopkins University School of Hygiene and Public Health. An executive committee managed the project; it consisted of representatives of management, unions, and members of Baltimore's "alcoholism community." Pressures were continually exerted to extend services, research, and new directions. The large staff of the executive board was concerned with funding and sustaining itself. Considerable energy was expended in balancing and satisfying the perceived needs of the participating interest groups. Thus, it collapsed.

The successful EAP coordinator is especially attentive to the needs of the vested supporters and sponsors as well as the participants. Further, as analyzed in Cooper and Payne (1980), evaluation is supremely stressful in its own right. One may legitimately wonder if the costs of evaluation do not swamp the ambiguous benefits (numerical products) of the activity when these measures often deal with presumed effectiveness and not the political realities.

FUTURE DIRECTIONS AND RECOMMENDATIONS

Two important future directions for EAPs include more intensive dealing with the special needs of federal managers and supervisors and the general upgrading of services. The bias of this chapter is that new forms of EAPs and development of more extended policy statements and new manuals will add little to the improved effectiveness of the services performed by EAP staff. On the other hand, improved selectivity of coordinators and counseling staff could make a profound difference in the future. The author's experience in dealing with persons who run "successful" EAPs and with those who appear to be dominated or swamped by their difficulties is that the competence and experience of the coordinator is a major factor. The coordinators who can relate to managers on their own level, can "eyeball" aggressive occupational physicians, can relate to members of the AA fellowship, can negotiate with the alcoholism "industry," and can cut through red tape by virtue of their ability to identify and relate to critical organization staff are the ones who can succeed and perform the greatest service to user ogranizations. Perhaps the most important act that EAP consultants and coordinators can perform over the coming years is to *not* dictate the characteristics of acceptable EAPs and their staff. Formalizing credentials will probably do more to inhibit the innovative, developmental and entrepreneurial skills of EAP managers than it will to upgrade the quality of our service products.

A major protracted issue is that of the frustrations and anger of the federal manager. The frustrations are many and the anger is unitary, usually directed within. Many senior executives earn considerably less than their industrial counterparts with whom they often must deal. Many have not had a raise in salary for four years, as of spring 1981, and the purchasing power of their salaries is declining steadily. Several strata of executives receive the same salaries. If the rewards of federal employment at senior levels are not financial then they must be symbolic, including *hope* for future nonfederal higher-paying employment. Current symbols include an illusion of power over subordinates, which usually consists of withholding information, dispensing "perks," and distributing furniture, office space, equipment, travel, and positive performance evaluations. Given the nature of most managerial influence, ambiguities of many agency products, and the caprice of the political process, as well as negativity brought to the workplace from outside sources, it is no wonder that management radiates its discontent both laterally and downward. The widespread climates of stress and depression one often encounters in a federal setting are challenges to EAPs. A major task of this profession is to develop superior methods to train managers and supervisors to discharge or at least reduce inner tension and conflict in a productive and effective manner. If this is accomplished everyone will benefit.

REFERENCES

Bayer, J.M. and H.M. Trice. 1978. *Implementing Change: Alcoholism Policies in Work Organizations*. New York: The Free Press.

Brasch, P. 1980. *"A Helping Hand from the Boss." Parade,* June 8.

Cooper, C.L. and R. Payne. 1980. *Current Concerns in Occupational Stress.* New York: John Wiley.

Local Government Assistance Task Force, Federal Laboratory Consortium, Far West Region. 1979. *Stress: A Survey of Emotional Health Management*

Programs. Report compiled by San Diego Science and Technology Applications Center. December 1, 1979.

Masi, D. 1979. "Combating Alcoholism in the Workplace." *Health & Social Work* 4(4): 41–59.

Munter, P.K. 1978. "Occupational Psychiatry: A One-Man Program." *Psychiatric Annals* 8(4): 38–39, 43–45.

Phillips, D.A., A.J. Purvis, H.J. Older. 1980. *Turning Supervisors on to Employee Counseling Programs.* New York: Hazelden Press.

Rouseau, Denise. 1978. "The Relationship of Work to Non-Work." *Journal of Applied Psychology* 63(4):513–17.

Shain, M. and J. Groeneveld. 1980. *Employee-Assistance Programs, Philosophy Theory and Practice.* Lexington, Mass.: D.C. Heath & Company.

U.S. Office of Personnel Management. 1980. *Employee Assistance Program, Coordinator's Handbook.* Manual prepared for the U.S. Department of Agriculture.

9 Credibility, Confidentiality, and Ethical Issues in Employee Counseling Programming

Marilyn Puder, Ph.D.

The occupational setting has been gaining recognition as a site for clinicians providing counseling services. For economic, legal, and humane reasons, employee counseling programs have come of age and are seen as one of the vehicles employers can set up to promote the mental wellness of employees.

Underlying the enthusiasm, however, lurks occasional ambivalence. Although there is a general recognition of the importance of fostering mental wellness for employees, there can still be doubts about the credibility of employee counseling efforts. Some doubts seem directed primarily at ethical issues, such as concerns over possible violations of the privacy of employees as they "bare their souls" to the occupational clinician (O'Toole, 1980).

Faced with a plethora of employee counseling approaches and models, a burgeoning body of literature on occupational stress and mental wellness programs, and an array of professional, paraprofessional, and nonprofessional practitioners, the time is ripe to reinforce the importance of credibility as one of the cornerstones in the viability of any employee counseling effort. This chapter will address the issue of credibility, equating it with the clinical concept of the therapeutic/working alliance.

This chapter is not intended as a handbook or exhaustive review of professional legal/ethical issues involved in employee counseling programming, nor will it provide comprehensive guidelines on developing a credible program. Good sources are available for those readers wishing to explore these issues in greater detail. In addition to other chapters of this volume, readers are advised to seek knowledge from the Springer-Verlag series on industry and health (Springer-Verlag, New York 10010) and the Addison-Wesley series on occupational stress

(Addison-Wesley, Reading, Mass., 01867). In addition to being familiar with all the professional standards and ethics promulgated by the professional associations, readers are advised to obtain knowledge on the federal and state rulings and statutes affecting the mental health profession in their areas.

Before proceeding, certain key terms need clarification. *Employee counseling program* (ECP), as used here, is a global term for a wide variety of program models, all of which provide confidential service on a voluntary basis. This chapter will, however, distinguish among the personnel who can carry out the counseling. *Clinician* is used in this chapter as a synonym for *counselor* and includes in its definition only those practitioners who are duly qualified and licensed members of a mental health profession. This focus on professionals does not mean that nonprofessionals and paraprofessionals have no relationship to ECPs. It is my opinion that whatever the program model, there should be at least one member of the counseling team who is a licensed professional. That individual is responsible and held accountable for the program's adherence to ethical standards. It is, therefore, this unique contribution by professionally trained and licensed clinicians that is being distinguished in this chapter, especially in light of the discussion of legal/ethical issues.

WORKING ALLIANCE

Much of our training and experience as clinicians has been in learning about and developing "therapeutic alliances." These alliances in their most positive and constructive sense have involved two-way working alliances between ourselves and our clients (Greenson, 1967). We have learned that the alliance is a partnership founded on: the client's positive anticipation regarding receiving help and his or her capacity to trust, the clinician's professional skills, a judicious combination of warmth and empathy, and a consistent adherence to professional standards and ethics in practice.

The clinician in the occupational setting must use clinical tactics in developing and maintaining a similar trusting working alliance with the host organization (as well as with individual clients). In addition to having the professional skills that fit the specific needs of the ECP, the clinician needs to possess the rational and intuitive perceptiveness necessary for straddling the worlds of business and mental health. The clinician, in addition, should have the sensitivity and maturity to have personally integrated outer-directed business values with the more inner-directed humanistic ones.

In the outreach efforts undertaken by the clinician and other program staff to "market" the ECP, it is essential to highlight the interrelationship between these two value systems. It is critical that the ECP is not viewed as another human resource "fad." The direct relationship between humanistic and business goals needs to be communicated; that is, if a person is helped in coping with problems in living, his or her personal effectiveness and competence and productivity will be either maintained, restored, or enhanced.

It is the premise of this chapter that the credibility (and utilization) of an ECP will develop and be maintained to the extent that the clinician (and other program staff) possesses a judicious combination of clinical and business skills and develops, communicates, and adheres to a specific code of ethics. This code serves as the framework for the legitimacy and stability of an ECP.

ETHICS AND SHADES OF GREY

Philosophers have approached the definition of ethics for centuries. The great prophets themselves chose to outline their precepts as frameworks for conduct. Ethics, although more subjective than the law, but nevertheless often overlapping it, reflect this concern for good conduct and behavior.

The mental health professions each have standards and codes of ethics to guide the professional whatever his or her specialty or setting. This uniformity may be partly responsible for the lack of specifics in some of these guidelines.

Cohen (1979) in his discussion of legal/ethical issues for mental health professionals points out that in addition to vague ethics, the legal statutes and licensing regulations of mental health professionals are often confusing and chaotic, varying as they do from state to state. He states that activities that are legal and considered to be ethical in one state may be illegal and considered ethically improper in another state.

This state of affairs, according to Cohen, "begs ordering." He writes:

> Working closely with responsible public representatives, professional organizations need to formulate specific professional guidelines and then disseminate those guidelines to members of the profession and the public. Until such guidelines are prepared, mental health professionals must practice within the relatively nonspecific guidelines of their professional organizations, monitor . . . lawmaking activity in the area, and remain responsive to an internalized code of ethics. . . . (1979, p. 100).

Although all mental health professionals should be concerned and aware of the situation highlighted by Cohen, it is my belief that occupational clinicians may have to be even more concerned. Occupational clinicians may be faced with potential dilemmas of divided loyalties and "Catch-22" situations involving balancing the needs of individual clients against others more often than the private practitioner.

The occupational clinician, in addition, may confront more intense and ubiquitous initial resistances than a clinician in a traditional mental health environment. This resistance may be caused by general ignorance and/or prejudice concerning the role of a clinician within an occupational setting. Fears and concerns about privacy, intrusion, as well as the stigma over mental illness also contribute to the resistance.

Due to these factors, the occupational clinician must assume and communicate a greater ethical responsibility in order to work through this resistance and insure a constructive working alliance in the occupational setting.

CONFIDENTIALITY

Nahrwold (1980) points out that the most crucial ethical issue in an ECP is confidentiality, primarily because violations in this area will destroy a program faster and more decisively than anything else. Consistent adherence to ethics regarding confidentiality will, correspondingly, be decisive in maintaining the credibility of an ECP and the alliance between the clinician and the host organization.

Privileged Communication

Some issues in confidentiality have already been determined by federal and state statutes. State statutes, for example, have provided for a form of extension of the constitutional right to privacy ("taking the fifth")–the right to have kept private those communications made to someone with whom the communicator shares a special relationship. The right of "privileged communications" has been extended in many states from attorney-client relationships to include relationships between mental health professionals and clients.

For example, the confidential communications between a licensed psychologist and his or her client are privileged under New York State law. A psychologist in New York may only disclose privileged information at the request of his or her client. The privilege belongs to the client not the psychologist. The psychologist may not disclose the communications that took place unless the client consents. But, as pointed out by Mariano and Feldman (1980), legal counsel to the New York State Psychological Association, the area of privileged communication is complex and varied. Certain conditions must be met before the privilege arises (e.g., the communications must have been in the course of the professional relationship between the licensed psychologist and the client where no strangers are present and the communication must not relate to the commission of some crime or civil wrong).

Mariano and Feldman also suggest that a slight variation in the facts of a case could cause privilege to rise or fall, since there are several instances where the privilege is not recognized.

Cohen (1979) explains that privileged communication relates to law as confidentiality relates to ethics. Professional codes of ethics provide for professional-client confidentiality as a standard of conduct. The statutes give the ethical standard legal status. Although applicable statutes vary from state to state, in regards to counselors they relate only to licensed mental health professionals who are included and who can state that their relationships (if conditions are met) are privileged under the law.

Breaching Confidentiality and Duty To Warn

The area of disclosure of confidential information is also complex. The law does not hold that privilege is absolute. There do exist situations in which disclosure without the client's consent of confidential information is permissible, even mandated. Professional ethical codes provide for the breach of confidentiality under extraordinary circumstances just as the law provides exceptions to rules against disclosure.

For example, according to the 1974 ruling of the California Supreme Court in the landmark *Tarasoff* v. *The Regents of University of California,* "protective privilege ends when public peril begins" (Cohen, 1979, p. 62). The Tarasoff decision legally compels California mental health professionals to breach confidentiality when this "public peril" begins. This legal "duty to warn" when a client is perceived by a clinician as possibly homicidal is one of the major and probably most controversial exceptions to the rule of privilege (Barton & Sanborn, 1978; Saxe, 1980). For example, in New York, the State Psychological Association (*New York State Psychologist,* 1980) is presently studying what should be required by law in terms of this "duty to warn" and is asking the Regents of the State to consider legislative problems in drafting a law on this issue.

Where does the clinician's obligation to his or her individual client end and to that of the corporation and society at large begin? How do we define peril?

One of the problems in determining answers to the above questions is the lack of specificity that exists in the law, as well as in professional codes of ethics in the area of breaching confidentiality. Cohen (1979) points out that hints exist in many of the professional codes, but they are certainly not very clear! For example, the American Medical Association code states that:

> Confidence . . . should never be revealed unless the law requires it or if necessary to protect the welfare of individuals or the community . . . . (Ibid., p. 63)

The American Psychological Association's code (1977) states that safeguarding information about an individual that has been obtained in the course of professional practice is a "primary obligation" of psychologists and that such information is not to be communicated to others unless certain conditions are met. One of the conditions in which revelation of confidential material is deemed appropriate is "after most careful deliberation and when there is clear and imminent danger to an individual or to society."

In 1976, the American Occupational Medical Association adopted a code of ethics for physicians providing occupational medical services. Although the principles are also quite general, they have been made a little more specific to the occupational setting. The following is a principle regarding confidentiality:

> Treat as confidential whatever is learned about individuals served, releasing information only when required by law or by over-riding public health considerations, or to other physicians at the request of the individual according to traditional medical ethical practice; and . . . recognize that employers are entitled to counsel about the medical fitness of individuals in relation to work, but are not entitled to diagnoses or details of a specific nature. . . .

The next section highlights some procedures and/or principles that the occupational clinician can use to deal with the oftentimes grey area of ethics.

DEVELOPMENT OF SPECIFIC ETHICAL PRINCIPLES

As a program model is tailored to the structure and needs of an organization, a "code of ethics" should be developed and tailored to the specific ECP. The clinician responsible and accountable for the program should, prior to the development of a code, consult with the respective professional organizations and corporate counsel and become familiar with the federal and state statutes relating to privileged communications as well as the ethical standards and conflict of interest policies of the corporation (host organization).

This consultation and research should give the clinician a framework from which to develop the code. The code should include principles similar to those promulgated by the clinician's respective professional association but made as specific as possible to the occupational clinical setting and the specific ECP services.

The code should specify the philosophy and policy governing the ECP, list the principles regulating program procedures, and include a statement on the *limits* of confidentiality (what specific situations warrant breaching confidentiality), on the status, retention, and access of program records, on the limits on collection of information, and on the release of information to internal and external sources. The code should specify principles regarding program staff conduct, responsibility, and competence.

In this section, some principles and procedures that are worthy of general consideration in drawing up a code are included.

On the *collection of information* during an initial interview with a client in an ECP, Nahrwold writes:

> It is generally unethical to collect unnecessary information on clients. Counselors who do so are often voyeuristic or seeking to surround themselves with an aura of omniscience.... Every counselor must make a series of pragmatic ethical judgments on the type and amount of information collected and make sure it is truly necessary, relevant, and accurate. (1980, p. 116).

What makes the information necessary and relevant would depend upon the level of assessment required, and that would depend on the focus and types of services provided by the ECP. Although diagnostic skills are a must and intelligent assessments do require sufficient probing of presenting and contributory problems/concerns, these clinical tools are often streamlined in many programs. These programs tend to see the "worried well" in greater numbers than the "ill." The primary reason is because potential clients are for the most part productive employees who, however distressed they may be by problems in living, still have sufficient ego strength to work. Therefore, many ECPs have a wellness focus that involves an appreciation of quality of life issues and concern for an individual's sense of well-being and that individual's ability to adapt effectively in the face of psychosocial stressors. The focus is on the maintainence of adaptive functioning and the prevention of more serious problems. If on-site counseling is offered in addition to information and referral services, it is usually of the "psychological first aid" variety (Puder, 1979). Intrapsychic change rarely is the goal, since long-term treatment is seldom offered. Typically, referrals to outside mental health professionals are offered if long-term treatment is indicated.

In light of all this, assessment as well as counseling services may be dynamic, but they generally remain pragmatic. Lengthy, in-depth intake evaluations are rarely necessary to arrive at intelligent assessments and provision of short-term services.

In terms of *case records,* Nahrwold (1980) points out that employees feel more comfortable if they believe ECP records are separate from other company records. A code of ethics should specify the status of program records and define those who can have access to them. The sole ethical situation is to limit the right of access to counseling staff *only.* The clinician should take strong precautions to safeguard confidentiality of records by denying access to noncounseling staff.

In his discussion of *conflict of interest situations,* Nahrwold highlights situations that involve balancing the needs of management with those of individual clients. The balancing act is inevitable since any in-house ECP serves two clients—the individual and the organization. It is critical that the code contain guidelines that specify ways of handling typical "Catch-22 ' situations.

For example, if the ECP accepts management referrals, what is the staff's obligation to management in terms of feedback on the employee? A general principle (similar to the American Occupational Medical Association's code of ethics) may be that management can be told that an employee came for his or her appointment, but confidential information derived during the visit should never be shared unless informed consent is given.

Nahrwold points out that there is no justifiable policy except one that makes *release of individual information* contingent upon the verbal and/or written *informed consent* of the client. The release of aggregate information that is used generally in utilization analyses and that preserves anonymity of clients should not be considered to be unethical.

Often occupational clinicians monitor and *supervise* paraprofessionals, nonprofessionals, and unlicensed professionals and can be held liable for their staffs' negligence. It is critical to stress in the ethical code the limit of services provided based on demonstrated competence of program staff. Clinicians should not take lightly their role as mentors providing clinical supervision as often and as responsively as possible. This attentiveness to staff serves not only to prevent potential legal/ethical problems, but it enables staff to grow and develop—leading to provision of *higher quality counseling services.*

Since *referral* is a frequent service offered by the ECP, the clinician has to make as certain as possible that the person or institution to which the client is being referred is appropriately licensed and equipped to handle the client's needs. This principle should be part of an ECP code. Clinicians should also avoid potential conflict of interest dilemmas by referring to *many* professionals and institutions rather than to a few.

The clinician, in arriving at the ECP policy on *limits of confidentiality,* should consult legal counsel to make certain the policy complies with the law. Program staff should be expected to consult with the clinician in charge prior to taking action, even in situations in which the breach of confidentiality appears warranted.

Although not directly related to drawing up a code of ethics, a word should be said about insurance. It is a good idea not only for the clinician to carry his or her own professional liability insurance, but also to arrange for the ECP to be covered under corporate liability insurance. This insures that corporate and individual staff interests will be protected in the event of litigation.

COMMUNICATION OF CODE TO ALL CONCERNED

In summarizing the first ten years of the American Psychological Association's professional liability program, Wright (1981) noted that the substantial number of malpractice cases involved the professional failing to *communicate* clearly to the client the nature and extent of professional services provided.

It is essential that the occupational clinician take a proactive stance regarding the development of a specific "code of ethics." Once developed, the standards and principles need to be clearly set forth in writing. Management should be made aware of the code. Clients should be given a verbal statement about the program's policy on confidentiality, including a statement of those situations that would warrant breaching confidentiality, prior to a discussion of their problems. Program staff should understand that job disciplinary action follows any violations of the code.

CONCLUSION

Within this decade, we hope to witness an increase in the trend toward professional comprehensive mental wellness efforts within corporate America. There can be tremendous potentials for creative, innovative programs, along with career opportunities for clinicians. But in our enthusiasm, let us never forget that the success of our efforts depends upon the development and maintainence of credibility and a positive working alliance.

REFERENCES

American Occupational Medical Association. 1976. *Code of Ethical Conduct for Physicians Providing Occupational Medical Services.* Board of Directors. New York: Author.

American Psychological Association. 1977a. *Ethical Standards of Psychologists* (Revision). Washington, D.C.: Author.

———. 1977b. *Standards for Providers of Psychological Services.* Washington, D.C.: Author.

Barton, W., and C.J. Sanborn, Eds. 1978. *Law & The Mental Health Professions.* New York: International Universities Press.

Cohen, R.J. 1979. *Malpractice–A Guide For Mental Health Professionals.* New York: Free Press.

Greenson, R. 1967. *The Technique & Practice of Psychoanalysis.* New York: International Universities Press.

Mariano, W.E. and S.J. Feldman. 1980. "Privileged Communications." *Annual Reference Diary.* New York State Psychological Association.

Nahrwold, S.C. 1980. "Ethics in Industrial Mental Health Programs." In *Mental Wellness Programs for Employees,* edited by W.B. Goldbeck. New York: Springer-Verlag.

New York State Psychologist 32 (December, 1980).

O'Toole, P. 1980. "The Menace of the Corporate Shrink." *Saavy Magazine,* October, 1980.

Puder, M. 1979. *"A Clinician Meets Industry."* Paper presented at the annual meeting of the American Psychological Association, New York City.

———. 1980. *"A Professional Employee Counseling Program: Credibility Issues."*

Paper presented at the annual meeting of the American Psychological Association, Montreal.

Saxe, D. 1980. "Must Psychotherapists Warn About Released Patients." *New York Times,* February 12, 1980.

Wright, R. 1981. "Psychologists & Professional Liability." *The Clinical Psychologist* 34 (Winter).

10 Why Programs Fail

Steven C. Nahrwold, Ph.D.

Current literature on industrial mental health care programs has little to say about program failure. Most articles discuss past successes or outline approaches that may lead to future success. Program failure, however, may be caused by obvious errors–such as neglecting basic duties or violating accepted standards of professional practice. But more often than not, the causes of program failure are less clear and deserve careful analysis.

"Failure" does not necessarily mean the complete collapse of a program. Even poor programs rarely cease to exist. Like "quack" therapies, some may even flourish for awhile and die only in the glaring light of public exposure. Most "failures" are simply programs that help some people but that are for the most part mediocre and marginally effective. They survive, hobbled by misguided policies or other inadequacies; more significantly, they fail to accomplish what *can* be done.

Background for this examination of program failure does not include an extensive list of formally documented case histories. However, direct experience in managing a large corporate program, discussions with directors of both successful and problem-plagued programs, and considerable reflection about avoidable pitfalls contribute to this analysis. While exposure to mental health programs in a union environment might add a special perspective, it seems safe to assume, even without direct experience, that these programs share many of the problems encountered in nonunion organizations. Their unique problems will be mentioned but not discussed in depth.

BREACH OF ETHICS

Nothing will destroy a program faster than disregard for ethics. Confidentiality is the most important of ethical standards and must be protected rigorously. To guard against breaches of confidentiality, program information and data should be maintained separately from all other company records–including regular medical reports and especially routine personnel records. Access should be limited to program staff, and no information should be divulged without verbal or, preferably, written consent. *Only* in the case of extreme homicidal or suicidal risk should confidentiality be breached–and then, whenever possible, with the client's foreknowledge.

Confidentiality applies to information supplied by management as well as to data on a company's problems as revealed in program practice. In the course of daily business, management often shares information with program staff that is, at the time, considered confidential. This information may concern future plans, reorganizations, office politics, promotions, transfers at high levels, etc. Although such information can be very helpful in counseling at a later date–particularly if job stress is a major factor–management has an equal right to confidentiality that must be respected. Whatever policies are concerning confidentiality, they should be clearly communicated to both clients and management.

Professional ethics have practical program applications beyond the protection of confidentiality. These will be cited later in this discussion. Basics are covered in the professional ethics code of the American Psychological Association, as well as in the various state and federal codes that apply to both mental health and alcohol and drug rehabilitation programs. Every industrial clinical psychologist should be thoroughly acquainted with these laws and documents.

LACK OF TOP-LEVEL SUPPORT

Every mental health program needs management support to survive. In most cases, management is responsible for at least half of all program referrals. In fact, most alcoholism programs rely on management awareness, identification, and referral.

Business organizations are usually hierarchical, and managers take their cues from superiors. While hierarchy is not always completely rigid, many organizations develop a strong structural emphasis not unlike a military chain of command. Given this reality, it is very important for the program to have top-level management support–preferably from the chief executive officer.

Union shops or highly decentralized companies may be different, but in most instances, a program that is intended to be taken seriously by first-line or middle management must be important to upper management, or be perceived as such. When building support, every program director should start at the top of the hierarchial pyramid and work down.

Of course, the director should avoid identifying the program too closely with one chief executive officer. As soon as possible, it should become part of an overall personnel policy and be integrated fully into the "company's way of dealing with problem employees." But endorsement from the top remains essential.

Program directors can labor for years to build grass-roots support for their programs without building top-level management support. Many of these programs are struggling to survive. This is especially true in companies with high labor turnover because the continuity that management can provide is lacking.

As noted, union shops possibly are different. Although first-hand program experience might reveal subtle differences, union support is obviously as crucial as management support, though probably not an adequate substitute for it.

STAFF INCOMPETENCE

Staff incompetence is a broad problem, but most staff inadequacies result from inaccurate self-assessment. As Clint Eastwood said in the movie *Dirty Harry,* "A man ought to know his limitations." Perhaps because psychotherapy and counseling are more of an art than a science, people with insufficient training sometimes overestimate their skills. This exaggerated perception is highly unethical and can lead to many problems with clients. Most professionals have heard of poorly trained counselors getting in "over their heads" with extremely sick clients and causing more problems in the attempt to extricate themselves from the mess. They begin to take responsibility for their clients' lives, encourage pathological dependency, or involve themselves in hopelessly tangled countertransference.

Staff incompetence also can have a major impact on the success of referrals. Problems begin when a counselor uses psychological tests with which he or she is not sufficiently experienced, leading to a misinterpretation of results. Counselors should be sufficiently skilled in both diagnostics and therapy, because referral is an intelligent process requiring adequate training. It is not as simple as giving out a name and telephone number.

Successful referrals first require that clients be adequately prepared, and that includes giving them some understanding of their problems, how therapy works, and how to contract for services. Second, staff members need a thorough knowledge of various types and theories of psychological treatment. They should know which types of treatment are most appropriate for different types of problems. For example, it is inappropriate to refer a manic-depressive illness to a psychotherapist when this disorder is best treated medically and by a psychiatrist. Third, a competent staff person knows his or her resources well and avoids fads and quacks.

A good general rule to follow is *don't try to do more than you're trained to do!* False claims of expertise, mishandling clients, and inappropriate referrals that do not "take"—all these can destroy staff and, ultimately, program credibility. If these errors go uncorrected, the program will fail.

CRUSADING

There is much disagreement on whether "crusading" should play a part in mental health programs. "Crusaders" are staff members who display an evangelistic fervor in their dedication to locating and reducing a particular problem—usually alcoholism. Most mental wellness programs in industry began as alcoholism programs, and most still identify this as their principal concern. These programs generally operate with an aggressive sense of urgency, attempting to locate alcohol abusers even before obvious performance problems can be documented. While this enthusiasm is generally laudable, the ultimate desirability of such an approach is questionable.

The case for or against crusading goes deeper than program "style." The fundamental question is one of intent and degree: how proactive or intrusive should a program be? Most mental health professionals are reactive and wait for patients to come to them. That approach is too passive for industry.

Yet programs are best when they "tilt" toward the reactive side. Although they encourage employees to seek help early, these programs project an image of objectivity, of having no ax to grind. They do not appear to exist for the sole purpose of eradicating any particular problem or disease, and they do not need aggressive management involvement in detecting illnesses. While the general "mental health" image itself carries some stigma, a program with an alcoholism or drug abuse image can hold more of a stigma.

For example, in advising an employee to seek program assistance, there is a kind of "implied diagnosis" if that program already is recognized as one specifically designed for alcoholics. Implied diagnosis is less of a problem if the program projects a broad concern for personal well-being and social service. It's not surprising that programs with this more benign image receive more referrals and more voluntary requests for assistance. While active crusading will not destroy a program—and may even create a "look" of success—this evangelistic approach may very well reduce the number of people seeking help.

Intrusive, proactive programs also seem less professional. They convey the notion that industry is one more arena for locating and confronting a specific disease (e.g., alcoholism). A more reactive, benign program identifies as its proper concern *anything* that disturbs a person's well-being or hinders performance. The task of an employee counseling program is to help employees solve their problems, not to try and eliminate some specific social ill.

EXCESSIVE ADVOCACY

Any industrial mental health program must be especially concerned with its neutrality and objectivity. While providing confidential assistance to an employee usually serves the interest of both the employee and management, there are times when counselors face agonizing conflicts of interest. These conflicts often arise between the needs of treatment or rehabilitation—usually involving time off the job or reduced responsibilities—and the current demands of the client's job. Another example is the difficulty in advising a valued employee to change jobs because of current job stress.

Whether directly stated or not, the expectation is that mental health care programs should be very sensitive to the needs of management. There is nothing inherently wrong with this idea, but it adds a difficult dimension to the single-minded client concern characteristic of private practitioners.

Most of the time, there is no conflict between management and employee expectations regarding a mental health program. A manager often suggests that an employee visit the program after the employee has confided a personal problem. Or an employee comes to the program on his own, and management heartily supports whatever help is necessary to ensure that employee's personal well-being. Fortunately, most managers have been trained to be sensitive to human needs and to maintain an enlightened attitude toward subordinates. This attitude could be viewed as paternalistic, and to some degree it springs from that management style. Yet, concern for employee welfare is an enduring force behind mental health care programs.

It should be recognized, however, that the relationship between labor and management in the United States historically has been one of competition and conflict. If the United States is to compete economically today and in the future, that adversarial relationship must give way to a spirit of cooperation and mutual respect. Yet due to that past conflict, employees often are suspicious of any program supported and financed by company management. Thus, in union shops, it is essential that the program have union endorsement as well as management support. In nonunion environments, it is equally essential that programs maintain an image of neutrality and a recognizable concern for the objectives and needs of both sides.

Any knee-jerk, automatic advocacy of either management or employee interests will destroy a program. If the program is *perceived* as an ally or extension of one side, it will lose the support of the other. Hence, it is helpful to be physically located in a neutral setting like the medical department. To enhance this image of concerned neutrality, some companies contract with outside agencies to provide mental health care in off-site offices. This is not really necessary; most major companies have succeeded in maintaining programs in-house. But the importance of evenhandedness, both in practice and appearance, cannot be emphasized enough.

While there are numerous legitimate occasions that warrant intervention in job-related matters, program staff should be wary of individuals who try to "use" the service for their own ends. Counselors can expect to encounter—on a daily basis—employees who attempt to be relieved of responsibility for poor attendance or performance because of personal factors. Some try to use the program to redesign their jobs, engineer transfers, or even obtain promotions. Questions like "Don't you agree that my boss' demands are unrealistic?" are not uncommon. Counselors must be very cautious about judging the job performance of either employees or their managers. It is best to stick to the data made available through the counseling activity itself. Staff members who are quick to put psychiatric labels on employees and exempt them from personal responsibility for their behavior—or who trace all employee stress problems to job pressures—have lost their objectivity and become employee advocates.

Managers may also try to "use" the program for their own purposes. For example, when the case against an employee is weak or poorly documented, a manager may push program staff to make a negative judgment on the employee or to "fire" him or her on medical grounds. When managers do not have the courage to terminate an employee or to alter employee responsibilities, they may turn to the mental health program, asking that the employee be declared permanently disabled or too ill to work at his or her present job. The manager is then in a position to lay the burden of judgment on the program when informing the employee of demotion or termination.

Counselors should be very careful about pitfalls like these that can lead a program toward a disastrous advocacy position.

ANTIBUSINESS ATITTUDES

Negative attitudes about the purpose and nature of business present an even greater threat to program success. While employee advocacy can result from either an "authority problem" or an indiscriminate sympathy for the underdog, doubts about the value and legitimacy of business—or even capitalism itself—present more fundamental problems for program staff.

There are historic prejudices with which program staff must contend. Since the mid-1960s, many books, journal articles, and public pronouncements by social scientists have depicted businesses as amoral, greedy, polluting, exploitive (or even fascist) organizations that sacrifice human values and social responsibility to increase profit. To counter criticisms portraying them as Dickensian villains, business people in turn have characterized social scientists as naive, bleeding heart academics or crypto-Marxist social agitators seeking to overturn capitalism.

Clearly, most of these epithets are mindless stereotypes. Social or behavioral scientists who wish to operate company programs should examine their attitudes and perceptions of business.

It is not sufficient to bear no particular grudge against the business world. Some counselors manifest an antibusiness attitude (or an incredible lack of social awareness) in their dress. Attempting to look "liberated" and "anti-establishment"—or simply refusing to adopt appropriate dress—will have a major impact on program credibility and acceptance.

Staff members will probably be more comfortable in business if they readily accept some of its values and goals. For example, it is assumed that they will not be antagonistic to the profit motive, provided it doesn't overshadow all other values. Perhaps the old cliche beginning "when in Rome . . .," or the biblical admonition to be "in the world but not of the world" can serve as helpful guides in developing the proper perspective.

Counselors need not become conservative Republicans in order to work with management—or liberal Democrats to work with unions. In fact, if staff members identify too strongly with all aspects of their company's culture, how can they be of help to the casualties of that culture's excesses? Every business culture has both healthy and pathological aspects, and counselors should have the wisdom and professional distance to know which is which. They can then help those who are wounded by the pathology. Effective staff members are able to "blend in" with their organization's culture and dress, affirming the positive, remaining critical of the negative, and effecting change in a manner that is both charitable and discreet.

Hostile attitudes and avant-garde dress are not the only possible forms of counterproductive behavior. A more subtle kind of professional arrogance—one that assumes that "helping people" is vastly superior to the "mundane" materialism of business—is another destructive posture. Professional counselors worry as much about their salary as do business people, and false distinctions between social service and other business professionals are patently hypocritical. Arrogance of that sort will not go unnoticed and will severely inhibit a program's effectiveness.

Hostile attitudes also are revealed in staff ignorance about the business of the organization that the program serves. Counselors need not try to become experts, but they should take the time to visit various areas or their organization in order to learn about its activities. In addition to generating considerable goodwill, showing a genuine interest over coffee or lunch with key people in various areas, asking questions, and trying to understand the demands and pressures of various types of work will be most helpful to program staff when clients come from those work areas for counseling.

In short, if counselors have little respect for or interest in the company they serve, they are poorly equipped to work in the programs sponsored by that company.

OVERPROMISING RESULTS

Psychology has more than its share of "snake oil salesmen" and quacks who offer a plethora of fringe theories and therapies. Eventually, most of them are discredited. As in most professions, genuine depth and experience in the field of psychology or psychiatry fosters profound humility and a realistic sense of limitations. Seasoned, honest professionals understand the uncertainty and difficulty of the attempt to make significant changes in human personality. While industrial mental health programs do make a difference, program staff members must always remain cautious about promising results. The temptation to overpromise is especially strong in industry, where the pressure for results is stronger.

The temptation to create unrealistic expectations can take several forms. The problem first arises in "selling" these programs to industry. Program counselors or agencies feel compelled to promise a certain penetration rate or cost savings to encourage the adoption of a program or to justify its expense. They then virtually guarantee to locate and assist a specific number of alcoholics or emotionally disturbed employees. Or they promise a specific dollar-and-cents return on every employee who receives assistance. But like research on the benefits of psychotherapy, most cost-benefit studies are inconclusive and can trap the unwary. As selling tools for industrial mental health programs, "tight" compelling studies are nearly impossible to devise.

Setting cost-benefit standards is not only difficult but also dangerous, because the mental health program could be continually forced to justify its existence on the basis of those standards, while other company programs, in training and development or medical, for example, are not required to do the same.

The problem of overpromising also surfaces in exaggerated claims made about the treatment to which an employee is referred. Sometimes such claims reflect the staff member's desire to make a successful referral when limited time prevents thorough handling of all the client's fears and objections to treatment. Unlike private practitioners, program counselors seldom have time for numerous sessions with each client. This is due to high volume of clients or a company mandate for short-term counseling only. Within the limits of a few sessions, it takes a great deal of skill to identify core problems and motivate clients to seek further assistance. The natural and strong temptation is to shorten the necessary preparation (pretherapy) process by exaggerating the results of referral treatment.

Sometimes overpromising treatment results is used to encourage management to refer clients to the program or to enlist management support for a particular employee's treatment—especially when that treatment involves time away from the job. Whatever the reason for making exaggerated claims, this practice will seriously damage credibility and can cause program failure. Counselors must always give an honest prognosis and should discuss openly the client factors (motivation, patience) so necessary to therapeutic success.

Advocating one form of treatment to the exclusion of all others is a shortcoming closely related to overpromising results as well as to incompetence and unethical behavior. Usually poorly trained and inexperienced, counselors who fall prey to this error have one tune in their repertoire and sing its praises as the only valid treatment for any illness. All clients are referred to this type of therapy, often with exaggerated promises of recovery. If this type of treatment is one of the numerous fringe therapies, the credibility of the entire program could be destroyed and its staff liable to a well-deserved malpractice suit. Further, if a staff member attempts to persuade clients to discontinue legitimate therapy to make way for this "favorite" treatment, he or she has committed a serious breach of professional ethics.

POLITICAL FAILURES

For many, the word "politics" conjures up images of the dark and devious. And most professionals in industrial programs probably would prefer not to become involved in this inescapable aspect of corporate culture. Yet, programs can surely fail as a result of extreme attitudes toward company politics—either by ignoring political situations or becoming too involved in them.

"Politics" means many things. On the positive side, it can mean understanding an organization's informal structure of power and influence. In program practice itself, it can mean attending to a "public relations" image in every sense of that phrase, as well as maintaining a good working relationship within all chains of command. In short, "politics" properly refers to the active preservation of a network of contacts and the careful cultivation of support and goodwill toward the program. This is the kind of "politics" in which program staff members should be involved.

At the same time, there are political games that program staff members should never play. These games involve all the dishonesty, aberrant attempts at publicity, breaches of trust, and unjust means of advancement that are well known—and often tempting. The most reprehensible tactic is to use the program as an "intelligence unit" to gather politically sensitive information for the benefit of company management. Evidence of such behavior will quickly destroy a program. To prevent abuses of confidential information, program data or test results should be reserved for counseling or clinical purposes only. Avoiding political gamesmanship includes withholding program information from placement or promotion decisions. If used for this purpose, program data should not be released without the explicit consent of the employee in question.

Program counselors face one further "political" temptation—probably most seductive for its clear benefits and comfortable rationale. In nearly all organizations, the power and prestige accorded to an individual are contingent upon several factors: budget size, importance and number of customers served, size of area managed, etc. Another determinant of prestige is the position of colleagues or clientele. If an individual regularly associates with upper-level managers or works closely with them—especially in a professional service capacity—that person generally enjoys a high social position within the organization. It follows that program staff members who regularly counsel or consult with higher management will probably be accorded higher positions and income. Pursuit of these advantages is very tempting because, ostensibly, the motive is still "human service" and perhaps a chance to influence "the system."

But as noted earlier, not all "political" behavior leads to program failure. If approached properly and kept within limits, these kinds of contacts can help maintain the upper level support so necessary for survival. They become destructive if the program's attention and energy are so focused on this particular clientele that broad service to all employees suffers. Such elitism eventually will damage the program's image with the majority of employees, and usage will decline.

Any sacrifice of a program's ethics, principal goals, or broad outreach is a destructive form of political maneuvering. All program directors must be sensitive to and differentiate between appropriate and inappropriate politics.

CONCLUSION

Most of the factors contributing to the failure of industrial mental health programs—like those that help them succeed—are intangible. Describing the elements common to most successful therapies, Jerome Frank, in his book *Persuasion and Healing,* discusses some of these intangibles, which include hope, faith, and human support, as well as the personal qualities of the therapist. Along the same lines, the World Health Organization Committee on Mental Health maintains that "the most important single factor in the efficiency of treatment in a mental hospital appears to be an intangible element which can only be described as atmosphere" (Jones and Sidebotham, 1962, p. 118). For an industrial mental health program, intangibles like staff personality, attitudes, prudence, judgment, and social and political awareness are crucial factors in maintaining a successful working relationship with both management and employees.

Because of their humanitarian intent, mental health programs have become both popular and well-publicized. Positive publicity has prompted business firms across the nation to establish such programs, and a host of new agencies have appeared, offering mental health services on a contract basis. Along with some businesses' lack of sophistication in evaluating services and staff, this current popularity has made it relatively easy for programs to survive. Growing interest has also produced a variety of program models, and in practice, a wide diversity in levels of staff training. But few guidelines have emerged for comparing programs or evaluating their success.

The need for a critical perspective may come sooner than expected. Trends in business in the United States signal not only increased concern for employee welfare, but also a harder look at employee benefits. In the changing economic environment of the 1980s, productivity, resource allocation, cost-benefit analysis, and a general "trimming" of wage and benefit "fat" are playing a more important role in strategic planning. Formerly accepted as standard, many employee programs will be subject to closer scrutiny than ever before.

Marginal programs may not survive that scrutiny. But out of increased emphasis on evaluating objectives and measuring results can come basic critical guidelines lacking in the profession today. The development of such standards would represent a milestone in the field of industrial mental health care and could contribute to the survival of a very good idea. Industrial mental health care *is* a good idea—not simply because it's an enlightened policy, but because it makes good business sense. With a relatively small investment in a mental health program, an organization can realize major gains in both employee welfare and cost control. Programs fail when they fail to produce the gains that are well within their grasp.

REFERENCES

Dunnette, Marvin S. 1976. *Handbook of Industrial and Organizational Psychology*. Chicago: Rand McNally.

Egdahl, Richard H. and Diana Chapman Walsh, Eds. 1980. *Mental Wellness for Employees.* New York: Springer-Verlag.

Frank, Jerome D., 1970. *Persuasion and Healing.* New York: Schocken Books.

Jones, Kathleen and Roy Sidebotham. 1962. *Mental Hospitals at Work.* London: Routledge and Kegan Paul.

Noland, Robert L., Ed. 1973. *Industrial Mental Health and Employee Counseling,* New York: Behavioral Publications.

11 The Metamorphosis of a Corporate Emotional Health Program

James S.J. Manuso, Ph.D.

Corporate emotional health programs are becoming increasingly common in the United States. There are a number of criticisms regarding such programs, stemming as they do from misunderstandings regarding the purpose, the staffing, and the experience of such programs. It is often felt that an in-house counseling program becomes an arm of management, that there is a basic conflict of interest for the practitioner. It is felt that management can whimsically mandate a broach of confidentiality on the part of the practitioner and that the interest of the corporation always takes precedence in every such transaction. It is also sometimes stated that short-term therapy is not effective, that this is merely a band-aid approach to highly difficult problems, and that such programs are primarily serving low socioeconomic status employees and women, who are stigmatized already. It is also sometimes stated that those who do stoop to use such a program are stigmatized and their jobs will soon be in jeopardy, if they are not already.

Based on a variety of corporate experiences and emerging research, these misunderstandings may now be properly addressed. Staff members of in-house emotional health programs function as practitioners with an existing code of ethics at all times, never broaching confidentiality and always respecting state law and professional, ethical practice. The patient comes first in every interaction, this always being the case regardless of the fleeting desires of management. In fact, any such program that did not meet these standards would soon find itself with a considerable paucity of clients (Manuso, 1979a). It is also clear that interventions employed by such programs are, indeed, highly effective, short-term and cost-beneficial (Cummings, 1977; Manuso, 1978). It is also being reported that executive level and lower level employees and males and females are using emotional health programs in exact proportions equal to their representation in the workforce. In some instances, minority employees, who must undergo considerable adaptation to the corporate environment, use employee counseling programs to a slightly greater extent than others. Finally, those employee counseling programs that have earned the respect and trust of employees tend to experience considerable demand for services. In some instances, research has shown that employees experience an increased rate of promotability after program interventions (Manuso, 1979b). Where there was stigma, now there is trust. In fact, the Government Services Administration recently mandated that the Potomac Electric and Power Company establish an employee counseling program as part of its affirmative action compliance.

Having already dispelled some myths regarding employee counseling programs, this chapter will go on to review five major issues. First, it will review the reasons for the development of employee counseling programs at this time in the history of the United States. Second, it will examine the history of the emotional health program for employees of the Equitable Life Assurance Society of the United States, from its founding in 1956 to the present. Third, it will discuss the services currently being offered by the Equitable's emotional health program, offering a profile of program users and their program utilization patterns. Fourth, based on the Equitable's experience, guidelines for program staffing patterns will be outlined. Finally, a number of general developmental trends in employee counseling programs, once they are founded, will be presented.

Why is it that employee counseling programs are rapidly developing in corporate settings at this time in the history of the United States? In our increasingly secular society, we come into contact with organizational life at every step along the developmental road. As a result, we are subject to those facets of the organizational structure that both enhance and detract from our quality of life. The organization has evolved into a site for the delivery of a multitude of human services, previously located in the exclusive domain of government. Modern U.S. corporations, perhaps the best examples of highly developed organizational structures, are increasingly finding themselves in the position of mental health care provider. The corporate experience is demonstrating that preventive services are the most cost-effective and viable in an institutional setting. In the future, more corporate mental health programs and policies will reflect this discovery.

Large organizations, in an effort to maximize their incrementally decreasing return on investments in human resources, have recognized their role as a stressor to their citizens. Because large organizations are dynamic, the stressors they generate are frequent, intense, and sustained over time, creating an environment conducive to the development of stress-related disorders. In turn, such disorders bring about significant deficits in the application of employees' social, intellectual, and learned skills, which are particularly important in organizational life. Moreover, these deficits are communicable in a social environment, bringing about measurable productivity declines. Since this means a measurable net loss to the employing organization, the selfishly altruistic need to correct the problem in a cost-effective manner consistent with sound business practice becomes paramount. This is fortunate for the mental health industry, which needs to become more cost-effective and preventive in its applications. Indeed, recent research shows that 50 percent of the daily stressors reported by employees originate at the worksite (Manuso, 1979b).

There are other social, legal, and economic reasons for a growing cottage industry of corporate mental health policies and programs at this time in our history. U.S. society has become increasingly complex, demanding rapid change, both interpersonally and institutionally. Previously avoidable confrontations because of the full emancipation of women in minorities, job changes, new sex roles, social alienation, divorce, relocation, greater competition, and new technologies and management systems are no longer avoidable. It should come as no surprise that the President's Commission on Mental Health (1978) suggests that 25 percent of all Americans are suffering severe emotional stress, that the majority of Americans are dying from stress-related disorders, primarily through hypertension, coronary artery disease, and associated heart attack, and that one-third to one-half of all general practice patients, including those seen in corporate medical departments, are presenting with stress-related problems. Americans, feeling more health conscious and seeking a higher quality of life, are recognizing the importance of associated behavioral change for their employees. Psychological health care is becoming less of a stigma and more popularly accepted; people feel that they need not be sick in order to get better and are more preventive in their approaches to personal health care. Employees, corporations, and unions are all being educated as to the benefits of preventive mental health measures. The "new breed" of employees, the younger, more politically and socially sensitized people, is more insistent on the corporation's demonstration of social responsibility and its associated services. This is a direct reflection of the new psychology of entitlement, now being recognized in the nation's board rooms.

From a legal perspective, with the advent of affirmative action and equal employment opportunity come the corporation's responsibilities for insuring the success and development of women, minorities, and the disabled in the organization. Thus, the vast problems of innercity minorities, who have historically received the least and the worst mental health care, become the problems of the employing corporation. People cannot be fired, nor can hiring be denied, for health-related problems that affect an employee's overall performance. The maintenance of confidentiality with respect to employee health records has encouraged employees to make use of corporate mental health programs. And corporations continue to eschew governmental mandate, preferring to act before being acted upon.

From a purely economic perspective, profit-minded corporations can no longer afford to close their eyes to the stress-related genesis of costly employee lateness and absenteeism, poor decisions, terminations, dissension in work groups, lost sales, lowered worker morale, overtime costs, disciplinary actions, grievances, and the like. And the corporate bill for our nation's health care costs and employee benefits (now one-third of salary and increasing) is emerging more and more on the balance sheet. On the services end, there are more mental health practitioners available, practitioners trained in interventions that are typically short in duration, making use of drugs and new technologies that are more effective and less expensive. Finally, because most corporations already sponsor employee medical departments, it becomes a relatively inexpensive task to intergrate a mental health program into an already existing health service. Some initial cost-benefit analyses of employee counseling programs are reporting cost-benefit ratios of one dollar invested to $5.50 return on that investment in regained productivity, lowered medical care utilization, and less time away from the job. (Manuso, 1979b).

The Equitable Life Assurance Society of the United States, the third largest life insurance company in the country, employs approximately 7,000 people at its New York based home office. There were three distinct phases of the Equitable's emotional health program. It began in 1956, with the advent of an alcoholism program. It was staffed with a half-time physician, who later became the chairman of the National Council on Alcoholism, and one recovered alcoholic who functioned as a counselor. This program was expanded in 1969 to include other substance abusers, primarily narcotics addicts. The guiding policy has remained unchanged; namely, that substance abuse per se is a medical and psychological problem requiring appropriate treatment and administrative monitoring. Once identified by management, a substance abusing employee is referred to a program staff member who decides upon the nature of treatment indicated by the medical and psychological extent of substance abuse. The employee is then offered the opportunity to undertake treatment or to face the administrative consequences of his or her behavior. The overwhelming majority of identified substance abusers opt for treatment and are followed-up periodically by emotional health program personnel. As with all health center transactions, visits are completely confidential. Thus, the early phase program was primarily a reconnaissance and referral service, tending to not treat employees in-house.

The social and economic successes of the substance abuse program and the realities of emotional problems among employees prompted the Equitable to further develop its commitment to the troubled employee. Thus, in 1972, the groundwork for the current emotional health program was initiated. A group of psychologists and consultants was contracted in order to study and report upon the problem of troubled employees, to offer short-term treatment and referrals, and to train certain personnel and medical department employees in the recognition and handling of the troubled employee. The overwhelmingly positive response of management and employees to the presence of an effective and confidential psychological service led to the third, present-day phase of the emotional health program.

At the Equitable, it is corporate policy to provide a program of health care for employees during the working day and to assist management in handling problems in which the physical or emotional well-being of an employee may be involved. The overall employee health program is the responsibility of the employee health services department at the New York home office. The emotional health program of the employee health services department is dedicated to the detection, prevention, education, treatment, referral, and follow-up of troubled employees. All services are completely confidential, free of charge, and on company time. Indeed, employee health problems are recognized as treatable and are not to jeopardize one's job. The emotional health program is physically housed in the employee health services department, thereby enabling the delivery of multimodality (psychological and medical) services. Company physicians and nurses work closely with emotional health program staff. Emotional health program staff size varies from one practitioner for every 2,000 employees during times of "business as usual" and one for every 1,000 employees during times of major organizational change. At the time of this writing, the program is staffed with one full time psychologist and two full-time psychology interns. Consultant psychiatrists and psychologists are "on call" for the program.

The emotional health program offers a variety of optional and confidential services to employees. Short-term psychological treatment (i.e., ten sessions or fewer) for anxiety and depression, the stress-related disorders, phobias, sexual dysfunction, and related nonpsychotic problems is offered through two major modalities: (1) conventional insight-oriented and cognitive-behavioral psychotherapy and (2) the stress management training program utilizing industry's first in-house biofeedback laboratory, founded at the Equitable in 1975, wherein clients are neuromuscularly reeducated, or taught to achieve and maintain low levels of psychological and physical arousal in the face of stressors. Psychological diagnostic testing is offered but not for purposes of employee selection. In the substance abuse program for self-referred or otherwise identified alcohol and other drug abusers, clients are offered the option of treatment with follow-up or of facing the administrative consequences of their drug-induced behavior. The overwhelming majority of identified substance abusers opt for treatment. Emotional health program staff members are always on immediate call for acute crisis situations involving, for example, suicidal or homicidal threats, psychotic episodes, and aggressive behavior. The managerial training program offers presentations to managers and supervisors regarding the recognition, proper handling, and appropriate referral of troubled employees. Advisory and consultative services are available to management for assistance in solving social and psychological problems encountered in their work. For example, the program has been consulted regarding the issues of relocation, job abolishment, decentralization, employee morale, and even environmental design. Employees requiring or requesting longer-term or highly specialized care are referred to the proper outside agency, institution, or practitioner. Follow-up is always a necessary part of referral out. In order to maximize the quality of health care offered to employees, liaisons are maintained with major teaching and research institutions in major U.S. cities. And whenever a common problem, such as job abolishment, is shared by a large number of employees, some form of group intervention may be undertaken (Manuso, 1977).

Though not formally a part of the emotional health program, there exists a significant number of additional corporate programs that are ultimately preventive in their mental health impacts. For example, the equal employment opportunity office assists women and minorities with job-related difficulties, serving as advocate, educator, and negotiator on their behalf. An upward communications program facilitates employees' airing of their job-related concerns, when they feel they have been inappropriately dealt with by the corporation. On a regular basis, the chief executive officer hosts advisory panels in order to maintain contact with employee morale, concerns, and attitudes. Other programs assist managers and supervisors in appropriately exercising their responsibility for others who report to them. The personal concerns program, a hotline and referral service, is intended to assist employees and their family members with medical and psychological problems throughout the United States. Whenever legal or financial problems impact an employee, consultations are arranged with in-house professionals. In addition, a preretirement counseling program offers employees aged 55-56 the opportunity to discover alternatives that they may consider in their retirement years. Finally, a career counseling program is available to employees who are considering changes in their careers.

The experience of the emotional health program shows that the vast majority of troubled employees present not with job-related problems, but with personal, situational, or interpersonal problems. In decreasing order of frequency, the problems seen are anxiety disorders (25 percent), depression (20 percent), stress-related disorders, including headache, generalized tension, myalgia, etc. (15 percent), substance abuse (15 percent), situational problems such as a death in the family, financial dilemmas, etc. (10 percent), and all others (15 percent). Although males and females use the services of the program in equal proportions, males tend to require more sessions of treatment than do females. This is because males tend to minimize or ignore the warning signals of emotional problems, whereas women respond quickly to emotional disequilibrium and seek out the proper care sooner, thereby not allowing symptoms to progress. The program's experience demonstrates that the group reporting the most severe problems was composed of white or Hispanic males in their 20s or 30s, married, with five or more years of service, working in presupervisory and premanagerial jobs. It is here, during the takeoff phase for one's family and career lives, where the occupational stressors and others have their greatest additive impact.

As to the actual quantities of employees utilizing the program, in 1978 a staff of five saw 500 individuals in approximately 2,500 visits. This represented approximately 13 percent of the home office employee population. The group was composed of 58 percent females and 42 percent males. A recent study indicated that 60 percent of all employees who received mental health services stated that these services were very helpful in terms of positive changes in the initial problem, their life in general, attendance, job performance, and job satisfaction. Of that same population, 30 percent said that the services were somewhat helpful, 8 percent said they were not helpful, and 2 percent did not respond. Therefore, 90 percent of emotional health program services are found to be concretely helpful on the part of employees. Thus, it has been demonstrated that employees suffering mental health problems may be effectively treated at their worksite, this being a form of prevention.

The Equitable experience suggests a number of points regarding the staffing patterns of corporate emotional health programs. First, the program director should report to a level as close to the top of the organization as is feasible, and the program should not be confused with the monitoring and selection activities of personnel departments, with whom a coequal alliance should be shared. Staff composition should include appropriate female, minority, linguistic, and age group representation, given the composition of the employee population. Staff members' prior work history should include experience in a corporate environment, in a medical setting, and with innercity problems, and their educational background should be at the doctoral level in psychology, psychiatry, or clinical social work. Staff members should certainly be skilled diagnosticians and practitioners of short-term group and individual psychotherapy. The program itself should be located in an occupational medical center in order for staff members to coordinate treatment with physicians and nurses. The personal characteristics of staff members should be "suitable" with respect to the highly sensitive nature of their work, the contact with senior executives, the need for clients to trust them, and the dynamic needs of the organization. Advanced training and other forms of professional involvement should be undertaken by staff members and financially underwritten by the corporation on an annual basis. Staff members should be encouraged to complete cost-benefit research for each new emotional health project initiated. Again, it cannot be overstated that client confidentiality should never be jeopardized and that staff members should be fully committed to ethical practice.

In a very general sense, emotional health programs such as the one at the Equitable tend to evolve in specific directions over time. There is a tendency to move from a curative (i.e., disability oriented) stance to one of prevention and health enhancement. There is a movement away from addressing only the most severe problems with gross consequences to recognizing the importance of working with milder problems that, nonetheless, evidence significant hidden costs. There is a tendency to refer out less and offer more in-house, short-term treatment to employees. Staff size correspondingly increases. From a one-on-one orientation in intervention, there develops a willingness to work with groups of employees simultaneously. As such programs grow, they become more powerful in the host institution, establishing more liaisons with external resources, particularly with universities. Internship programs develop, and research begins to emanate from the program. There develops an access to senior management, and program roles expand. As a critical mass of practitioners is achieved, a more aggressive marketing of the program to employees takes place. Although more passive counseling strategies typically characterize the beginning program, a mature program begins to offer active interventions based on behavioral modification approaches. The staff, originally paraprofessionals to a great extent, are replaced with mental health professionals. The program, originally cloistered and silent in the corporation, becomes much more visible and communicative; there are more interactions and coordinations with other departments in the organization and a greater willingness to address the press, including the production of films and radio programs. The original practitioner evolves into an administrator and manager as the staff size increases. The program, providing it has proven its worth in the competitive corporate arena and thereby earned the respect of the corporate system, enjoys a "free agent" status in the organization and is trusted by the corporation.

Any corporation is a stressor to its employees. Corporations may be distinguished from one another, not in terms of the presence or absence of stressors, but in terms of their response (or lack thereof) to the problem. It appears that the corporation's central objectives are to maximize profits in a competitive market and to thereby perpetuate itself, its growth, and its power through the management of employees by way of rational and authoritarian organizational structures and systems. It is clear that corporations are not in the business of curative mental health. However, mental health promotion and preventive policies and programs are wholly consistent with corporate goals and, in fact, enhance their achievement, as some corporations are learning.

The epoch of preventive health care, of wellness and of self-regulation of behavior, is truly beginning in corporate America. Increasingly, corporate employee health programs are serving as the earliest tier of preventive health service delivery. Government will no doubt encourage this development further, through financial and other incentives and, perhaps, through mandate. The tasks of developing and managing efficient, cost-effective preventive mental health programs will be met by the private sector—corporations must tame their creations for their own survival. Corporations are learning the ultimate in management. They are learning how to manage the stress they of necessity engender in their employees.

REFERENCES

Cummings, N., 1977. "The Anatomy of Psychotherapy under National Health Insurance." *American Psychologist* 32 (9): 711–18.

Manuso, J. 1977. "Coping with Job Abolishment." *Journal of Occupational Medicine* 19 (9):598–602.

———. 1978. Testimony to the President's Commission on Mental Health, Panel on Costs and Financing. *Report of the President's Commission on Mental Health, Volume II, Appendix,* p. 512. U.S. Superintendent of Documents, Washington, D.C.

———. 1979a. "Staffing a Corporate Emotional Health Program." In *Employee Mental Wellness Programs,* edited by Boston University–Washington Business Group on Health. New York: Springer-Verlag.

———. 1979b. "Stress Management Training in a Large Corporation." Unpublished manuscript.

President's Commission on Mental Health. 1978. *Report of The President's Commission on Mental Health, Volumes I and II.* U.S. Superintendent of Documents, Washington, D.C.

SECTION FOUR

Specific Focus Counseling

Oftentimes, a corporation and/or its employee counseling program will opt for some limited form of crisis intervention, remedial action or other counseling involving a specific focus. The "need" for a particular specific focus counseling program is often generated through marketing efforts on the part of practitioners and through the desires of top management for filling a particular need or solving a particular problem. Generally, specific focus counseling is offered by an external consultant and for a limited period of time. Accordingly, the external consultant is usually identified with a specialty, and it is this expertise that the organization is buying. Sometimes the specific focus counseling will involve attention in a particular population; otherwise, the counseling will involve teaching a particular skill to a wide variety of participants. In fact, sometimes different divisions of a corporation will employ an external consultant to offer employees a brand of specific focus counseling that is not in any way identified with an employee counseling program, if there is one.

In the first chapter of this section, Dr. Joseph Yeager develops "A Model for Executive Performance Coaching" relying heavily on the neurolinguistic programming technique. Dr. Yeager wisely avoids any psychological terminology in presenting his intervention to potential clients. Rather than being a psychotherapist performing psychotherapy, Dr. Yeager becomes a consultant in executive performance coaching. Dr. Yeager's chapter reviews how one obtains clients and how to make accurate assessments of the situation giving rise to the request for a clinician to be brought in. Dr. Yeager's "Want to, How to, Chance to" model of performance problem assessment is intriguing in its simplicity and compelling in its depth of organization. The important distinction between business and therapeutic criteria is discussed, along with the types of business alternatives contingent on a performance problem. Dr. Yeager argues for behaviorally based performance appraisals and labels in order for such information to be of assistance to managers undergoing performance coaching and for those to whom the person reports. The chapter reviews the neurolinguistic programming approach to in vivo performance coaching for behavior change, outlining a series of specific techniques. Seven brief case histories are presented; the role of the internal consultant is examined, along with the degree in appropriateness of management involvement, confidentiality with limits, and the importance of power issues while working within an organization. Dr. Yeager ends with his view of treating the situation and all its actors as the client in his intervention model.

Although performance coaching is generally aimed at a "problem" employee, assertiveness training is generally earmarked for enhancing the range and suitability of an employee's response repertoire in various situations. In his chapter, "Assertiveness Training for Corporate Executives," Dr. Mitchell Clionsky begins with a review of the four major response alternatives (assertiveness, passivity, aggression, and passive-aggression) and their results before examining the application of assertiveness as a training methodology having significance for business situations. Dr. Clionski also describes his epidemiological study of assertive behavior in 20 executives. Dr. Clionski then outlines his 15-hour executive assertion training model, wherein participants are first taught how to discriminate response styles before developing assertive skills. Practical considerations are presented, ending up with a statement as to the felt effectiveness of executive assertion training.

Allied to the enhancement focus of assertiveness training is the enhancement afforded an individual undergoing career counseling. Dr. Mark Carsman, in his chapter, "Individual Career Planning and Counseling," presents to the clinician a four-stage individual career planning model, consisting of career expiration and counseling, education and training, job search and placement, and career assessment focusing on the future. Dr. Carsman then outlines the potential roles for clinical psychologists: providing career counseling services, assessment with respect to career issues, and the roles of promoting, developing, and administering programs and services. Dr. Carsman's chapter methodically educates the clinician in the various theories and practices required of a career planner and counselor. Clinicians should certainly not promote themselves as having these and related skills unless they are assiduously developed and cultivated over an extended period of practice.

One of the most difficult situations an organization and its employees must face from time to time is that of job abolishment, requiring the "outplacement" of staff found to be unnecessary for any variety of reasons. Because outplacement has become increasingly more common, and because health problems have been found to bear a direct relationship to unemployment, organizations have become more attentive to the need for humanitarian pragmatic programs for easing the outplaced employee's adjustment. In his chapter, "Coping with Job Abolishment," Dr. James Manuso presents research regarding the effectiveness of a workshop for 16 employees whose jobs were abolished, demonstrating that a small investment of time and effort can positively affect a number of dimensions of psychological change making participants more positive, realistic, certain regarding their career capabilities, and positively hopeful vis-à-vis the future. This chapter ends with a series of recommendations regarding the process of job abolishment.

Although an in-house workhouse may be helpful with respect to the initial adjustment of job-abolished employees, what is required is a longer-term sequencing of outplacement counseling. In his chapter, "Outplacement Counseling: Business and Profession," Dr. Donald Monaco defines outplacement counseling and reviews its origins, noting the present day reasons for larger numbers of employee terminations and subsequent outplacement counseling service growth. Dr. Monaco presents retrospective research regarding the successful impact of outplacement counseling, which serves to follow and assist the terminated employee from the time of termination up to the finding of a new job. The psychological effects of unemployment are discussed, and the stages of unemployment are likened to the phases approaching death. The different phases of the outplacement counseling process are presented, and three case studies are cited. Dr. Monaco ends his intriguing chapter with a proposed profile on the qualified outplacement counselor and encourages the reader to look upon outplacement counseling as a profession with a good future, given that this type of counseling is still in its infancy.

Related to outplacement counseling, through a process that is frequently freestanding, is that of employee relocation counseling. Dr. Martha Sherwood and Ms. Judith DeSimone, in their chapter, "Relocation Counseling: Current Status and Potential," open with a dramatic recounting of the extensive costs of relocation to the host corporation, pointing up the importance of a successful relocation from a purely financial point of view. This sets the stage for the recent development of relocation counseling. A profile of the typical relocating employee is generated, pointing out that there is an increasing resistance on the part of employees to transfer that is coupled with the recent advent of organization reluctance. Recent trends in relocation management are examined, and the different forms counseling may take are presented. From the organization's standpoint, the most compelling reason for offering relocation counseling is to save staff time that would otherwise be spent in managing the relocation and in assuring that a relocation will "stick." Disparities between the personal and organizational priorities with respect to relocation are outlined, as is the recent appropriate attention being paid to the spouse of the relocated employee (this latter factor is particularly important in dual career marriages). Perhaps the suicide of a female psychologist married to a recently relocated McGraw-Hill employee could have been prevented had there been adequate preparation and relocation counseling taking into account her professional and employment needs (the psychologist jumped to her death from her husband's Sixth Avenue office in McGraw-Hill!). The authors argue in favor of the need for professional intervention in relocation counseling, which is typically administered by non-professionals. They close their chapter with a review of a number of innovative trends in relocative counseling, leaving us with a number of significant considerations for the future.

The last chapter in this section, "Affirmative Action and Corporate Emotional Health Programs," by Dr. James Manuso, addresses the unique set of stressor circumstances facing women and minorities in organizational life and reviews one corporation's set of responses to those unique problems. The chapter develops a series of recommendations aimed at assuring the success of minority employees in organizational life.

Because many corporations cannot afford in-house programs, specific focus counseling will become increasingly popular. This is especially true because the majority of U.S. corporations employ 100 people or fewer. The clinical psychologist with one or more of the specific skills mentioned in this section would do well to orient those skills in such a way as to be suitable for the occupational arena, in order to better serve U.S. organizations.

12 A Model for Executive Performance Coaching

Joseph Yeager, Ph.D.

The rising interest in employee health programs is generating a trend toward the behavioral scientist acting as a clinical consultant within the business organization. The following discussion presents some of the major differences involved between private practice and organizational practice. When working with executives on the job site (i.e., making "house calls") the rules are different.

The organizational context calls for a rethinking and reframing of the one-on-one practitioner's point of view. "Clinical" methods must be adapted to the context and expectations of the clients. The emphasis of this discussion is on an aspect of one-on-one performance management that is useful to call executive coaching.

HOW DOES ONE OBTAIN CLIENTS?

A client executive can emerge from virtually any source. The boss may think someone's performance is declining. The lack of desired results may be puzzling in a seasoned executive. There may be doubt about a person's ability to handle more responsibility. A person may be eliciting conflicts or stifling results or interrupting routines. In other words *any* performance issue can be a reason to use a clinical practitioner, to attempt to find an answer.

One of the problems facing the practitioner is to "sell" the organizational decision makers on the fact that these performance questions are indeed the domain of the clinician. Selling is necessary because there are management solutions such as terminations that *do* solve the problem in one sense. The result is that clinical services must compete with established practices and programs. Much of what follows in this chapter will help to orient the clinician's point of view toward seeing *how* clinical services can be very useful in response to performance questions without necessarily having *anything* to do with conventional notions of "pathology" or "symptoms."

ASSESSING THE SITUATION

The approach to assessment in the organizational setting is different than the usual diagnostic clinical testing. There is heavy reliance on the interview with the client, his peers, and superiors as well as *in situ* treatment, with little or no testing. The first item on the agenda is to find out about the client's behavior from as many sources of information as possible. In the search for what is wrong, a few generic questions can yield an outline of the situation, while further probes can flesh out the data. Examples of such generic questions are:

- What is the person doing?
- When did the behavior begin to change or become a problem?
- What events were occurring then and just prior to the changes?
- What work is the person supposed to do?
- What work is the person *not* doing to standards?
- What behavior is the person displaying that's problematic?
- What is the effect of the job context?
- Who is establishing the criteria defining the problem behavior?

These questions are only suggestive. To have a coherent means of questioning, a framework suitable to the business setting is required. The primary sources of such data are colleagues, superiors, and subordinates, since the interdependence of the members of an executive team makes coworkers observers of the client as well as customers for the results of his or her work. Executive performance, in this sense, is public information, and the observations of coworkers can be very useful.

When these sources exist it is mandatory to inquire about their perspective on the situation even though one might not reveal the reason for the inquiry and one would usually be quite oblique in this fact-finding survey. Often a red herring issue, such as a new program, is the overt topic, while the covert subject is to inquire about the client. Data are assembled much like building a mosaic. Eventually the picture emerges. These sources are often critics of the client and rivals. As such *they* are defining what is wrong by telling the consultant their *response* to the client. Part of the task is to help the client generate new and more acceptable responses in those he or she must work with. That is, to help the client *manage* the attitudes and behavior of others. In a real sense others can define a person as a problem even if the person is quite comfortable with his or her own behavior. This is typically the reason why self-referral is less often made than supervisory referral in certain organizations.

THE "WANT TO, HOW TO, CHANCE TO" MODEL

In assessing an individual client, it is necessary to have a model or rule of thumb for formulating questions to ask. Questions must generate information relevant to performance prescriptions and relate to both the individual, his or her context, and their interaction.

In the business context, the frame of reference used by the consultant-practitioner is especially important. It is likely to be different from that used in private practice. The "Yeager model" (Yeager, 1980a) is offered as a very simple one that is useful, although it is recommended that consultants experiment with others of their own choosing. Sometimes it is called the "Want to, How to, Chance to" model.

The model poses three broad strategic questions that focus detailed questioning. An assumption implicit in the model is that the individual needs to be assessed in the context of the job and the corporate hierarchy, not in the abstract or with theoretical models. The questions are:

1. Does the individual *want to* do the job?
2. Does the individual know *how to* do the job?
3. Does the individual have the *chance to* do the job?

Some expansion should clarify this rule of thumb model intended to touch on both the individual and the environment. In the organizational context, or in any other, it is important to have specific relevant ways to focus on what you are looking for in order to recognize it when you find it.

Want to:

First, at the root of many performance problems is a camouflaged motivation: The client doesn't *want to* do the job. Sometimes neither the client nor management have any notion that this is the reality. Value changes, domestic events, life stage, etc. can cause a change in what a person wants. Sometimes it is so subtle that the investigation can be detoured to other unproductive directions.

Conflicts can be unearthed with clinical observational and elicitation techniques at this facet of a case, where the traditional clinical skill of acute sensitivity to the "subjective" side of the person is very useful. Interviews and other clinical data gathering tools are appropriate here. For example, gathering information on performance inhibiting mood states (e.g., depression, agitation) is an objective in this facet of the inquiry. As a management problem, motivating a person who doesn't *want to* do what is required is much like pushing a wet noodle. The specific questioning techniques presented by Bandler and Grinder (1975) are exceptionally useful in uncovering the relevant subjective variables to be managed.

How to:

Second, in many volatile, fast growing organizations, individuals will be promoted, inadvertently, before they have the seasoning to have absorbed the prerequisite management skills needed to perform the content aspects of their work. Assessment centers and related techniques can sometimes tease out these deficiencies in functional repertoire. Management skills are nearly invisible and can be very hard to identify, especially if they are overlaid or driven by "personality" variables.

For example, if an executive is offensively aggressive in meetings and as a result cannot elicit the cooperation of his peers, it is a performance problem in *how to* run effective meetings. It may also be that a "personality" problem is the source of the inappropriate aggressiveness.

An intrapsychic subliminal strategy that precedes an externally observable behavior is often the cause of such a problem. Performance and personality are often synonymous in the executive suite. Executive skills, such as interpersonal effectiveness, decision making, etc., are known to be generated by subjective experiences and sequences of behavioral events, as has been demonstrated by Bandler, Grinder, et al., (1980) and have been discussed by Yeager (1981a, 1982) under the rubric of "subliminal strategies" noting their preeminent impact on executive behavior.

The effect of subliminal strategies and their behavioral derivatives on the matters of performance and the resulting superior/subordinate relations has been discussed by Yeager (1981b) citing the impact of the hierarchically related strategies on the degree of agreement possible among superiors and subordinates within the framework of performance appraisal systems and management by objectives (MBO). It is important to note that the majority of any given individual's subliminal strategies can be elicited in systematic way by using the questioning techniques of the Meta model (Cameron-Bandler, 1978) and related tools of behavioral elicitation. The fact that this facet of an individual's behavior is by definition out of that individual's awareness (i.e., subliminal) makes the task one of separating the *how to* of subliminal strategy impoverishment from the motivational issues involved in the *want to* aspect of the performance problems' elicitation.

There are numerous ways to assess for the skills in question. Interpersonal skills, planning, budgeting, project management leadership, and related generic skills are included in this area. Intrapsychic skills (the subliminal cognitive skills) of problem solving in their many forms and strategizing are pursued at this point in an inquiry. Then, too, the consultant must enlist the help of peers of the client to assess the client's technical skills by asking appropriate process questions. This can lead those who know what to look for in the right direction until the problem is confirmed to exist or not.

Chance to:

The third aspect of the questioning involves the tentative assumption that the person *wants to* do the job, *knows how to* do the job, yet is prevented from doing it by not having the *chance to* do the work. Many factors in organizations can prevent an individual from performing. Sometimes it is an overwhelmingly intimidating boss, political rivalries, lack of budget, authority, time, or other resources, punitive incentive systems, conflicting demands of equal priority or not receiving information to execute a necessary task on time, and so on. The context is a *very* big factor in determining performance. The boss-subordinate relationship is a major window on the determinants of performance and must be given special attention, as Yeager has explained (1981b).

In this third arena of assessment, one looks at the interface of the organization and the person. At times the practitioner will recommend a change in the organization rather than in the person. Sometimes both need to change in some way. Remember, all is not self-evident in the points where individual and organization mesh.

BUSINESS CRITERIA VERSUS THERAPEUTIC CRITERIA

For a practitioner to approach an organizational context case from the point of view of traditional therapeutic criteria of *wellness* is inappropriate. The criteria are *performance* and *productivity* in the organization. Interim objectives, such as keeping a rare clinically agitated person calm, are useful, occasionally. But the end product is to have the person "fit" one or more of the administrative actions that are available and/or possible. The chosen alternative (transfer, training, firing, etc.) then becomes the criterion toward which the therapeutic intervention must address itself. The more severe the crisis, if there is one, the fewer the alternatives that are likely to be considered. The executive needs his team to *perform* so his team can *win.* Helping a person "self-actualize" (Maslow, 1964) or become "Theory Y" (McGregor, 1960) oriented, for example, are totally useless criteria in the business setting.

The limits and potentialities of the situation must be mapped out early in the process. The tolerance level of the decision makers, legal ramifications, precedent, and business pressures must all be assessed for their influence on the eventual shape of the solution and the clinical goals. *In fact, the business alternatives will determine the clinical goals.*

TYPES OF DECISIONS

There are a number of administrative decisions that can be made in any human resource situation. The following are examples:

- Transfer the employee to another job.
- Demote the employee.
- Terminate the employee.
- Rehabilitate the employee in the current job.
- Downgrade or otherwise redesign the job.
- Retire the employee.
- Enroll the employee in a disability program (mental or physical).
- Grant a leave of absence.
- Create a temporary job.

Business priorities, degrees of humanitarianism, and similar factors will determine which of the administrative decisions the consultant will work toward. Of course, the consultant's evaluation of the likelihood of success of any of the decisions affects the desirability and weighting given to the alternatives in discussion with the client's superiors or other decision makers who may be involved (e.g., a disability program administrator or the legal department). And it is part of the consultant's task to recommend appropriate alternatives, especially when management's occasional reflexive decision is ill-advised.

Because managers are trained to manage and *not* to psychologize they will make the decision based on the variables that are clear to them. Since their focus is on a set of criteria that are productivity oriented they can and do make suboptimum decisions (for the company and the client). Psychological information from the consultant can tilt managers toward an ultimately happier choice for all parties. A major influence of the consultant can be to produce a different decision alternative based on behavioral, as opposed to administrative, criteria and data. The consultant's salesmanship becomes important here.

PERFORMANCE APPRAISALS

The next major issue is that of establishing the employee's record of performance, his or her appraisal history. Questioning deviates from traditional clinical models by focusing on what the person is being told about his or her performance and status. The reason for this line of questioning is that, as experience demonstrates, bosses find it very difficult to confront people with performance problems in even the best of circumstances. It would be a rare exception if the person were being given an unvarnished and clear picture of his or her performance from the boss' perspective. Assertive skills are, interestingly, often in short supply in organizations. As a result in the majority of performance problem cases, the formal written performance appraisal of the person is officially satisfactory in spite of the fact that, defacto, it is not satisfactory. Nonverbal messages are bound to exist telling the person that he or she is being judged as deficient in some way, and the resulting incongruity is often the subtle source of many boss-subordinate conflicts.

The typically avoided item is the direct confrontation on the issues. There are also legal ramifications arising from the need to document performance should an employee resort to litigation as a result of any decision that may be made. And recent court decisions are tending toward imposing "salvage attempts" in many cases where an employee might previously have been scuttled (e.g., "protected classes" as legislatively defined by the Civil Rights Act of 1963).

LABELING

It is possible to use a diagnostic label to categorize a person's behavior as a form of shorthand for professionals to use in talking among themselves. One could call a person, say, obsessive compulsive. But if a practitioner wants to do any therapy or take any administrative action on a case, the label must be translated into specific behaviors, that is, behaviors to work with an order to take actions that would be appropriate. A label can also imply a negative professional judgment, thereby raising doubts about the labeled person in the ranks of management. This is not useful to building a supportive organizational environment. Having a label for a case adds nothing to the issues at hand.

The key criteria to consider are those Freud (1959) articulated; that is, a person is healthy if he can love and work, but only work is relevant on the job. A label can obscure the fact that in a business environment the person's ability to work is at issue, not a person's mental health according to a professional handbook. If a client is obsessed with an idea, it is a separate value judgment as to whether the obsession interferes with that person's love life. It may well be to the company's advantage and the client's advantage if the client is obsessed with success or is compulsive about meeting deadlines. It is a matter of the company and the client having mutually useful characteristics. Therefore, it is necessary to have techniques available that utilize existing client behaviors to accomplish a change rather than to waste time characterizing such behaviors with a label. In other words, it really is sufficient to say that something is wrong or that the person is causing trouble as a diagnosis. One then starts from that point to find out the specifics particular to that situation.

Another aspect of labeling has to do with the idea that the title the practitioner uses is important. One may choose from a wide variety: therapist, practitioner, consultant, behavioral scientist, expert, third party, coordinator, specialist, clinician, psychologist, organization developer, and more.

Managers, as a population, are frequently gun-shy of people who wear credentials and titles like badges. Often there is suspicion of what psychologists or "shrinks" of any variety are really doing. A way to avoid unnecessary resistance is simply to choose a label that blends in with the executive environment. Professional ego trips are short journeys in the executive world. A title such as consultant or organization development specialist is much better than, say, psychologist or therapist. Fewer doors will be closed unnecessarily.

A title also has to do with issues of confidentiality and the more subtle fact that the practitioner must be able to behave in a way that is consistent in all of these various titles. He must also be able to work in various far-flung company locations with various licensing laws defining what is and isn't "psychological" under local jurisdiction. An interesting aside is that neuro-linguistic programming (NLP) technology, discussed below, is defined as *training* by its founders and as such is not therapy in the usual sense.

In some cases it is better to operate as a consultant, either internal or external, and in other locations and situations it is better to use one of the other labels to define oneself. Some laws make it prudent to be a consultant, others give the priority to "psychologist." Consultant is preferable due to its flexibility and freedom from unnecessary restraint.

There is also a legitimate ethical problem in defining when one is changing behavior by training, coaching, career planning, or teaching methods as opposed to when it is being accomplished by overt therapeutic methods. Pop-psychology has certainly taken a great deal of therapy out of the practitioner's office and put it in the business environment via management development media. For example, assertive training, transactional analysis, T-groups, and the like are techniques many managers might use.

Then too, looking at B.F. Skinner's (1953) work on behavior, it is instructive to consider the impact of environmental change on behavior. By changing the shape of the maze, one changes the behavior of those who run that maze. Thus, when an executive reorganizes a business unit he is, for all practical terms, changing behavior, and it may or may not have "therapeutic" effects. Many traditional clinical definitions fall apart in the organizational setting.

FROM ASSESSMENT TO BEHAVIOR CHANGE

It has been stated that testing and traditional nomothetic assessment instruments are usually very limited in usefulness in organizations. Any performance problem will be defined idiographically and in terms of the organization's particular setting and productivity objectives since problem performance is relative to the setting and the person. For instance, a traditional clinical MMPI (Minnesota Multiphasic Personality Inventory) will generate virtually no data of value for the development of a treatment program for performance related behaviors. The executives in decision-making positions will decide the criteria, and *criteria are relative,* not absolute. A problem person in one setting under a given boss will be a very valued person in another setting. Performance, like beauty, is in the eye of the beholder. In organizations this means that persons in higher authority decide according to subjective and very changeable criteria. It may not be "fair," but it is true.

When one has effective prescriptions, testing can be relegated to its secondary role. Beware of overusing testing when one's armamentarium of behavior change techniques is limited or ineffective. Conventional insight therapy takes too long and is too ineffective to use in this setting. Rapid behavior change techniques are crucial. One assesses for ultimate results, not data or research.

SELECTING BEHAVIOR CHANGE METHODS

The main criteria for therapy in the business context is that the method *must fix the performance problem* and it *must fix it fast.* Conventional dynamic therapy methods do not wear well against these two criteria. Of course, many schools of therapy have evolved effective methods, for example, Gestalt (Perls, 1969), behavior modification (Wolpe & Lazarus, 1966), biofeedback (Brown, 1977), and rational emotive (Ellis, 1962). This discussion will be limited to the approach of neuro-linguistic programming (NLP) (Bandler, Grinder, et al. 1980) *because* it fixes the specific performance problem and it fixes it fast. For example, it is not at all uncommon, using NLP, for phobias and depressions to be remedied in less than an hour.

NLP is defined in several ways by its founders, in part because its development is so rapid that its parameters are still unknown. It has been defined as a technology of behavior change, as the study of subjective experience, as the study of human communication, and as a system for modeling or mapping of various perceptual world views. Notwithstanding its fluid definition, NLP is useful for altering either states of consciousness (moods or emotions) or for altering cognitive behavior (judgment, creativity, learning, coping, problem solving, et al.). One of its noteworthy advantages in the business context is that one may approach the change of a client's behavior as an "ordinary" conversation either with or without the client's conscious awareness of the mechanisms being used, thus overcoming the often encountered phenomena of "client resistance." It also has the advantage of being so flexible that therapeutic interventions may be conducted at the intrapsychic, interpersonal, or organizational levels of behavior as is appropriate to the presenting problem.

NLP assumes that the client has all the psychological resources necessary to achieve the desired outcomes. This may or may not be true, but NLP has been demonstrated to work well under this assumption. The consultant, in a manner of speaking, "reorganizes" the client's resources (moods or cognitive patterns or both) in order for the client to have access to more responses, ones that are calibrated approximately to the wide variety of environmental demands that must be mediated in order to achieve valued goals. As Leslie Cameron-Bandler has noted (1981), NLP consists of four essential kinds of interventions. Regardless of the level of intervention, the consultant either *adds* a unit of behavior, *sepa-*

rates units of behavior, *combines* units of behavior, or *changes* the *criteria* that trigger the operation of a unit of behavior. For example, one might add the ability to observe colleague behavior by inserting it into a sequence of mental events that trigger criticism rather than, say, curiosity. One might separate an intense feeling such as fear from the mental image or actual presence of an intimidating boss. One might combine a motivation and a decision-making sequence of behaviors to elicit action rather than rumination. Or one might change the subjective criteria that causes a person to hold back in meetings so that he or she participates more readily.

SELECTED NLP TECHNIQUES OF RAPID BEHAVIOR CHANGE

At the risk of oversimplifying the NLP approach to behavior change, this section will briefly outline some of the techniques. The objective is to provide an orientation (not an explanation) to the mix of emotional and cognitive changes that are called for in some illustrative cases that suggest how one uses such a behavior change modality with a representative sample of symptoms found in the occupational setting. Table 12.1 outlines several specific techniques.

NLP methods expand a client's cognitive and emotional repertoire of behavior. Metaphorically speaking, they add many more paths to the peak of the mountains the client must climb. Thus, NLP appears to modify both cognitive and emotional memories, their triggers, their attendant memory processing mechanisms, and their resultant observable behavior.

NLP's emergence on the therapeutic scene is relatively recent. The publication of Bandler and Grinder's (1975) work entitled *The Structure of Magic,* in two volumes, grew out of their respective work in mathematics and linguistics and heralded the beginning of an explosive growth in the understanding of and ability to change human behavior in ways only wishfully dreamed of by helping professionals for generations. By using exquisitely precise and atypical methods, they analyzed the common denominators of *how* successful therapists managed to cause change and as a result have generated a new map of the world of human behavior as radical in its ramifications as the change from a flat world map to a round world map in the fifteenth century. Practitioners will be exploring the new worlds opened to them for generations, and the impact on the varieties of human experience can only be subject to speculation at this early point in time. Professional acceptance has been mixed because the NLP discoveries violate most of the rationales implicit in many other systems of psychological change. Its eventual warm acceptance is probably assured due to the repeatedly demonstrated fact that it works.

What follows is a selected list of NLP techniques (Table 12.1) and a selection of cases aimed at illustrating the types of people served and some frequently observed presenting problems.

TABLE 12.1.
Selected NLP Techniques*

Technique	*Purpose*
Change History	Restructuring the emotional facets of key, compelling memories that cause "limiting behaviors" such as dependence, naive idealism, prejudices, etc.
Reframing	Several varieties of this NLP technique use imaging to access unwitting limitations and to expand the number of positive responses available to a given stimulus. For example, unfulfilling defensive or repetitive behavior patterns of executives, such as stage fright or rigidity, are changed to flexible responses.
Metamodel	An entire armamentarium of linguistic and questioning methods that elicit behavior change.
Filmstrip	Using visual imagery a "filmstrip" of an emotionally charged memory is created to desensitize the client to the emotion. For example, the emotional reaction to public humiliation by a superior can be neutralized. This is analagous to systematic desensitization (Wolpe, 1966) in its effects.
Trance	The utilization of certain "natural" hypnotic phenomena allows highly leveraged access to unconscious learning resources. In this way, executives' behavior can be shifted from stereotyped response patterns to more flexible and adaptive ideas, plans, and relationships.
Chaining	A means of accessing and reorganizing cognitive-emotional sequences to alter states of consciousness. An individual may be moved from depression to alertness by connecting several overlapping states that allow the trigger pin depression to elicit the entire chain, ending up in the desired mood.
Therapeutic Metaphor	Telling specially constructed stories and analogies to access unconscious change mechanisms. For example, sports metaphors about competition translate well for naively idealistic, noncompetitive managers with technical backgrounds.

*All of these techniques are described fully in Cameron-Bandler (1978).

SELECTED CASES BRIEF:

None of the changes in any given case reviewed below required more than a half dozen sessions with the client for the NLP techniques to produce the desired outcome. The practitioner's liasion role with others in the organization can and usually does take more time than the treatment itself. Five and even ten hours of "environmental relations" with peers and superiors to one hour of therapy with the client is not very unusual.

Case 1.

A president was either "wishy-washy" with his ambitious staff or inappropriately angry. Reframing provided the assertiveness skills necessary for him to be in command by accessing dormant abilities that calibrated his responses more appropriately. Change history eliminated his resentment of perceived slights toward his authority in the past.

Case 2.

A scientist was the victim in a near fatal laboratory explosion, generating an extreme phobic reaction to the worksite. Filmstriping and reframing served to return the job-site response to normal levels by desensitizing him to the triggering stimuli.

Case 3.

An experienced writer suddenly developed debilitating and totally bewildering writer's block. His subliminal cognitive strategies were disassembled and repackaged to reinstall two missing steps squeezed out of his normal sequence of writing by transient domestic stress.

Case 4.

A president was alienating parts of his staff with blunt talking and incessant demands. With therapeutic metaphor, a persuasive strategy was elicited from his romantic life and applied successfully to the job context.

Case 5.

A senior division executive was drifting from project to project, year to year. A trance strategy elicited leadership skills, reframing elicited political skills, and metaphors provided strategic goal-setting skills resulting in a dynamic, growing division for the company.

Case 6.

An executive was unnecessarily dependent, clearing all his decisions with his superior and taking no initiatives on his own. Trance suggestions and therapeutic metaphors produced the desired self-sufficiency, initiative, and risk taking. Chaining produced an enduring state of self-confidence.

Case 7.

An abrasive executive was offending his peers and causing a political rift by widely distributing criticism of them in memos. Reframing and metaphors worked to change him rapidly into a valued "teamplayer" instead of an isolated critic. To onlookers it appeared as an "attitude" change.

THINKING IN THREES: THE INTERNAL CONSULTANT ROLE

To have a program that will help large organizations where there are regular recurrences of problem employees, it is useful to have in place access to three critical elements or roles. The three elements are:

1. The supervisor of the individual with the problem (and usually others higher up who participate in the discussions and the decision).
2. An in-house or external consultant with experience in the specific company and with expertise in behavior change methods.
3. An internal or external source of therapists or counselors who are able to handle the more extreme cases that can't be entirely handled on site, in the job context.

For the practitioner with the organizational experience and the therapeutic expertise, the second and third roles are often executed by the same person. For practitioners with multiple therapeutic and managerial competencies, and operating within the laws of the locale, the in-house consultant may wish to operate as an on-site therapist. Still, other professional therapeutic resources should be available in case a referral out of the office is appropriate. This would be useful, for example, when job and personal domestic issues interact, such as during divorce.

The internal consultant is the anchor person who works out solutions to problem performance with this model of case management. It is his or her job to assess the situation and to act as a liaison among the management staff and the external therapeutic resources (if needed) and the problem person in question. He or she can define the problem as requiring external therapeutic resources or not, as well as being able to diagnostically tease out the difference between when the person does or does not *want to* do the job, does or does not know *how to* do the job, or does or does not have the *chance to* do the job due to things beyond his or her control.

The anchor person can assist the therapist (or be the therapist if qualified) to help set work related priorities in the therapeutic goals in concert with the client and the management hierarchy. The anchor person can help interpret the situation to management in such a way as to generate a supportive climate for the person while he or she is on the job (and maintain confidentiality) and can help management define realistic plans for coping with the problem for its duration. The anchor person can also help by defining ways to make the appropriate management decisions that may need to be made at various points in the case. A good deal of supportive work can be accomplished with the client, too, by the practitioner being supportive and by acting as a helpful third party to lend a positive tone to a situation that would otherwise be threatening to most people. Maintaining a sense of humor among all those concerned can be helpful by defusing anxieties and is another role of the anchor person. The anchor person is usefully advised to tell both client and supervisor that the client will be encouraged to be the main source of data about the consultant's efforts in order to enhance communications between supervisor and client.

MANAGEMENT INVOLVEMENT

An important item to consider is that one must develop a positively packaged rationale about how the client is going to be told of the problems his or her superiors are having with his or her performance. It can be helpful to rehearse and role play a number of positive ways for the supervisor to conduct the discussions in order to ease the supervisor's embarrassment as well as to assure that the supervisor's rapport with and support of the employee is also communicated. The consultant is useful in working out the approach.

The choice of *who* should handle the interviews (consultant, personnel officer, or supervisor) is less important than insuring that the supervisor's attitude is supportive through an understanding of what is going on and how his or her unit's performance will be assisted by this problem-solving process.

The focus should build on the rapport that exists among the individuals involved as a means of handling discussions with the client. Supporting the client emotionally is crucial. If the organization is heavy-handed and threatening in its actions, the problems are only exaggerated. If there is little or no rapport and trust among the people, the consultant must bridge the gap. In any event, supervisory participation is crucial.

CONFIDENTIALITY

The patient-therapist issue of confidentiality is very important. Trust is built on it. Yet, in the organizational setting one must work to the mutual gain of individual and organization. There are two clients in any such intervention. The problems of what to tell who are more like those found in family network therapy (Haley, 1976) and marriage counseling than in individual therapy. Sometimes the practitioner works a hidden agenda that is not revealed to anyone involved in the situation.

If a client will confide in the consultant only under the contingency of "total confidentiality," the consultant has fallen into a trap. The performance problem is a function of a complex situation and must be solved in context. The client *must* be persuaded that the consultant's discretionary use of information will help resolve the problems. If the consultant cannot help superiors understand psychological causes and parameters, they will make decisions on administrative criteria alone. All too often such decisions involve termination, forced retirement, etc. at the expense of the individual's preferences.

The client's nervousness about potential embarrassment notwithstanding, performance is an observable fact, and peers will judge it, pro or con, no matter what the client wishes. As a practical matter, the client is trained to communicate progress to his or her supervisor in performance terms, and the supervisor is lead to accept the client as the main source of data instead of the consultant.

Thus, (since performance is public data anyway) one of the ways to deal with confidentiality is to encourage the client to want to reveal what is necessary (personally or via the practitioner) to the organization. Such data are useful in reaching personnel decisions aimed at restoring normal effectiveness and help define which options are realistically available to both parties. Usually generalities are enough for management anyway. It is all too easy for management to make a well intentioned, yet deleterious, decision for lack of knowledge about what is going on. The liaison role of the practitioner cannot be overemphasized in managing the situation. Naturally, confidentiality is a major part of maintaining the trust of both parties–individual and organization.

In a legal sense, the issue of confidentiality is handled simply by making sure one is officially offering human resource consulting–*not* psychotherapy. This is not deception. As a practical matter, when is one doing training and education as opposed to therapy, since both are based on the fact that all behavior change is a function of learning (organic pathology expected)? It is a noteworthy aside that the most skilled NLP practitioners are certified as "trainers" not therapists.

THINKING IN LEVELS OF POWER

Any time a person emerges from the normal routine to attract a manager's attention as a problem it is most useful for the third party consultant to look at the situation from the point of view of the power structure for at least three layers of authority upward in the hierarchy. At least the client, the client's boss, and the boss' boss will be involved, not to mention the personnel office and possibly others. The decision that will be made at any stage of the case, once it is opened, will be a function of the perceived business and operational problems. Customarily, no one manager will make the decisions alone.

Almost always the decisions are made on a consensus basis after a good deal of consideration of the issues. Without dealing with all three layers and any peer reactions that may be involved, the chances are poor of having a supportive organizational environment necessary to define and resolve the problem with an optimum solution.

Another aspect of organizational work is the fact that it is only sometimes the case that the client has any choice in decisions affecting him or her. At times it may be a matter of the degree to which the client can assert his or her preferences. People of superior rank will judge the client's behavior, have the power to take action on what they perceive, and do so routinely. Custom, courtesy, and at times fear prevent the wholesale use of this power, but the point to be made is that it is erroneous to assume that the client will have the key role in the decisions. A matrix of others, including the client, do the deciding. The real power is in the hierarchy of higher ranking decision makers.

Of course the client is always free to quit the company. When the client doesn't quit, he or she has consented to work within the organization's decision parameters and processes. Managing these variables is part of the practitioner's task.

As mentioned earlier, it is not uncommon for the consultant to spend ten or more hours working with the decision makers on organizational issues for every hour spent with the client in therapeutic activities. To some degree the amount of time spent structuring the environment is a matter of how comfortable one is in working with "political" variables as well as with interpersonal or intrapersonal variables, the latter of which is traditionally the arena for the clinical approach.

THE POWER CONTEXT

When inquiring about a case or when working on any facet of a case, it is *crucial* to look closely at the fact that all of the events at issue are taking place in an organizational hierarchy. In other words, the effects of hierarchical variables will pervade everything that happens, and it is an astute consultant who interprets events in the context. For instance, rivalries and upward mobility can be assumed to be driving forces in those who will supply data about a client. Yet, by using as many people as possible as sources, these effects can be moderated and the behavioral descriptions that emerge will be useful in spite of any motivational distortions that may occur. The meaning of the client's behavior *is* the response it gets. In other words, the way he hollers into the mountain (his behavior) is the way his echo comes back from his coworkers.

Another aspect of power is the fact that management, by its hierarchical nature, will make decisions that do not in any form resemble democratic processes. Advocates of participative management may take issue and feel that it should not be the case. But that argument is better addressed elsewhere. The fact is that the hierarchy exists in decision making and it determines therapeutic outcomes. This must be dealt with *as is* or the consultant would do better to keep to a traditional private practice.

In any case, the supervising manager of the client will be forced to make a decision regardless of the appearance of the consultant on the scene. It may turn out that the decision will be different as a result of the clinician's intervention. It may also turn out that the client is much improved in behavior and in his or her prospects for a career as a result of the hierarchy of superiors, rather than the client, being the site of an intervention. How one handles hierarchical interventions is best bypassed here as a complex subject too extensive to review in this paper (Yeager, 1980b).

WHO IS THE CLIENT: INDIVIDUAL OR ORGANIZATION?

According to the traditional clinical approach the problem performer would be the client. He may be only nominally the client in fact. It is probably more accurate to say that the *situation* and all its actors are the client in this model of thinking. The organization itself, or at least the work unit, is the client, too.

The range and rank of the people involved in a case is, in any open system, a matter of how the consultant defines the parameters of the system according to his or her knowledge of how decisions are made and other relevant characteristics of the organizational events that envelop the case. The shape of the organizational structure will determine how far afield from the client into the surrounding environment of the system one must go to control enough of the significant variables to cause the results and changes that are defined as desirable. Policies, politics, procedures, precedents, attitudes, business conditions, and other influences will affect the therapeutic goals and criteria that will be set.

SUMMARY

It is clear that private practice and organizational practice are different in both assumptions and procedures. Coaching calls for new ways to cause rapid behavior change that is relevant to performance.

It would be very difficult to overemphasize the degree of effect the organizational hierarchy has on the client. The client's performance is a function of tasks defined by "the system" and judged by "the system" as well. The client's performance is, in fact, interdependent with the needs of the organization.

All these things require a figure-ground ability for the practitioner to shift focus from system to person and back again in order to successfully practice in the organizational setting.

REFERENCES

Bandler, Richard and John Grinder. 1975. *The Structure of Magic,* volumes 1 and 2. Palo Alto, Calif.: Science and Behavior Books.

Bandler, Richard and John Grinder, et al. 1981. *Neuro-Linguistic Programming,* volume 1. Cupertino, Calif.: Meta Publications.

Brown, Barbara. 1977. *Stress and the Art of Biofeedback.* New York. Harper & Row.

Cameron-Bandler, Leslie. 1978. *They Lived Happily Ever After.* Cupertino, Calif.: Meta Publications.

———. 1981. Personal communication with the author.

Ellis, Albert. 1962. *Reason and Emotion in Psychotherapy.* New York. Lyle Stuart.

Freud, Sigmund. 1959. *Collected Papers,* edited by Ernest Jones. International Psychoanalytic Library. New York: Basic Books.

Haley, J. 1976. *Problem Solving Therapy.* San Francisco. Jossey-Bass.

Maslow, Albert. 1964. *Motivation and Personality.* New York: Harper & Row.

McGregor, D.M. 1960. *The Human Side of Enterprise.* New York: McGraw-Hill.

Perls, F. 1969. *Gestalt Therapy Verbatim.* Lafayette, Calif.: Real People Press.

Skinner, B.F. 1953. *Science and Human Behavior.* New York: The Free Press, Collier-Macmillan.

Wolpe, Joseph and Arnold Lazarus. 1966. *Behavior Therapy Techniques.* New York: Pergamon.

Yeager, Joseph. 1980a. *Diagnosing Problem Performance.* Executive Development Series. Princeton: Princeton Creative Research.

———. 1980b. *Winning the Minds of Your Peers: Overcoming Resistance to Change.* Executive Development Series. Princeton: Princeton Creative Research.

———. 1981a. *Executive Performance and Subliminal Strategies.* Executive Development Series. Princeton: Princeton Creative Research.

———. 1981b. *Who's in Charge Here?* Executive Development Series. Princeton: Princeton Creative Research.

———. 1982. "Coaching the Executive Team: or, Can you Teach an Old Dog New Tricks." *The Personnel Administrator*, in press.

13 Assertiveness Training for Corporate Executives

Mitchell I. Clionsky, Ph.D.

INTRODUCTION

Assertiveness training techniques are being widely used by behavioral psychologists to enhance individual self-esteem and functioning, modify problem behaviors, and improve interpersonal communication. The systematic application of assertiveness training holds tremendous promise for coping with organization and management problems in business and industry. This chapter presents an overview of assertiveness concepts and procedures, examines the relevance for corporate employees, and outlines a prototype assertiveness workshop that has been developed by the author. Special attention is given to the particular components of this type of workshop and to presentation features that create relevance and benefit for business populations.

THE NATURE OF ASSERTIVENESS

Fensterheim (1971) defines assertiveness as "the action of declaring oneself; of stating, 'This is who I am, what I think and feel'; [It] characterizes an active rather than a passive approach to life." Early formulations of assertiveness emphasized the reduction of discomfort and the acquisition of personal power. Based originally on the work of Joseph Wolpe, assertion was conceptualized as any expression of feelings other than that of anxiety. These expressions originally included "more or less aggressive behavior" (Wolpe, 1958) as well as friendly and affectionate feelings. With time and experience, writers enlarged the concept of assertiveness and emphasized the expression of personal rights. The most evident right was freedom from guilt when refusing another person's request, as the titles of two popular psychology books attest: Smith's (1975) *When I Say No I Feel Guilty* and Fensterheim and Baer's (1975) *Don't Say Yes When You Want to Say No*.

The most recent expansion of assertiveness theory and technique has broadened the universe of behaviors considered assertive and has excluded aggressive behavior from that realm. Contemporary writers and practitioners, most notably Lange and Jakubowski (1976) balance the power of outward expression with an emphasis on personal responsibility. With this reformulation, assertiveness is defined as *the relatively straightforward expression of thoughts and feelings, keeping in mind the rights of others*. In short, assertive behavior is characterized as any communication that is honest, direct, and fair (responsible).

A partial list of responsible assertive behaviors includes:

1. Stating beliefs, opinions, desires, and needs.
2. Standing up for legitimate rights.
3. Initiating and maintaining conversations.
4. Expressing the range of human emotions, including anger, sadness, anxiety, and happiness.
5. Making and refusing requests.
6. Giving and receiving compliments.
7. Offering and accepting criticism.

Fairness and responsibility are critical elements in distinguishing assertiveness from aggression. When behaving aggressively, the individual wins through intimidation and humiliation, seeks to "put down" others, and fails to take their feelings into account. While assertion is honest, direct, and fair, aggression may be brutally honest, tactlessly direct, and, more importantly, unfair. The basic message of assertion is "Both of us count. Both of our needs and feelings are important." By contrast, aggression's message is "You don't count. Only my needs and feelings are important."

Passivity is the behavioral option most often recognized as nonassertive. Through passive responding, the individual avoids conflict at all costs, gives in to the desires of others, and fails to make legitimate requests. Passive behavior is frequently dishonest, rarely direct, and typically unfair to the individual who continually places other people's needs first. "I don't count. My needs and feelings are unimportant" is the basic message behind passivity.

Often unrecognized, the fourth basic behavioral style is passive-aggression. Passive-aggressive behavior is aggressive in its lack of respect for others, while passive in its indirectness and dishonesty. Procrastination, "sniping," manipulation, sarcasm, sabotage, and guilt induction are common expressions of passive-aggression. By dishonestly presenting needs, indirectly handling conflicts, and unfairly attacking others, the passive-aggressive individual implies that "Neither of us count. My needs and feelings are not important enough to state directly and your feelings are not worth my consideration."

A summary of the four basic behavioral styles—assertion, aggression, passivity, and passive-aggression—appears in Table 13.1.

While we often speak of an "aggressive person" or a "passive person," these labels are actually shorthand descriptions of someone's most evident behavior style. Assertion cannot be viewed as a fixed or general personality trait. Rather, assertive behaviors are learned and, like many other behaviors, are situation-specific (Mischel, 1968). That is, they depend greatly on the situational context for the likelihood of their expression. As Jakubowski and Lange (1978) imply in their title, *The Assertive Option*, each person has a potential choice in expressing assertive or nonassertive behaviors. Through assertiveness training, an individual can develop enough skill in assertive responding to make assertion a viable option.

APPLICATION OF ASSERTIVENESS

Since its introduction, assertiveness has been an applied theoretical construct, a technique for creating behavioral change. Within the context of a behavior therapy setting, the therapist evaluates the client's problems with self-expression, instructs the client in appropriate assertive responses, and then prescribes a series of graded tasks requiring assertive behaviors. The evaluation process might range from an informal compilation of problem areas to a more formal assessment using one of many paper-and-pencil instruments or the client's spontaneous responses to preplanned role-play situations.* The formal instruction often includes information presented by the therapist and/or bibliotherapy to increase the client's awareness of appropriate assertive responses, help the client recognize and accept important personal rights, and motivate the client to make assertive responses outside of therapy. The therapist then coaches the client on necessary components of assertion, including nonverbal behaviors (appropriate eye contact, audible and confident voice tone, relaxed body posture) and verbal behaviors (entering conversations, making and refusing requests, asking for more information, stating disagreement, and many others). In some cases, the therapist and client role play or rehearse assertive behaviors in the office, with the therapist offering encouragement, criticism, and alternative approaches. The client's successes or failures in making these approaches will then determine his or her

---

*For a more detailed review of the development, assessment, and practice of assertiveness training, the reader is directed to the critical reviews of Fensterheim (1972) and Galassi and Galassi (1978).

TABLE 13.1
Summary of Response Alternatives and Results

	Basic Message	*Honesty*	*Directness*	*Fairness*
Assertive Behavior	We both count	Honest facts and feelings	Direct approach	Fair to both parties
Passive Behavior	I don't count	Dishonest denial of facts and feelings	Indirect approach	Unfair to yourself
Aggressive Behavior	You don't count	Tactlessly honest facts and feelings	Overly direct approach	Unfair to others
Passive-Aggressive Behavior	Neither of us count	Dishonest facts and feelings	Indirect approach	Unfair to both parties

readiness to apply them in real-life problem situations. Behavioral tasks are then given to the client in a graded hierarchy of difficulty. Because early successes create enthusiasm and continued assertive responding, the therapist rewards even minimal positive changes. Future sessions progress in speed and complexity as the client masters each situation.

Fensterheim (1972) has noted that the "social nature of assertive training suggests that it would be particularly effective in the treatment of groups" (p. 162). In the past ten years, group assertiveness training has become the predominant mode of treatment. The groups provide support and encouragement for their members, offer a variety of role models, promote a wider range of alternative suggestions and feedback, and allow for more economical use of the therapist's time.

Assertiveness training, individually and in groups, is now one of the major treatment modalities of the behavioral psychologist. The techniques provide a broad-based intervention for a number of interpersonal and communicational disorders. A review of the now-voluminous literature on clinical applications of assertion training finds therapists treating problems of anxiety (social anxiety, shyness and minimal dating, phobias, sexual inhibition), depression, psychosomatic illness, behavior control (anger management, alcoholism, sexual dysfunction and paraphilias), and communication/relationship processes (marital difficulties, social skills deficits). The techniques have been applied to a wide range of populations, including high school and college students, hospitalized and nonhospitalized psychiatric patients, women's groups, juvenile delinquents, alcoholics, and children with emotional or behavioral problems.

Results of controlled studies on the outcome of assertion training, using college student populations, show it to be a significantly effective change agent. Galassi and Galassi's (1978) extensive review of the clinical literature finds that, while psychiatric patients and alcoholics are treated with mixed success, "numerous studies have demonstrated the superiority of assertion training over alternative treatments and/or attention placebo and no treatment control groups in modifying nonassertive behavior . . . in college students" (p. 22).

RELEVANCE FOR BUSINESS

Fensterheim (1972) characterizes assertive behavior as "crucial" to healthy psychological functioning. He notes that "the individual's ability to assert himself, when appropriate, is associated with an active orientation, feelings of mastery, and the ability to communicate satisfactorily with others" (p. 61).

Activity, confidence, and effective communication are essential qualities in successful managers. Levinson (1978) lists activity, organizational involvement, comfort in exercising authority, articulateness, and sensitivity to other people's needs as five of 20 ideal characteristics describing chief executive officers. Using management terminology, the needs for greater assertiveness in executives have been described by writers in business journals: Harriman (1974) addresses the importance of open communication channels; Josefowitz (1980) points out the need for managers to set limits and refuse unreasonable requests; Quick (1980) encourages managers to listen openly to their subordinate's concerns; Bartolomé (1972) suggests that executives avoid unnecessary stoicism and learn to express legitimate dependency needs; and Levinson (1978) describes the individual and organizational problems created by abrasive or aggressive executives.

The difficulties caused by passive, passive–aggressive, and aggressive employees are highlighted in a recent newsmagazine article entitled "Troublemakers in the Office" (*Time*, 1980). The report, which is based on the experience of management consultant Robert M. Bramson, describes several classes of "troublemaking" office workers and suggests strategies (many of them assertive) for coping with these individuals. But, while Bramson concludes that only 10 percent of the group are "relentlessly difficult," evidence gathered by this writer suggests that the number of employees who are moderately difficult because they characteristically behave nonassertively averages near 79 percent and may, at times, approach 84 percent.

In the first known prevalence study of assertive behavior in any population, this writer surveyed 38 executives who completed a 15-hour intensive workshop in assertiveness training (to be described in a later section). This survey asked the respondents to categorize the dominant behavior pattern of their immediate colleagues, superiors, and subordinates as either assertive, aggressive, passive, or passive-aggressive. Because these patterns are situation-specific, the respondents rated their coworkers separately on how they behaved with their colleagues, superiors, and subordinates. This produced a 3 × 3 × 4 matrix of persons, relationships (situations), and behavior style (e.g., the respondent's superior interacting with his or her superior in either an assertive, aggressive, passive, or passive–aggressive way). The respondents' ratings reflected the behavior of 135 middle-management colleagues (mean = 3.6), 93 upper-management superiors (mean = 2.5), and 316 lower-management or nonmanagement subordinates (mean = 8.5).

The results of this survey suggest that, regardless of position or role relationships, only a minority of business employees (generally less than a third) behave assertively on their jobs. As position and power increase, executives are more likely to be predominantly assertive (and, unfortunately, aggressive) and less likely to be passive. Also, their probability of assertiveness (and, again, their aggressiveness) increases as they deal with people of lesser status. Table 13.2 presents the complete results of this survey.

In evaluating the validity of this survey, the reader is cautioned that formal reliability of the instrument was not ascertained and that generalizability of results is limited by the size and characteristics of the respondent sample. Nevertheless, the respondents can be regarded as generally accurate on the basis of extensive training in identifying assertion, and they represent a range of management ranks, functional positions, and organization size. Even with moderate

TABLE 13.2
Prevalence of Assertive versus Nonassertive Behavior*

Persons	*Style*	*Relationship*			
		With Subordinates ($\bar{x} = 8.5$)	*With Peers* ($\bar{x} = 3.6$)	*With Superiors* ($\bar{x} = 2.5$)	*With Coworkers in General* ($\bar{x} = 6.3$)
Subordinates (n = 316)	Assertive	33%	19%	16%	21%
	Passive	31%	45%	54%	45%
	Aggressive	24%	16%	11%	16%
	Pass-Agg	12%	20%	19%	18%
Peers (n = 135)	Assertive	34%	25%	21%	27%
	Passive	15%	30%	45%	30%
	Aggressive	30%	19%	8%	18%
	Pass-Agg	21%	26%	26%	25%
Superiors (n = 93)	Assertive	38%	33%	19%	30%
	Passive	11%	20%	47%	25%
	Aggressive	30%	30%	9%	23%
	Pass-Agg	21%	17%	25%	21%
Average Executive (n = 544)	Assertive	34%	23%	18%	
	Passive	21%	37%	50%	
	Aggressive	27%	19%	10%	
	Pass-Agg	17%	21%	22%	

*Results based on responses of 38 executives.

deviations from the obtained statistics, it is clear that corporate employees are not as assertive as may be generally believed.

While there is clearly a need for executives to be comfortable and effective in using assertive approaches, very little has been written about occupational assertiveness training. In some popular psychology books, job-related problems are included with more general situations that involve family, friends, and service people (Jakubowski and Lange, 1978; Smith, 1975). A few books offer separate chapters on assertive techniques that can be used at work (Alberti and Emmons, 1970; Baer, 1976; Fensterheim and Baer, 1975; Lange and Jakubowski, 1976), although even these writings focus almost exclusively on ways to refuse unfair requests of supervisors, to develop job interviewing skills, or to negotiate for better salaries or positions. Rarely is assertiveness training offered as an approach to management problems. The few exceptions include a description of assertiveness training as one component of a management training program for women in an insurance company (Pilla, 1977), the use of assertiveness training in a stress management program for executives of a major hospital (Goldberg, 1978, pp. 117-18), and a segment on assertive behavior in a non-mediated occupational stress management package (Manuso, 1980).

With such clear need for assertiveness skills in management, executive assertiveness training should be a major part of a corporation's management development activities. Because occupational assertion has not been addressed specifically in the literature, the rest of this chapter will be devoted to a description of a prototype training workshop, the "Assertive Executive," developed by the author. This training model will illustrate the basic elements of a corporate assertiveness program and highlight special approaches which increase participant interest and application of the techniques to managerial situations.

AN EXECUTIVE ASSERTION TRAINING MODEL

The "Assertive Executive" is a 15-hour intensive workshop composed of five weekly three-hour sessions. Fifteen hours is sufficient to cover the major areas of skill development, and the time-divided format allows the leader to present the training in discrete and easily learned sections. The weekly training sessions enable participants to apply the concepts during intervening weeks and to report back to the group on their progress. In this way, participants can fine tune their newly acquired skills under the guidance of the leader and other group members. Of course, this scheduling is not inflexible, and some segments could be offered in pairs to facilitate day-long programming and a shorter overall training period. But sufficient time for practice between sessions must be allowed or learning is limited to intellectual awareness without much behavior change.

During the "Assertive Executive," participants learn the basic concepts of assertiveness and are taught to discriminate assertive from nonassertive behaviors. They also evaluate their own needs, set realistic goals, and develop particular skills through small group exercise, preplanned problem situations, and participant-relevant enactments of business situations they are likely to encounter. Each of these areas will now be discussed in detail.

Assertive Concepts and Discrimination

Basic to developing appropriate assertive behavior is a clear understanding of what assertion is all about. Participants are taught that assertion involves honestly and directly communicating thoughts and ideas, such as offering suggestions on a new production method, speaking up at meetings, or openly disagreeing with a policy or procedure. Assertive communication also permits individuals to make their needs known in ways such as requesting a deadline extension, asking for a redistribution of work load, negotiating for a salary or position change, requiring a subordinate to correct an error, or delegating tasks to others. Similarly, assertive executives set limits on unreasonable requests or intrusions into their time, give compliments for good performance, and appropriately criticize unfavorable performance.

Participants also learn that emotions are an integral part of all communication and that honest and direct expression of emotions is both important and desirable. Therefore, assertive managerial behavior might include expressing anger at unmet expectations or thoughtless intrusions, anxiety about new responsibilities, sadness at the departure of a friend, or happiness when there is success or accomplishment. In U.S. society most males, and particularly executive males, learn to suppress or to disguise their emotions. They consequently suffer a disproportionate number of stress-related problems in their physical and emotional health. Through assertiveness training, managers can learn to verbalize feelings in acceptable ways that retain the manager's prestige and avoid the need to bury feelings or "act out" in destructive ways. For example, assertively expressed anger can reduce the chances of hypertension or ulcers and can simultaneously prevent aggressive tirades or passive-aggressive "sniping."

A particular emphasis is placed on balancing honesty and directness with fairness. As previously mentioned in the general discussion of assertiveness, fairness is the pivotal distinction between assertion and aggression. Because the word "aggressive" has been used favorably in business settings (e.g., an aggressive marketing strategy) special care must be taken to explain that an aggressive, but not assertive, executive can alienate others, increase interpersonal conflicts, and ultimately reduce the effectiveness of the organization. Assertive fairness incorporates the attitudes of equality, mutual respect, personal responsibility, and caring for others. Most importantly, assertive fairness prevents misuses of personal power: it places the needs of each individual on an equal par with those of others and takes others into consideration when stating beliefs or sharing feelings. By adding fairness, assertive executives empathize with the concerns of coworkers, identify mutual goals when they disagree about the methods for achieving those goals, seek compromises to irreconcilable differences, and open the communication channels for others to assertively express themselves.

Underlying all assertive behavior is the recognition of personal rights and responsibilities. This explicit pairing of rights with responsibilities emphasizes that the right to make requests implies the responsibility to listen to the requests of others, that the right to refuse also gives others the right to refuse you, and that the right to make mistakes requires responsibility for those mistakes and an effort to correct them.

Teaching assertive rights and responsibilities helps participants to change attitudes that may have blocked prior assertive responding. Through societal proscriptions against assertiveness, individuals are taught to be passive (e.g., "Don't make waves" or "Always think of others first"), to be aggressive (e.g., "It's a dog-eat-dog world" or "Good guys finish last"), or to be passive-aggressive (e.g., "Don't get mad, get even"). Individuals may also think in ways that inhibit assertion. They develop irrational belief systems (cf. Ellis and Harper, 1975) that cause them to desire unqualified acceptance by everyone, perfection in all areas of their own behavior, and universal justice. The cognitive imperatives of *should, must* and *ought to* prevent their making assertive responses with which others might disagree, inhibit their taking reasonable risks for fear of failure, and create unnecessarily high levels of anxiety, anger, and depression.

Another important concept is that assertive behavior is situation-specific. Consequently, most people who are reasonably capable and who have attained responsible business positions already possess assertive skills in their behavioral repertoires. They may be quite adept at asserting themselves with family or friends, they may be assertive with subordinates but not with superiors, or they may be comfortable when expressing agreement but not criticism or disagreement. Therefore, it is important to clearly identify areas of strength and weakness and to promote transfer of training from areas of greater to lesser competency.

Allied with this concept is the idea that a person is not compelled to behave assertively at all times. Assertion should not be advertised as a panacea for all ills, nor should assertive effectiveness (making your point clearly) be confused with short-range practical success (getting what you want). The unstated demand that participants be perfectly assertive in all situations can raise significant resistance from those who prefer to be nonassertive in some situations or have found the risks of assertion too great to take. It is important here to identify assertiveness as just one behavioral option and to encourage participants to master assertive behaviors so that they can use this option when desired. I have found that a cost-benefit analysis can place this choice in perspective and can reduce resistance to practicing and applying assertive behaviors. The cost-benefit analysis focuses on personal risks and payoffs as well as on the emotional consideration of "How will I feel if I don't assert myself in this situation?"

In presenting these concepts, learning is enhanced by combining written material, self-assessments, lectures, and group discussion. Written material includes a chapter-long discussion of assertive principles and examples, along with a brief test to assess the reader's ability to discriminate among assertive, passive, aggressive, and passive-aggressive responses. The test, modeled on one used for general populations by Lange and Jakuboswki (1976) presents ten common occupational situations with four responses to each. After deciding which response typifies each of the four behavioral styles, the reader compares his or her choices with a list of correct answers that follows the test.

The second step in self-evaluation asks participants to complete the Executive Interaction Stress Inventory (EISI) (Nelson, 1980), a 24-item questionnaire modeled after the Assertion Inventory developed by Gambrill and Richey (1975). While the Assertion Inventory investigates assertive behaviors in a number of general areas, the EISI specifically targets occupational assertion problems. In completing the EISI, participants rate their degree of discomfort (on a 1-5 scale) in making an assertive response and, separately, the probability (also on a 1-5 scale) that they would make this response. Each assertive response is rated in the relationship context of dealing with their boss, an associate, and an employee or subordinate. Participants are then asked to circle the two or three situations that they will specifically work on during the course. A portion of the EISI is presented in Table 13.3.

Responses on the EISI provide a contextual view of participants' assertive profiles and help individuals commit themselves to particular areas for development. At this point, the leader may request participants to write a description of a recent or frequent problem situation based on the circled test items. These descriptions form the basis for future work via role playing.

Other written materials include handouts listing assertive rights and responsibilities, descriptions of cognitive and attitudinal "roadblocks" to assertive behavior, and information that clarifies or supplements the lectures. Lectures, when combined with slides or other audiovisual aids, effectively present many important concepts and increase participant interest.

Skill Development

Understanding assertion and differentiating it from nonassertion is not, by itself, sufficient to help most individuals behave more assertively. Specific assertive behaviors are mastered through exercise and practice. Because assertion involves nonverbal as well as verbal behaviors, participants are taught to project an assertive image. This includes practice (often with videotaped feedback) in making appropriate eye contact, standing or sitting in a sturdy and comfortable posture, monitoring fearful or aggressive facial expressions, and speaking in an audible and modulated voice tone. Short exercises are used to teach participants how to make requests and delegate responsibility, refuse requests and set limits,

TABLE 13.3
Sample Items from Executive Interaction Stress Inventory (EISI)*

B = *Boss*
A = *Associate*
E = *Employee or Subordinate*

Degree of Discomfort			*Situation*	*Response Probability*		
B	*A*	*E*		*B*	*A*	*E*
			1. Turn down a request for a meeting with your:			
			2. Admit fear and request consideration from:			
			3. Ask a favor of:			
			4. Initiate a conversation with a new:			
			5. Ask for constructive criticism from:			
			6. Turn off a talkative:			
			7. Compliment a:			

*Copyright 1980 by Sally J. Nelson; used with permission.

evaluate work and give criticism, and comfortably manage the criticism or anger of others. While participants are encouraged to deliberately use the pronoun "I" and are taught step-by-step process models for each of these situations, the primary focus is on meeting the criteria of honest, direct, and fair communicating. When these criteria are effectively met, few responses can be judged nonassertive.

To extend their skills from the basics taught in exercises, workshop members participate in simulated practical situations by using the technique of role playing. They begin by defining the problem situation (usually identified on the EISI) and then choose one or more group members to play the role(s) of the other individual(s). With the scene and cast clearly defined, the protagonist improvises an assertive approach and the respondent presents increasingly more challenging rejoinders until the protagonist is comfortable with his or her mastery of the situation. Other group members and the leader may model alternative approaches or offer supportive comments and suggestions to sharpen the protagonist's skills. At times, the actors may reverse roles so that the protagonist can more easily experience the clarity or fairness of his or her responses.

As a final step, participants are instructed to use their assertive responses on the job and to inform the group of their successes and problems. Reports of success build enthusiasm and motivation, while descriptions of problems provide opportunities for refining assertive approaches.

Practical Considerations

The design and implementation of a corporate assertiveness program can take many forms depending on the size of the organization, the management level of participants, and the interest of the group leader. Regardless, there are some factors that I have found to be essential for a successful program:

1. Participants must be volunteers or sufficiently cooperative to invest their energy in the group. Attendance by explicit or implicit coercion defeats the purpose of the group and engenders passive-aggressive sabotage. The leader must clearly express his or her expectations for group involvement, and participants must agree to keep the personal experiences of other group members confidential. Only through an atmosphere of trust and support can already cautious executives expose their communicational shortcomings and risk making the mistakes necessary for learning.

2. Participants must arrange their schedules around the group meetings. So much important material is presented in each session that absences seriously interfere with the outcome. Also, a group member who depends on the role-play involvement of another is penalized by that colleague's absence. Cooperation and support from upper management can help to avoid this problem.

3. Participants should have similar levels of management responsibility. In general terms, groups should be composed entirely of top managers,

middle managers, or line supervisors. While some mix of positions is possible, too much diversity of experience and position dilutes group cohesion and may discourage the involvement of atypical members.

4. The leader should encourage questions, comments, and general discussions from the group throughout the workshop. This feedback informs the leader about the clarity of the presentation and promotes a greater sense of participant involvement. During the presentation, some group members may ask for advice on handling a specific problem they have encountered. Though it is often tempting to dispense advice, it will often be better to encourage the group member to use that situation as the basis for a future role-play dialogue.

5. In directing the role plays, the leader aids the group by maintaining the focus on the core assertive interaction and not allowing the discussion to drift into concerns about specific personalities, the nature of an organization's product, or an historical narrative about previous interactions with that individual. The leader encourages positive group feedback to the protagonist and reinforces initial positive efforts even when they are not fully polished. It is important to reward the *minimally effective response* and then to "shape" the response to a more sophisticated level.

6. As a general rule, the leader should exemplify assertive responding by encouraging open expression of ideas, by communicating clearly, by giving compliments and constructive criticism, and by limiting unnecessary intrusions or digressions by group members.

Other practical matters concerning the size of the group and the physical setting of the workshop are more open to modification and experiment. Groups can be as small as six and as large as 20. When working with larger groups, it is helpful to divide participants into small subgroups, which simultaneously practice exercises and role plays among themselves. They can be rejoined into a large group for demonstrating principles. Workshops can be conducted "out-of-house" at a college, hotel, or consulting office, with participants drawn from different organizations. When conducting "in-house" workshops within one organization, the leader may wish to separate managers from their immediate superiors or subordinates or from competing colleagues. While in-house programs create a unique opportunity for general organization change, they may also stifle the participation of group members and compromise confidentiality.

Effectiveness of Executive Assertion Training

Controlled outcome studies on the effectiveness of the "Assertive Executive" have not as yet been made. This partly reflects the applied goals of the group rather than an interest in academic research. The latter demands strict methodological practices and the use of various control groups. There are also many difficulties inherent in any psychological outcome study, including questions about what constitutes change, what measuring tools are the most applicable and reliable, what components of the package are most powerful, and at what point in time change should be evaluated. Certainly, as more companies include assertion training in their management development programs, these questions and those concerning cost effectiveness will need to be considered.

Nevertheless, general evaluation responses from "Assertive Executive" group members are most encouraging. The 45 middle- and upper-middle management executives who completed the four most recent workshops represent New England business organizations ranging in size from small, privately owned companies to divisions of Fortune 500 corporations. They express enthusiasm regarding the overall usefulness of the training, with all of the participants rating the program as helpful or very helpful and 84 percent reporting that most of the material was relevant to their work situation (the remaining 16 percent stated they could use at least half of the material). In assessing specific aspects of the workshop, there was universal agreement that lectures and written material were beneficial to the learning process. While a number of individuals state that the role-play situations generated anxiety, 50 percent found them to be very helpful, and another 45 percent thought that they were somewhat helpful for skill development.

Anecdotal reports confirm that, with training and practice, executives feel an increased ability to manage difficult interactions, have increased comfort with negotiation, are more effective communicators, and gain improved listening skills.

In today's highly complex managerial climate, executives find that technical proficiency is just one part of being successful. They must also possess interpersonal skills of high calibre. Executive assertiveness training is one important way to achieve this goal. This statement by one 40-year-old corporate vice-president is typical: "When I started the course, I already knew how to be aggressive, passive, and passive-aggressive. But now I know that I can be so much more effective when I am assertive."

REFERENCES

Alberti, R.E. and M.L. Emmons. 1970. *Stand Up, Speak Out, Talk Back*. New York: Pocket.

———. 1974. *Your Perfect Right: A Guide to Assertive Behavior*, 2nd ed. San Luis Obisbo, Calif.: Impact.

Baer, J. 1976. *How to be an Assertive (not Aggressive) Woman*. New York: Signet.

Bartolomé, F. 1972. "Executives as Human Beings," *Harvard Business Review* (November–December): 62–69.

Ellis, A. and R.A. Harper. 1975. *A New Guide to Rational Living*. Englewood Cliffs, N.J.: Prentice-Hall.

Fensterheim, H. 1971. *Help Without Psychoanalysis.* New York: Stein & Day.

———. 1972. "Behavior Therapy: Assertive Training in Groups." In *Progress in Group and Family Therapy*, edited by C.J. Sager and H.S. Kaplan, pp. 159–69. New York: Brunner/Mazel.

Fensterheim, H. and J. Baer. 1975. *Don't Say Yes When You Want to Say No.* New York: Dell.

Galassi, M.D. and J.P. Galassi. 1978. "Assertion: A Critical Review." *Psychotherapy: Theory, Research and Practice* 15: 16–29.

Gambrill, E.D. and C.A. Richey. 1975. "An Assertion Inventory for Use in Assessment and Research." *Behavior Therapy* 6: 550–61.

Goldberg, P. 1978. *Executive Health.* New York: McGraw-Hill.

Harriman, B. 1974. "Up and Down the Communications Ladder." *Harvard Business Review* (September–October): 143–51.

Jakubowski, P. and A.J. Lange. 1978. *The Assertive Option.* Champaign, IL: Research Press.

Josefowtiz, N. 1980. "Management Men and Women: Closed vs. Open Doors." *Harvard Business Review* (September–October): 56–62.

Lange, A.J. and P. Jakubowski. 1976. *Responsible Assertive Behavior.* Champaign, IL: Research Press.

Levinson, H. 1978. "The Abrasive Personality," *Harvard Business Review* (May–June): 86–94.

———. 1980. "Criteria for Choosing Chief Executives," *Harvard Business Review* (July–August): 113–20.

Manuso, J.S.J., Ed. 1980. *Manage Your Stress.* New York: McGraw-Hill.

McCaskey, M.D. 1979. "The Hidden Messages Managers Send." *Harvard Business Review* (November–December): 135–48.

Mischel, W. 1968. *Personality and Assessment.* New York: John Wiley.

Nelson, S.J. 1980. "The Executive Interaction Stress Inventory." Unpublished test.

Pilla, B.A. 1977. "Women in Business," *Training and Development Journal* 31: 22–25.

Quick, T.L. 1980. "Counseling for Change," *Management Digest* (November): 8–11.

Smith, M.J. 1975. *When I Say No I Feel Guilty*. New York: Dial Press.

"Troublemakers in the Office," *Time*, March 17, 1980, p. 72.

Wolpe, J. 1958. *Psychotherapy by Reciprocal Inhibition.* Stanford, Calif.: Stanford University Press.

14 Individual Career Planning and Counseling

Mark J. Carsman, Ph.D.

In recent years, individual career planning has received considerable attention in the literature dealing with the management and development of human resources. The purpose of this chapter is to provide the occupational clinical psychologist with a brief introduction to the current "field" of career planning in organizations with special emphasis on the role(s) that she or he may want to or be called on to assume in that area.

WHAT IS INDIVIDUAL CAREER PLANNING

There appear to be many different theoretical definitions of career planning. Indeed, many writers disagree on the meaning of "career." Though important, these theoretical matters will be side-stepped here. If interested, the reader can pursue this issue elsewhere (e.g., Dyer, 1976; Gutteridge, 1980; Hall, Hall, & Hinton, 1978).

For the purpose of this chapter, Walker's (1980) definition is useful for both its brevity and its correspondence to programs and activities widely seen in the "real world" as being a part of individual career planning:

> Career planning is the personal process of planning one's life work. It entails evaluating abilities and interests, considering alternative career opportunities, establishing career goals and planning practical development activities. The process results in decisions to enter a certain occupation, join a particular company, accept or decline job opportunities

> (relocations, promotions or transfers, etc.) and ultimately leave a company for another job or for retirement. (p. 279)

Ferrini and Parker's (1978) model of the career change and development decision process is not inconsistent with the Walker definition. Their model specifies a four-stage career change process: (1) career exploration/counseling, (2) education/training, (3) job search/placement, and (4) career assessment/future options.

Stage I: Career Exploration/Counseling

This stage is further subdivided into three components: self-assessment, career identification, and action planning. Self-assessment often sets the stage for all further career planning and decision-making activities. It involves the determination of positive and negative personal qualities (e.g., abilities, skills, interests, and values), any special barriers (e.g., race, sex, age, disabilities), and external factors (e.g., financial needs and resources, family needs and support). Career identification yields the selection of a realistic career option after an investigation of specific careers. As part of this process, requirements for training, job entry and advancement, and job rewards are determined and compared with the individual's assets and liabilities, as determined in the self-assessment. Stage I concludes with the formulation of an action plan and timetable, which indicates the overall career goal and specifies all the steps (and times) required for their fulfillment. All practical matters relating to each portion of the plan (e.g., budgets) are made a part of this plan. Once formulated, the plan guides subsequent actions and is reviewed periodically and, where necessary, revised or completely reformulated.

Stage II: Education/Training

When training or education is specified in stage I, it is fulfilled in stage II. Experiences within this sphere (e.g., failure or lack of interest) may cause an individual to revise career goals, thereby returning to a stage I situation.

Stage III: Job Search/Placement

Where a new (or first) job is specified in the action plan, the search for it is the substance of this stage. It can involve the location and/or self-development of job openings, the use of friends, search firms, or other agencies. Furthermore, it can require the preparation of resumes or "sales letters" and the attainment and use of interviewing and negotiation skills.

Stage IV: Career Assessment/Future

After major specific career goals have been attained (e.g., placement in a desired career position), individuals should then assess, at regular intervals, whether their career is currently meeting expectations in all personally important matters: for example, job satisfaction, extrinsic and intrinsic rewards, demands on abilities and interests, impact on family and general lifestyle, and general values. While Ferrini and Parker conceive of this as a separate stage, it is highly similar in content to the self-assessment phase of stage I. Indeed, they indicate that an outcome of stage IV work could be the decision to identify new or modified job or career objectives and thus begin the career change and development cycle again.

In their survey, Ferrini and Parker found that organizations have begun to provide support to employees in the tasks involved in each of the four stages. Figure 14.1 presents their four stages and typical issues or tasks subsumed within each. In addition, the figure also shows the type of organization-provided programs that have been created to support the individual in each stage.

In summarizing their findings, they note:

> Although the career change model described here is fairly straightforward when it is utilized by individuals, its relevance to organizations is not always evident. Career change programs in most educational institutions and business and industrial firms do not fully address all of the tasks that most individuals must perform. In many cases, only one or two of the major functions will be evident within a specific organization. (p. 16)

Walker and Gutteridge's (1979) survey of career planning practices in predominantly private sector organizations provides us with a clearer view of the scope and diversity existent today. Their findings include the following:

1. There is greater support for career planning programs on a conceptual, rather than a practical, level.
2. Almost all of the survey respondents reported that they are or will soon provide some form of career planning assistance.
3. Two basic types of programs were widely reported:
    a. Informal counseling by personnel and supervisory staff.
    b. Communication programs regarding the company's existing career-relatable programs, such as educational assistance, affirmative action programs, and job requirements.
4. Reported intentions to strengthen career programs largely focus on communication programs or career related matters, such as job information and career path data.
5. Where employees are given career counseling assistance, it is provided in many ways:
    a. Informal counseling by personnel staff (currently done by 88.7 percent of the companies; 5.0 percent are planning to do this).

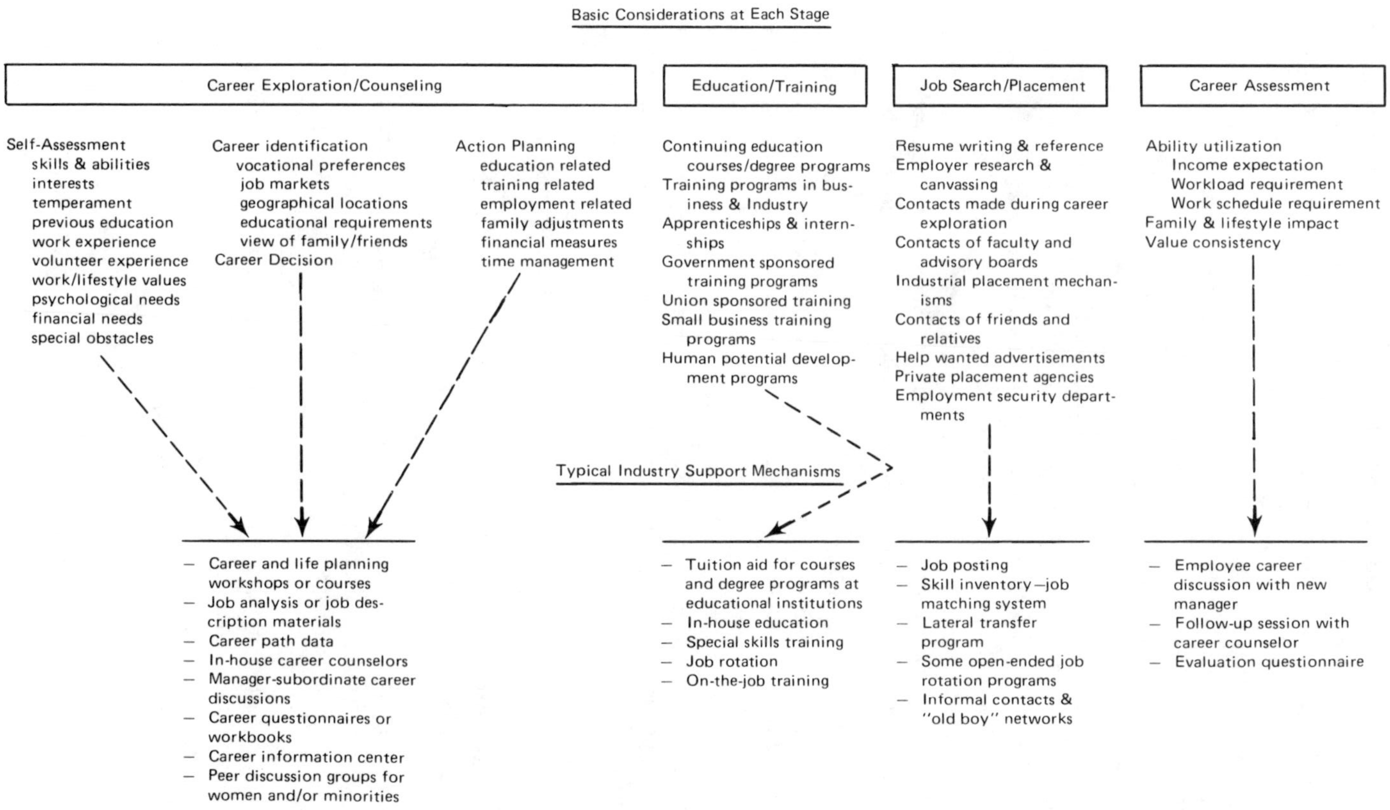

Figure 14.1. The four stages of the career change process and typical programs found in industry supporting each stage. (This material adapted from Ferrini and Parker, 1978.)

b. Career counseling by specialized staff counselors, such as a staff psychologist or a trained guidance counselor (20.5 percent, 7.6 percent).
c. Referral to external counselors at related services, such as specialists, career centers, university personnel. (29.2 percent, 3.8 percent).
d. Career counseling by supervisors (55.8 percent, 17.5 percent).
e. Life and career planning workshops (11.4 percent, 17.1 percent).
f. Individual self-analysis and planning using workbooks, etc. (15.6 percent, 18.5 percent).
g. Psychological testing and assessment (35.1 percent, 8.0 percent).
h. Testing and feedback regarding aptitudes, interests, etc. (32.7 percent, 9.6 percent).
i. Outplacement counseling/related services (37.3 percent, 1.9 percent).
j. Workshops and communications on retirement preparation (33.5 percent, 24.1 percent).
k. Job performance and development planning workshops (42.4 percent, 21.9 percent).

POTENTIAL ROLES FOR CLINICAL PSYCHOLOGISTS

As seen in the above discussed surveys, and that of another survey by Griffith (1980), current and contemplated career planning programs do not rely heavily on the services of "professional" counselors of any type. Indeed, there seems to be a strong and continuing interest in using supervisors or general personnel staff as career counselors.

Despite this, opportunities do exist for the prepared clinician in several capacities, including: (1) provider of comprehensive or selected career counseling services to individuals or groups, (2) developer and/or facilitator of career programs, and (3) administrator of career programs and services.

Provider of Career Counseling Services

On the face of it, this role would seem the most obvious one for a clinician to assume. We will first examine the nature of career counseling, the basic competencies required in its practice, and relate them to the "typical" clinician unschooled in this area.

Defining career counseling. On a most pragmatic level, career counseling could be defined as the process in which one person seeks to help another in pursuing individual career planning (cf. the Walker, 1980, definition of individual career planning). Career counselors, then, would be those individuals (whether credentialed or not) whose position or personal perspective defines them as a helper to others in career planning.

In the terms of Ferrini and Parker's conceptual model, career counselors would likely be those individuals who help others with one or more of the following: self-assessment (of interests, abilities, values, needs, special obstacles, or deficits), career identification (including career decision making), and action planning.

Definitions of career (or vocational) counseling encountered in the psychological/academic literature are not usually in complete agreement, or clear-cut for that matter. Nevertheless, an informal "content analysis" of a few scholarly definitions can be useful.

Lofquist and England offer the following operational definition of vocational counseling:

> Vocational counseling is a continuous learning process involving interaction in a nonauthoritarian fashion between two individuals whose problem solving efforts are oriented toward vocational planning. The professional vocational counselor and the counselee with a problem are concerned not only with solution of the immediate problem, but also with planning new techniques for meeting future problems. While the counselee has need for anxiety-reduction concerning his vocational problem or set of problems, psychopathology is not involved, and the counselee is capable of learning new attitudes and appraising vocational reality with reference to his unique assets and liabilities, without first requiring a major restructuring of his personality. Psychotherapy may result in some measure, but vocational planning, not psychotherapy, is the primary orientation of the process. The vocational counselor serves in this learning process as the reinforcing agent, facilitator of counselee activity, resource person, and expert on techniques for discovering additional data relevant to the vocational planning. The counselor, also, learns continuously in the process, but keeps his need satisfaction demands at a level subservient to those of the counselee. (1961, p. 5; authors' italics omitted)

For Brammer and Shostrum (1977), career counseling is part of the general field of counseling that "seeks to help a client become aware of his assets, limitations, and opportunities in all possible areas so that he will make wise choices and will use his unique talents if he cares to do so" (p. 390). They assert that career counseling is no longer concerned with a single occupational entry decision; instead, it now reflects the reality of a changing workplace by being concerned with continuous change over life. They believe that vocational psychology cannot be singled out as a special branch of counseling and psychotherapy "largely because career counseling must be accomplished in the context of the individual's total life style and in relationship to the client's sub-culture. Optimally effective career counseling, therefore, cannot be an isolated and mechanical process of matching people and jobs" (p. 391).

They also provide three career counseling goals: (1) confirmation of the choice already made by the client (the most commonly seen goal in career counseling), (2) clarification of vocational objectives, and (3) facilitation of the discovery of new or previously unconsidered facts about self and the working world.

Tyler writes that the purpose of career (and other) types of counseling

> *is to facilitate wise choices of the sort on which the person's later development depends.* Counseling should not be *just* for persons who are anxious, unhappy, or unable to cope with the circumstances of their lives.... But the depth of understanding and the interest in the full complexity of personality characteristic of psychotherapy at its best should be built into *every* counseling relationship. (1969, p. 13)

Tyler also offers a classification system to be used with clients seeking counseling in the "developmental areas" of work, interpersonal areas, and aloneness. She believes that "a wise and skillful counselor" should be able to classify all clients into one of three case categories: "choice," "change," or "doubtful."

"Choice" cases primarily involve decision making and one or both of the counseling goals of: (1) a comprehensive survey of possibilities, which in turn supports (2) a decision or commitment. Counselor activities in these cases include: "exploratory interviews," "testing," "gathering situational information," "gathering prognostic information," and "planning and evaluating tryout experiences."

"Change" cases involve the need for "considerable psychological change" to take place before any choice or commitment can be successfully made. As an example, a painfully shy client would probably require change in this area before any appropriate career decision could be made or carried out. Counseling goals in "change" cases involve (1) removal of obstacles blocking possible avenues of choice and/or (2) the creation of new possibilities. Counselor activities in these cases include "interviews for future planning," "therapeutic interviews," "desensitization procedure," "arranging for medical (or other) treatment," and "arranging for education or training" or "experimental social innovation."

"Doubtful" cases are those that can not be immediately placed as a "choice" or "change" case. These require a "search for structure" as an initial counseling objective, supported by such counseling activities as the "client-centered interview," "study of case records," and "testing and observation of life situations."

Even though career counseling is not typically defined as being psychotherapy, the clinician with a psychotherapeutic orientation is likely to see much in common in his or her work with that of a career counselor. After all, what clinical psychologist in practice with mildly disturbed clients does not deal with "choice" or "change" cases? What clinician is alien to the basic assessment techniques and case management practices included in her definition of career counseling?

The common bonds between the two areas may become more evident when one considers the goals that Sundberg, Tyler, and Taplin found to be emphasized by a wide variety of schools of psychotherapy:

> 1) strengthening the client's motivation to do the right things, 2) reducing emotional pressure and anxiety, 3) releasing growth potential, 4) modifying cognitive structure, 5) increasing self-knowledge, 6) changing habits, and 7) improving interpersonal relationships. Therapists of different schools all attempt 1) to lower the client's anxiety level, 2) to establish a strong personal relationship and 3) to facilitate communication. What therapists say to clients during interviews can mainly be classified as reflection of feeling, interpretation, or teaching, and the proportions of each vary somewhat from one theoretical school to another. (1973, p. 309)

They also indicate that systematic appraisal of the client (often with tests) is typical in psychotherapy to facilitate decisions about whether and how to best serve the client.

Based on the descriptions of counseling and psychotherapy, it seems that many clinicians are likely to possess a core of competencies that are necessary but *not* sufficient to permit them to function as a career counselor. They do tend to possess critical skills regarding client contact and management (including attitudinal and behavior modification). In addition, they are typically trained in the general methods and supporting theories and techniques regarding client assessment.

What appears to be missing from the repertoire of the skills of the typical clinician for the practice of career counseling are one or more of the following: (1) a well founded and explicit stance regarding the theories and research surrounding career development and adjustment, (2) expert knowledge of career related assessment instruments and their uses, (3) knowledge of the realities of job markets, and (4) an expert command of occupational information.

Theories of career development. In his book on *Theories of Career Development,* Osipow (1973) states that all counselors have some ideas about the workings of human behavior, since such ideas are necessary to their ability to function. Counselors differ from each other in the degree to which they use explicit and systematized ideas (e.g., theories) or implicit and probably less systematized ideas.

The organizing ideas that a counselor holds are very important since, explicitly or not, they will determine: (1) the assessment procedures used, (2) the type of diagnosis made, (3) the interpretive meaning of any test results, and (4) the type of service provided.

Osipow provides some examples. Counselors believing that the process of career choice is one of matching skills and interests of a person to the requirements of a position will act quite differently than counselors who view career development as an elaboration and extension of the self. In the former case, the counselor is likely to use tests of ability and aptitudes and to employ other methods directed at clarifying the self; additionally, the client would be encouraged and aided in exploring careers through literature and visits to career settings. In the latter case, the counselor would tend toward creating an interview environment that facilitates self-exploration and self-expression and will probably eschew the use of tests and occupational information as being an interference to or distraction from this process.

The interested reader is directed to the Osipow work and Crites (1981) for an elaboration and critique of the major theories and approaches to vocational development and counseling (see also: Holland, 1973; Hopson and Hayes, 1968).

Assessment. Assessment procedures seen in career counseling tend to fall into four categories: (1) formal tests of client ability, interest, aptitude, personality, values, et al., (2) structured exercises in reflection on the self in the above mentioned areas, (3) interviews (to determine client's self-perceptions, social maturity, general knowledge, etc.), and (4) reviews of historical and/or incidental data regarding the client (e.g., work history, educational history—including grades—prior test data, medical history, family's socioeconomic standing and history, et al.).

Formal test instruments often used in the career counseling of adults include: (1) Allport-Vernon-Lindzey Study of Values (Houghton Mifflin); (2) Edwards Personal Preference Schedule, a quasi-personality inventory (Psychological Corporation); (3) General Aptitude Test Battery (U.S. Employment Service); (4) Holland's Self Directed Search, a self-scored and self-interpreted personality based interest inventory (Consulting Psychologists Press); (5) Kuder Occupational Interest Survey (Science Research Associates); (6) Strong-Campbell Interest Inventory, an interest inventory organized in accord with Holland's (1973) personality types (Stanford University/Consulting Psychologists Press).

The above mentioned instruments are far from the only ones specifically available for career counseling purposes. In addition, instruments used in clinical settings (e.g., the Rorschach or the MMPI) can be and are used by appropriately trained career counselors.

Structured exercises (e.g., "name your three fantasy jobs") are also very frequently used in career counseling. These frequently involve clients in reflecting upon their past achievements (as perceived by them) and then factoring out the underlying competencies, attributes, and values used in these situations. Structured exercises are often used to yield a written profile of the individual, which is then used to produce a portrait of an ideal position. That information is then used as an anchor in the search for potential occupations, to evaluate the client's present occupation or for comparative purposes in making occupational decisions.

A number of popular self-help guides can provide an excellent illustration of this process; unlike much of the academic literature on counseling, the self-help guides are quite clear and useful in providing a concrete framework within which to work. These include: Bolles, 1978, 1979; Burack, Albrecht, and Seitler, 1980; Campbell, 1974; Ford and Lippett, 1972; Hagberg and Leider, 1978; Haldane, 1974, 1975; Jackson, 1978; Kotter, Faux, and McArthur, 1978; Souerwine, 1978; Storey, 1976.

Of these, Bolles' *What Color is Your Parachute?* has been exceptionally popular and requires special attention as a model of a counseling process and as a direct and indirect source of occupational information. The self-help program of Kotter, Faux, and McArthur is also of interest, given its use of several formal test instruments like the Strong-Campbell Interest Inventory; as such it provides a good example of how test and nontest data can be derived, arrayed, and used.

Tests in counseling can evoke more problems than they solve. Thompson (1976) believes that the appropriate value and purpose of tests in vocational counseling are frequently misperceived by clients. One of the typical client misconceptions he cites is that tests can tell a person what they *should* do or in what they will *succeed.* These and the other typical misconceptions discussed serve to illustrate the content and challenge of vocational counseling.

For further information about the nature and use (on a theoretical and practical basis) of the full spectrum of tests used in vocational counseling, the reader is advised to consult Goldman (1971) and Super and Crites (1962). Though somewhat dated, these works serve as an excellent introduction and reference. The discussion on assessment by Prediger (1974) is also helpful.

Expert knowledge of the world of work and occupations. Expert knowledge of occupations and work settings is of critical importance in career counseling; unfortunately, it is a difficult area to master. Figure 14.2, from Brammer and Shostrom (1977), illustrates the vast scope of the area.

Occupational data are available from certain major sources: (1) the federal government, (2) commercial publishers, (3) trade associations, and (4) special information centers or libraries.

For the federal government, the Bureau of Labor Statistics and the Bureau of the Census are the primary sources of data. The major references published by the federal government (U.S. Government Printing Office) are the *Dictionary of Occupational Titles (D.O.T.)* and the *Occupational Outlook Handbook.* The *D.O.T.* names and describes thousands of jobs and classifies them as to how they involve "people," "data," and "things." It also describes the personal attributes and abilities used in each job. The *Handbook* provides an indication of trends in opportunities in specific occupations.

TREND DATA
(job loss, growth, openings, etc.)

- Local surveys
- State employment/economic surveys/studies
- U.S. *Occupational Outlook Handbook*
- U.S. Bureau of Labor regional/national reports
- Business or trade press
- Professional or trade associations

COMPENSATION
(monetary & nonmonetary)

- U.S. Bureau of Labor reports
- Personnel or compensation journals
- Trade/professional association studies/reports
- Business/trade/professional press

ENTRY LEVEL POSITIONS

- *Dictionary of Occupational Titles*
- Job announcements or advertisements

BARRIERS OR RESTRICTIONS
(sex, age, handicaps, etc.)

- Vocational rehabilitation literature
- Personnel journals
- General occupational literature
- Political/social action organizations
- State bureaus of professional/vocational standards

JOB DESCRIPTIONS
(work performed, hours, travel, setting, etc.)

- Recruitment literature
- General occupational literature
- U.S. Bureau of Labor Statistics (including *Occupational Outlook Handbook)*
- Job analysis studies

WORKER FUNCTIONS
(skills and capacities)

- *Dictionary of Occupational Titles*
- U.S. Employment Service studies
- General occupational literature
- Job announcements/advertisements

WORKER QUALIFICATIONS
(education/training)

- Trade/professional associations
- College reference books, e.g., Lovejoy
- College catalogues
- Job announcements/advertisements

REGULATORY REQUIREMENTS (licenses, degrees, certificates, etc.)

- State bureaus of professional/vocational standards
- General occupational literature
- Trade/professional association

JOB STRUCTURE

- U.S. Census
- U.S. Employment Service

Figure 14.2. A summary of nine types and selected sources of occupational data needed in career counseling. (This material adapted from Brammer & Shostrum, 1977.)

The American Personnel and Guidance Association (Falls Church, Virginia) publishes career information data for counseling purposes and can be a source of information about other publishers. Trade associations often publish data for career decision making, but they must be contacted on an individual basis. Some states or other governmental units have established centers for career information. One would have to investigate this potential source of help at the local level.

Assuming that one is willing and able to gain and keep current a workable hold on the enormous volume of occupationally relevant information, there remains the tricky task of assisting a client in translating test and nontest data into the names of occupations worthy of consideration. (Tests only match a person on some dimension to a portion of all job titles.)

While such a translation may turn out to be more art than craft in many cases, Holland (1973) has helped with this problem by providing a basis for directly translating a client's personality typology to a *range* of occupations within the *D.O.T.* Both the Self Directed Search and the Strong-Campbell Interest Inventory employ Holland's personality classifications, and Bolles' (1979) work uses a modified form of it.

DEVELOPER/FACILITATOR AND ADMINISTRATOR ROLES

Clinical psychologists working in industry are likely to be familiar with or experienced in the basics of promoting, developing, and administering programs and services. The development process basically involves identifying a need, determining and proposing a solution to that need, and using a perspective and form of communication that will convince the relevant authority to provide the requested organizational support and resources.

While needs and concerns will vary across organizations (and must be addressed accordingly), it may prove useful to note some of the underlying motivations that have been reported or suggested as being operative in the support of career planning programs.

The Walker and Gutteridge (1979) survey found that companies adopting career planning programs do so primarily to serve management oriented needs, including: the shortage of management talent, a desire to develop and recruit from within the organization, a desire to improve productivity or to reduce turnover.

Morgan, Hall, and Martier (1980) note that many such programs begin with the purpose of addressing the needs of "special groups," such as women and minorities; after operating successfully, they are expanded to include all employees.

The clinical psychologist wishing to develop or promote such programs would be well advised to examine the history, nature, and operation of existing programs carefully. The Ferrini and Parker (1978) study provides a detailed look at programs in business and other settings and provides and sketches many others, most of which are specifically identified. Walker (1980) also identifies the following companies as being pioneers in introducing career planning: Gulf Oil, IBM, General Electric, Xerox, TRW, and General Motors. He also suggests a process for introducing and developing such programs as organizational innovations. Morgan, Hall, and Martier (1980) also speak to this issue and provide an example of a specific career planning workshop.

Clinical psychologists may also consider the role of administrator of career planning programs and personnel (e.g., trained career counselors who are neither clinicians or certified/licensed). Such a role does not appear to be the mode; however, neither would it be proscribed.

CONCLUSION

It is important to emphasize that the entire area of career planning and counseling varies considerably across organizations. Even within the formal area of vocational/career counseling, considerable diversity exists between theories of vocational adjustment and across practitioners. Because career counseling is not psychotherapy (although it may result from it, lead to it, or accompany it), it can be practiced by anyone. There is no protected market for the licensed clinical psychologist (or the Ph.D. counseling psychologist, who is often trained and experienced in career counseling).

On the other hand, the clinical psychologist wishing to embrace this area is limited only by his or her motivation to acquire the additional knowledge and skills. For those so motivated, Otte (1980) provides a listing of sources of training programs for individuals interested in learning to implement career development programs.

In addition to the references provided here, the reader is urged to keep current with periodicals in the area of personnel, e.g., *Personnel* and *Personnel Journal,* and with the publications of the following organizations: the American Personnel and Guidance Association (Falls Church, Virginia), e.g., *Measurement and Evaluation in Guidance, Personnel and Guidance Journal,* and *The Vocational Guidance Quarterly;* The American Society for Training and Development (Washington, D.C.), e.g., *Training and Development;* The American Psychological Association (Washington, D.C.), e.g., the *Journal of Counseling Psychology.*

A further source of information on career development is *The Career Development Bibliography* (1979) of the Center for Research in Career Development of the Columbia University Graduate School of Business and its periodical, *The Career Development Bulletin.*

REFERENCES

Bolles, R.N. 1978. *The Three Boxes of Life and How to Get Out of Them.* Berkeley, Calif.: Ten Speed Press.

———. 1979. *What Color Is Your Parachute? A Practical Manual for Job Hunters and Career Changers,* rev. ed. Berkeley, Calif.: Ten Speed Press.

Brammer, L.M. and E.L. Shostrum. 1977. *Therapeutic Psychology: Fundamentals of Counseling and Psychotherapy,* 3rd. ed. Englewood Cliffs, N.J.: Prentice-Hall.

Burack, E.H., M. Albrecht, and H. Seitler, 1980. *Growing: A Woman's Guide to Satisfaction.* Belmont, Calif.: Lifetime Learning Publications.

Campbell, D.P. 1974. *If You Don't Know Where You're Going, You'll Probably End Up Somewhere Else.* Niles, Ill.: Argus Communications.

The Career Development Bibliography. 1979. New York: The Center for Research in Career Development, Columbia University Graduate School of Business.

Crites, J.O. 1969. *Vocational Psychology: The Study of Vocational Behavior and Development.* New York: McGraw-Hill.

———. 1981. *Career Counseling.* New York: McGraw-Hill.

Dyer, L., Ed. 1976. *Careers in Organizations: Individual Planning and Organizational Development.* Ithaca, N.Y.: New York State School of Industrial and Labor Relations, Cornell University.

Ferrini, P. and L.A. Parker, 1978. *Career Change.* Cambridge, Mass.: Technical Education Research Centers.

Ford, G.A. and G.L. Lippett. 1972. *Planning Your Future.* La Jolla, Calif.: University Associates.

Goldman, L. 1971. *Using Tests in Counseling,* 2nd ed. Santa Monica, Calif.: Goodyear.

Griffith, A.R. 1980. "A Survey of Career Development in Corporations." *Personnel and Guidance Journal* 58:537–43.

Gutteridge, T.G., Ed. 1980. *Career Planning and Development: Perspectives of the Individual and the Organization* (annotated bibliography). Madison, Wis.: American Society for Training and Development.

Hagberg, J. and R. Leider. 1978. *The Inventurers: Excursions in Life and Career Renewal.* Reading, Mass.: Addison-Wesley.

Haldane, B. 1974. *Career Satisfaction and Success.* New York: AMACON.

———. 1975. *How to Make a Habit of Success,* rev. ed. New York: Warner Books.

Hall, D.T., F.S. Hall, and R.W. Hinton. 1978. "Research on Organizational Career Development." *Human Resource Planning.* 1: 203–33.

Holland, J.L. 1973. *Making Vocational Choices: A Theory of Careers.* Englewood Cliffs, N.J.: Prentice-Hall.

Hopson, B., and J. Hayes, Eds. 1968. *The Theory and Practice of Vocational Guidance: A Selection of Readings.* Oxford: Pergamon.

Jackson, T. 1978. *Guerrilla Tactics in the Job Market.* New York: Bantam Books.

Kotter, J.P., V.A. Faux, and C.C. McArthur. 1978. *Self Assessment and Career Development.* Englewood Cliffs, N.J.: Prentice-Hall.

Lofquist, H.H., and G.W. England. 1961. *Problems in Vocational Counseling.* Dubuque, Iowa: Wm. C. Brown.

Morgan, M.A., D.T. Hall, and A. Martier. 1980. "Career Development Strategies in Industry: Where Are We and Where Should We Be?" In *Managing Career Development,* edited by M.A. Morgan. New York: Van Nostran Reinhold.

Osipow, S.H. 1973. *Theories of Career Development,* 2nd ed. Englewood Cliffs, N.J.: Prentice-Hall.

Otte, F.L. 1980. *Implementing Career Development Programs: Results of a Survey of Seminars/Workshops for Trainers.* Atlanta: Author. (Available from Dr. Fred L. Otte, associate professor of vocational development, Georgia State University, University Plaza, Atlanta, GA 30303).

Prediger, D.J. 1974. "The Role of Assessment in Career Guidance." In *Vocational Guidance and Human Development,* edited by E.L. Herr. Boston: Houghton Mifflin, 1974.

Souerwine, A.H. 1978. *Career Strategies: Planning for Personal Achievement.* New York: AMACON.

Storey, W.D. 1976. *Career Dimensions* (4 vols.). Crotonville, N.Y.: General Electric Co.

Sundberg, N.D., L.E. Tyler, and J.R. Taplin, 1973. *Clinical Psychology: Expanding Horizons,* 2nd ed. Englewood Cliffs, N.J.: Prentice-Hall.

Super, D.E. and J.O. Crites. 1962. *Appraising Vocational Fitness,* rev. ed. New York: Harper & Row.

Thompson, A.P. 1976. "Client Misconceptions in Vocational Counseling." *Personnel and Guidance Journal* (September): 30–33.

Tyler, L.E. 1969. *The Work of the Counselor,* 3rd ed. Englewood Cliffs, N.J.: Prentice-Hall.

Walker, J.W. 1980. "Does Career Planning Rock the Boat?" In *Managing Career Development,* edited by M.A. Morgan. New York: Van Nostrand Reinhold.

Walker, J.W., and T.G. Gutteridge. 1979. *Career Planning Practices.* New York: AMACON.

15 Coping with Job Abolishment*

James S.J. Manuso, Ph.D.

Reorganization, regionalization, and technical innovation sometimes require corporations to abolish a number of jobs within a short time period. The loss of one's job, a primary source of self-esteem, and the resultant anger that is often suppressed, are conducive to the development of effective depression. And, when a working unit is abolished, there may be a group-reinforced maintenance of that depression. Either nearness in work position or a commonly shared dilemma, or both, are known to favor interaction and friendship, (Festinger, Schachter, & Back, 1950) and individuals tend to want the same positive or negative relationship to an attitude, idea, or value that is held by another individual with whom they have a positive relationship (Heider, 1958). Thus, if a whole work unit is abolished and the reactions of a few employees are negativistic and depressive, others with whom they share relationships may adopt these "unhealthy" reactions, especially at a time of uncertainty. The result is that a diffusion of depressive thought patterns may occur.

Depression is especially pernicious when the separated employee is seeking a new job, a time when he needs to mobilize all his personal resources in order to sell himself to a new employer. Feeding on itself, it diminishes self-esteem and augments anger that is usually suppressed. The feeling of worthlessness and the anger are almost inevitably communicated during job interviews. Since the mood and attitude of the job applicant weigh heavily in his evaluation, the individual

*Originally published in *Journal of Occupational Medicine* 19 (September 1977): 598–602. Reprinted with permission.

may not get the new job; this will confirm his feelings of inadequacy and escalate his frustration and anger, thereby initiating a self-fulfilling prophecy. When this happens to members of a peer group, these "depressive elements" gain force and may produce a more widespread depression in mood. This is especially true among marginal populations in complex urban environments and at times of economic downturns.

It is widely acknowledged that psychological stress and tension increase the incidence of disease in any population and cause people to seek medical care. Dr. Robert J. Haggerty of the Harvard School of Public Health recently indicated that "stress works to increase the susceptibility to disease" and that "accidents and abuse have been shown to be two to three times as common in families with frequent moves, recent deaths, and evidence of social dysfunction, such as unmarried mothers, marital problems, and unemployment." (*New York Times,* 1976). Indeed, stressors come in many forms—even the gasoline shortage of 1974 was observed to directly create and exacerbate frank psychiatric symptomatology (Shwed & Ruvin, 1976). Dr. Hans Selye's work on the General Adaptation Syndrome shows that stress can both cause and be caused by emotional reactions, through a series of corticoid secretion mechanisms (1955). Particularly relevant to the present study, Dr. Sidney Cobb found that "there are meaningful changes in norepinephrine excretion and in serum creatinine, serum uric acid and serum cholesterol associated with the stress of job termination" (1974). These "changes" are typically "increases" unless the individual whose job was terminated had strong psychological defenses and a meaningful social support system (such as family, friends, and relatives). Thus, the undefended and unsupported employee who is terminated is a likely candidate for functional symptoms and exacerbations of chronic or latent medical disorders.

Recently, the Equitable Life Assurance Society of the United States, historically considered an organization offering considerable job security, found it necessary to abolish a number of technical jobs in the same department. This provided the opportunity to develop, in collaboration with personnel staff, a "job-attainment training program," the most significant clinical features of which were the "stress management workshop" and individual follow-up interviews with workshop participants. This report summarizes that experience and examines four experimental questions. They are: (1) Is job abolishment more likely to serve as a template for depression among employees than is a precipitous change in their management, job responsibilities and work methods? (2) Is there a group-reinforced propensity for the development of depressive thought patterns? (3) Is a stress management workshop a significantly effective instrument for helping employees minimize the probability of developing stress-related disorders, including depression, following job abolishment? (4) How can the treatment effects of the workshop be explained?

To answer these questions an experimental, job abolishment workshop group was compared to a control "precipitous change"—no workshop group on the basis of visits to the employees' health center three months before and three months after job abolishment or precipitous change. For the experimental group members, a pre- and post-workshop version of the Thematic Apperception Test (TAT) (Murray, 1943) was administered, content analyzed by a "double-blind" method, and then compared on four overlapping psychological dimensions and on a fifth composite dimension. The dimensions developed for investigation by the researcher were: (1) positive and negative views of oneself as a functioning employee; (2) psychological distance from or closeness to the reality of job abolishment, i.e., realistic acceptance and unrealistic denial; (3) felt certainty and uncertainty regarding one's capabilities in a continuing career; and, (4) hope and despair. The fifth composite dimension pooled the data across these four dimensions.

SAMPLE

The 16 participants (15 white, one black) were employees whose computer-operator jobs were being abolished. They had been working in the organization for a minimum of six years to a maximum of 27 years; the average length of service was 15 years. They ranged in age from 30 to 55; with an average of 39 years. All but two were married and had families; most had considerable fixed financial obligations. They were in the fortieth percentile of the nonofficer grade and salary range, and all were high school graduates. Eleven of the employees knew and had worked with one another prior to the workshop. Ideally, a stress management workshop should be limited to eight to ten participants. A commonly shared occupational dilemma, albeit job-related moving (Olive, et al., 1976) or job abolishment, appears to be the essential criterion for the selection of participants.

Since all job-abolished employees participated in the workshop, the records of 91 employees who had previously experienced the stressor of having their management, job responsibilities, and work methods changed precipitously, and had not participated in a workshop, were used as the best available control condition. The control group employees, 32 males and 59 females, ranging in age from 18 to 56, held similarly semi-skilled, technical jobs, and averaged the same educational, grade, and salary levels as the experimental group.

OBJECTIVES

The goals of the workshop were fivefold: (1) to elicit the individual's and group's most negative feelings in an uncritical, socially supportive, and accepting environment, all the while respecting the reality that the jobs had indeed been permanently abolished; (2) after surfacing of these depression-loaded feelings, to assist the participants to gain insight and, by working the feelings through, to learn to cope with their tendencies to self-sabotage; (3) to assist participants in recognizing and articulating the array of personal choices that they now confront, e.g., to opt for outplacement, to actively seek jobs on their own, to consider early retirement, etc.; (4) to demonstrate specific stress-management and antidepression techniques and to explain and offer to make available as needed the full resources of the Equitable's emotional health program; (5) to evaluate the program and to solicit feedback from the participants in order to improve it The first four goals were thus aimed at lessening the stressor effects of job abolishment and the required readjustments.

The individual follow-up interviews were intended to further detect and prevent depression and, if necessary, to encourage into treatment those employees suffering depression.

METHODS AND MATERIALS

The author, assisted by a female organization development consultant, met with the 16 employees for the two and one-half hour workshop four days after they had been notified of job abolishment. This was on the third day of their full-time, week-long job-attainment training program, which helped them to understand the job abolishment policy and drilled them in writing resumes and in developing effective job-interview techniques. Employees were to receive their full salaries over the three months following notification of job abolishment unless outside jobs were accepted. Each employee also had the assistance of three staff members of the human resources department in arranging a transfer to another department and of a consultant agency for placement with other companies.

The four-day delay before meeting with the employees allowed the initial shock of job abolishment to wane and permitted the development of a readiness for grappling with the pertinent issues. At the time of the workshop the participants were found to be at relative ease with one another, thus facilitating the group process.

In the first phase of the workshop, lasting approximately five minutes, participants, seated in a large circle, were asked "to write a career or job-related story, explaining the past, present and future," in response to one of the three Thematic Apperception Test (TAT) pictures. The TAT presents ambiguous, primarily interpersonal drawings of people of different ages and sexes in various settings, and the mood and present life situation of the subject are reflected through his responses. Picture cards depicting a farm scene (card 2), a medical operation (card 8BM), and a conversation between two men (card 7BM) were used as stimuli.

An incomplete sentence technique was used in the second and longest (1 hr, 50 min) phase of the workshop. Participants completed emotionally charged sentence stems and then one-by-one for each sentence stem, shared their final sentences and their thoughts and feelings with others in the workshop. Some of the sentence stems used were: (1) My first reactions to my job being abolished are . . . ; (2) the worst/best thing that could happen to me as a result of my job being abolished is . . . ; (3) my career . . . ; (4) my boss . . . ; (5) if I could do my career all over again, I would . . . ; (6) to get a new job I need to . . . ; (7) when I get depressed I . . . ; and (8) my family . . . . Group interaction was encouraged. During the participants' discussions, the author and coleader maintained a supportive, problem-solving group focus on the realities of job abolishment, anger, depression, and the responsibility for exercising personal choice.

In the third phase of the workshop, lasting 30 minutes, methods of coping with stress were examined. For example, tense-slow-relax exercises were presented, the importance of talking out emotional problems was highlighted, and methods of self-assertion were reviewed. Employees were also encouraged to take advantage of the opportunity for individual consultations with members of the emotional health program.

Finally, in the workshop's last (5 min) phase, employees were again asked to write a career or job-related story in response to any one of the three TAT pictures. In this way, employees' pre- and post-workshop moods and their attitudes toward their life situations could be compared.

RESULTS AND DISCUSSION

Analyses of group discussions and of the pre- and post-workshop TAT stories written by participants indicated that the session was successful in significantly modifying participants' moods and attitudes. Table 15.1 records the results of the 12 (scorable) pre- and post-workshop TAT stories across the four dimensions of possible psychological change and for a fifth composite dimension. A two-tailed Z score testing for statistically significant differences between pre- and post-workshop dimensions of possible psychological change at the .05 level revealed that participants began and ended the workshop with a genuine awareness and acceptance of the realities of their dilemma. It was their shared reaction to this reality, their moods and attitudes, that changed following the workshop. The workshop was most successful in facilitating group members' shift from uncertain and despairing attitudes and feelings regarding their job abolishment to more certain and hopeful ones. Although there was a presumably workshop-induced shift of three group members, or 25 percent, from a negative to a positive view of the self, it is not statistically significant. For the composite dimension, there was the most significant shift, from negative, unrealistic, uncertain, and despairing outlooks to more positive, realistic, certain, and hopeful ones.

These observations were confirmed by the group discussions. Employees freely released their anger and frustration when encouraged to do so, and began

TABLE 15.1
Pre- and Post-Workshop TAT Responses

Dimensions of Possible Psychological Change	*Pre-Workshop No.*	*Pre-Workshop %*	*Post-Workshop No.*	*Post-Workshop %*	*Pre-/Post-Workshop Z - Scores*
1. Positive self-view	5	42	8	67	Z = 1.22[a]
Negative	7	58	4	33	
2. Realistic acceptance of job abolishment	9	75	11	92	Z = 1.10[a]
Unrealistic denial	3	25	1	8	
3. Felt certainty of career capabilities	1	8	10	83	Z = 3.65[b]
Felt uncertainty	11	92	2	17	
4. Hope	3	25	8	67	Z = 2.04[b]
Despair	9	75	4	33	
5. Composite:					
I. Positive, Realistic, Certain, Hopeful	18	38	37	67	Z = 3.93[b]
II. Negative, Unrealistic, Uncertain, Despair	30	62	11	33	

[a]Z is not significant at the .05 level for a 2-tailed test (where ± Z .025 = ± 1.96).
[b]Z is significant at the .05 level for a 2-tailed test (where ± Z .025 = ± 1.96).

to look progressively forward to attaining new jobs. The first three objectives of the workshop, namely, for participants to bring out, identify, and work through the depressive material and become able to make meaningful choices regarding the immediate future, were thus satisfied.

The fourth objective, of instructing participants in helping themselves and in seeking external assistance, was achieved partially in the workshop but primarily in subsequent individual interviews with members of the emotional health program. Three of the participants were found to be clinically depressed and were subsequently treated by staff members of the emotional health program. Of these three, two were single and lived alone, lacking the social support provided by a spouse and/or family. One of the depressed employees presented a recent history of situational trauma, which the abolishment of his job had apparently compounded. Another was found to be characteristically depressive in response to change. The third, an employee with considerable length of service and at a critical stage of life, was experiencing disbelief in reacting and adjusting to his job being abolished. Thus, the extent of a participant's pre-workshop predisposition to depression was decisive in determining whether or not a depressive reaction occurred, given the depression-inducing elements of job abolishment.

The last objective, of learning from the participant's job-abolishment experience, was readily met. The employees cited two major concerns: The exit interview was felt to be hurried and not informative; and most felt they had not been sufficiently prepared for the possibility of a job abolishment. For many, the news came as a shock.

For different periods of time preceding termination, those employees who decided to pursue the possibility of being transferred within the organization were placed on temporary assignments. The majority of these assignments translated into concrete job offers. Employees choosing outplacement received their salary at regular intervals until they accepted new jobs and were not expected to take temporary internal assignments.

A six-month follow-up revealed that four of the employees had chosen to be and were outplaced. All of the remaining employees had been transferred within the organization, at no cut on salary. Some took better jobs at higher salaries. The three depressed employees were appropriately treated in short-term psychotherapy and recovered successfully.*

It was also found that the mean number of participants' combined visits to the organization's health center remained unchanged over the three-month periods of time before and after job abolishment. This contrasts with retrospective measurements made of the control group's 91 employees. Their combined emotional health visits to the health center three months before and three months after their management and work methods were changed precipitously evidenced a 716 percent increase, from six to 43. In decreasing order of incidence, the majority of the control group's visits were for hypertension "exacerbation," gastro-intestinal disorders, anxiety, and myalgia. There were no instances of depression among control group employees.

The data support the conclusion that job abolishment, albeit with the assurance of a replacement job, serves as a template for depression among employees, whereas a precipitous change in management, job responsibilities, and work methods does not. These latter changes were observed to be more effective in eliciting psychophysiological expressions. Therefore, anxiety is more likely to be allayed through depression after one's job is abolished, or "lost," than if an employee's same job is changed. The necessary adaptation or readjustment atten-

*All three underwent short-term insight and supportive psychotherapy averaging four visits each. One of these employees also received a mild antidepressant, Norpramin, for six weeks.

dant to job loss must be greater than that following from changes in the same job. This is supported by the fact that being "fired at work" is ranked eighth in severity on Holmes and Rahe's Social Readjustment Rating Scale (Holmes & Rahe, 1967) whereas a "change in responsibilities at work" ranks twenty-second, and a "change in work hours or conditions" ranks thirty-first.

It may be inferred that there was a group-reinforced propensity for the development of depressive thought patterns among employees whose jobs were abolished. This inference is partially based on a comparison of pre- and post-workshop TAT responses, especially those relative to felt certainty and uncertainty of one's career capabilities. It may be hypothesized that, when an employee is feeling uncertain of himself, in a group sharing the same feelings, there arises a need to focus on the available certainties in the environment, a need to seek out that which is undeniable and in the present. For those whose jobs were abolished, the only immediate "external" certainty was that they would no longer hold their jobs. Through group interaction, this awareness or realistic acceptance of job abolishment may be translated into uncertainties concerning one's capabilities in a career. The pre-workshop cognitive appraisals of participants may have been as follows: "I am certain that I am capable of performing my job; My job has definitely been taken away; therefore, like the other members of this group, I am now uncertain that I am capable of performing in a job." Pre-workshop TAT responses on dimensions (2) and (3) support this view. Participants overwhemingly accepted the fact that their jobs were abolished and felt uncertain about themselves as a result. This caused them to focus again on the harsh fact that their old jobs were gone forever. Whenever they assembled, they were more likely to discuss that which they shared in common, the loss of their jobs. And, if group interaction in the workshop could readily change participants' moods and attitudes, then a similar mechanism may be held accountable for the initial dynamic of accepting job abolishment and feeling uncertain about one's job capabilities, regardless of previous performance.

Since employees whose jobs were abolished participated in the workshop, it is problematical as to whether or not they would have developed acute anxiety and its psychophysiological expressions in the absence of a workshop as did members of the control group. And, since depression is insidious and progressive in its development, it is also open to question as to whether or not more than three of the 16 employees whose jobs were abolished would have developed reactive depressions in effect in the absence of the workshop. It will be recalled that those three employees who evidenced depression were more predisposed to doing so before job abolishment notification than were the other 13. Their depressive reactions might have worsened had the workshop not been held. These observations, along with the fact that the workshop was successful in modifying participants' moods and attitudes relative to job abolishment, from more depression-inducing to less so, suggest that the workshop served to detect and prevent, but not treat, depression. The data also suggest that the workshop may have been a sufficient condition for preventing the onset of additional anxiety and associated psychophysiological disorders for all participants.

By design, participants' interactions in the workshop were aimed at encouraging the recognition and disclosure of moods and attitudes relating to job abolishment, particularly those found to be self-defeating and conducive to the development of the stress-related disorders, including depression. Once this was accomplished, individual and group missions were defined, namely, to get another job and to avoid stress. The reality of job abolishment remained unchanged, yet workshop participants discovered alternative ways of responding to this reality. They no longer saw their self-systems as being "abolished" along with their jobs. Participants underwent a cognitive restructuring (Lazarus, 1971)—in changing how they thought about themselves as a result of job abolishment, they also changed their moods and, therefore, the likelihood of (further) developing psychological or emotional reactions, stress, and its physiological expressions.

RECOMMENDATIONS

From the pilot workshop, the following recommendations were developed for job-abolishment programs.

1. Professionally supervised stress management workshops, such as the one described above, should become a part of any program held for employees impacted by mass job abolishments. A variation of such "training" is also appropriate for individuals.

2. As contrasted to exit interviews for the employee who voluntarily quits and/or takes another job, such interviews should be longer, more intensive, and more descriptive for the employee whose job is abolished. Employees should be provided, via checklist evaluations and recommendation letters, with information regarding their strengths and weaknesses in the various jobs they held for the last five years. This permits them to make realistic self-evaluations and plan future goals. Performance feedback must be continuous and maximal prior to notification of job abolishment. In facing a new situation the employee must be armed with realistic appraisals of his abilities, habits, and attitudes. Self-awareness necessarily precedes conscious self-control of behavior.

3. Advance notification of job abolishments and the encouragement of voluntary job relinquishment should be considered. This would assist in accommodating the goals of those employees wishing to transfer or be outplaced and of those desirous of remaining in their jobs. Moreover, bringing

the real facts out into the open somewhat obviates the "grapevine terror" accruing to covert communications and rumors.

4. Managers and supervisors charged with the responsibility of informing employees of their job abolishment should be trained in interview techniques by a knowledgeable emotional health professional. Anxious managers tend to minimize contact, whereas the person whose job is being abolished experiences a need for more information, less uncertainty, and longer contact.

5. Future job-abolishment and job-attainment training programs should make use of employees who have themselves successfully weathered a job abolishment. Such "veterans" could serve as role models, group leaders, tutors, and counselors.

6. As Basil R. Cuddihy (1974) notes, employees whose jobs are abolished should meet with an emotional health professional shortly after notification.

7. All departmental meetings and memoranda addressing job abolishments should make note of the specific goals and methods of those abolishments, this for the benefit of affected employees. An informed employee is less preoccupied with negative, unfulfilling activity and fantasy aimed at decreasing the uncertainty of his or her situation.

CONCLUSIONS

It appears that the effects of job abolishment serve as a template for an occupationally induced depression, particularly so for employees who are previously predisposed to depression and in an organization expected to offer continuing job stability. When a work unit is abolished, a group-reinforced propensity for the development of depressive thought patterns may obtain. These occasions for stressful depression may be anticipated and controlled, through stress management workshops, in such a way as to modify attitudes and moods in a positive direction. The present workshop served two major functions: to detect and prevent stress-related disorders, including depression, not to treat these disorders; and to bolster employees' psychological resources at a time when these resources were needed most.

It is advisable for the organization that must abolish jobs to provide stress management workshops for those whose jobs are abolished. The benefits are that employees placed internally readjust to their jobs with renewed commitment and hard work; interviews indicate that employees whose jobs are not abolished do not feel overly threatened by the prospect of job abolishment should it affect them—stress levels decline and the work focus goes uninterrupted in a more forthright organizational atmosphere; the organization maintains its respect in the job market for future employees; and it may be that the probability of making disability payments to employees for stress-related disorders is lessened.

Harry Levinson (1976), in his *Psychological Man,* recognized that even promotions, when they usurp from the employee his or her avenues of self-esteem, can result in affective depression. This is especially true of job abolishment.

REFERENCES

Cobb, Sidney. 1974. 'Physiologic Changes in Men Whose Jobs Were Abolished." *Journal of Psychosomatic Research* 18: 245–58.

Cuddihy, Basil R. 1974. "How to Give Phased-Out Managers a New Start." *Harvard Business Review* (July-August).

"Family Stress Called a Menace to Health." *New York Times,* October 20, 1976, p. 27.

Festinger, L., S. Schachter and K. Back. 1950. *Social Pressures in Informal Groups: A Study of Human Factors in Housing.* New York: Harper.

Heider, F. 1958. *The Psychology of Interpersonal Relations.* New York: John Wiley.

Holmes, T. and J. Rahe. 1967. "The Social Readjustment Rating Scale." *Journal of Psychosomatic Research* 11: 213–18.

Lazarus, A. 1971. *Behavior Therapy and Beyond.* New York: McGraw-Hill.

Levinson, Harry. 1976. *Psychological Man.* Cambridge, Mass.: The Levinson Institute.

Murray, Henry. 1943. *Thematic Apperception Test.* Cambridge, Mass.: Harvard University Press.

Olive, L., J. Relsey, M. Visser, and R. Daly. 1976. "Moving as Perceived by Executives and their Families." *Journal of Occupational Medicine* 18: 546–50.

Selye, Hans. 1955. "Stress and Disease." *Science* 122: 625–31.

Shwed, H.J. and S.F. Ruvin. 1976. "Some Psychological Implications of the Gasoline Shortage of 1974." *Journal of the Medical Society of New Jersey.* 73: 857–60.

16 Outplacement Counseling: Business and Profession

Donald A. Monaco, Ed.D.

Outplacement counseling (OPC) or career continuation counseling are terms that describe a new management consulting service and individual career planning/job search endeavor that is struggling to achieve a professional clinical identity and status. Outplacement counseling is a service a corporation provides to employees who are terminated. It includes personal counseling, assessment, strategy development for job search, and coaching until a new position is found (Furler, 1980). Unfortunately, due to the nature of the lucrative business aspect of this service it could lose the struggle for a professional rating and eventually tarnish the image of its dedicated practitioners. One reason for the struggle is that OPC is a seductive business for ambitious management consultants looking to expand profits and offer their behavioral science expertise to other businesses, industries, corporations, and governments. Another reason for the struggle is that its current need and popularity have attracted highly trained individuals and incompetents alike. In fact, a typical profile of an outplacement professional can look much like that of a used car salesman (Buchanan, 1980). At any rate, the rapid evolution of outplacement counseling has catapulted a new hybrid management consultant into prominence—the outplacement professional.

There are ample trade journal articles describing the concept and process of outplacement services (Cuddihy, 1974; Driessnack, 1978, 1980; Erdlen, 1978; Lee & Hecht, 1978; Morin, 1977). In addition there are two books on the subject (Morin & Yorks, 1981; Sweet, 1975). For outplacement to attain and maintain a respectable professional status and remain a profitable, quality control business, professionalism of its practitioners must be achieved. This has not been fully addressed in the literature or in the strategic planning of its business managers. The purpose of this chapter is to review the historical development of OPC and to address the issue for the need of having high level professional counselors to provide OPC services. With this objective, the chapter will review the following:

- Origins of outplacement.
- Reasons for termination and OPC growth.
- Statistical overview.
- Psychological effects of unemployment stress.
- Outplacement: processing or counseling.
- Different OPC programs.
- Three typical OPC clients.
- Profile of a qualified counselor.
- Profession with a future.

ORIGINS OF OUTPLACEMENT

Outplacement counseling is a systematic process in which a terminated individual is trained and counseled in the latest skills and techniques to find new employment. It provides a smooth transition from the termination process to relocation of a new position with the minimization of trauma. It also imparts to the individual affected the necessary and appropriate skills, the guidance, and the support in their efforts to find a meaningful position within a reasonable period of time.

The earliest origins of outplacement date back to post-World War II, when the government provided extensive reemployment services to veterans leaving the military. Early industry efforts to assist departed employees were extended both by in-house personnel as well as outside executive recruiters who had vested interests in grooming their candidates for acceptance by potential employers. In those formative years there were no clinical efforts to assist the individual in coping with depression or loss. Outplacement as a more formal process began taking form in the aerospace industry during the mid to late 1960s. Broad scale layoffs of engineers and other technical specialists resulted from government spending cutbacks and diminution of our commitment to the space program.

The 1969–70 recession put pressure on organizations to release droves of executives who were overhired during the expansive 1960s. This recession created the need for profits and in turn necessitated large-scale personnel cutbacks. Corporations looked for assistance from outside executive search experts and other management consulting firms to help redundant employees relocate to new positions.

Today, outplacement has become a vital part of the management process and has been integrated into many companies' philosophies of human resource management.

REASONS FOR TERMINATION AND OPC GROWTH

The significant benefits and advantages of OPC services have been firmly established (Driessnack, 1978). It is proven that employees that are counseled mobilize more quickly and find suitable positions in shorter periods of time than terminees without OPC. Companies and employees alike are increasingly turning to this service as an effective and positive solution to performance or interpersonal relationship issues.

Corporations and other organizations are increasingly receptive to using OPC services, particularly when the termination concerns any of the following:

- *Corporate reshuffling*—mergers, departmental cutbacks, across-the-board cutbacks or relocations of facilities.
- *"Peter principled" employees*—executives and managers who were promoted beyond their capabilities resulting in poor or inadequate performance.
- *The "plateaued out"*—individuals who were promoted into jobs with no advancement possibilities who became frustrated or bored, leading to unsatisfactory performance.
- *The mismatch*—a general term that covers any disparity between a job's demands and the individual's capabilities. This includes jobs that are not demanding enough.
- *Poor chemistry*—different personality styles between superior and subordinate can lead to an abrasive relationship and a "political" termination.
- *Behavioral trait problem individuals*—subordinate clearly has a personal problem needing professional assistance, for example, marital discord or alcohol abuse.

There are a number of reasons contributing to OPC growth. Of central importance is the fact that OPC services offer companies increased flexibility, cost savings, and manpower alternatives; the "shelf sitter" or "plateaued" individual need not continue to interfere with a company's growth. It is also increasingly common to find organizations with a "corporate conscience." They feel the need to provide a support package for the severed individual. And the increase in use and effectiveness of performance appraisals is leading to the identification of and the willingness to terminate a consistently poor performer.

However, higher level executive positions are becoming increasingly temporary, a condition helping to create the mobile executive phenomenon wherein many executives spend only a short time, approximately one to two years, in any one corporation.

STATISTICAL OVERVIEW

Results of a two-year statistical review (Monaco, 1979) attest to the effectiveness of OPC efforts. Over 200 OPC clients were served and especially tracked for purposes of analysis. The results showed that within an average of 4.5 months, 71 percent ($N = 212$) of the counselees who found employment accepted proper positions at significantly higher salaries than ever before.

Would these clients have found their new positions within the short time frame and in an emotionally unscathing manner? The probability is no! Although not provable to the satisfaction of the hard-nosed and empirically minded, OPC counselors are aware of the "hidden control group" of uncounseled outplacements. OPC counselors are constantly appraised of the "horror stories," the misfired attempts and stalled search campaigns of uncounseled terminees. Human resource personnel in corporations are acutely cognizant of this problem.

In-house OPC counselors are frequently effective and helpful with resourceful terminees or individuals with lower level skills. The in-house OPC consultant has disadvantages that the outside consultant does not have. The external counselor has a better chance at achieving a trusting rapport with terminees and has the unlimited time to provide the support, career planning, and skills training required to meet the terminees' privacy and need for confidentiality.

Out of the 212 individuals surveyed (1977–78) the following pertinent statistical findings were gleaned:

- Counselee average age was 45.
- Salary range was from $25,000 to $250,000.
- Average salary was $51,000.
- Ninety-five percent were male.
- Number placed at lower income than original income was ten.
- Number placed at same income was 21.
- Fifteen made career changes (most left corporate life to pursue their own businesses).
- Number placed at a higher salary was 166.
- The best source of initial lead to new position was the use of personal relationships, i.e., colleagues, friends, other professionals (90 percent).
- Executive search assistance accounted for approximately 13 percent of job lead source.

- Seven percent found positions, collectively, either through newspaper advertisements or direct mailing without personal referral.
- OPC consultants identified and dealt with a significant amount (30 percent) of terminees who presented special challenges, i.e., either behavioral or personality trait problems.

The last statistic should come as no surprise since the President's Commission on Mental Health (1978) suggests that 25 percent of all Americans are suffering severe emotional stress to the point that professional psychological intervention is needed. One can well imagine the overwhelming emotional taxation on a terminated individual who was probably already stressed and highly anxious about his or her performance prior to the termination.

PSYCHOLOGICAL EFFECTS OF UNEMPLOYMENT STRESS

There is ample evidence to substantiate that a jobless status is often experienced as a highly stressful life adaptation. The stress caused by unemployment has been determined to rank high on the stress scale of traumatic personal events and life changes. In comparison to as many as 61 life changes, unemployment stress ranks between seventh and ninth in the degree of stress created and measured on the Holms and Rahe (1967) Social Readjustment Rating Scale. Unemployment stress fosters nearly the same degree of stress to an individual as a divorce, the death of a loved one, or the loss of a close friend. The emotional impact of the jobless state, from a depth psychological perspective, could be equivalent to the child feeling the sense of loss and abandonment of a rejecting parent (Kaufman, 1981). The psychological consequences for both adult and child are significantly depleting for the individual's sense of self-worth, confidence, and self-esteem.

The weight of research evidence indicates that executives, managers, and highly skilled professionals identify more strongly with their work than do other workers (Kaufman, 1981). Work activity, therefore, becomes a potential medium by which either frustration or satisfaction can be experienced by the professional. Unemployed professionals consistently manifest more stress than their employed colleagues with approximately two out of five experiencing emotional impairment extreme enough to require psychological counseling.

A seasoned outplacement counselor who has had several years' experience consulting a variety of terminated executives and professionals will confirm that there is a high percentage of terminees who manifest interpersonal difficulties, character disorders, and behavioral trait problems, at worst, and ineffective coping capabilities, at best. Professionals affected by stress are likely to show one or more of the following symptomatic behaviors needing either referral to an outside mental health professional or skillful handling by the outplacement counselor:

1. Debilitating anxiety.
2. Displaced anger and aggression toward others.
3. Devalued self-esteem.
4. Irrational thinking.
5. Self-defeating behavior.
6. Overexaggerated self-aggrandizement.
7. Depression and withdrawal leading to work inhibition.
8. Helplessness and emotional vulnerability.
9. Excessive dependency.
10. Psychosomatic disorders.
11. Alcohol abuse.
12. Occupational rigidity or inability to role change.

Kaufman (1981) in his voluminous work on coping with unemployment stress concludes:

> The reaction of many professionals to unemployment can be understood in terms of a societal model in which an environment that devalues self-esteem and diminishes the individual's control can result in low levels of achievement and satisfaction in addition to aggression toward oneself and others. Widespread unemployment creates just such an environment and it is the resulting loss of self-esteem and the emergence of helplessness that appears to be central to the psychological consequences among professionals.

Based on his research efforts, Kaufman (1981) also identified four stages of unemployment that a terminee is likely to experience. Note the similarity between the stages of unemployment and the phases approaching death (Kubler-Ross, 1969).

Stage I: Shock, Relief, and Relaxation

After the initial shock subsides, the terminee regains a positive mental attitude and anxiety is reduced momentarily. There is also a period of anticipation and uncertainty that lasts approximately one to two months.

Stage II: Concerted Effort

The terminated individual's anxiety level is dependent on financial security and the available social support system. Psychological adjustment continues to improve, while there is almost total concentration on finding work. There is much effort in the attempt at being in control. Among the unemployed professionals whose self-esteem is low, the most devastated are those between the ages of 30 and 40, that point in the male life cycle when a man is achieving personal status and reaching long planned for and sought after objectives and goals. Extreme frustration and personal failure can be experienced at this "midpoint" in the career path due to unemployment stress. This stage lasts approximately three months.

Stage III: Vacillations, Doubt, and Anger

After five to six months of unemployment, the terminee experiences deep frustration and questions his or her ability to find a job. The greatest danger is the deterioration of a positive mental attitude. The job search becomes erratic and desperate, while the individual becomes more prone to psychosomatic disorders and suicidal thoughts.

Stage IV: Resignation and Withdrawal

The individual could, after six or more months, be resigned to being jobless. There is low initiative, reduced aspiration, inability to role change ("occupational rigidity"), lower self-esteem, loss of control, hopelessness, and helplessness. Worst of all, the individual avoids job search activity. Psychosomatic disorders and premature death could occur.

Braginsky and Braginsky (1975) found that unemployed men, mainly middle managers, engineers, and skilled professionals, were left with deep emotional scars, vis-à-vis faith in our institutional way of life, lower personal worth, and lack of confidence in the social order and its predominant political beliefs. These researchers tapped into the deep impact of an unemployed status and found that the long lasting effects of this trauma are a threat to the cherished ideals, beliefs, and values that made this country viable and democratic.

OUTPLACEMENT: PROCESSING OR COUNSELING?

An outplacement program, generally, and the outplacement counselor, specifically, attempt to assist the terminee to find the right job, so that stages III and IV outlined above are not reached. If the time of unemployment reaches beyond four or five months, the outplacement counselor provides the guidance and support needed as well as "technical" and strategic advice for the job hunt.

The efforts of the outplacement counselor are quite basic, as is true in other counseling situations. Outplacement is a "counseling process." Any counseling function is an interactive relationship and a learning process designed to assist people with such problems as choice, action, and role definition (Stefflre, 1965). The outplacement counselor, due to the high stress factor inherent in the termination event, must apply psychological sophistication in counseling skills to establish and maintain effective relationships. The counselor must be "psychotherapeutic," not "psychonoxious," that is, emphatic, sensitive, and able to create an atmosphere of trust, support, and attunement with the terminee. Above all, the counselor must attain a high degree of professionalism, avoiding the pitfalls of either perfunctory "processing" of terminees or the pandering to excessive dependency demands. Perhaps the most challenging terminees are hostile and depressed individuals.

The high level of counseling skill required in outplacement has not received broad scale recognition in the author's view. Some outplacement practitioners and firms are not committed to this point of view. Herein lies the danger for the business and the profession. Assisting terminated individuals to feel in control, optimistic about the future, confident, and resourceful requires of the counselor the skills, talents, and knowledge of a professional. A good measure of psychological sophistication along with an ability to understand the fine nuances of human motivation and defense mechanisms is a minimum requirement for an outplacement counselor. Later in the chapter, the profile of a qualified OPC counselor will be discussed.

DIFFERENT OPC PROGRAMS

Because of the potential high profit margin, more individuals and firms are entering the OPC marketplace. Those with established reputations are making substantial advances in sales volume and clientele. Although the leading OPC firms have burgeoning programs, these programs vary depending on consulting philosophy and commitment to imparting job search techniques. There are three kinds of OPC services, each effective in its own way. The first kind of service offers career change counseling with emphasis on linking a client's background and skill with job openings. Resumes are written for the individual, along with other correspondence. Firms are usually identified by their aggressive newspaper advertisements in employment sections. The client population tends to be lower level personnel. Comprehensive assessment and career development are not typical in this type of program.

The second type of OPC program emphasizes a didactic training approach, assisting clients to master job search skills. Generally, this program has been completed in a week's time, with follow-through counseling until final placement. Although this type of OPC program is effective; the emphasis is on speed as opposed to extensive career development planning. This fast rate of counseling can, and often does, produce a high "bounce rate" (the person is not successful in the next position).

The third kind of OPC program is typified by extensive and in-depth assessment and planning over a three-week period. Consideration is given to personal/vocational appraisal, interview training, and evaluation in matching individual needs to specific work settings and organizational climates.

John D. Erdlen, a management counsultant expert, succinctly outlined the criteria desired for a comprehensive OPC program in his article "Guidelines for Retaining an Outplacement Consultant." Erdlen (1978) concluded that "While the job hunting programs of each consulting firm may differ considerably in their methods, the particular counseling steps are an integral part of every plan. Anything less will not get the job done."

A quality OPC program should encompass the highlights described below.

Pretermination Consulting

The OPC consultant counsels the organization and the person who will terminate the employee prior to the termination date. The purpose of pretermination consulting is to ameliorate any anxiety, undue stress, and guilt feelings for both employer and terminee.

Self-Appraisal and Preparation

The assigned consultant works personally with the terminee to formulate a career enrichment program tailored to the needs of the individual. "The primary function will be to furnish assistance in planning a meaningful program that will facilitate an improvement in the person's career status" (Erdlen, 1978).

In this important phase, the consultant, in tandem with a licensed psychologist, assesses the individual through in-depth interviews, career-oriented tests, and identification of practical achivements and functional competencies. Developmental needs (personal shortcomings and limitations) are equally subject to scrutiny and counsel.

Setting Objectives and Market Planning

Following the rigors and gains of the self-appraisal phase, a positive action plan is formulated. The client's objectives in this phase are to:

1. Construct a concise, results-oriented resume that gives a dynamic view of the client's strengths.
2. Prepare letters designed to attract the right prospective employers.
3. Build a personal contact network.
4. Become adept in resources appraisal (search firms, advertisements, research material, etc.).
5. Develop a marketing strategy.

Enhancing Professional Self-presentation

Analysis of interviewing skills and thorough audiovisual training is conducted by the counselor. Coaching is provided on how to diagnose one's own and an interviewer's personal communication style in order to help create a positive "chemistry." The closed circuit television role-play/feedback technique has proved effective in developing a crisp self-presentation and in avoiding potential problem areas.

Continuous Counseling to Placement

The counselor extends continuous counseling as needed until successful placement occurs. During the follow-through phase, the consultant helps the client maintain a positive and assertive posture. Other issues often discussed are general progress, obtaining leads and interviews, and salary negotiations.

The terminating organization should become familiar with the differences in style, content, and approach of OPC programs. Just as OPC firms differ, client expectations and needs vary significantly. A small percentage of the executive-managerial OPC population prefers a more abbreviated, less career assessment and planning approach. Since it is a time in the terminee's life to plan carefully and objectively for this next and perhaps last job, many select a comprehensive, in-depth program. Still other terminees should receive an extensive, detailed program along with specific psychological intervention.

Experience suggests that program flexibility and special consulting expertise are required to meet successfully the variety and diversity of client needs. Two-thirds of the population studied in a statistical survey (Monaco, 1979) rallied in a few weeks and found suitable jobs on an average within four to six months. Even with this group, the consultant frequently had to provide both ego support and assertiveness training, that is, instructing individuals how to employ effective techniques in getting interviews with key employers. The other third of this OPC client population had individuals with personal difficulties ranging from minor behavioral problems to major interpersonal conflicts. In the future, consultants should be psychologically sophisticated and sensitive to such problems. The consultant must be skillful in recognizing a wide array of problems and in making the client receptive to the concept of using the services of other professional specialists. Clients debilitated by alcoholism or complications involving marital discord also require help from the OPC consultant.

THREE TYPICAL OPC CLIENTS

An example of the typical OPC client is John R., a 47-year-old chief executive officer. John had many positive qualities, some of which were high intelligence, analytical ability, and a flair with words. He was well liked and had several personal contacts. His particular need was direction for a vaguely formulated career goal. Once assisted through the basic OPC program, a goal became crystallized, and he was quickly able to analyze and decide upon the appropriate work environment. John generated several offers that enabled him to locate his best opportunity within four and one-half months.

Marie S., an attractive, single woman in her late 50s, represents an OPC client population that faces career change as well as preretirement considerations. Marie lost her position as a financial analyst with a large international organization. Her need was intensive career counseling supplemented by sensitive guidance involving preretirement information and preparation. Her consultant had to be attuned to the multidimensional aspect of Marie's concerns. In six months, Marie accepted an administrative post on a hospital staff near her home, and she felt relaxed about her future retirement plans.

A third type of OPC client represents an extreme challenge to the consultant. Marvin M., a 37-year-old legal expert, got fired due to his "arrogance and the devastation of people under him." Although his knowledge and technical competence were above reproach, he "got the job done, but left legions of shattered egos." It was clearly evident that Marvin was obtaining "results" on the job by overcompensating for deep feelings of inadequacy and vulnerability. His personal conflicts were mainfested by an oscillating love-hate ambivalence toward himself. Unfortunately, he externalized his deep problems and was unable to develop or maintain positive, trusting human relationships. The consultant, after persistent efforts, was able to direct this client to seek psychotherapeutic assistance. Marvin found an excellent position (after eight months) in which he nearly doubled his former salary. He also continued in psychotherapy.

PROFILE OF A QUALIFIED COUNSELOR

Experience suggests that program flexibility and special counseling expertise are required to successfully meet the variety and diversity of terminee needs. As of this writing, outplacement counselors are not expected to be professional psychologists, but the counseling aspect of the consulting relationship requires that the counselor be adept and insightful and understand the complexity of human motivations. Incompetent counselors can be harmful. Unfortunately, at this juncture, there are no graduate degrees, licensing procedures, accredited competency certificates, or professional societies for outplacement counselors. There are some early signs, however, that the competing OPC organizations are willing to form a consortium to establish professional qualifications and training considerations for its practitioners.

The following are some desirable characteristics of a qualified OPC counselor:

- Ability to interview skillfully and establish effective/positive relationships.
- Familiarity with executive, managerial, and technically professional positions and career paths.
- Sensitivity to organizational ("political") dynamics.
- Astuteness in job hunting procedures.
- Ability to counsel people under pressure.
- Ability to motivate, support, and rebuild confidence in others.

- Assertive and able to follow through on details.
- Possession of a broad range of business and industry experience.
- Familiarity with the managerial labor market.
- Possession of career and personal counseling experience.

In toto, the outplacement counselor has to be an ambidextrous ombudsman, versatile, adaptable, and knowledgeable about industry, corporate, and organizational dynamics, the business milieu, and job specifications and functions.

PROFESSION WITH A FUTURE

The theme of this chapter has been the high level of capability and skillfulness required in professional outplacement counseling. This perspective has not received genuine acknowledgement in all quarters. Outplacement will survive as a professional counseling activity if the business manager, and some practitioners, commit themselves to the concept that OPC counselors must be of the caliber discussed above.

Outplacement has become as important for organizations and society as employment/recruiting activities are today. Lee and Hecht (1978) wisely conclude:

> Outplacement counseling is in a sense nothing more than a professional way for an organization to mesh with the larger society in regard to a natural, inevitable and healthy process: exchanging employees with other organizations. There is nothing shameful or embarrassing about it—if it is done gracefully and humanely. The expectation of a 40 year-old career with one employer is ending; the day of second careers, high mobility and rapid change is already here. Outplacement counseling will emerge as a professional way to facilitate these processes. (p. 32)

REFERENCES

Braginsky, and Braginsky. 1975. "Surplus People: Their Lost Faith in Self and System." *Psychology Today,* (August): 68–100.

Buchanan, W. 1980. "Outplacement Counseling." *Career Planning and Adult Development Newsletter* 2 (November).

Cuddihy, B. 1974. "How to Give Phased-Out Managers A New Start." *Harvard Business Review* (July–August): 61–69.

Driessnack, C. 1978. "Outplacement: A Benefit For Both Employee and Company." *Personnel Administrator* (January).

———. 1980. "Outplacement—The New Personnel Practice." *Personnel Administrator* (October).

Erdlen, J. 1978. "Guidelines For Retaining An Outplacement Consultant." *Personnel Administrator* (October).

Furler, C. 1980. "Outplacement: A Blessing in Disguise." *American Journal of Psychotherapy,* 34 (July): 363–73.

Holms, T. and J. Rahe. 1967. "The Social Readjustment Rating Scale." *Journal of Psychosomatic Research* 2: 213–18.

Kaufman, H. 1981. *Professionals In Search of Work: Coping With The Stress of Job Loss and Underemployment*. New York: Wiley Interscience.

Kubler-Ross, E. 1969. *On Death and Dying.* New York: Macmillan.

Lee, R. and R. Hecht. 1978. "Divorce Executive Style–The Role of the Outplacement Counselor." *Training Management Motivation and Incentive* (Fall).

Monaco, D. 1979. "Outplacement Consulting: State of the Art." Unpublished article.

Morin, W. 1977. "Outplacement Counseling: What Is It?" *Personnel and Guidance Journal* (May): 553–55.

Morin, W. and L. Yorks. 1981. *Termination and Outplacement: A Positive Approach*. American Management Association publication.

President's Commission on Mental Health, Panel on Costs and Financing. 1978. *Report of the President's Commission on Mental Health*, vol. 2, Appendix, p. 512. U.S. Superintendent of Documents, Washington, D.C.

Stefflre, B. 1965. *Theories of Counseling*. New York: McGraw-Hill.

Sweet, D. 1975. *DEcruitment: A Guide For Managers*. Reading, Mass.: Addison-Wesley.

17 Relocation Counseling: Current Status and Potential

Martha B. Sherwood, Ph.D., and Judith A. DeSimone, M.B.A.

Current issues that surround the relocation of industrial employees have opened up another potential area for counseling and psychotherapy in occupational settings.

THE COSTS OF RELOCATION

One of five people change their residence every year, making the United States the most highly mobile nation in the world. Positions at the highest corporate levels are attained by those who are ready and responsive to mobility. It is approximated that 500,000 corporate transfers are made annually, which would include family members and thus involve 2 to 2.5 million people. Current costs for the transfer for one of these employees and his or her family are estimated to be between \$26,000 to \$30,000, with an additional \$2,000 to \$20,000 necessary if a mortgage interest differential allowance is provided. This can be compared with the average cost in 1960, which was \$6,000, and to \$10,000 in 1970 (Guillet, 1980).

Recognizing the financial burden a move usually places upon an employee, employers have been bearing some of the obvious and incidental costs of transfers. Homequity, the country's largest relocation firm, says that in 1980 relocation costs were up 50 percent. The average cost to move a family of four 900 miles is \$35,000. Of course, costs are directly related to salary, so many companies operating in higher cost locations are well above this average (Bell, 1980). AT & T's base cost figure is \$40,000 per move, and Exxon estimates a base cost of $60,000 for a senior manager ($100,000 with the tax absorption feature included) (DeSimone, 1981a). Employers are also adding inducement bonuses and compensation payments to their packages for the spouse's loss of income. Mortgage money is currently hard to come by, and banks are requiring transferees to provide paychecks as proof of employment in place of letters of intent from the employer. The Equitable Life Assurance Society is implementing a mortgage money fund for its employees as a last resort (DeSimone, 1981b).

When the relocation compensation runs out, the employee is left to bear the increased housing and mortgage costs. At best, increases in salary may just cover these costs, making it difficult to realize an increase in discretionary income. It remains to be seen what effect new legislation and deregulation of the banking industry will have on the interest rates and where and how much mortgage money will become available.

In response to these uncontrollable costs, both AT & T and IBM, who have a heavy volume of transfers, have announced policies to reduce the number of moves by 20 to 25 percent, or to limit the number of moves per individual (*New York Times*, 1981).

THE CURRENT RELOCATION SCENE

Transferees of the 1980s are typically between 25 to 40 years of age, married, and with children. However, an increasing proportion of transferees are women, with estimates presently ranging from 3 to 10 percent of the total transferred population. Whether male or female, before reaching the age of 30, the typical transferee probably has already moved once or twice and may expect to move again every three years or so for the next 10 to 15 years. It is also presently estimated by experts that people are going to be permanently spending 30 to 40 percent of their income for housing, which is unlike the last decade when they were spending 20 to 25 percent of their income on housing (Brett and Werbel, 1980).

The relocation scene is changing radically for two reasons. The first reason involves the transferees themselves. There is no question that there is an increasing resistance to moving for a number of reasons, which will be discussed later. Second, there is a reassessment of relocation policy on the part of corporations due to the excessive costs and also due to the resistance of their people.

There are numerous issues that affect the degree of one's mobility, but the three that surface as most critical are the dual-career couple, lifestyle and geographic preference, and costs to both the employee and the employer. In addition, the degree of one's mobility varies in relation to occupational function and age. The Employee Relocation Council found that the major distinction between employees who accept and those who reject a job transfer is willingness to move (Brett and Werbel, 1980). Employees are most willing to move when the new job promises to be a challenge and a contribution to their career development. Younger employees are more willing to move than older ones. Sales and marketing people are more willing than those in other functions. Wives who are willing to move experienced little difficulty associated with their previous move and, if working, were not very involved in their own job. The wife's willingness to move was not related to whether she worked full- or part-time, nor how much she earned, but how involved she was in her work. The more educated she was the less she was willing to move.

An immediate response to the escalating cost of transfers on the part of large companies is a reduction in the number of moves. Several major corporations have publicly stated their intentions to reduce the number of moves. Relocation experts estimate that relocation activity is currently down 20 percent. The director of the Executive Relocation Consultants states that it has become more difficult to move people—many more people are turning down moves than ever before (*Business Week*, 1981). There has to be a very compelling reason for an executive to pack his or her bags.

As noted earlier, IBM is reformulating its relocation policy. The company, famous in the past for its highly mobile executives, is cutting the percentage of its 200,000 person work force that it moves each year from the 5 percent rate of the mid-1970s to less than 3 percent. The company also plans to reduce the number even further (*New York Times*, 1981). This is being seen more and more in industries that have typically relocated large numbers of employees as the forces mentioned earlier begin to take their toll. Even with these problems, however, most corporate decision makers still see relocation as an opportunity to broaden the experience of their employees and give them a better feel for the organization as a whole. Thus, relocation will continue to be a way of life for corporations, though the scope and frequency of transfers may be limited.

RELOCATION MANAGEMENT TRENDS

Increasingly corporations are developing in-house relocation departments or contracting third-party relocation management firms to deal with the problems of relocating their employees (Levenson and Hollman, 1980). The primary reason for the inclusion of such services is to deal with the financial aspects of relocation, those that probably have the single greatest impact on corporate relocation policy. Other issues have also contributed, however, such as women's rights, environmentalism, and parenting; these factors have played an active part in forming the new corporate relocation market place.

Relocation management specialists are presently employed by many companies to handle the increased paper work and staffing, as well as related benefits and services. It is currently estimated that from one-third to one-half of relocation requests are met with objections or resistance on the part of employees

(*Business Week*, 1981). Employee attitude and behavior constitute the latest and most primary challenge facing those involved in relocation. There is no question that blind allegiance to the job and the employer has decreased among corporate workers. Leisure activities, individual interests, family needs, community involvement, and educational/spiritual resources are taking on greater importance for these people in the 1980s.

Corporate executives have found the use of relocation services to be cost-effective since it saves staff time. The indications are that the relocation revolution is only beginning and that relocation costs will continue to rise at an inflationary rate. A current approach to relocation cost is referred to as zero-based relocation, which involves selectively analyzing each planned relocation to determine whether it is cost-effective and appropriate (Tavernier, 1980). Many companies have turned to zero-based relocation in which all transfer situations are individually reviewed and approved prior to making an offer to the employee. This review consists of the following:

1. A study of cost-of-living differentials.
2. An examination of career ramifications.

These two tests then form the basis for zero-based relocation policy.

Most independent relocation services today are affiliated with larger parent companies, such as the Merrill Lynch relocation unit of the nation's largest brokerage firm. The Employee Transfer Corporation is a subsidiary of Lincoln National Bank; the Equitable Relocation Service is part of the Equitable Life Assurance Society; Executrans is a subsidiary of Sears, Roebuck; Home Equity is connected with the PHH Group, Inc.; the Transamerica Relocation Service is a part of the Transamerica Corporation. Their growth has made relocation companies a new force in the real estate market. Needless to say, the access to national networks and capital make the connection with a parent company very useful. The newest entrant into the third-party relocation field is a Chemical Bank subsidiary that has recently opened shop and is instituting a program for counseling the spouses of relocated employees. Other relocation firms are exploring this area as well. Equitable Relocation Service presently has a pilot study underway.

A number of studies have been launched to analyze statistically what is taking place in the area of relocation. For example, a multiple correlation analysis was used to test the variables in explaining postjob transfer satisfaction (Frank, 1978). Among a sample of managers, preference for location of residence emerged as the predominant predictor of postjob transfer satisfaction, with size of city ranked also as a major predictor among managers and their spouses. Moving employees is a complicated, dynamic process that needs much more understanding if certain pitfalls are to be avoided and if dangerous and undesired side effects are to be anticipated and forestalled.

A recent survey has highlighted the primary reasons for employees' unwillingness to relocate and has listed these in rank order (Brett and Werbel, 1980). They are:

1. Cost of living.
2. Mortgage related problems.
3. Housing costs.
4. General unwillingness to relocate.
5. Spouse.

The same survey also focused on the primary reasons for willingness to relocate. They are:

1. New opportunities.
2. Increased income.
3. Environment.
4. Climate.
5. Cost of living.
6. Company reputation.

In this survey, shortage of mortgage money emerged as the primary difficulty for 79 percent of the responders, and 83 percent of the respondents said that their company had recently reevaluated its relocation policies, in most cases in the past six months.

PERSONAL AND CORPORATE PRIORITIES

There is a new and strengthening attitude toward lifestyles and sex roles. Priorities are shifting. The past two decades have seen a persistent change in values. The traditional work ethic has given way to a "me-ism/us-ism" quality-of-life ethic. This does not necessarily imply a weakening of values but rather a broadening of them. One's sense of identity encompasses far more than that which come from one's occupation or profession. Leisure pursuits and avocational interests occupy a greater proportion of an individual's time and devotion, and they contribute to a great extent to one's sense of self-worth and contentment and are not readily surrendered.

Children and their interests and pursuits also play an important role in decisions to move. In order to avoid negative adjustment responses, parents are seriously considering the academic, career, extracurricular, and social needs of their children. When children are involuntary participants in a relocation, they become predisposed to unfavorable consequences (Jenkins, Lewis and Ellis,

1978). So, as children reach the age of 10 or 11 years they will participate in the decision.

Closely tied to lifestyle preferences (recreational, cultural, and leisure pursuits) is where a person lives. These concerns, as well as technological developments in telecommunications and information processing, will greatly influence where a company conducts its business. Energy costs, mass transportation systems, support systems for certain lifestyles, and an appropriate labor source will determine the desirability of certain locations for both the organization and the employee—married and single.

Mature central cities are becoming upper middle class enclaves with substandard schools and transportation and a serious lack of access to a "support skills" labor pool. While still viable, housing costs will continue to escalate in nearby suburbs. As they become saturated, advantages they have to offer will diminish. The sunbelt is experiencing some difficulty absorbing an uneven pattern of growth. Organizations seem to be looking more favorably upon ex-urban regions, evidenced by the recent move of Tyco Labs, Wheelabrator-Frye to New Hampshire and Union Carbide to Danbury, Conn. (Wheelock, 1979). In general, companies are seeking more compact metropolitan areas with suitable and complete living and working environments. In addressing the issue of office location and dispersion of management, priorities will be operational vitality, control of operating costs, and the ability to capitalize on efficiencies.

In addition to these factors, there also seems to be a difference in perception between companies and their employees as to what the issues are surrounding mobility. In a survey funded by Exxon of 400 companies and 815 dual-career couples, *Catalyst* (1980) found that while the great majority of companies believed that men increasingly felt the need to share parenting duties and were in favor of flexible work hours, weeks, and places and that cafeteria-style benefits and support for child-care facilities were more in demand, only a small percentage of organizations had programs to deal with these issues. Two-thirds of these companies are experiencing increased resistance to relocating. They recognize that the spouse's career is the number one reason for resistance and that the number of two-career families will increase—yet only 5 percent of the companies have a policy of assisting the spouse. An additional 29 percent said they would help if the employee requested it.

Many employees will resist moving (thereby taking themselves out of the running for promotions) because of lack of information, misinformation, and apprehension about handling the move (DeSimone, 1981a). They may be reluctant to discuss their concerns with the company. They fear they might be perceived as uncommitted or as a high-risk mover. They further assume that company policies are firm, that no one else seems to have these concerns, or that they are expected to find their own solutions. The length of time a person has to make a decision and to move is a critical factor, especially for the first relocation.

INCREASED ATTENTION TO NEEDS OF THE SPOUSE

Corporations today are placing more emphasis on the role of the mobile manager's spouse. Over 50 percent of all married women are working today, and by 1990 this figure is expected to rise to 75 percent. Two-career couples are forcing corporations to attend to the relocating employee's problems that naturally result from this condition (Hayghe, 1981). Several ways of handling the employment of spouses have been tried:

1. Identifying employment agencies in the new location.
2. Providing employment counseling as part of the relocation service.
3. Using the corporation contacts informally within the new community.
4. Formal corporate networking, which provides cooperating companies with information about job openings.

Corporations are traditionally reluctant to intrude on the private lives of employees, and at the same time employees are reluctant to ask for help for fear they will appear less than enthusiastic about the move and perhaps be treated punitively. With a formal relocation program that incorporates counseling, corporations can offer employee assistance to the spouse as one of the components of a larger package of relocation services and leave it to the individual employee to take advantage of the services or not.

The two-income family is a fact of life, and young people are beginning their professional careers with the intention of planning their personal and professional lives as one package. Currently, almost 55 percent of married couples are dual earners. The median age for men in these couples is 39; it is 36 for women. Of this group, 42 percent have very young children. Transferability of skills and commitment to career are major factors in mobility. In 1979, 46 percent of men with professional or technical jobs had wives with professional, technical, or managerial jobs, while 33 percent of male managers had wives with managerial, professional, or technical jobs (Hayghe, 1981). These numbers will continue to increase because there is a 30 percent female enrollment in M.B.A. programs today.

An examination of the reasons for the increase in the number of dual-career couples will underscore the necessity for focusing attention in this area. Men and women desire to achieve a better way of life and to offset the effects of inflation and higher living costs. The women's movement has provided support and encouragement to women who are seeking the same professional growth, advancement, and recognition as men. EEO programs have stimulated recruitment and created opportunities. Advances in technology have lessened the time necessary for housekeeping chores and provided more sophisticated family planning aids. The rise in the divorce rate encourages women to think about being able to support themselves. Two incomes are necessary to maintain as high a standard as possible after retirement. Current conditions are forcing people to carefully plan their careers and to demand a greater voice and control over where and when they move. Married couples are supporting each other's careers. They are inventive, but their lifestyles are changing faster than the institutions with which they have to live. They are taking turns subordinating each other's career or setting time frames on whose career comes first, and, in general, they will turn down a transfer if there are more disadvantages than advantages to the whole family.

The president of Korn/Ferry observes that clients are learning that to attract many of today's brightest young executives they have got to find career opportunities for the spouses as well, and it is becoming increasingly the case that more executives are limiting their options geographically because of their wives (Hall and Hall, 1978). Assurances of job placement for a spouse will be a major factor in the decision to hire on or to relocate.

THE NEED FOR PROFESSIONAL INTERVENTION

Given the current state of affairs, it becomes increasingly clear the field of relocation is in need of fresh perspectives. Psychologists, social workers, and personnel professionals all have an opportunity to apply their skills to counsel relocated employees and provide more humanistic relocation policies for corporations. Counselors are presently employed both by the corporation itself through their in-house relocation departments and also by the independent relocation management firms. The recognition of the need for professionals will definitely be on the increase as all of the pressures combine to make the process of relocation more complicated for all parties concerned.

There is no question that there must be a thorough examination of ways of minimizing the undesirable side effects of relocation. Corporations, employees, and their families should all be aware of the variety of potential effects inherent in moves ahead of time and be able to thoroughly discuss and weigh them before final decisions are made. Such discussions should involve representatives from management as well as both the employee and his spouse. As mentioned earlier, at least two-thirds of executives report that they experience family problems as a result of frequent moves. Corporate leaders are gradually and painfully becoming aware of the fact that organizational life and family life are symbiotic. The key to a successful mobility policy is to determine the needs and values of the family members and to measure their propensity and ability to adjust to relocation before the relocation occurs. This determination must be measured from economic, social, and psychological perspectives.

Family lives and the business environment cannot be completely separated, although many corporations have operated in the past as though they could be. A major void at present is the lack of supportive counseling offered as a standard component of relocation packages. In the meantime, corporations lose hundreds of thousands of dollars because there is no mechanism through which human concerns can be voiced. They have shied away from the need to hire trained professional counselors to provide preventive counseling services in the past. However, competitive relocation policies are gradually now including such things as third-party home purchase, home finding, and cost-of-living benefits. It is certainly only a matter of time until the counseling component becomes an integral part of relocation policy. The aim of corporations should be to eliminate unnecessary transfers and sufficiently support the necessary ones. Consideration of the spouse and his or her career can only have favorable results on the employee and on his or her productivity (Manuso and Sherwood, 1980). Trouble at home is usually reflected in employees' performance on the job, and corporations can do much about these problems and with little expense by recognizing the "trauma" of relocation and being willing to provide resources to alleviate that trauma.

SOME INNOVATIVE TRENDS

What are companies doing now? TRW, Pepsico, and American Can Company allow employees to choose the type of fringe benefits and insurance protection that will best meet their needs (i.e., vacation time versus overlapping insurance coverage) (Randolph, 1981). Twenty-three percent of large companies get involved in some type of informal job assistance for spouses. (A New York based national manager of home searches who is involved with a spouse-counseling program says that the cost of this service—$700 to $1,500 per spouse—prompts companies not to "advertise" the existence of this service.) AT & T has a six month child-care leave for any employee. Sixteen percent of large companies (up from 6 percent in 1977) have flexible workday and workweek policies. Some companies (usually with a large female work force) provide subsidized day-care facilities (DeSimone, 1981b).

Organizations will feel the impact of these trends and factors in the areas of recruiting, career development, benefits, conflicts of interest, negotiations with employee, and spouse relationships. Most companies are handling the situation on a case-by-case basis, but the trend is toward integrated programs with a designated coordinator or facilitator. The following are components of a proposal based on a survey recently conducted at one Fortune 500 corporation (DeSimone, 1981a).

Dual Career Audit

Through surveys and personal histories, data can be collected on how many employees are in dual-career situations, for how long, in what fields, and in which career stage. Additional information about how employees perceive company policy, career trends and opportunities, and the degree of support and flexibility would also prove useful.

Special Recruiting Techniques

A preselection job preview for couples can help to avoid a poor couple/company fit. Recruiting husband and wife teams and couple counseling and orientation can help to identify potential conflicts.

Revision of Career Development and Transfer Policies

An examination of the way in which a company provides its employees with exposure and experience may reveal alternate approaches, which if given an adequate test may prove entirely satisfactory. These may include short-term field assignments (two to three months), geographic limitations of transfers, task forces and special team projects, condensed workweeks and staggered schedules to aid long-distance commuting, and skills analysis to determine what skills are essential to get ahead and where and how these skills can be developed.

Assistance for Couples in Career/Life Management

Creative solutions are necessary to retain valued employees. Each move should be viewed as part of a complete career plan.

Consultants versus In-House Service

The advantages and drawbacks of each method should be weighed in light of the company's volume of transfers and capacity to provide a total package of services. Probably a combination of the two works best and allows for the most flexibility. In either case, a program service evaluation technique must be established to gather continuous feedback from transferees.

Training of Supervisors to Counsel Employees

Since the supervisor/manager makes the transfer offer, it is important that he or she be equipped to handle each situation. Basic interpersonal skills and awareness of issues can be developed through training and case study analysis. The ability to evaluate and select the appropriate services is also important.

CONSIDERATIONS FOR THE FUTURE

Opening effective lines of communication regarding relocation policy is most essential at this time. Relocation policies ought to address three areas:

1. The basic issues associated with the relocation policy, such as the necessity of the transfer.

2. The basic economic issues, such as the cost of the move and the change in real estate market.
3. The basic psychosocial issues, such as the two-career marriage, life-style(s), and concerns about children.

One study has specified five reasons for the increasing resistance to transfer: (1) more independent employees, (2) greater concern for the quality of life, (3) more women employees, (4) working wives, and (5) nonworking wives who resent corporate seduction of their husbands (Renshaw, 1976). This study cites one local and hopeful solution to this problem. A nurse at a mental health center near Pittsburgh formed a self-help group called SOS to deal with wives with "transfer trauma." Regular meetings include discussion on the difficulties of moving, and future programs will include speakers to help the participants become familiar with the area. Given the success of such a relatively spontaneous movement as this, it certainly appears that the potential is present for in-house facilities to provide for these kinds of services before, during, and after the move, not only to show concern on the part of the corporation but also to deal with the very real needs that occur.

The Levinson and Holmann study (1980), which was recently completed, attributed a high number of present relocation turndowns partly to a lack of systematic career planning or pathing programs on the part of corporations and the absence of candid face-to-face discussions of the career implications of the proposed transfer, as well as the absence of a clearly stated policy on the risk employees' face in turning down transfers. It is becoming increasingly clear that career path plans can no longer be effective unless cost-of-living differences among locations are taken into account. With these considerations in mind some factors that can contribute to the development of policies and programs to ease the stress of relocation would be:

1. Increased information: formalized career pathing programs that can provide information on the likelihood of relocating the spouse and the provision of accurate and specific data to transferees and their families on the resources available and the quality of life in the new location.

2. Early communication with the spouse and the acceptance of his or her role in the decision-making process.

3. A reexamination of current policies and procedures concerning the refusal to relocate and the consequence of turndowns (e.g., not viewing the turndown of a relocation as a sign of disloyalty to the company with punitive consequences).

Above all in importance, corporations transferring their employees should supply them with a counseling program. However, this program should not emphasize emotional problems because such an emphasis could result in stigmatizing the participants. Instead, factors that need to be considered in relocation of employees are: (1) preparation for the differences in the local cost of living, climate, and customs, (2) family counseling, and (3) assistance to the working spouse.

A viable relocation counseling program should look at factors that are central to the family's acceptance or rejection of location. Studies have shown these factors include:

1. The number of moves the family has made and their frequency. Research shows there is increasing rather than decreasing hostility to each subsequent move.

2. The attractiveness of the new locations; for example, the West and sunbelt are currently most attractive, and the Northeast is the least attractive.

3. The children's attitude toward the move. Here again research shows that children between the ages of 3 to 5 and teen-agers between the ages 14 to 16 have the greatest trouble with relocation.

Therefore, the alert counselor working within a relocation program can detect and be able to deal with the early warning signals of conditions that deter an employee from relocating or cause family problems subsequent to the move (Tavernier, 1980). The early warning signs include:

1. Presence of teen-agers.
2. Involvement in civic activities.
3. Locale involved in past mobility.
4. Marital values.
5. Inflation.

Each step in the relocation process brings a need to identify and evaluate the options and needs of those involved. As mentioned earlier, relocation should not be viewed as a problem but as a normal sequence of events, and there is a predictability about what those going through relocation will experience. One survey reports that 97 percent of transferees reported psychological burdens resulting just from buying and selling a home (Tavernier, 1980). These and other difficulties encountered in relocation can be extensive, and there is no question that there is need for training and counseling in regard to these difficulties. Educational programs or workshops, counseling sessions, printed material and information forms that deal with these issues can help the corporation, employee, and the family separate fact from assumption and have a clear view of what the situation will entail.

One recent example of a move in this direction is a pamphlet published through the Equitable Relocation Service (ERS) called *The Human Dimension in Relocation* (Manuso and Sherwood, 1980). This pamphlet is part of the relocation package available to ERS clients that deals with identifying and controlling the stress related to relocation. Other relocation companies such as those run by Chemical Bank are looking at spouse involvement in relocation. And in-house departments such as Merrill Lynch's relocation service employs professional counselors as consultants when it is deemed necessary. There is no question that there is a strong move in this direction, and it will only expand over the next few years.

REFERENCES

"America's New Immobile Society." *Business Week*, July 27, 1981.

Bell, Theodore. 1980. "Dealing with the Costs of Employee Relocation." *Financial Executive* (August).

Brett, Jeanne M. and James D. Werbel. 1980. "The Effect of Job Transfer on Employees and Their Families." *Employee Relocation Council* (November).

"Corporations and Two-Career Families: Directions for the Future." *Catalyst*, 1980.

DeSimone, Judith. 1981. *Mobility*. Unpublished report prepared for the Exxon Corp.

———. 1981b. Personal communication.

Frank, Robert H. 1978. "Family Location Contracts and the Geographic Distribution of Finale Professionals." *Journal of Political Economy,* 86(1).

Guillet, Denise. 1980. "Getting Employees to Relocate . . . When They Won't." *Administrative Management* (October).

Hall, Francine S. and Douglas J. Hall. 1978. "Dual Careers—How Do Couples and Companies Cope with the Problems?" *Organizational Dynamics* (Spring).

Hayghe, Howard. 1981. "Husbands and Wives as Earners: An Analysis of Family Data." *Monthly Labor Review* (February).

Jenkins, James L., Bobby D. Lewis, and Alton M. Ellis. 1978. "Effects of Mobility on Quality of Parental Relationships." *Psychology Reports* 38.

Levinson, Myra and Robert Hollmann. 1980. "Personal Support Services in Corporate Relocation Programs." *Personnel Administrator* (September).

Manuso, James and Martha Sherwood. 1980. *Human Dimension in Relocation*, Equitable Relocation Service.

"More Workers are Getting a Chance to Choose Benefits Cafeteria Style." *Wall Street Journal*, July, 1981.

"Mortgage Miseries Shift the Mobile Society's Gears." *New York Times*, May 17, 1981.

Renshaw, Jean. 1976. "An Exploration of the Dynamics of the Overlapping Worlds of Work and Family." *Family Process* (March).

Tavernier, Gerard. 1980. "The High Cost and Stress of Relocation." *Management Review* (July).

Wheelock, Keith. 1979. "Office Relocation in the 1980's." *Personnel* (September–October).

18 Affirmative Action and Corporate Emotional Health Programs

James S.J. Manuso, Ph.D.

Using the New York home office of the Equitable Life Assurance Society of the United States as a model for corporations in general, this chapter addresses four major areas concerning the psychology of success or failure of minorities in newly acquired "corporate elite" jobs: (1) the nature of the corporate mandate for making affirmative action work, (2) the stressors unique to minorities in corporate life and the effects of such stressors, (3) the Equitable's response to its minority employees' stress-related symptoms, and (4) recommendations aimed at assuring the success of minority employees in organizational life.

The Equitable Life Assurance Society's affirmative action program incorporates an effort to hire and upgrade minorities and women with the long-range goal of employing in all major job categories, minorities and nonminorities and men and women in approximately the same proportions as they appear among all the people qualified for the types of work Equitable offers and available in Equitable's various labor markets. It is clear that the federal government is the prime mover in connection with affirmative action. However, the organization ultimately decides the "spirit" in which this is undertaken. Without the vigorous support of top management, affirmative action programs are doomed to failure.

Given the political and institutional rationales for affirmative action, the host corporation must of necessity attend to maximizing its returns on investments in its minority employee human resources. In order to achieve this objective, special measures must be considered. The minority corporate employee must cope with and adapt to a much wider array of stressor situations than the nonminority corporate employee.

CORPORATE STRESSORS AND THEIR EFFECTS ON MINORITIES

Minorities newly introduced into the corporate setting must face and adapt to those stressors that have been previously identified as characteristic of the corporate world. For example, in a direct demonstration of the relationship between corporate stressors and stress, Weiman (1977) studied 1,540 managerial employees and found that four job factors were positively correlated with heavy smoking, hypertriglyceridemia, essential hypertension, arteriosclerotic heart disease, hypercholesterolernia, exogenous obesity, and peptic ulcer. The four factors were: (1) too much or too little to do, that is, work overload or work stagnation, as perceived by the employee; (2) extreme ambiguity or extreme rigidity in relation to one's task, or not knowing what to do or how to do it as opposed to having every attribute of the job strictly spelled out; (3) extreme role conflict or little conflict, pointing up the importance of the consistency or lack thereof of one's job with one's other work and social roles; and (4) extreme amounts of responsibility (especially for people) or little responsibility, another form of the overload-underload dimension. Another study (Caplan, et al., 1975) reported two additional commonly occurring occupational stressors: low social support from supervisors and from others at work, and a high amount of unwanted overtime with a subjective sense of quantitative work overload. Manuso (1977) reported on a group of office employees' visits to the corporate health center for stress-related problems three months before and three months after their management and work methods had been changed precipitously. A 716 percent increase in such visits was observed. In decreasing order of frequency, the majority of visits were for exacerbation of hypertension, functional gastrointestinal disorders, generalized anxiety, and muscular tension. In the same study, it was found that employees whose jobs were abolished experienced depressions regardless of the fact that they had been promised a possibly better job within the same organization. Thus, job changes, management changes, and organizational changes are corporate stressors.

When 699 manager-members of the American Management Association were queried, they most frequently identified those factors that led to negative competition at work as a lack of consideration for others, a need for recognition and approval, greed for power, envy, and a fear of criticism (McLean & Jillson, 1977). "Negative competition," an unhealthy form of one-upmanship that involves the denigration of another's achievements in order to elevate one's self, was reported to characterize over 90 percent of the managers' organizations. It has been some time since it was first recognized that the necessity of adapting to the subtleties and complexities of social interactions within a hierarchically structured corporate environment is also a potent stressor (Levinson, et al., 1962).

Although large urban centers where corporations are typically located are often more liberal and "mixed" than elsewhere, there are certain corporate stressors that are unique to minorities. Minority employees must contend with racism and discrimination, both real and perceived, which is often subtle and always insidious (Willie, Kramer, & Brown, 1973). Subordinate minorities must sustain the interpersonal effects of fears, reaction formations, lowered expectations, and unwitting and deliberate backlashes on the part of white middle management, to whom they report.

Thanks in part to the "old boy" network of middle-aged, white middle management, minorities must face de facto segregation, hierarchically, within the power structure and, microgeographically, within a single office. At Equitable, as in the case of most corporations, minorities are typically employed in support functions (29 percent) and least often in professional, official, and managerial jobs (10 percent). Although minorities appear mainly in the unofficial staff positions, their large proportion is perceived as a threat by whites in that environment (Wrightsman, 1975). In reaction to this, minority group formation is rigidified, thereby perpetuating segregation (Simmel, 1955).

Referred to as the "crossover phenomenon," and occurring in all biological specimens exposed to environmental pressure, it is a well-known fact that the death rate of blacks as a percentage of the death rate of whites is a constant at infancy and above age 65, yet is significantly higher from age 35 to 44 (Calloway, 1973). A possible extension of these data is that the same relationship holds for the incidence of the stress-related disorders, which are known to hinder advancement in corporate life. It is during these ages 35 to 44 when employees are most often selected for advancement to higher management posts. These are also the years when the mid-life crisis tends to occur. Thus, the "crossover phenomenon" may serve as a detriment to the advancement of minorities in their host corporations. That is to say, reflective of the comparatively high death rate of blacks to whites during this mid-career, ten-year span, it may be that for every white person suffering the symptoms and effects of stress-related disorders, such as headache and generalized anxiety, 2.6 black people are succumbing to similar disorders. At a time when individuals are likely to need as much psychological and physical stamina as possible to advance in their chosen fields, the black person may be experiencing a form of psychophysiological discrimination that places a double barrier to striving toward success.

A related stressor is the absence of minority mentors or senior role models for minority employees to emulate, given the difficulties with peers due to the effects of negative competition. Minorities do not yet have a network to rely upon.

The largest segment of corporate-employed minorities, those found in support functions, appear to have developed a common means to control the white supervisor and express anger indirectly. Minorities often engage in covert contracts to regress to a mean level of performance. A negative group expectation may be perpetuated, with the possible result that the negative effect diffuses through the social milieu of minority in-groups, as in the case of whites whose jobs are abolished (Manuso, 1977). This could hinder productivity, the "bottom line."

Stemming from their previous contacts with large, white-dominated institutions imbued with the "plantation syndrome" ("we" must fix "them"), minorities seem to have learned to be distrustful and disbelieving of large institutions. This attitude may be transferred to the host corporation, with the effect that minorities' involvements in various activities are avoided. An extreme example of this potential effect is the minority employee whose job must be in critical jeopardy before he or she requests the assistance of an affirmative action office.

In order to comply with federal government rules, tokenism in hiring practices may take place. This inevitably leads to the minority being given an inappropriate job, for which the person is either overqualified or underqualified. This is a significant stressor.

In addition to the aforementioned stressors, minorities are more likely to enter the corporation with health, educational, social, and cultural deficits vis-à-vis the white establishment. The overall effect is to further increase the concentration of stress carriers within minority groups. Of special note is the fact that particular minority subcultures, such as minority women and upper managers, have unique problems and stand alone in their respective arenas, lacking any form of social support from peers.

What, then, are the effects of multiple stressors on minority groups? Because stressor situations are additive in their impact on the organism they affect, when sustained they have the capacity to induce the stress response and its accompanying symptomatic expressions (Dicara, 1974). On a national scale, it is known that minorities show the worst health profiles of all Americans, (*Health, U.S.,* 1975), particularly with reference to mental health, although they tend to receive the least and the poorest mental health care (President's Commission, 1978). Indeed, psychic distress and vulnerability is highest for the low-income minority groups (Bishop, 1979). Thus, for example, blacks tend to have higher rates of restricted-activity days, bed-disability days, and work-loss days than do whites, (*Disability Days,* 1975) though this may be the effect of minorities' holding low-status jobs (Gerson & Skipper, 1973).

Thus, multiple stressors have significant impacts on the physical, psychological, and social health of minorities; these factors in turn affect performance, productivity, and attendance. These observations are borne out in the experience of the Equitable home office, where 25 percent of employees are minorities, yet where 33 percent of the patients seeing a psychologist in the emotional health program of the Employee health services department are minorities. Such are the effects of stress, of lower income levels, and of being inappropriately perceived as "mentally disturbed" by white male managers, who are generally unable to recognize and address the frustrations peculiar to their minority subordinates.

The corporation, unless it is willing to address these problems, must face the consequences of its inactivity. Negative employee attitudes have a damaging financial effect on the corporation (Mirvis & Lawler, 1977) as do psychological problems of employees (Rappaport, Dolan, & Clementi, 1977). There are political ramifications as well, as in the case of the Potomac Electric Power Company, which was required by the Government Services Administration to offer an employee counseling program in order to comply with affirmative action guidelines.

THE CORPORATE RESPONSE TO THE PROBLEM

The Equitable has responded aggressively to the problems inherent in incorporating minority group members into its traditionally conservative structure. At the institutional level, the chief executive officer hosts ongoing meetings with minorities employed at many levels in the organization in order to keep himself appraised of their unique problems. An affirmative action office, directed by an officer of the corporation, serves an advocacy role for minorities with job-related difficulties, mediating between the minority and management when necessary and facilitating upward communication. The affirmative action office also employs a variety of consultants to management to deal with the problems and employment of minorities, while hosting educational workshops for minorities and enhancing the slow development of a minority "old boy" network. The emotional health program, dedicated to the detection, prevention, education, treatment, referral, and follow-up of troubled employees, enhances these institutional efforts by educating new supervisors in the recognition and proper referral of troubled employees, by advising senior management on mental health issues, by identifying pockets of stressor overloads and recommending a form of intervention, and by offering workshops for management regarding stressor situations.

Two programs of particular importance to minority groups are the stress management training program and the substance abuse program. The frequency of heroin addition and the stress-related disorders of generalized anxiety, hypertension, and headache is inordinately high in the minority group population of emotional health program users. In a recent study of drug abusers in the substance abuse program at Equitable, 65 percent were minority group members (Graham & Gottcent, 1977). Based on a 99 percent confidence level (using a standardized score to test the differences between two proportions from independent samples), the study concluded that ex-drug abusers, if carefully selected for skills, if ready for employment, and if offered an ongoing substance abuse program consisting of regular counseling and follow-up, are no different from other similar employees who have no known history of drug abuse with reference to their job retention rate, promotions, punctuality, and performance.

A random sample of participants in the stress management training program, which treats employees suffering generalized anxiety or headache, or both, found that 40 percent of the subjects were minority group members. Employees participating in this program learn, through behavior modification and biofeedback techniques, how to mobilize the antistress response in appropriate situations. Tests showed that subjects successfully decreased the absolute value and variability of forehead muscle tension level, decreased symptom frequency and intensity (thereby decreasing the interference of symptoms with productivity), and decreased medication intake and visits to the health center for stress-related and other disorders. Subjects also significantly increased their capacity for hypnogogic mentation or fantasy formation along with their verbalized proprioceptive awareness. Before treatment, the equivalent of 26 percent of subjects' salaries were being spent on visits to the health center and on the interfering effects of symptoms on their productivity and on the productivity of their supervisors, coworkers, and subordinates. After treatment, this figure dropped to 6 percent. Cumulative cost-benefit ratios demonstrate that for every dollar invested in this program there is a $5.52 return on that investment per person per year.

It is clear that psychologically based problems affecting minority groups can induce stress-related disorders, which, in turn, can be effectively and economically treated by the host corporation for its own benefit. Experience shows that corporations with aggressive affirmative action programs and an existing employee counseling program with a good performance record (as measured by its reputation among the employees and respect for confidentiality) and with minority group representation on staff tend to see higher proportions of minorities in their caseloads than do corporations with limited affirmative action programs and new employee counseling programs with no minority representation (Manuso, 1981).

SUMMARY AND RECOMMENDATIONS

With the influence of governmental mandate, some of the structural barriers to managerial jobs for minorities disappear. Emotional, health-related, cultural, attitudinal, and social barriers remain, however. This calls for the employees' adaptation to new stressor situations without the benefits of social support or role models and without deficits in productivity. In the absence of assistance, it appears that such a task is virtually impossible. Following is a series of recommendations that are intended to increase the likelihood of success of corporate affirmative action efforts.

1. Avoid tokenism at all costs. This serves as a stressor to the minority and antagonizes and alienates whites.

2. Make some arrangements for an effective employee counseling program, before governmental agencies mandate that this be undertaken.

3. Educate senior management. Make sure that all understand the nature of systematic discrimination (which can result from corporate hiring and advancement practices and systems (Sparks, 1975)), stressors unique to minority employees, the financial, political, and organizational costs of multiple stressors on minorities, and what can be done about these problems.

4. Seek the support of the chief executive officer for any such programs.

5. Anticipate and design a strategy for overcoming human resistances to affirmative action organizational change efforts (Kotter & Schlesinger, 1979).

6. Cultivate minority participation by having adequate minority representation on the staff of the employee counseling program.

7. Assure that all members of the management and supervisory teams understand that affirmative action is being undertaken as a business objective, for economic reasons, for selfish reasons, reflecting that the organization is concerned with self-perpetuation and growth, while complying with the law.

8. Assure that minorities have a noncompetitive and comfortable access to one another and to appropriate mentors, regardless of race. Encourage the slow development of a minority employee "old boy" network.

9. Throughout the early phases of affirmative action compliance, engage the services of appropriate consultants in order to teach each party about the resistances of the other and the psychology of facilitating more appropriate relationships.

10. Assure that the affirmative action staff has qualified white members in order to identify with the dilemmas of white middle managers in connection with compliance and problems.

11. Install a mechanism for upward communication of all employees in order to guarantee that minority employees' job-related problems have a forum.

12. Give special attention and assistance, in terms of additional benefits or an increased frequency of medical checkups, to minorities in the "critical" 35 to 44 years age range.

13. To dispell the "we" versus "them" mentality, direct employees' attentions to the common goal of ridding society of additional stressors,

which in the long run can have only negative impact upon the health of one and all.

14. Avoid any pockets of de facto segregation. Better interracial attitudes and resultant relations can be assured by the interracial mix of equal status employees with common goals (Blanchard, Weigel, & Cook, 1975).

REFERENCES

Bishop, J. 1979. "Age of Anxiety." *Wall Street Journal* 193:1.

Blanchard, F., R. Weigel, and F. Cook. 1975. "The Effect of Relative Competenence of Group Members upon Interpersonal Attraction in Cooperating Interracial Groups." *Journal of Personal Social Psychology* 32:519–530.

Calloway, N. 1973. Health Problems of the Black Minority. pp. 7–12. In *Wingspread Report, Health Issues and Minority Communities.* Racine, Wisc.: The Johnson Foundation.

Caplan, R., S. Cobb, J. French, et al. 1975. *Job Demands and Worker Health: Main Effects and Occupational Differences.* U.S. Department of Health, Education and Welfare, Publication No. (NIOSH) 75–160.

DiCara, L., Ed. 1974. *Limbic and Autonomic Nervous Systems Research.* London: Butterworths.

Disability Days. 1975. U.S. Department of Health, Education and Welfare, Publication No. (PHS) 78–1546.

Gerson, L. and J. Skipper. 1973. "Job Status and Expectations of Exemptions from Work Due to Illness." *Journal of Occupational Medicine* 15:633–634.

Graham, R. and R. Gottcent. 1977. "Restoration of Drug Abusers to Useful Employment: Experience of the Equitable Life Assurance Society of the U.S." Presented at the National Drug Abuse Conference, San Francisco.

Health, U.S. 1975. 1975. U.S. Department of Health, Education and Welfare, Publication No. (HRA) 76–1232.

Kotter, J. and L. Schlesinger. 1979. "Choosing Strategies for Change." *Harvard Business Review* 57:106–114.

Levinson, H., C. Price, K. Munden, et al. 1962. *Men, Management and Mental Health.* Cambridge, Harvard University Press.

Manuso, J. 1977. "Coping with Job Abolishment." *Journal of Occupational Medicine* 19:598–602.

———. 1981. "Corporate Mental Health Programs and Policies." In *The Promotion of Health; New Trends and Perspectives*, edited by L. Ng. and D. Davis, New York: Van Nostrand Reinhold Company.

McLean, P. and R. Jillson. 1977. *The Manager and Self-Respect–A Follow-Up Survey.* New York: AMACOM.

Mirvis, P. and E. Lawler. 1977. "Measuring the Financial Impact of Employee Attitudes." *Journal Applied Psychology* 62:1–8.

President's Commission on Mental Health. 1978. Task Panel Reports Submitted to the President's Commission on Mental Health, Volume 3, Appendix. U.S. Government Printing Office.

Rappaport, M., M. Dolan, and T. Clementi. 1977. "Psychological Problems in an Industrial Setting." *Journal of Occupational Medicine* 19:659–663.

Sparks, G. 1975. "How to Identify Systemic Discrimination." *EEO Today* 4:43–51.

Simmel, G. 1955. *Conflict and the Web of Group-Affiliations*. New York: The Free Press.

Weiman, C. 1977. "A Study of Occupational Stressors and the Incidence of Disease Risk." *Journal of Occupational Medicine* 19:119–122.

Willie, C., M. Kramer, and B. Brown, Eds. 1973. *Racism and Mental Health: Essays*. Pittsburgh: University of Pittsburgh Press.

Wrightsman, L. 1975. *Social Psychology in the Seventies*. New York: The Free Press.

SECTION FIVE

Transitions: Stress Management, Health Enhancement, Psychology, and Leadership

Beyond alcoholism treatment, employee counseling programs, and specific focus counseling, occupational clinical psychology has begun a series of transitions wherein occupational clinicians translate their knowledge of behavioral medicine and leadership training to worksite interventions and/or for worksite concerns. Most of these transitions have been prompted by organizational concern for health systems cost containment. This development has paralleled the recent concern on the part of psychologists with the need for health enhancing approaches to clinical work. Because of the magnitude of some of these interventions, only long-range research and observation will chart the effects on morbidity and mortality. We can be sure that the nation's insurers and large organizations with significant employee health costs will be watching and waiting.

Dr. Gary Schwartz, in his chapter, "Stress Management in Occupational Settings," reviews the stress concept and its linkage to psychophysiological disorders and the stressors unique to large organizations. The chapter reviews relevant research and introduces the reader to stress management procedures and research based clinical outcomes. Dr. Schwartz challenges us with future potentials of applying behavioral medicine interventions in large organizations.

One of the most comprehensive and exciting outlets for psychologists' clinical expression is the occupational health enhancement and health promotion arena. Dr. Murray Naditch, in his chapter, "The StayWell Program: Health Enhancement at Work," discusses the issue of worksite health promotion using as his example the largest corporate commitment to health enhancement thus far in the United States.

Dr. Naditch establishes the rationale for such a program, namely, productivity enhancement and health care cost containment. The risk intervention model, or wellness program, attempts to facilitate employees' positive behavioral changes with respect to five major risk factors. The complete program is outlined, and the parameters for program evaluation are discussed. Cost effectiveness concerns are highlighted, and the key factors necessary for an effective lifestyle change program in an organizational setting are detailed. Dr. Naditch ends with a discussion of future developments in the StayWell program, which will involve heavier reliance upon interactive, computer-based programs. There is no one model for wellness, and new orientations with respect to this area are developed regularly. Following a complete evaluation of the effectiveness of various types of interventions, more effective models will be developed.

Beyond their work in behavioral medicine, psychologists interested in occupational issues have begun to address the issue of how to develop more effective leaders, which are so critical. Three of the founders of the California NEXUS Foundation, Donald Michael, John O'Neil and Dr. Kenneth Pelletier, in their chapter, "NEXUS," address the history and present revolution in the interface between the individual and organizational life, with particular attention devoted to the issue of leadership. The need for bridging psychology and leadership is pronounced, and the founding of the California NEXUS Foundation in early 1981 by the California School of Professional Psychology was intended to assist in the development of that bridge. NEXUS, through its three-day seminars, aims at bringing together leaders to work on common problems of organizational life and at developing better leadership skills as a result. This experiment is in its infancy and will surely stand as a significant trailblazer in the movement to prod psychology into assisting in the development of better leaders.

Increasingly, pragmatic Americans with specific psychosocial needs are banding together formally and informally in a variety of self-help groups. The importance of this movement cannot be underestimated in terms of its long-range impact on the practice of occupational clinical psychology. One of the best examples of this process is the women's networks movement, wherein leadership skills and social interactions are cultivated with the aim of helping women advance in their careers. Naturally, there are a number of roles an occupational clinical psychologist might play in organization-based self-help movements. In her chapter, "The Networking Process: Informal and Formal Networking, with a Corporate Case Study," Alina Novak, one of the founders of the nation's first corporation-based women's network programs, discusses how networking helps women to learn self-help survival skills. Whereas men have typically learned goal setting through their acculturation, women have had to "catch up" in their business training. The precedents for the networking movement are assertiveness training and consciousness raising, but networking endures because it is based on women's needs and skills being continuously exchanged in a mutually supportive atmosphere. Ms. Novak outlines the formal and informal networking processes, aimed at self-promotion through informal follow-up. Naturally, the networking goals are mutually advantageous to group members. In reviewing the Equitable Life Assurance Society's networks organization, it becomes clear that the survival of such a corporate-based program depends on three critical factors: (1) support from the chief executive officer, (2) a corporate climate conducive to and supportive of the networking process, and (3) continuing grass-roots support and leadership on the part of networks members. This chapter makes it clear that Americans are beginning to tap into the most effective stress management tool of them all—social support—for self-betterment. How organized psychology responds to the self-help movement on its different fronts, will, at least in part, determine the future usefulness of psychology to American society.

As a science develops, it becomes more capable of rendering meaningful services to the society of which it is a part. And certainly, the structure of scientific revolutions is such that practical applications result in the long run. Psychology is now being tested by American society. This is particularly so in the organizational context, where the need for systems interventions is great. We can and must meet this challenge effectively.

19 Stress Management in Occupational Settings

Gary E. Schwartz, Ph.D.

Substantial progress in documenting the role of psychosocial stress in the etiology and development of physical and mental disease has been made in the past ten years. It is now known that not only are the classic psychosomatic disorders—such as hypertension, ulcers, and asthma—strongly influenced by psychosocial stress, but even susceptibility to and recovery from infectious and genetic disorders (ranging from the common cold to cancer) are determined, at least in part, by stress in the environment and the person's way of coping with stress (Selye, 1976; Weiner, 1977).

Also in the past decade, substantial progress has been made in documenting effective behavioral approaches to the management of psychological and physiological responses to stress. We now know that various behavioral techniques, including relaxation, meditation, biofeedback, and other psychological self-control procedures, can be helpful in treating some persons with mental and physical disorders (Williams and Gentry, 1977). These behavioral techniques, when integrated within a comprehensive, biobehavioral approach to health and illness, can also (1) enhance the effectiveness of biomedical treatments such as drugs and, in the process, reduce the dosage needed to produce a given clinical effect and (2) decrease susceptibility to future disease by promoting positive approaches to health. In other words, stress management procedures are not only useful in treatment, but they also may be useful in the prevention of illness.

---

*Originally published in *Public Health Reports* 95 (March–April 1980): 99–108. Reprinted with permission.

It should be recognized at the outset that most of the research conducted to date that links stress to illness is not based on data derived from occupational settings. Although a growing body of literature specifically documents the effects of occupational stress in the etiology and development of physical and mental disease (McLean, 1974, 1977), data that directly tests the effects of stress management procedures in the treatment and prevention of stress-related disorders in occupational settings are scarce (McLean, 1979). The relative lack of data in this area is neither surprising nor discouraging, because it is only recently that basic and clinical research on stress has developed to the point of seriously justifying research and applications in occupational settings. Furthermore, industry just recently became aware of (1) its role in promoting and sustaining health and (2) the potential benefits that may accrue by industry, labor, and science working together to promote health in occupational settings.

The challenge facing industry, labor, and science today is to design stress management programs that can be clinically effective and cost-effective and then to carefully evaluate these programs in occupational settings through systematic research. The promise of positive results emerging from collaborative research in this area is substantial and should be pursued vigorously, despite the numerous problems in conducting such research.

We are witnessing today a major change in our conception of health and illness. In the past, psychological and biological models of health and illness were couched in separate scientific languages and practice by separate disciplines —now these separations are being broken down. Behavioral and biomedical sciences are beginning to join forces to tackle health problems that require a multidisciplinary approach to their solution. The concept of stress and its implications for health and illness is a key factor bringing these disparate disciplines together.

The extent of this change in orientation can be seen, for example, in the emergence of the new field of behavioral medicine. Formally established at the Yale Conference on Behavioral Medicine in February 1977 (Schwartz and Weiss, 1978b) and extended at a meeting hosted by the Institute of Medicine of the National Academy of Sciences in April 1978, which founded the Academy of Behavioral Medicine Research, behavioral medicine has been defined as follows:

> Behavioral Medicine is the interdisciplinary field concerned with the development and integration of behavioral and biomedical science, knowledge, and techniques relevant to health and illness and the application of this knowledge and these techniques to prevention, diagnosis, treatment and rehabilitation. (Schwartz and Weiss, 1978a, p. 250)

Two words in this definition, "development and integration," need to be emphasized, because they highlight the pitfalls and promises of stress management as applied to health and illness in occupational settings. Although the present data are encouraging, many key basic and applied questions still need to be answered. The development of this knowledge will hinge on the creative integration of behavioral and biomedical approaches. When applied to the occupational setting, the development of this knowledge will further hinge on the integration and collaboration of industry, labor, and science. As Dr. Neal Miller, one of the pioneers of behavioral approaches to health and illness, said concerning behavioral medicine's future, we must be "bold in what we try, but cautious in what we claim." In this spirit, I will review what is and what is not known about stress management in occupational settings, suggest some of the directions to be considered for future research and applications, and indicate the cautions that must be considered in light of our present state of knowledge.

The literature linking occupational stress to disease is reviewed by McLean in a 1974 volume and in the proceedings of a 1977 conference sponsored by NIOSH. Some of the major classes of psychosocial stress facing workers have been summarized recently by Dr. James S.J. Manuso, director of the emotional health program of the Equitable Life Assurance Society:

1. Work overload, or work stagnation
2. Extreme ambiguity, or rigidity in relation to one's tasks
3. Extreme role conflict, or little conflict
4. Extreme amounts of responsibility (especially for other people), or little responsibility
5. Cut-throat and negative competition (or one-upmanship), or no competition
6. Constant change and daily variability, or a deadening routinized stability
7. Ongoing contact with "stress carriers" (e.g. demanding workaholics, highly anxious people, indecisive individuals), or social isolation
8. That the corporation, for its own survival, encourages its employees to define their egos in terms of the organization, to contain emotional reactions, and to depend upon it, and
9. The interaction of one's stage of career development, career opportunity, and management style. (Manuso, 1981)

According to Manuso, "It is not surprising, then, that 58% of the men and 36% of the women in a sample of 95 Emotional Health Program participants at the Equitable Life Assurance Corporation stated that job-related factors, at least in part caused or contributed to their problems."

A recent paper by Chesney and Feuerstein (1979) highlights some important research on sources of stress. For example, while using a homogeneous population of 1,540 white-collar workers (84 percent male) in a large financial institution, Weiman (1977) examined Selye's (1956) hypothesis that both overstimulation and understimulation are sources of stress and are associated with a higher level of disease or risk. Weiman confirmed this hypothesis, observing a U-shaped relationship between stimulation (measurement by an index of work load, role conflict, task ambiguity, and responsibility) and an index of disease or risk (including smoking, hypertriglyceridemia, hypercholesterolemia, atheroschlerotic heart disease, essential hypertension, exogenous obesity, and peptic ulcer). It is of considerable interest that both overstimulation and understimulation can result in an increase in stress-related disorders and behaviors associated with health risk. Chesney and Feuerstein (1979) comment that research on the health of occupational groups, whose jobs are characterized by understimulation, such as blue-collar assembly workers, would further establish this important U-shaped relationship between environment and disease.

Zorn, Harrington, and Goethe (1977), in a study of West German sea pilots, observed excess cardiac mortality in this occupational group compared to the cardiac death rate of the male population of Hamburg. Although numerous studies report a relationship between stress and heart disease, the mechanisms linking these two factors remain unknown. To explore the hypothesis that increased catecholamine levels contribute to the relationship between job stress and cardiac death, Zorn and coworkers measured urinary catecholamines in five sea pilots before, immediately after, and 24 hours after a stressful river piloting operation. They found a significant elevation in catecholamines between the pretrip and posttrip collections and a subsequent drop in catecholamines 24 hours after the operation.

A related study linking catecholamines and job stress was recently conducted by Dutton and coworkers (1978), who compared a group of paramedics with a group of firefighters. Although both groups had similar scores on the Schedule of Recent Life Events—a general life stress scale that predicts susceptibility to disease (Holmes and Rahe, 1967)—the paramedics scored significantly higher than the firefighters on a job stress questionnaire designed specifically for the study. The paramedics, importantly, also had significantly higher levels of epinephrine and norepinephrine on work days than on nonwork days.

Chesney and Feuerstein (1979) recognized that although these studies suggest an association between environmental stress and disease, certain cognitive, personality, and behavior characteristics of the employee (mediated by the brain) interact with characteristics of the environment and influence this association. In collaboration with Chadwick, Chesney, and Feuerstein (1981), they attempted to define the relationships between job and life stresses, personality characteristics and behavior patterns, job and home environments, physiological strain variables, and coronary heart disease risk and status; they assessed these variables over a one and one-half year period for 397 men who were examined at their worksites. The data indicate, for example, that higher levels of catecholamines correlated with job stress as measured by the work pressure subscale of the Work Environment Scale (Moos, Insel, and Humphrey, 1974) and impulsiveness as measured by the Eysenck Personality Inventory (Eysenck and Eysenck, 1968). Although not mentioned in their report, the implication is that persons high in job stress and high in impulsiveness will more likely evidence health risk factors than persons high in either one alone. The need for multi-measure, interactive analyses is critical if the effects of job stress on health are to be understood and therefore controlled.

It must be recognized that combinations of factors within and outside of the work situation interact and contribute to disease. Because the work setting may be either a primary determinant of risk, or it may interact with serious stresses in the worker's personal life, the study of the relationship between job stress and illness is complicated. On the other hand, the control role that the work situation plays in people's lives increases the potential impact that industry can have in motivating persons to change their lifestyles for the sake of their health. Industry may, for its own purposes, wish to reduce absenteeism, enhance productivity, and reduce insurance and medical costs. However, providing stress management training as part of a more comprehensive health enhancement program may not only help the worker in the work situation, but also may help the worker to deal with significant problems occurring outside the work situation. In this way, industry can potentially make a greater contribution to society at large.

INTRODUCTION TO STRESS MANAGEMENT PROCEDURES

Numerous procedures are documented by research that can influence response to stress. Some procedures are geared toward helping people change their environment to be more healthful. For example, various studies document how assertiveness training can be used to help people take better control of their lives and in the process reduce tension and hence decrease the physiological responses of strain due to excessive anger or anxiety, or both (Novaco, 1975). The goal of assertiveness training programs is not to make people more aggressive, but rather to help them assert themselves more appropriately in order to reduce the likelihood that they will engage in health risk behaviors reinforced by peer pressure, or to help them modify their jobs (through appropriate channels) to be more healthful. Often, assertiveness training programs consist of combinations of behavior therapy, imagery, role playing, and other techniques aimed at improving people's ability to communicate their concerns, which helps them change the groups in which they work–not only to better meet their individual needs, but also to improve the functioning of the group as a whole.

Other stress management procedures are geared toward helping people cope with an environment that cannot be changed. These coping procedures involve various mental and psychophysiological techniques including relaxation, meditation, biofeedback, and guided imagery. For example, progressive relaxation involves teaching people to tense and relax each of the major muscle groups of the body–a "somatic" procedure (Jacobson, 1938), while autogenic training involves teaching people to imagine particular sensations—such as one's limbs being warm and heavy—a "cognitive" procedure—with the goal of reducing autonomic arousal (Schultz and Luthe, 1969).

Other techniques combine various mental and somatic relaxation procedures. The most well known of these procedures was developed by Benson (1975), who proposes that the harmful effects of prolonged psychosocial stress are mediated by excessive elicitation of a hypothalamically controlled "fight or flight" response, with its attendant increased sympathetic nervous activity. Benson further proposes that a reaction opposite in its physiological effects to those of the "fight or flight" response is an integrated "relaxation response" also mediated by the hypothalamus. The relaxation response is presumably elicited by a variety of relaxation and meditation techniques. Goleman and Schwartz (1976) also have documented the effectiveness of relaxation response procedures.

Benson's technique draws on a combination of processes to promote the relaxation response. It includes (1) relaxation of all skeletal muscles, (2) attention to breathing in a relaxed fashion, (3) saying a simple word ("one") after each breath (to help remove distracting thoughts), and (4) adopting a passive attitude (thereby further removing the requirement to respond to one's own images). It should be noted that this simple technique, which can be taught by any trained health professional or paraprofessional in a single session and can be supported by simple cassette tape instructions and reading materials, actually combines mental and skeletal muscle relaxation, as well as expectancy and "placebo" effects.

Carrington (1977) proposes a similar procedure in terms of the basic component processes. However, her procedure differs from Benson's in a number of important respects. Whereas Benson recommends that people practice his technique 15 to 20 minutes in the morning and evening, Carrington recommends that people practice on a more ad lib basis, and, ideally, they should practice in actual stressful situations. In addition, Carrington encourages persons to select their own "mantras" so as to make the procedure more personally relevant and pleasant. Carrington claims that these changes, plus others, lead to increased adherence. However, there are currently no published studies that carefully compare the different relaxation procedures in terms of their actual clinical efficacy and long-term adherence.

Biofeedback has evolved over the past ten years as a means of teaching specific voluntary control over particular muscles or visceral responses (Schwartz and Beatty, 1977). As shown in Figure 19.1, biofeedback can be seen as the use of electronic sensors to make normally unconscious physiological feedback processes conscious, and thereby increase the capacity of the person to exercise self-control. Whether biofeedback training procedures substantially augment the effectiveness of various relaxation procedures used by themselves is controversial (Silver and Blanchard, 1978). It is likely that biofeedback training is,

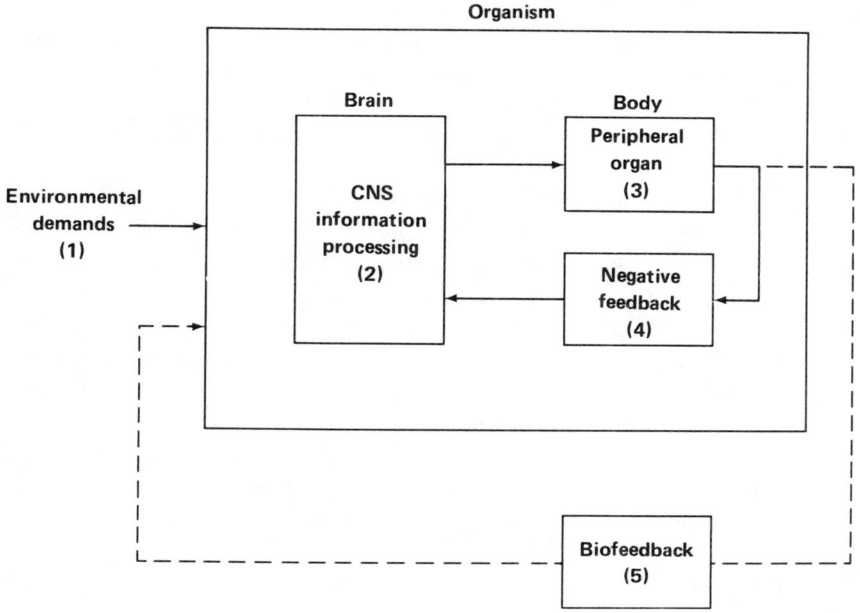

Figure 19.1. Simplified block diagram depicting (1) environmental demands influencing (via exteroceptors, not shown), (2) the brain's regulation of its (3) peripheral organs, and (4) negative feedback from the periphery back to the brain. Disregulation can be initiated at each of these stages. Biofeedback (stage 5) is a parallel feedback loop to stage 4, detecting the activity of the peripheral organ (stage 3) and converting it into environmental demands (stage 1) that can be used by the brain (stage 2) to increase self-regulation. (Adopted from Schwartz, 1977.)

per se, not essential for many patients with stress-related problems. However, research does suggest that biofeedback is important as an adjunct to stress management procedures for at least two major reasons:

1. It helps convince the patient that he can actually voluntarily control his physiological responses, and that psychosocial stress does, in fact, elicit stress responding.

2. It provides reinforcement for the patient and therapist regarding the patient's progress over time.

It allows both patient and therapist to discover what relaxation procedure (or combination of stress management procedures) is or is not effective in reducing the physiological symptoms of stress responding. As Schwartz (1978) emphasizes in this context, biofeedback should not be used simply as a self-regulation training technique, but rather as a clinical "research" tool essential to effective and responsible clinical practice.

Various mental self-control procedures have been devised for helping patients decrease stress responding. In addition to systematic desensitization, where anxiety provoking imagery is coupled with deep muscle relaxation to reduce stress, specific stress "inoculation" programs have been developed for helping people cope with pain and distress (Meichenbaum, 1977). For example, Turk (1976) used an experimental pain task to document that stress inoculation training (consisting of imagery-rehearsal role playing and specific mental self-statements) resulted in a 100 percent increase in the subject's ability to endure the pain, whereas morphine alone led to only a 30 to 60 percent increase in the subject's ability to endure the pain. It should also be noted that hypnosis and various other suggestion procedures are sometimes used to further enhance such effects.

It is generally accepted that specific combinations of stress management techniques can help certain people reduce their response to stress and that these effects are not due to simply expectancy or "placebo" factors. However, the research has not advanced to the point that enables clinicians to predict with any precision what kind of person, with what kinds of problems, will respond best to what combinations of procedures. Furthermore, little research has been conducted to date that has combined, for example, relaxation training with assertiveness training with the explicit goal of changing the person and the environment in a balanced fashion.

However, most significant for this discussion is that at present, only one published study systematically evaluated the use of a stress management technique in a work setting (Peters, Benson, and Porter, 1977; Peters, Benson, and Peters, 1977). However, a few additional studies have been either completed but not published, or they are in progress. A review of these studies follows.

CLINICAL ASPECTS OF STRESS MANAGEMENT

Benson and colleagues recently published a major study comparing the effects of daily "relaxation breaks" on five self-reported measures of health, performance, and well-being (Peters, Benson, and Porter, 1977) and measures of systolic and diastolic blood pressure and heart rate (Peters, Benson, and Peters, 1977). The work was done at the Converse Rubber Company, a subsidiary of the Eltra Corporation. For 12 weeks, 126 volunteers filled out daily records and reported for biweekly blood pressure measures. After four weeks of baseline monitoring, they were divided randomly into three groups: group A was taught Benson's technique for producing the relaxation response; group B was instructed to sit quietly and relax any way they wanted, and group C received no instructions. Groups A and B were asked to take two 15-minute relaxation breaks daily.

After an eight-week experimental period, the greatest mean improvements on every index occurred in group A, the least improvements occurred in group C, and group B was intermediate. Differences between the mean changes in group A versus group C reached statistical significance ($P < .05$) on four of the five indices: symptoms, illness days, performance, sociability-satisfaction. The relationship between amount of change and rate of practicing the relaxation response was different for the various indices. Although fewer than three practice periods per week produced little change on any index, two daily sessions appeared to be more than necessary for many persons to achieve positive changes. Interestingly, somatic symptoms and performance responded with less practice of the relaxation response than did behavioral symptoms and measures of well-being.

The results for blood pressure paralleled the self-report measures. Although the subjects generally were normo-tensive, the decreases in systolic blood pressure from the beginning to the end of the study were −11.6 mm Hg for group A, −6.5 mm Hg for group B, and +0.4 mm Hg for group C; mean diastolic blood pressures decreased by −7.9, −3.1, and −0.3. Moreover, within group A, the higher the initial blood pressure, the greater the decrease with relaxation training.

An interesting, serendipitous finding occurred for the blood pressure data. Both systolic and diastolic blood pressures rose in all three groups for session 6 and fell again for session 7 in groups A and B but not group C. The project was apparently initiated shortly before the company experienced the effects of a nationwide economic recession. As a result, the company initiated a series of layoffs, most of which were implemented on three consecutive Fridays, beginning at session 5 and ending at session 6. Although only 5 percent of the total corporate staff were laid off, another 10 percent were offered and accepted other positions in the company. During sessions 5 and 6, many participants mentioned their anxiety about their job security or increased work load or their concern for colleagues who had been forced to move or leave. Benson and coworkers (Peters, Benson, and Peters, 1977) hypothesized that stress mounted over those weeks, and blood pressure increased accordingly. Other investigators (Kasl and Cobb, 1970) have reported such increases in blood pressure during the anticipation phase of factory shutdowns among employees who eventually lost their jobs. Benson and coworkers (Peters, Benson, and Peters, 1977) also offered the intriguing hypothesis that blood pressures may have returned to the original levels more rapidly in groups A and B than in C (session 7) due to some effect of the relaxation practice.

The preceding data are clearly encouraging and beg to be replicated and extended under more controlled conditions. Benson and coworkers (Peters, Benson, and Peters, 1977) pointed out some of the limitations of their experiment, including the lack of control for positive expectancy effects, the lack of follow-up data, the lack of actual data regarding subsequent use of health services, and so forth. Furthermore, their study was not performed on patients who were seeking help for specific stress-related disorders. On the other hand, the data illustrate the potential of incorporating a relatively simple relaxation procedure into an industrial setting, which could have beneficial effects on health and work performance. Benson and coworkers noted that if the relaxation response proves capable of maintaining lowered blood pressure in normotensive subjects, "it might become a most useful component of preventive as well as therapeutic programs."

Regarding cost, Benson and coworkers commented:

> The relaxation response is particularly attractive as a preventive measure since it costs only the time involved to practice, has no known side effects, and is reported to be a pleasant and personally rewarding experience by those who elicit it regularly.

However, precise cost-benefit ratios have not been computed.

In Benson's studies cited, the relaxation training was purely voluntary. The company did not reinforce the employees for learning stress management by giving them, for example, time off from work to learn and practice the skills. However, an excellent model of a corporation-supported, comprehensive approach to stress management was developed by Manuso and colleagues for Equitable Life Assurance Society of the United States. They have established an emotional health program, staffed with a clinical psychologist, a psychiatrically oriented physician, a clinical psychology intern, and a counselor. Liaisons are maintained with outside mental health practitioners, universities, and hospitals. The program is more than just a referral service. It is concerned with the detection, prevention, education, treatment, referral, and follow-up of troubled employees. All services are free and on company time, along with all other medical services. The emotional health program is physically housed in the employee health services department, thereby enabling the delivery of multimodality (psychological and medical) services. All services are confidential, ensuring that the workers can freely pursue and therefore, it is hoped, resolve their problems.

Manuso has just completed his first study examining the clinical and cost effectiveness of providing biofeedback and other stress management procedures in the treatment of 15 subjects with headaches and 15 subjects with general anxiety. These subjects held a wide variety of job responsibilities, from filing to upper managerial jobs. Their average annual salary was $14,000. The subjects were included in the study if their average annual symptom activity and their symptom's history met a minimum standard; namely, if symptoms had been present for at least five years and if the average symptom activity for a two-week baseline period (assessed by using a daily log procedure) was "moderate" to "severe." A unique feature of this study was that an additional and different subject population of 30 was used to report on the extent to which significant others at the worksite with stress-related symptoms interfered with the respondent's ability to work. From their percentage estimates, a quantitative effect of interference could be generated. Bosses, closest coworkers, and subordinates were used as significant others at the worksite.

The experiment consisted of three phases: a pretreatment baseline phase, during which two no-feedback, electromyographic (EMG) measurement-only sessions were administered; the treatment phase, consisting of five weeks of frontalis EMG biofeedback training with three sessions per week (the average number of treatment sessions per subject was 13); and the posttreatment follow-up phase, which consisted of two no-feedback, EMG measurement-only sessions over a two-week period, taking place three months following the last treatment phase session. Subjects were grouped according to primary diagnosis (headache versus anxiety) and served as their own controls.

Numerous before and after measures were taken in this study, including personality scales, health center medical records, daily logs (including medicine used), total interference and work interference due to the presence of symptoms, and so forth. The stress management training included muscle relaxation, breathing exercises, imagery techniques, as well as the biofeedback training. Since a complex stress management package was used, it is not possible to attribute the results to any one component or combination of components in the treatment package.

The results were striking because, on the average, improvement occurred in every measure taken. Both groups showed statistically significant decreases in symptoms and increases in work-related satisfaction and effectiveness. Importantly, both anxiety and headache subjects significantly decreased their visits to the health center for both stress-related and other complaints from the period three months before treatment (5.75 visits per subject) to three months after treatment (1.70 visits per subject). Whereas during the three pretreatment months, all subjects had visited the health center because of stress-related symptoms, only five anxiety subjects and two headache subjects visited the health center during the three posttreatment months.

These initial results, although striking, must be viewed with caution. There were no control groups in the study. Therefore, one cannot conclude with certainty that similar results would not have been obtained if the subjects had been, for example, placed on drugs (or a "new" drug with potential placebo effects). Furthermore, the follow-up period is short. On the other hand, only subjects who had longstanding symptoms were selected, and all subjects were currently being seen for traditional biomedical treatment. This argues in favor of the interpretation that sizable decreases in headaches and anxiety observed in these patients were due, at least in part, to the comprehensive stress management program.

Manuso is careful to consider the cost-benefit aspects of this work.

> The estimated average annual pretreatment corporate costs of employing one person with chronic anxiety or headache was found to be \$3,394.50. The costs to corporation of an experimental subject–employee are considerable though not patently obvious. The costs involved four factors: namely, visits to the Employee Health Center (\$473.14), time away from the job in order to visit the Health Center (\$56.61), work interference due to symptoms (\$2,206.95), and meta-interference affecting bosses (\$72.80), co-workers (\$542.88) and subordinates (\$42.12). These costs were present even though subjects were receiving traditional medical treatment, involving diagnosis, prescription of appropriate medications and follow-up by a physician. It will be noted that absenteeism figures are conspicuously absent from this accounting. This is because, on the average, Anxiety and Headache subjects were absent only 4.27 days per year, which is not significantly different from the overall corporate average of 3.92 (two-tail Z = 1.00).
>
> The estimated average annual post-treatment corporate costs of employing one person with chronic anxiety or headache were found to amount to \$532.68. These costs, when compared to the corresponding pretreatment costs, indicate average savings of \$2,861.82 annually per subject. By extrapolation, the expected 3-year savings to the corporation afforded by reduced symptom activity for all 30 subjects would amount to \$202,945.05 minus the cost treatment of \$24,622.50, which equals \$178,322.55. Whereas earlier work (Manuso, 1978) indicated a 1:3 cost–benefit ratio, taking into account a 23% dropout rate, the present research suggests that the ratio averages 1:5.52 for each of the first three years following treatment. This represents a considerable return on investment.

These figures must be viewed as tentative, and they are probably overly optimistic. They do, however, illustrate the potential for stress management programs to have some cost as well as clinical effectiveness. They also point to the need for more comprehensive clinical studies to be conducted in the future.

SUGGESTIONS FOR THE FUTURE

With our current knowledge, it is appropriate to consider incorporating various stress management techniques into occupational settings on an experimental basis. Despite the promise of present findings, much needs to be learned through future research that is relevant to industry, labor, and science. Although it is tempting to simply bring some stress management consultants into an industrial setting to conduct a program or two, this approach will not prove valuable in the long run. What is needed are clinical research studies in which relevant health and work variables are measured concurrently, with appropriate short-term and long-term evaulation included as a necessary component of the program. Evaluation should not be viewed as necessary only for the initial developmental stages of such programs. Rather, evaluation (both clinical and cost-effective) should be incorporated as a standard component of such programs if future research proves them to be valuable in occupational settings.

Clearly, industry needs to consider how it can promote stress management (as well as health more broadly) by changing its incentive structure. In fact, it may even prove cost-effective to reinforce workers to take "relaxation breaks" (Peters, Benson, and Porter, 1977; Peters, Benson, and Peters, 1977), which may take a variety of forms (including mental and physical relaxation exercises, plus other recreational-relaxing activities). It may prove cost-effective also to change the work setting to better match the needs and physiological limits of the people working in the settings. It is probable that labor will resist simple stress management programs if these programs are offered in the absence of other needed changes in work settings. Requiring the worker to continue to cope with more and more job stress is not a final solution. At some point the strain will become too great, and everyone (both management and labor) will suffer the consequences. Industry must strive toward reaching a balance between the requirements of the work setting and the worker's capacity to meet those requirements. Industry could make a major contribution to society at large by providing an incentive for health behavior.

Stress management should not be isolated. Stress management training can have positive spinoffs, such as reducing drug usage, improving diet, and promoting exercise. Moreover, health programs aimed specifically at changing drug usage (including cigarettes and alcohol), diet, and exercise can have positive spinoffs by helping persons cope with stress. As noted by Benson (1975), Carrington (1977), and Meichenbaum (1977), stress management is a skill useful to any person. The work setting is but one setting, albeit a significant one, where such skills are of value. It should also be recognized that stress management need not be viewed only as a means of preventing illness, but also as a means of promoting health. Many of the relaxation and cognitive exercises are inherently pleasant and bring other personal rewards, as does regular exercise.

As noted by Manuso (1981) one way that industry may be able to promote the development of stress management programs is to offer predoctoral or postdoctoral fellowships in clinical and health psychology and related disciplines. Most clinical psychologists, for example, do not have experience in occupational settings. To encourage psychologists and other health professionals to apply their skills to problems relevant to occupational settings, a training-incentive program should be established. It should be recognized that developing such internship programs is also cost-effective in that interns typically work more hours for less pay as part of the training experience. Nurses and physicians also can be trained to administer some types of stress management programs, and this option too should be pursued.

It is not possible to present in this chapter detailed suggestions regarding specific directions for future research and applications, including possible alternative structures for incorporating stress management programs into occupational settings. However, I have provided a general introduction to the problems and promise of stress management as applied to occupational settings. The challenge is becoming clear. Whether the challenge will be met depends on the cooperation and collaboration of industry, labor, government, and the behavioral and biomedical sciences in the context of the emerging field of behavioral medicine (Schwartz and Weiss, 1978a, b).

REFERENCES

Benson, H. 1975. *The Relaxation Response*. New York: William Morrow.

Carrington, P. 1977. *Freedom in Meditation*. New York: Doubleday.

Chadwick, J.H., M.A. Chesney, and M. Feuerstein. 1981. *Psychological Job Stress and Coronary Heart Disease*. National Institute of Occupational Safety and Health, Cincinnati, Ohio.

Chesney, M.A. and Feuerstein, M. 1979. "Behavioral Medicine in the Occupational Setting." In *Behavioral Medicine*, edited by J. McNamara. Kalamazoo, Mich.: Behaviordelia.

Dutton, L.M., et al. 1978. "Stress Level of Ambulance Paramedics and Fire Fighters." *Journal of Occupational Medicine* 20: 111–15.

Eysenck, H.J. and S.B.G. Eysenck. 1968. *Eysenck Personality Inventory*. Education and Testing Service, San Diego, Calif.

Goleman, D.J. and G.E. Schwartz. 1976. "Mediation as an Intervention in Stress Reactivity." *Journal of Clinical Consulting Psychology* 44: 45–466.

Holmes, T.H. and R.H. Rahe. 1967. "The Social Readjustment Scale." *Journal of Psychosomatic Research* 11: 213–18.

Jacobson, E. 1938. *Progressive Relaxation*. Chicago: University of Chicago Press.

Kasl, S.V. and S. Cobb. 1970. "Blood Pressure Changes in Men Undergoing Job Loss: A Preliminary Report." *Psychosomatic Medicine* 32: 19–39.

Manuso, J. 1981. "Psychological Services and Health Enhancement: A Corporate Model." In *Linking Health and Mental Health: Coordinating Care in the Community* (vol. 2, Sage Annual Reviews of Community Mental Health), edited by A. Broskowski, et al. Beverly Hills, Calif.: Sage.

Mason, J. 1975. "A Historical View of the Stress Field." *Journal of Human Stress* 1: 6–12.

McLean, A. Ed. 1974. *Occupational Stress.* Springfield, Ill.: Charles C. Thomas.

McLean, A. Ed. 1977. *Reducing Occupational Stress.* Proceedings of a conference. DHEW Publication No. (NIOSH) 78-140. U.S. Government Printing Office, Washington, D.C.

———. 1979. *How to Reduce Occupational Stress.* Lexington, Mass.: Addison-Wesley.

Meichenbaum, D. 1977. *Cognitive-Behavior Modification.* New York: Plenum.

Moos, R.H., P.M. Insel, and B. Humphrey. 1974. *Work Environment Scale.* Palo Alto, Calif.: Consulting Psychologists.

Novaco, R. 1975. *Anger Control: The Development and Evaluation of an Experimental Treatment.* Lexington, Mass.: D.C. Heath.

Peters, R.K., H. Benson, and J.M. Peters. 1977. "Daily Relaxation Response Breaks in a Working Population. II. Effects on Blood Pressure." *American Journal of Public Health* 67: 954–59.

Peters, R.K., H. Benson, and D. Porter. 1977. "Daily Relaxation Response Breaks in a Working Population. I. Effects on Self-Reported Measures of Health, Performance and Well-Being." *American Journal of Public Health* 67: 946–53.

Schultz, J.H. and W. Luthe. 1969. *Autogenic Training: A Psychophysiological Approach in Psychotherapy*. New York: Grune and Stratton.

Schwartz, G.E. 1977. "Psychosomatic Disorders and Biofeedback: A Psychobiological Model of Disregulation." In *Psychopathology: Experimental Models,* edited by J.D. Maser and M.E.P. Seligman. San Francisco: W.H Freeman.

———. 1978. "Research and Feedback in Clinical Practice: A Commentary on Responsible Biofeedback Therapy." In *Biofeedback: Principles and Practices for Clinicians,* edited by J. Basmajian. Baltimore: William and Wilkins.

Schwartz, G.E. and J. Beatty. Ed. 1977. *Biofeedback: Theory and Research.* New York: Academic Press.

Schwartz, G.E. and S.M. Weiss. 1978a. "Behavioral Medicine Revisited: An Amended Definition." *Journal of Behavioral Medicine* 1: 249–52.

Schwartz, G.E. and S.M. Weiss. 1978b. *Proceedings of the Yale Conference on Behavioral Medicine.* DHEW Publication No. (NIH) 78-1424. U.S. Government Printing Office, Washington, D.C.

Selye, H. 1956. *The Stress of Life*. New York: McGraw-Hill.

———. 1976. *Stress in Health and Disease*. Wolburn, Me.: Butterworths.

Silver, B.V. and E.B. Blanchard. 1978. "Biofeedback and Relaxation Training in the Treatment of Psychophysiological Disorders: Or Are the Machines Really Necessary?" *Journal of Behavioral Medicine* 1: 217–39.

Turk, D. 1976. "An Expanded Skills Training Approach for the Treatment of Experimentally Induced Pain." Doctoral dissertation, University of Waterloo, Ontario.

Weiman, C.G. 1977. "A Study of Occupational Stressor and the Incidence of Disease Risk." *Journal of Occupational Medicine* 19: 119–122.

Weiner, H. 1977. *Psychobiology and Human Disease*. New York: American Elsevier.

Williams, R.B. and W.D. Gentry. Ed. 1977. *Behavioral Approaches to Medical Treatment*. Cambridge, Mass.: Ballinger.

Zorn, E.W., J.M. Harrington, and H. Goethe. 1977. "Ischemic Heart Disease and Work Stress in West German Sea Pilots." *Journal of Occupational Medicine* 19: 762–65.

20 The StayWell Program: Health Enhancement at Work

Murray P. Naditch, Ph.D.

The rate of disability and death from chronic degenerative diseases has reached epidemic proportions in the United States and in other industrialized countries. More than half of all deaths in the United States are accounted for by cardiovascular diseases alone. The major drop in deaths caused by acute infectious diseases between 1900 and 1970 has been accompanied by a rise of more than 250 percent in deaths from major chronic diseases such as stroke, heart disease, and cancer during that period (Califano, 1979). The Surgeon General's report on health promotion and disease prevention calls for a second public health revolution, a movement that will focus on today's major killers such as heart disease, cancer, and stroke by affecting the lifestyles or habits that relate to the etiology of these diseases. There is an emerging consensus that the most efficacious way to reduce unnecessary death and illness in the United States is to focus on our lifestyles—the cigarettes we smoke, the food we eat, the exercise we don't get, and the safety practices that we ignore.

The growing consensus on the part of government, academic, and public health institutions on the efficacy of prevention in stemming the tide of chronic degenerative diseases in the United States has been accompanied by heightened awareness and a more active role by corporations in the private sector focusing on this problem. Programs of focused lifestyle change in organizational settings represent a unique coming together of opportunities for effective intervention as well as for more effective collaboration between academia, public health, and the private sector.

Organizational settings provide a unique opportunity for intervention because of access to populations who spend a significant portion of their lives assembled in one place. Health lifestyle change programs in a workplace setting provide potential cost effectiveness advantages as well as a unique opportunity for designing effective programs. Workplace settings allow programs to focus on changes in the work culture itself that have a major impact on health behaviors and the opportunity to foster a highly supportive environment in which to initiate and maintain positive health behaviors.

Corporations themselves are very interested in lifestyle change programs because these programs offer corporations the chance to introduce programs that are perceived very positively by individual employees to make profitable investments in the health and performance of their own employees. In addition to concerns that corporations have about the welfare of their employees, there are some clear economic advantages to the introduction of workplace programs of lifestyle change. Although the hard data is not in, it would appear to most analysts a very good bet that workplace programs will turn out to be a profitable investment for those companies that introduce them. Health care costs have become a major area of expenditure for most U.S. companies. The spiraling costs of health care in the United States is borne mainly by U.S. corporations. Health care spending in the United States has gone from $27 billion in 1962 to an estimated $212.5 billion in 1980 (Kaplan, 1980). These spiraling health care costs have resulted in health care premiums increasing by as much as 20 percent annually for the last few years. To the extent that lifestyle change intervention programs affect mortality and morbidity, they represent one possibly very cost-effective way of stemming the tide of these health care costs.

Cost savings that could potentially accrue to a company that implements a health lifestyle change program include direct health care costs as well as replacement costs for key personnel and costs associated with work performance. It has been estimated that it costs between $250,000 and $500,000 to replace an upper level manager (Harris, 1978). Delay or prevention of a premature coronary incident among one or two upper level managers could more than pay for the total costs for a lifestyle change program for all of a company's employees.

Productivity has also been a key concern in recent years among the nation's employers. One hypothesis being tested in a number of settings is whether lifestyle intervention programs may be a cost-effective way of increasing productivity. Lifestyle change intervention programs may result in decreased absenteeism and turnover, decreased downtime spent in smoking behavior, and improved employee satisfaction with the company's benefits program.

A number of companies have initiated wellness programs in recent years. These include substantial programs on the part of Johnson & Johnson, Equitable Life, and Control Data. The largest and most comprehensive effort in this area has been the StayWell program at Control Data Corporation (CDC).

Control Data initiated its StayWell program on a pilot basis in two cities in 1979 and has delivered the program to approximately 14,000 of its employees and their spouses in 12 U.S. cities as of 1981. Control Data Corporation plans to offer the program as a free corporation benefit to all of its employees and their spouses in 1984.

THE RISK INTERVENTION MODEL

The Control Data program is based on the premise and evidence that lifestyle and behavior have an important impact on health and that individuals can be helped to change those harmful behaviors. The focus of the program is on long-term changes in behavior. Although there are major awareness and educational aspects of the program, the key emphasis is on assisting people in creating the skills that they need to change their behaviors and on creating an environment in the workplace conducive to the initiation and maintenance of positive lifestyle behaviors. The program focuses on five key risk areas: smoking cessation; weight control; nutritional practices related to reduction in cholesterol, salt, and sugar; fitness behavior; and stress management.

Successful implementation of a major wellness program such as StayWell requires cooperation and endorsement of middle as well as upper management. StayWell is initiated at each new plant with an extensive presite preparation phase that begins months before employees are introduced to the program. A key element in that phase is an extensive communication program for managers, consisting of special management orientations and individual contact by key members of the StayWell team. The objective is not only to help management understand the purpose and nature of the program, but also to enlist an active management support. Every effort is made to enlist managers as program participants so that they can serve as role models for employees. Communication between managers and StayWell staff is a two-way street. Implementation of the program is planned in order to minimize any disruption of work schedules and to accommodate needs of each facility.

This period of intense preparation is followed by a promotion and orientation program for employees. Employees receive two mailings informing them about the program. The mailings are followed by special orientation sessions, during which employees and spouses learn about the program and have the opportunity to enroll. The orientations focus on positive benefits of lifestyle change and explain the program to employees. Employee enrollment in the program has been very high and ranges from 65 to 95 percent of the work force, with higher enrollment at sites where people do less traveling.

Those employees who do enroll in the program are scheduled for a health screening session. At that screening a professional health team collects data on each participant, including blood pressure, height, weight, health history, lifestyle, and a small sample of blood. Data from the health screening are used to generate a confidential health risk profile.

The health risk profile is a computer-generated analysis of each participant's most significant health risks. Each participant receives a report that compares their chronological age with their risk age (how old they really are in terms of risk) and their achievable age (how old they could be if they decide to make the appropriate changes in their health-related behaviors.)

Control Data has a very strict confidentiality policy. No one at the company has access to any individual data, except a physician who reviews the data for abnormalities. Individual participants decide when they register for the program whether they would like any findings suggesting potential abnormality sent to their personal physician.

Health risk profiles are interpreted for employees at group interpretation workshops. Workshops help individuals identify their health risks and suggest specific actions. After completing the interpretation workshops, StayWell participants can enroll in a variety of activities related to their individual needs. These activities include: educational and lifestyle change courses, support groups, and a variety of other group activities.

The program includes a series of one-hour wellness education courses. These courses heighten awareness and assist employees in becoming more knowledgeable about the relation of lifestyle to health. These courses include such topics as self-health management, coronary heart disease, hypertension, breast self-examination, and alcohol.

Lifestyle change courses are longer, more comprehensive workshops that teach employees the skills they need to change life-long habits such as smoking and improper eating habits. There are lifestyle change courses on smoking cessation, stress management, weight control, nutrition, and fitness. Courses are taught by health educators, psychologists, exercise physiologists, and other health professionals trained by CDC to deliver the program.

A unique part of the Control Data StayWell program is the social support activities offered through the employee participation groups. These groups are composed of employees and spouses who are interested in taking a more active leadership role in the program. The purpose of these groups is to change the worksite environment in a manner that will create norms and expectations about more positive health-related activities on the part of employees.

Participation group activities can take the form of task forces in which groups of employees work with the company to change some part of the work environment to make it more conducive to positive health-related behaviors. Employees have formed task forces to change food in vending machines for more nutritious selections; to initiate classes in low calorie cooking or aerobic dancing; to form clubs for activities such as running, walking, hiking, bicycling, and cross country skiing; and to promote a large number of other health-related activities.

Other employees have joined support groups. Support groups are formed at the end of each lifestyle change course. These groups assist members in implementing, continuing, and maintaining the difficult job of changing health-related behaviors. Support group activities include group sharing of experiences, innoculation against failure techniques, and other activities whose purpose is to provide a supportive, sympathetic environment in which to continue to initiate or maintain hard won changes in health behavior habits.

There has been a strong positive response on the part of employees to participation group activities. Approximately five times as many people have become involved in participation group activities as there are enrolled in courses.

Participation groups are open to all employees whether they are enrolled in StayWell or not. In sites where the StayWell program is working most effectively participation group activity is usually highly visible. These activities are very attractive to employees; they increase awareness, establish positive health related norms, and attract employees into the program who may not have joined solely because of a desire to modify behaviors that put them at risk for chronic degenerative diseases. Participation groups give people an opportunity to socially interact with one another, extend opportunities for program entry, and give people an opportunity to build a program momentum at a particular worksite.

Orientation and screening sessions are on company time. Interpretation workshops, courses, and participation group activities are on the employee's time. Most classes and activities take place during the lunch break, although activities are also offered before or after work.

PROGRAM EVALUATION

The evaluation includes formative as well as summative components. The formative component of the evaluation focuses on various aspects of the program and how well they are working. The summative evaluation focuses on changes in attitudes, health related behaviors and behaviors related to productivity, and actual health care costs.

The evaluation design focuses on examining long-term changes in health related behaviors that are affected by the program. Participants are tracked for a minimum of 36 months in the program, and there are plans to track some participants for a considerably longer period.

Attitudes and behaviors are measured through a variety of self-report assessments. One unique approach to the collection of this data is through the use of a health diary. Control Data Corporation has collaborated with Arbitron, a wholly owned subsidiary company, to develop and implement individual health diaries. Arbitron is one of the leading companies in the collection of data related to media use through diaries. Cooperative work with Arbitron has produced a health behavior diary currently administered by Arbitron separately to program participants, their spouses, children of employees, nonparticipants and their families, as well as to a national sample of non-Control Data people. Psychophysiological measures are also included as part of the health risk profile on a yearly basis.

Changes in baseline attitudes, behaviors, and health costs in StayWell sites among participants and nonparticipants are compared to individual responses from employees who are at matched control sites. Control sites are matched to experimental sites in order to examine urban versus rural differences and manufacturing versus white collar facilities and to include reasonable race, age, and sex heterogeneity in the population.

RETURN ON INVESTMENT MODEL

A major premise underlying workplace health promotion programs is that those programs will be cost-effective for the companies who sponsor them. Control Data Corporation is in a unique position to assess the cost effectiveness of the StayWell program because the company is self-insured and processes its own health care insurance claims. The health care claims data base has been included as part of the StayWell evaluation process, and the program is currently examining the relation between behavioral risks and health care costs and the relation between changes in health related behaviors and health care costs borne by the company.

This evaluation is being done in the context of a mathematical simulation model. The health care cost saving simulation model uses data from a variety of sources in order to estimate both the long-range as well as the short-range impact of the StayWell intervention. The model uses epidemiological and health economic data to estimate the future cost savings inherent in behavior change occurring in a one- to two-year period. For example, if the intervention impacts chronic degenerative diseases such as heart disease, the potential cost savings would only show up after a considerable number of years have elapsed. By using epidemiological data, the model estimates what changes in the disease rate will look like as a function of stable changes in behavior. The model defines stable changes in behavior as behavior changes that have lasted for 12 months or longer.

For example, the effect of StayWell on smoking behavior and the costs of that intervention are estimated using Control Data Corporation data. The effect of changed smoking behavior is then linked to lung cancer and heart disease rates using epidemiological data. The long-run cost impact of StayWell on lung cancer rates and heart disease rates can be projected directly from these calculations using costs associated with various disease entities from health economics data. The model looks at the cost savings inherent in changes in health behavior as cost savings inherent in decreased absenteeism, hiring, training, and other indirect costs.

The mathematical model allows the company to vary assumptions underlying the model and to look for the sensitivity of those assumptions on the cost-effectiveness projections. For example, if a 20 percent smoking cessation rate is projected in the model, the model allows the company to see what impact a 10 percent or a 30 percent smoking cessation rate would have on its return on investment.

QUALITIES ASSOCIATED WITH AN EFFECTIVE LIFESTYLE CHANGE PROGRAM IN AN INDUSTRIAL SETTING

There are at least five attributes of a sound lifestyle change program in an industrial setting that are overlooked in many programs and, thus, warrant further discussion. To have a maximum probability of success, a workplace program should:

1. Focus on behavior change, not just information dissemination.
2. Focus on long-term, rather than short-term changes in health related behaviors.
3. Be designed so that it attempted to affect the cultural context for health behaviors and not just individual behavior.
4. Be part of a long-term evolutionary process in which rigorous evaluation data and continued improvements in design result in a continually more effective program.

Focus on Behavior Change

Programs of health behavior change are attempting to change deeply held lifelong habits. Many industrial programs are based primarily on increased awareness, education, and information dissemination. Although these aspects of a program are very important, most people who are overweight or who smoke are already aware of the potential adversive consequences of these health related behaviors and would like to be able to change these behaviors. An effective program has to provide skills training, social support for change, and maintenance of new behaviors, as well as a supportive social environment.

Focus on Long-term Changes in Behavior

Long-term positive changes in health behaviors are often much more difficult to achieve than short-term changes. Most people who are able to stop smoking are smoking again within a year. Most people who lose weight gain it back. Consequently, both program structures and program evaluation have to focus on the effectiveness of long-term changes in behavior. In the StayWell program, for example, the maintenance phase includes support groups as well as a variety of other activities that keep the behavior change issue salient, teach individual innoculation coping strategies to handle the inevitable setbacks and failures, and use peer support to create a supportive environment to initiate and continue change.

Emphasis on Cultural and Normative Change

Cultural norms about health related behaviors exert an extremely powerful influence on an individual's behavior in any sociocultural setting. Workplace norms about health related behavior are very important in influencing and maintaining both positive and negative health related behaviors. A program that focuses exclusively on individual changes in behavior and ignores social and cultural aspects of the behavior change process has a greatly reduced chance for success. Individuals may make heroic attempts to change their behavior, only to have normative pressures and expectations erode hard won progress in health behavior change. In an industrial setting, for example, it is often normative to have high calorie, high cholesterol food in the cafeterias and vending machines or pastries at mid-morning coffee break. It is difficult for an individual to stay on an effective program of weight control in a nonsupportive environment.

The issue of individual change in a cultural context has been discussed in a number of articles (Allen, 1980). At least two workplace programs have a culture change focus; both the Control Data program and the Johnson & Johnson program do place emphasis on this issue. In the Control Data program, for example, volunteer employees take an active role in the program through task forces organized by the program. These volunteer groups promote changes in the workplace environment as well as influence norms about health related behaviors.

Some evidence is beginning to accumulate in the Control Data program that health related normative behavior in StayWell sites has begun to change in a positive direction after the first 12 months of the program. Perceptions of health related norms are more positive at the implementation (experimental) sites than in the control sites after the first year. At the implementation sites, perceived normative change was strongest among employees enrolled in the program. There were also significant changes of a lesser magnitude among nonenrolled employees in the implementation sites. This latter finding suggests that cultural changes in the worksite are at least perceived by, and therefore likely to affect, nonprogram as well as program enrollees.

Commitment to Long-term Program Evolution

Workplace health behavior change programs must be successful in creating positive health behavior change as well as be cost-effective. Programs will have to be shown to produce more cost savings to companies than they cost to implement if these programs are to disseminate to large numbers of sponsoring companies. Industrial organization-based programs that make inappropriate claims of potential effectiveness or that are put together on a one-time basis may do a major disservice to this field of endeavor. A program of health behavior change in an industrial setting that is effective in changing and assisting people in changing behavior over the long term and that can be shown to be a cost-effective intervention will take many years to develop and will occur in an evolutionary manner. This type of program evolution will require that programs can be implemented with state-of-the-art knowledge, rigorously evaluated, and that this evaluation data be used to modify and change the program in order to make it more effective.

The evolutionary aspect of behavior change programs in industrial settings offers a unique opportunity for collaboration between academicians, programs of public health, and the private sector. Clearly, the evolution of knowledge in this area is related to the same basic fundamental factors related to the evolution of knowledge in any scientific area. Sound theory, rigorous testing of hypotheses, and cumulative knowledge from a series of trials are essential if there is to be significant advances in the state of knowledge in the field. In the Control Data StayWell program, for example, design of the program content and its evaluation has been done in collaboration with a number of major academic institutions and scientists in the field of behavioral medicine. CDC expects to publish the results of evaluation studies and to continue to redesign, evaluate, and evolve various aspects of that program for five to ten years.

FUTURE DEVELOPMENTS

Control Data is currently designing and developing a *computer managed program* of health behavior change. That program uses unique aspects of computer technology to enable it to solve some problems that cannot be effectively solved with more traditional kinds of programs. It is a highly individualized, tailored approach to behavior change in which individuals are matched with the programs most likely to be effective for them. Programs are also modified during the course of any particular individual's participation as a function of that person's behavior change and compliance to the program.

Increased recognition of the importance of individual differences in response to health behavior change programs is an often cited area of needed inquiry in behavioral medicine. Clinically and academically based programs have not been able to respond to this obvious need to more individually tailored programs because most clinical samples are too small to perform the kinds of complex, multivariate analysis required to determine which interventions work with what kinds of people to what extent. Control Data has a large enough population of people who will be using the computer managed program (in excess of 20,000) to be able to match preprogram individual differences and within-program behaviors to outcome measures. Matching of individual differences to programs will be systematically updated based on the efficacy of success predictions in earlier trials.

The computer managed program also enables effective branching and effective program differentiation because various combinations and permutations of program approaches are tailored and delivered to people in a highly individualized manner. The Control Data Corporation computer based approach also enables people to have more frequent access to support groups via the computer.

REFERENCES

Allen, R.F. 1980. "The Corporate Health-Buying Spree: Boon or Boondoggle?" *S.A.M. Advanced Management Journal* (Spring).

Califano, J.A. 1979. *Healthy People. The Surgeon General's Report on Health Promotion and Disease Prevention.* U.S. Department of Health, Education and Welfare, Public Health Service.

Harris, L. and Associates, Inc. 1978. *Health Maintenance*. Pacific Mutual Life Insurance Company.

Kaplan, J. 1980. "Wellness Epidemic Sweeps Companies." *Business Insurance* (September).

21 NEXUS

Donald M. Michael, John O'Neil and Kenneth R. Pelletier, Ph.D.

It has never been clear how the behavioral sciences were meant to work together in attacking lively social issues. Clinical psychology has turned its intervention strategies toward the individual, and it has been more than easy to leave to sociology the study of organizations and the larger society. Obviously, the science of psychology is stretched in its yearnings to learn more about the inner workings of humankind, and it is hardly fair to criticize its inadequacies regarding the treatment of the individual within a contextual framework.

Social scientists discovered the importance of motivation (Roethlisberger & Dickson, 1939), leadership style (White & Lippitt, 1960), and informal social groupings (Homans, 1950; Miller & Rice, 1967) on productivity and morale. Regularities in intragroup processes were found, and two crucial dimensions of work group processes—task and maintenance (social-emotional) functions—were identified (Bales, 1950). The National Training Laboratories and the Institute for Social Research of the University of Michigan developed laboratory methods for interpersonal skills training and led the way in applying laboratory findings and methods to business and to human services agencies. Methods for attitude surveying and data feedback were developed and refined. Scientist-practitioners eventually developed guidelines for human process consultants (Argyris, 1970; Beckhard, 1969; Bennis, 1969). Organizational development, the utilization of a variety of human processes, and structural interventions that are designed to improve both morale and productivity became popular in the private sector and subsequently in human service agencies. By mid-century, managers were frequently using consultants to assist them in such interpersonal processes as leadership, communications, group relations, and conflict. The technological, social, and psychological processes of organizations became accepted domains for consultation (Gallessich, 1982). Recently, the work of Seymour Sarason at Yale on the organization as health affecting (1972, 1977) and the work being done by Kenneth R. Pelletier (1979, 1981, 1982) on the efficacy of institutional health programs have focused on the importance of the organization as a factor in individual health.

At the present time, there is a revolution taking place in every aspect of individual and organizational life. In every discipline, ranging from recombinant DNA to corporate management, it is evident that we are shifting rapidly away from a mechanistic, reductionistic, cause and effect view of the universe toward one that is systemic, vital, and having an emphasis upon interconnections and interdependence. All of this would remain an academic exercise if it were not for the fact that this shift toward a more holistic view of ourselves and the world around us already has had such dramatic, pragmatic, and practical consequences as: (1) a recognition of planetary ecology; (2) ethical and moral issues raised by basic laboratory sciences, for example, recombinant DNA–the Manhattan Project of the next decade; (3) an economics based upon nonmaterial wealth and voluntary simplicity where the quality of life reigns over the quantity of salary; (4) an extraordinary move in health sciences away from a fixation on biomedical technology and pathology management to a true health care system; and innumerable other examples ranging from molecules to multinational corporations, in the greater context of organizations and a dynamic social system. Central to this shift in world view has been the role of "leaders" who envision the future and in that vision also have the unique ability to actually implement pragmatic changes. In essence this is the function of the archetypal hero and for the new world leaders. However, the perils and tolls exacted for being such a leader are staggering.

It is the organization leaders who today have the responsibility for integration of the conflicting values and needs of our pluralistic society (Drucker, 1980). Their challenge: to go beyond a "satisfied" policy (Simon, 1947). The incipient power of the leader in large-scale organizations has been rediscovered as both the failures of large scale institutions and the inadequacies of management theory have crashed into one another. A recent book by Pascal and Athos, *The Art of Japanese Management* (1981) discusses seven "s's" of leadership: strategy, structure, systems, superordinate goals, skills, style, and staffing. The authors tell us that the last four–which they term the "soft s's"–have been neglected by U.S. scholars and practitioners. As a result, we have witnessed the phenomenon of Japan becoming a giant in world commerce, while the United States and other countries have reeled under unprecedented inflation and a feeling of lost confidence. In actuality, the success of Japan is an illusion, for there are many factors contributing to that success that would not be viable or desirable in the United States where individualism reigns over regimentation. Virtually every study has found deficiencies in the way management is carried out in the United States, and although other factors, ranging from inappropriate depreciation tables to a psychological ennui, are involved in a productivity/motivation crisis gripping this country's industrial machine, these deficiencies are seen as paramount. According to Pascal and Athos, "Let us avoid false expectations. We may not expect to borrow wholesale and directly from the Japanese . . . but we can incorporate some of their approach which will strengthen our areas of weakness." That is a deceptively simple task. Simple because it can be achieved quite readily—as quickly as a shift from figure to ground perception. Deceptive because doing it requires a shift in how we see ourselves, our role as leaders, and the effect of viewing our organizations and society as interrelated systems.

John Gardner has assured us that there is something emerging in the way of problem definition which we shall call "the leader's dilemma." It seems to have three parts: (1) the leader possesses too many options and too few guidelines for decision making; (2) the leader senses a loss of organizational vitality in himself; (3) the leader pursues the mission of the organization with great enthusiasm but, in the pursuit, loses his regard for the whole of society.

Such tendencies or symptoms leave wide open the questions of serious psychological breaks. Management literature tends to describe the individual within the organization in either one of two modes: productive or not productive. But what are the subtle psychological factors at work in the blinding variety of complexities that exist between the individual, the organization, and the larger society? Our earth's environmental turbulence and pressures from contradictory ideologies are tremendous. Sound decisions are difficult because of constant changes, the multitude of relevant factors to be considered, and conflicting values.

Traditionally and conventionally, leadership—in the West particularly—developed in response to and contributed to a world view of things as separate from one another, whether it was the state and the nation, business and government, person and organization, or as psychological variables. Psychologists seemed to have an image of a human being as a bag full of separate balls each labeled as a variable. In that kind of a world, individuals think of themselves as separate from their setting. "I am me; I do my own thing." Indeed this was the whole mode of the 1960s and 1970s. It was a world in which scientific information gained through social or physical research was going to enlighten us because it would give us knowledge of causes and effects. A competent leader would know the relation between causes and effects. A leader, thereby, could control the situation whether it was comprised of people, finances, products, or whatever. Because the world was seen as comprised of separate causes producing separate effects it was also a linear world: the natural way to structure relationships between humans and their environment or between humans and humans was hierarchically. This structure fit a linear mode of control where a competent leader was one who could "command" causes in order to produce specific effects.

Lastly, it was a world in which progress was by and large inevitable: things were expected to get better because more knowledge, brought to bear on more issues, would improve the situation. That, then, was the world view in which the traditional concept of power developed as it was applied. For the most part, it is still how the world is perceived and how power is applied.

What is the world today and as far as any of us are concerned, what is the world in which leaders must be competent? What does power mean now? It is a world of limits to growth, a world needing the attention of both the left and right globes of our brains, a world better managed via Japanese management style. It is a world wherein everything is connected to everything else; everything is interdependent: where one can't do just one thing at a time, or where one should be concerned, if one is going to be effective, with everything–ranging from what is going on inside of oneself to what is going on on a planetary scale. It is a world where everything is multiply caused and where seeking to attend to, to control, a simple course, results in unanticipated reverberations. Therefore, social research not withstanding, one cannot identify outcomes as due exclusively to any finite set of causes. It is a blurred world where causes aren't clear and effects aren't clear. It is a world, ironically, where information leads to *more* uncertainty rather than less. Understandably, this came as a great and unpleasant surprise to a lot of people who predicted that computers were going to make life easier for executives because they would have more information, hence more control capability. It is a world, then, where more information leads to less felt control (and usually less actual control) and thereby to more uncertainty. It is a world where progress is highly problematic, no longer to be taken for granted–a world that holds hopes both for the future and is full of potential disasters. It is certainly not a world where progress can be assumed.

Thus, this is the world in which leaders aspire to be competent: a world where the burdens of leadership are increasingly arduous, where the question, "How can I be meaningful?" is facing more and more leaders in all organizations.

What has been the responses of psychology and behavioral sciences generally to these problems of leadership? First, many of the responses have been mechanistic, especially those related to measuring and matching workers to the job to be done. While modern theorists bemoan Taylorism, it seems that at times we have simply brought Taylor's bizarre notions to a sophisticated extreme. Second, in spite of the proliferation of psychologically oriented management consultants, psychology has failed to have an impact on management because of its simplistic concepts and reliance on packaged solutions. Macho leaders not only fail to get help, but fail to understand the nature of psychological trouble. Third, as Warren Bennis has reminded us in recent times, the people charged with bringing the behavioral sciences' contributions into organizations are often obtuse and overly theoretical and have little sense of the overall organization. Many behavioral scientists eschew finance, production, marketing, and the other disciplines that are central to the vitality of the organization.

Lately, a movement focused on bridging psychology and leadership has been gathering momentum. Its unit of study is not the effect of organizations on individuals; rather, it is interested in the effect of the individual, particularly the leader, on the organization. It seeks through psychosocial experience to empower the leader to create more effective organizations and healthier members.

A leader in this movement is the California NEXUS Foundation, which was established early in 1981 by the California School of Professional Psychology, based in San Francisco. Through a program of seminars and research undertakings, NEXUS seeks to explore and to foster new ways of promoting psychological health among leaders and their organizations. Its approach can be described as follows:

1. Institutional leaders and behavioral scientists as well as other scholars come together to work on the common problems of organizational and social malaise and lowered productivity of the leader. There is an agreement that there are no packaged answers.

2. The leaders and their colleagues from the behavioral sciences focus on the positive aspects of psychological intervention rather than the disease-oriented approach of the medical model.

3. Organizations are examined as very special cultures beset by extremely complex problems that must be approached with great respect by various disciplines. In many of the NEXUS seminars, philosophers, system specialists, organization development practitioners, planning experts, and anthropologists work with psychologists and leaders in a common assault on the elusive problems of leadership.

The California NEXUS Foundation sees itself as providing research and training for the next generation of professionals involved in organizational change. These professionals, in NEXUS' view, will not be simply extruded versions of clinical psychologists. Rather, they will be specially trained, hydra-headed, well-balanced professionals.

For those leaders who want to serve, who seek to be meaningful in an interdependent world of multiple causes where the old mode of control doesn't make sense because it won't work, NEXUS is helping leaders begin to shift from defining their competence as dependent on their ability to control to using their ability to enhance society's resilience. (Resilience isn't the same as control, in that old rigid linear sense; it is a kind of survival mode where you learn as you go.)

At first, NEXUS sought those leaders who were in pain. They were recruited by a sort of snowball procedure, beginning with those known to NEXUS organizers; through them, others were contacted. Over time, the NEXUS seminars attracted other leaders who were not in pain but who were well aware that things would have to be different, including what they themselves were to become: meaningfully effective in a turbulent society and in their organizations.

The typical NEXUS seminar is a three-day experience, involving about 15 leaders and six faculty, plus supporting staff. The location is a comfortable, attractive, natural setting, preferably in an isolated location. This kind of setting is arranged so that participants and faculty share amenities and have an opportunity to become acquainted in low-key, informal surroundings. (Indeed, in some settings to date, participants have helped each other prepare breakfast.) The word "faculty" is perhaps a misnomer. In fact, NEXUS has not found an appropriate term to differentiate those who pay to participate and those who are paid to participate. The former are powerful contributors in their own right and expect to be. The latter have as much to learn as they have to teach.

However, faculty members are expected to have three exceptional characteristics: (1) each views the world through multiple perspectives. None presumes the usual professional arrogance of theatrical or disciplinary myopia. Yet each is highly accomplished professionally. (2) Each is an active learner seeking to understand self and the world. (3) Perhaps most important, each is a caring person committed to NEXUS because of its focus on the leader as a *person.*

In this setting, most if not all participants are able to begin to reperceive their situation as public leaders and private persons, to engage the "nexus" of self, organization, and society from new and rewarding perspectives. They come to see the acknowledgment of uncertainty or the opening of new options rather than the revealing of failed competence. They find that becoming a learner is a crucial criterion of a new competence. So too, as part of that new competence, is attention to managing their stress and attending to the transitions that characterized their lives and that of their organizations and, indeed, society.

They discover that, contrary to their previous impressions, they are not alone: there are others like them, perhaps even in their own organizations, but surely among their peers. They also discover that it is good and necessary to be supported in their search and to support others in their search for meaning. (This has been more of a revelation and relief for men than for women; women have known it all along.)

These realignments of self as leader are aided by the environmental and interpersonal nurturing the occasion itself provides, as well as by lectures, exercises, and small group discussions around several specific topics. It bears emphasizing that by careful preplanning each topic is explored at all levels and each topic is linked to the others. The content of some of these topics is described in these typical agenda notes:

> How the turbulent and interlocked transitions underway in society, in organizations, and in ourselves result in a profound crisis in the norms

and conduct of governance at all levels. What are the new problems and opportunities for leaders produced by this crisis?

How uncertainties, frustrations, and overloads threaten our physical and psychological well-being and that of those we lead. Much can be done to minimize or eliminate these effects. (Some "on the job" stress management methods will be demonstrated and experienced.)

The myths that give meaning and direction to our private lives and to society are disintegrating. This results in deep anxiety. What does this mean for those in leardership roles?

Throughout each seminar program, there is emphasis on "what does this all mean for *you* in your work and nonwork worlds? What are you going to do about all this when you get back?"

What, then, has evolved to date from the NEXUS programs, from all this thinking and experiencing, caring and sharing? Invariably, the seminar has been an emotionally, indeed for some, spiritually deepening and enriching experience, if for no other reason (and there are many reasons) than that each participant found that he or she was not alone; there were others to depend on. As a result, some of these leaders have continued to turn to each other for both moral and intellectual support, long after their seminar ended. For many, there has been the relief and excitement of beginning to be free of the gratuitous constraints that go with hiding or denying uncertainty about the role and meaning of leadership in a turbulent and obscure world. They have begun to see the possibilities of leading by virtue of becoming learners about the questions to be asked rather than being those who knew the answers.

Very importantly, many have come away with new operational insights and intentions. Since returning to their life and work situations, some have introduced changes in their activities or elsewhere in their organizations that have had significant consequences.

Out of these many experiences, NEXUS hopes to create an international, ongoing network of leaders who will call upon each other for specific counsel as well as personal support. Takeo Fujisawa, cofounder of Japan's Honda Motor Company has stated: "Japanese and American management is 95 percent the same and differs in all important respects." NEXUS believes that this vital difference resides in the recognition of human values and a holistic perspective as profits and productivity for the individual, the organization, and society as a whole.

Those who guide the California NEXUS Foundation believe that through the NEXUS seminars they have developed a prototype, which will continue to evolve, of how to help leaders and management in organizations to understand and implement their unique, high energy fusion of humanistic values and economic efficacy.

REFERENCES

Argyris, C. 1970. *Intervention Theory and Method: A Behavioral Science View*. Reading, Mass.: Addison-Wesley.
Bales, R.F. 1950. *Interaction Process Analysis*. Reading, Mass.: Addison-Wesley.
Beckhard, R. 1969. *Organization Development: Strategies and Models*. Reading, Mass.: Addison-Wesley.
Bennis, W.G. 1969. *Organization Development: Its Nature, Origins, and Prospects*. Reading, Mass.: Addison-Wesley.
Drucker, P.F. 1980. *Managing in Turbulent Times*. New York: Harper & Row.
Gallessich, J. 1982. *The Profession and Practice of Consultation*. San Francisco: Jossey-Bass.
Homans, G.C. 1950. *The Human Group*. New York: Harcourt Brace Jovanovich.
Miller, E.J. and A.K. Rice. 1967. *Systems of Organization*. London: Tavistock.
Pascale, R.T. and A.G. Athos. 1981. *The Art of Japanese Management: Applications for American Executives*. New York: Simon and Schuster.
Pelletier, K.R. 1979. *Holistic Medicine: From Stress to Optimum Health*. New York: Delacorte and Delta.
———. 1981. *Longevity: Fulfilling our Biological Potential*. New York: Delacorte and Delta.
———. 1982. "Corporate Health Promotion Programs." Ongoing study.
Roethlisberger, F. and W. Dickson. 1939. *Management and the Worker*. Cambridge, Mass.: Harvard University Press.
Sarason, S. 1972. *The Creation of Settings and the Future Societies*. San Francisco: Jossey-Bass.
———. 1977. *Work, Aging and Social Change: Professionals and the One Life-One Career Imperative*. New York: The Free Press (MacMillan).
Simon, H.A. 1947. *Administrative Behavior: A Study of Decision-Making Processes in Administrative Organizations*. New York: MacMillan.
White, R.K. and R. Lippitt. 1960. *Autocracy and Democracy: An Experimental Inquiry*. New York: Harper.

22 The Networking Process: Informal and Formal Networking, with a Corporate Case Study

Alina Novak, B.A.

Networks. It's a new kind of group that is structured in a formal or informal way and whose main goal is to facilitate the networking process. This process can be defined as the planned acquisition of contacts for mutual support, the exchange of information, and the transaction of business.

Over the past five years, the concept of networking has been popularized by women who have emulated the "old boys" networks. The "old boys" have met, played, and studied in the right Ivy League schools, on team sports, and in exclusive, all-male clubs from childhood to adulthood.

In contrast, women have only recently begun to use the process. Whether they have joined existing networks or set up their own, women are meeting each other as adults and trying to experience the team and club atmosphere. Although the experience of connecting is predominantly restricted to other women, men are part of the networking process.

Historically, connections in a network have always been important. As the dictionary defines it, a "network" is "anything resembling a net in concept or form, as by being dispersed in intersecting lines of communication: espionage network, network of railways."

The women and men who built up our country banded together in wagon trains to conquer new territory and in settlements and forts to preserve what they had from the elements. The Abolitionists introduced a new kind of network called the underground railroad. Its purpose was to transport blacks from slavery to freedom. And, during World War II, connections were set up to move food and milk from the farms to the war-torn cities and ghettos of Europe.

Every immigrant family that has come to the United States since the turn of the century has reached out to relatives and friends in order to survive. Finding a job, locating an apartment, and learning where to shop were tasks that were more quickly mastered through connections. By having to learn the language, customs, and taboos of business, women seeking success in business find themselves very much in an immigrant situation.

The language men use in business often contains terms that are derived from team sports and the military, which are foreign to most women. Many women were brought up to fulfill the custom of marriage and no other. In fact, for many women getting married was the only goal they ever had. In contrast, success in the business world implies performance goals, territorial expansion, and a mastery of the game of office politics.

Thus, the process of networking has been important not only in the past for both men and women, it's a crucial part of the success equation in business. Knowing the right people at the right time is a skill that can be developed and maintained. But, what is most interesting is the way women have as a group pioneered networking for their business experience. How networking has evolved informally as a process and been formalized as a structure will be explored further.

Successful men in business have always known how to use each other to get ahead. As women move up in business, they are expected to develop connections. In fact, the process is often so informal that men are unaware of women's historical isolation and assume that women are connecting when, in fact, they aren't.

Traditionally, women have not been conditioned to the requirements of business: bonding through play in team sports, sharing in the military, and having one's self-confidence reinforced socially through the expectation of business success. In contrast, it has been said that girls play with other girls because they like them, while boys play with other boys because they bring skill to the game. The "old boys" networks that endure are based on need and skill rather than on popularity.

The skills that are prized in boys' sports are part of the goal of winning. Through these games, boys absorb the art of goal setting. In the past, girls usually lacked this experience while growing up. As women, they often have had a hard time setting goals other than personal ones. The business environment demands clear goal setting, as does the process of networking.

As women have made decided strides in their progress over the last decade, they have become aware of the powerful results men achieve through networking. In addition, the enriching experience of women supporting women through consciousness-raising groups and in assertiveness training has been a precedent to women's networking.

In business, women are using the networking process in two ways. The formal route involves joining a network as a member who attends meetings, pays dues, and links up with other network members. The informal way is to individually set up one's own system of networking. Most men have done both; women are learning to do the same.

SETTING UP YOUR INDIVIDUAL AND INFORMAL NETWORK

One of the primary ways that the process of informal networking can be activated is by exchanging business cards when meeting people on a one-to-one basis. For many women, getting business cards is an exercise in assertiveness because it means self-promotion. For others, it signifies creativity by designing one's own card and having it reflect one's profession or avocation.

Contacts made by trading business cards can be classified according to the naure of the contact, date and place met, and anything else that might help identify the person. Often this is a game of odds; in the insurance business, the chances are that out of 100 cold calls, 16 will visit with the insurance agent and one will buy an insurance product. These numbers are similar for the person who exchanges 100 cards at a convention or seminar. Perhaps a dozen of these new contacts will develop into a lunch or dinner appointment. Depending on the exchange, one or two will become part of one's network.

The scheduling of lunch or breakfast has always been a favorite with business people. Women are now regularly connecting and sometimes inviting a few people on a regular basis. These kinds of informal luncheon or breakfast groups are a way to network without setting up a formal organizational structure.

Top-level women will often reserve a private dining room for a select group of women with whom they can meet to exchange ideas and lend support. By invitation only, these get-togethers provide a mentoring experience for the group. Also, the top-level woman acts as a role model.

Networking between men and women is often a function of the industry they are in. More and more men have supported women's networking as they have realized that it's an important ingredient to all business success.

Also, it should be noted that many immigrant and minority men were never allowed into the "old boys" networks either. They often are involved in setting up parallel organizations and clubs or trying to break into the old-line networks.

So far, for the most part, the networking process has been developed and implemented by women seeking to better their chances in the business area where who you know is as important as what you know.

During the initial encounter, a number of questions are asked between the lines. What information might be exchanged? Can mutual support be developed? Is a business connection possible? How can we use each other? These and other questions are explored further in subsequent meetings.

Further analysis will usually focus on where the contact fits in with respect to one's relative position. In other words, are you networking horizontally with a peer, vertically upward to a mentor/expert, or, perhaps, vertically downard to someone junior or less experienced than you.

Networking goals clarify the outcome. People network for a variety of reasons. One reason is to practice making contacts with people at all levels, somewhat in a random fashion. Others have a specific need to make connections around a particular project. This could be part of exploring a career change, running a political campaign, getting increased visibility to demonstrate executive skills, or just keeping up with office politics.

Somehow, setting a goal for one's networking is not enough. One must estimate the correct mix of needed contacts. Most women want to network upward and find someone who will mentor and support their careers. Almost everyone finds the exchange with one's colleagues to be a crucial part of getting ahead. Oftentimes, peer support can make a difference in moving up. Leaders usually cultivate a following of supporters in addition to their relationships with peers and mentors.

The number of people one cultivates depends on many factors. Some situations foster networking for quantity. Sales and public relations are examples where knowing many people is paramount. However, it is in the quality of contacts that corporate payoffs begin to reach women. Finding a mentor or having the support of the right select few is a special kind of focus that women in particular need.

At this point, if you are interested in networking on the individual level, you should set up a special file of index cards for the 100 most important contacts in your career and personal life. If there are not 100, start cultivating more people. These 100 contacts should be broken down, using a management system of prioritizing. This means establishing groups by priority.

The first group should contain all the contacts that you consider vital over the next 12 months. Examples would include people with whom you work closely, your mentor, key contacts, personal friends, and family. The second group is made up of those people who are part of your two-to-five year career plan or long-term networking strategy. This category would include past supervisors, members of your social club and professional organizations, and acquaintences.

The third includes a miscellaneous classification for anyone who doesn't fit either of the first two groups. Your lawyer, neighbors, or country club friends might fit this category. Finally, the last group is made up of enemies and people who are not to be trusted. These contacts are often dangerous but necessary and need to be handled carefully. Sometimes, a military alliance is possible.

Once you have defined who you know in addition to what you know, you'll be ready to consider where the bodies are buried, who's who, and which way is up. The next step is to develop a networking plan of action that takes into account your time commitments, budget, and lifestyle. An exercise of listing the ten people with whom you spend most of your time, either face-to-face or on the phone, can be revealing. Good networkers are disciplined and organized. They add contacts as well as discard them.

Women often are concerned about using people. Confusion exists with respect to the difference in using versus abusing someone. Often, the mutual support of other women can make it easier to clarify the situation. Networking is not "making nice." It's not necessarily being friends. Sometimes friendships develop but not as a rule. It's not necessary that you like the person; respecting someone is the key. Using each other is a win/win situation for both.

Part of the networking process is to identify one's financial emergency network. Here, a list is made of the people you could call out of the blue for financial assistance or, better yet, a list of the people who would be willing to extend credit in a crisis.

Another important network to consider is that of people who can help you make your next career move. In this case, developing a strategic plan is a must. Office politics, timing, and support from the right people can pay off. In fact, the hidden job market has been estimated at 70 to 90 percent of the jobs above entry level. The "old boys" network usually manages to corner the market on filling these jobs. Women are trying to be part of this inner circle to whatever degree possible and are setting up parallel "good old girls" networks.

Most men respond to money, power, or fame in their quest for success. Up until the last few years, women did not react well to these goals. In seminars today, women pick money and power, 50 and 40 percent respectively, with fame trailing at 10 percent.

The identification of people in our networks who are driven by money is valuable, especially if one then presents ideas to them with a bottom-line orientation. Power-hungry people should be approached with a different agenda. And, those seeking fame hear another drummer.

Success in making contacts can depend on your networking style. Here you should analyze the way you sell yourself. If you wanted to meet a few new people in the next month, would you call, write, use a referral, or approach them face-to-face? Identifying your preferred style involves listing the order in which you make your contact. Some people always call, others write. Those who use others to introduce them are different from those who would walk right up and introduce themselves.

Since networking is a two-way street, researching the other party's networking style is invaluable. There are phone people, and there are those who you'll never see unless the right person introduces you. Others respond best to something in writing. Finally, there are those who prefer a face-to-face approach.

Relative strength plays an important part in deciding one's strategy. It also helps to know how that profession or industry operates. Proper networking necessitates a firm grip on the goal of the encounter. As indicated earlier, goals are essential to the success of any endeavor. Then, you must ask yourself these questions: Is your goal reasonable? What about the timing? Has the preparation been adequate? What are the risks?

The networking process assumes an agenda. People who practice networking soon refine the topics they want to discuss. Gossip, trade secrets, and anything politically suicidal is usually avoided. Personal confidences are also a no-no. One way that you can prepare is to make a list of ten subjects to discuss and then pair up with a buddy to role play. Advancing the role play to bragging, each person talks for five minutes nonstop about herself and why she is successful.

The experience in bragging is foreign to many women who have a restricted task orientation and prohibitions against bragging about themselves. Men often socialize where bragging is part of the process. Too often, however, the listeners are women. Some executive search people feel that anyone unable to brag about their accomplishments for 15 minutes will not get the job. Studies show that women have not been socialized to brag or promote themselves. Their self-confidence often is unrealistically low. A support network usually helps in raising a woman's self-esteem.

Knowing and using basic self-help survival skills are what networking is all about. Knowing someone from whom one can get support is vital. Exchanging information hones one's communication skills, and transacting business creates a successful climate for winning.

Finally, setting up one's own informal, individual network involves setting goals, assessing one's contacts, and developing a networking plan of action.

A CORPORATE CASE STUDY

Although hundreds of women's formal networks have sprung up all over the country, less than a dozen are in corporations. Most networks are geographically based or made up along professional lines. They involve a formal structuring, which includes regularly scheduled meetings, dues, and a steering committee. The rarest network is that formed in the corporation by women employees.

These conditions notwithstanding, it is this kind of network that is most needed by women in business. Even though the network is organized around work-related issues, members respond to each other's needs by extending emotional support to one another.

Much vital information in the corporate hierarchy is passed down by word of mouth. Hearing the ideas of top executives can be invaluable to women who rarely have easy access to top echelons. Women executives who have made it can reach a wider group of women when the company has a women's network. Business women who have discussed various issues in a support-group setting find themselves better prepared to exchange ideas. Leadership and communications skills are practiced by active network members.

The structure of women's corporate networks varies from exclusionary to open to all. Membership may be restricted to women at certain corporate levels or open to anyone who pays dues. Most large networks include managers and secretaries, although some are restricted to middle-management women. Some networks are public and official, while others are underground and not recognized by management.

The in-house corporate networks that exist today all have a number of similar traits. Each has top-level support or permission, which may include a budget for operating costs. Usually, the beginning of the network was timed and executed with care by the initial founders. Most of these networks were started by women who were not newcomers and who had already networked informally to set the stage. Another important point is that the goals of the network must be clear to top management and the network must stick with its goals.

An example of a successful corporate network can be found at the Equitable Life Assurance Society, the third largest life insurance company in the country. With more than 16,000 employees nationwide, close to 6,000 work in the home office. Approximately 70 percent of the total work force are women Middle management includes more than 30 percent women, and top management greater than 10 percent.

Started in 1976, "Networks," a self-formed group, has more than 400 women and men members who pay annual dues of $1.00 and meet monthly in the home office to hear program speakers. The company subsidizes operating costs of "Networks" with an annual budget of $3,000.

Topics of most interest revolve around career planning, money, and discussions with top Equitable executives. In-house speakers often get a better turnout than outsiders. It seems members have great interest in what is happening inside the corporation.

One early decision, to meet during lunch, has made the "Networks' " programs a place to brown-bag-it. Using lunch hour for meetings makes the group accessible to employees at all levels in the home office.

Although women started the group, men asked to join in the first year. "Networks" evolved until, today, approximately 10 percent of the membership is male. Members often can be seen having lunch in small groups or in pairs, where the art of informal networking is practiced.

Personal development has been very important to members. A recent survey (24 percent of the membership responded; 96 percent women, 4 percent men) showed that 60 percent felt their involvement with "Networks" had assisted them in their personal development. Close to 22 percent relied on "Networks" for job leads within Equitable. The survey respondents rated as "very valuable" the following: monthly programs, 72 percent; information exchange, 79 percent; and publications, 92 percent.

In terms of the occupational classifications of the members of "Networks," 23 percent are clerical; 29 percent, nonsupervisory; 13 percent, professionals and supervisors; 28 percent, managers; and 8 percent, officers. More than 41 percent of the members have been employed at Equitable for more than ten years; 28 percent, six to ten years; and 30 percent, five years or less. In terms of education, 11 percent have a high school degree; 37 percent, some college; 32 percent, a college degree; and 20 percent, an advanced degree.

In looking back over the five years that "Networks" has existed, three things stand out. First, without the support of Coy Eklund, then president and CEO, the group would never have gotten started. It was after reading Coy Eklund's speech, "Women in Business: What Business Must Do," that I began in the summer of 1976 to meet with various women to discuss the idea of forming a women's group. Six months later, having spoken with the proper people in personnel, a room was booked and the first meeting called.

It was at this meeting that we discussed Coy Eklund's words: "I think a sensitive management today must be aware that women moving up in business need reinforcement from each other; they need role models, and they need contact with other professional women at higher levels. This kind of reinforcement need can be met to some extent by holding meetings for women only, and even more easily by making facilities available for self-formed groups who wish to meet on their own, just to share their feelings and their daily experiences with each other. . . ."

Second, the corporate climate over the last few years has been of major influence. Equitable has put in place rotating advisory panels made up of women, blacks, and Hispanics who each met with the president regularly, sponsored women's and minority workshops, and invited appropriate speakers.

In addition, Equitable's first female vice-president was appointed in 1974. Today, of 531 upper level executives, 57 are women. This number includes: 43 assistant vice-presidents, 13 vice-presidents, and one executive vice-president. Also, four women are on Equitable's board of directors. These numbers are higher than those of any other major corporation.

It was in this climate that the first steering committee formulated its goals, which are to: "open informal channels for the exchange of information both within and among the Equitable departments; enable the Equitable, at all corporate levels, to take full advantage of its human resources; and enable members to form groups for support, information, or business."

Third, the women and men who have volunteered their time to serve on the steering committee over the last five years include dozens of people who have kept the organization going.

In summary, the ingredients in forming a corporate network include: (1) top management support, (2) a corporate climate where the goals of a network fit in, and (3) the leadership among employees to be able to start and maintain such a group.

The future of corporate women's networks probably will involve an evolution similar to Equitable's "Networks," namely, men will join in and begin networking with the women. Perhaps this will not happen in great numbers, but the men who become involved will share similar concerns about their careers.

For additional material on the subject, you may look to the sources listed below.

REFERENCES

Kleiman, Carol. 1980. *Women's Networks.* New York: Ballantine Books.

Stern, Barbara. 1981. *Is Networking For You?* Englewood Cliffs, N.J.: Prentice-Hall.

Welch, Mary Scott. 1980. *Networking: The Great New Way for Women to Get Ahead.* New York: Harcourt Brace Jovanovich.

SECTION SIX

Beginnings Revisited: Clinical Research and Psychological Assessment in Organizations

Psychology began as an experimental discipline and should never neglect the importance of this genesis with respect to its current work. Clinical psychology, in turn, can chart its early development to psychological assessment of individuals. These important bases for the development of psychology must be integrated into all forms of present practice in order for the field to grow and prosper. This is particularly so in the case of occupational clinical psychology, which, since its variegated inception, has not generated much research reporting on and justifying its existence, nor has it until only recently made assessment tools available in an understandable form to managers. Proving a new field's usefulness and pragmatism is one of the most difficult aspects in a developmental sense.

Drs. Michael Smith and Lawrence Schleifer, in their chapter, "A Guide for Conducting Mental Health Research in Occupational Settings," introduce the reader to the history of worksite research, noting those facets of the organization making it an ideal site for mental health research. The various types of research that may be employed are discussed. Most importantly, this chapter assists the would-be occupational clinical researcher in setting up a study, given the significant differences between a laboratory or other in vivo research and that occurring at the worksite. The need to establish objectives, controls, and liaisons is presented. The selection of subjective and/or objective methodologies is examined. Conducting the study and disseminating its results are critical in the occupational environment, and appropriate provisos are offered. The experienced researcher will be struck by many of the important differences between worksite and other-site research. All too often, significant research projects are turned down by organizations due to the researcher's naiveté with regard to the occupational setting. This guide should help in reorienting that problem.

Our last chapter, "Contemporary Psychological Assessment in Organizational Settings," by Drs. Robert Most and Howard Glazer, gives the reader a complete overview of the place of new forms of psychological assessment in organizations. The chapter takes us quickly from a history of psychological testing to the recent trends in computerization. A section on using psychological testing for selection examines criterion issues, the use of personality inventories for selection purposes, federal law and psychological testing with respect to equal employment opportunity, screening in an employee counseling program context and possible litigation concerns, screening in an occupational context where public safety is involved, executive selection, and a rationale for employing psychological screening today. Placement and career development instruments and methodologies are also addressed. The chapter ends with a discussion of human resource development psychological instruments—those that assist in the personal and vocational development of employees. This excellent chapter shows the important and multifarious uses to which contemporary psychological testing may be put in occupational settings.

Thus, the psychologist interested in occupational clinical work need not disregard the training received in research and psychological testing. To the contrary, these aspects of the profession are critical to occupational clinical psychology.

23 A Guide for Conducting Mental Health Research in Occupational Settings

Michael J. Smith, Ph.D., and Lawrence M. Schleifer, Ed.D.

INTRODUCTION

Background

In the last two decades there has been an explosion of mental health services at the workplace. Increasingly, employers are providing their employees with mental health services such as alcohol and drug abuse counseling, career counseling, crisis intervention and stress management. The mental health needs of the worker are receiving more attention than at any time since the industrial revolution. The impetus for providing these services is in part due to the growing recognition that corporations have a social responsibility toward their employees. In addition, quality of working life has become a major contract or bargaining issue for today's workforce. Workers are demanding and are successfully obtaining mental health services as a standard employee benefit.

A growing appreciation of the social and economic costs associated with employee alcohol and drug abuse and other psychological disorders is another factor in the growth of mental health programs at the workplace. Corporate managers now recognize the adverse economic impact of mental health problems on worker absenteeism, motivation, and productivity. Moreover, since employee health insurance benefits often include the treatment of psychological disorders many employers have a financial incentive to be the primary provider of mental health services.

During the economic boom of the 1960s and the 1970s, the social and economic value of mental health services was implicitly assumed. Under these conditions, corporate managers were willing to give fledgling employee mental health programs the opportunity to establish themselves and demonstrate their utility to the corporation and its employees. The added costs associated with these programs were considered to be minimal when compared to the potential benefits that would accrue from good employer-employee relations.

Unfortunately, the current economic conditions in the 1980s are less favorable for employee assistance programs. Corporate decision makers are preoccupied with the problems of inflation, low productivity, and declining profits. They are therefore more likely to be skeptical of the social and economic value of mental health programs. They are becoming more interested in how mental health services affect profits and losses, productivity, and corporate well-being. Given this new economic and social environment, the ability to demonstrate the efficacy and efficiency of mental health programs may be crucial to their survival.

The purpose of this chapter is to provide direction to the clinical practitioner in how to organize and conduct a research project in an industrial or large organizational setting. Increasingly, the practitioner will be called on to engage in research as well as provide clinical services. Questions often arise regarding who is most in need of treatment given limited availability of resources. Many times the practitioner must determine whether a particular treatment approach is effective. Given limited resources, the practitioner may be forced to cut costs by administering individually oriented therapeutic techniques in a group setting. The issue of whether the innovative application of these techniques is appropriate must be evaluated. Inevitably, the practitioner will be required to define, clarify, and verify the basic assumptions of treatment approaches as well as their effectiveness. This chapter will provide a limited description of this process. It will review the basic mechanics of planning and conducting various types of mental health research in industry. It is not a definitive resource or a cookbook because of space limitations. Rather, it will provide a general perspective on the methods, strategies, and tactics that are involved in the conduct of such research.

The Workplace as a Laboratory

The industrial setting has several compelling characteristics that make it an excellent location to conduct mental health research. First and foremost is the relatively easy access to a large, diverse population. There are few institutions that offer the opportunity to examine such a large number of individuals with diverse personality and physical attributes under a range of organizational and environmental conditions. Second, it provides subjects that are "normal." That is, they are capable of daily functioning in society, yet they also manifest symptoms of emotional distress. Finally, environmental influences, such as working conditions and organizational features, are now recognized as powerful contributors to mental distress in "normal" persons and may also play a significant role in inducing "abnormal" responses and in reducing the overall quality of our nation's mental health.

The history of clinical research in industrial settings is very limited. Certainly, there are many excellent clinical mental health programs at the workplace that have been in existence for many years. However, there have not been many organized attempts to define the need for these programs and still fewer attempts to evaluate their impact. One area that has received a good deal of attention is that of occupational stress. There have been a wide range of studies to define relationships between specific working conditions and employee mental and physical health. Reviews of this body of research can be found in Cooper and Marshall (1976) and Smith (1981). Other job stress studies have attempted to evaluate the effectiveness of stress reduction programs in industrial settings (Manuso, 1979; Peters, Benson, & Peters, 1977; Murphy, 1981; Schleifer, 1981). Occupational stress research is growing at a rapid rate due to the increased awareness among worker and management groups of its adverse health implications. This area of research is making a significant contribution to all occupational mental health endeavors. However, the increased awareness by the public also brings closer scrutiny of occupational mental health programs and pressure for justification and assessment of quality.

Types of Research

There are two basic types of mental health research that are conducted in industrial settings. These are quasi-experimental studies and experimental studies. The quasi-experimental studies often do not utilize many of the basic principles that are required for scientific rigor—such as control groups, statistical analysis, or random sampling. The main purpose of such research is not to confirm a particular hypothesis but rather to identify significant issues that may need to be evaluated at another time. Essentially, this research can be characterized as fact-finding. Questions such as, "Is there a need for an alcoholism program in our company?" or "How many employees of our company are feeling high levels of mental distress?" can be addressed by this type of research.

Experimental research is far more rigorous than quasi-experimental research in that appropriate subject sampling procedures are used, detailed statistical analyses are performed, and control and comparison groups are a basic component of the study. The main purpose of this research is to prove that treatment approaches differ or that changes in employee mental health occurred. The results can define a causal link between treatments and the observed changes in the employees.

SETTING UP A STUDY

Establishing Objectives

The first step in planning a study is to establish the objectives. In this regard, there are a number of factors that must be considered. First of all, "Who is being served?" Is the primary recipient the organizational manager of a high stress work unit, or is it the employee receiving stress-management training, or is it the corporation? In each case, the objectives may differ. For the individual, the major concern is maximizing the influence of his or her specific intervention, while for the manager it may be maximizing the therapeutic impact on a total work unit. Second, the objectives must fit within the goals of the organization in which the research is being conducted. If the organization requires evidence of a problem before an intervention can be undertaken, then the study objectives must fit within this organizational objective. If the study objectives are at odds with those of the organization, then the impact of the study results will probably be minimal and may endanger other worthy research efforts.

The next step in establishing objectives is to determine the desired breadth and scope of the study. Many times the availability of resources will dictate the breadth and scope, which will influence the types of objectives. In determining the breadth and scope and in establishing objectives, the desired end product must be kept in mind. The type of information that is needed at the end of the study (the questions you want answered) will dictate the complexity of the study design, data collection, and data analysis. Finally, the objectives must fit into the mental health needs of the individual employees.

Establishing Controls and Liaisons

Once the objectives of the study have been established and put in writing, there is a need to establish the organizational apparatus to carry out the study. No study can succeed without the blessing and involvement of the management that will be affected by the research findings. In order to facilitate this support there is a need to enlist the aid of "key persons" in the organization. The first "key person" is the highest manager in the affected organizational unit. Often research is generated by a request from such a manager. However, other times the request does not come from this manager and is seen by the manager as a threat or an indictment. In this situation, the manager has to be gradually won over. The most effective approach is to actively involve the manager in the research process. Such involvement can include helping set the objectives and participating in discussions concerning the best approach for implementing the study in the organizational unit.

A second "key person" is the corporate level manager who supervises the organizational unit managers and can ensure that study results will be supported at a corporate level. This person can provide positive support to the unit manager who may need reassurance and advice. The corporate manager can also exert favorable influence if the unit manager lacks in enthusiasm or fails to fulfill study requirements. Other "key-persons" include the representative of employees or union officials, the employees, and various individuals in support departments within a particular organization. The support individuals include the chief medical officer, the head of personnel, the director of training, and the director of industrial relations. These persons provide for smooth implementation of the study and should be involved to various degrees depending on the need for their influence and expertise. At a minimum, all of these persons should be aware of the study, its objectives, and its progress.

Once cooperation and involvement of "key persons" have been obtained the objectives will need to be reevaluated. Original objectives have a "purity" in that they don't involve any of the biases of the "key persons." Alternatively, the objectives are "naive" in that they may not take account of many of the practical exigencies in the daily operation of the workplace. Therefore, the "key persons" can be used to strengthen the objectives by directing their biases at the original objectives. Then adjustments can be made to account for "real-life" conditions. This is best accomplished through face-to-face meetings of all "key persons" with the researcher acting as a facilitator. At this point, it is expected that there will be a good deal of disagreement. Such disagreement is productive because it points out potential pitfalls and biases that the researcher may not have initially considered. However, if disagreement still persists after two or three of these meetings, then the research must take a definitive direction so that the study can move ahead. While consensus on the objectives is always a desirable goal, it is one that cannot always be attained. It is up to the researcher to make the final determination on what the objectives will be.

Now the process of implementing the study procedures can begin. This also requires a great deal of bargaining and compromise. The main purpose is to obtain the necessary organizational authorization and power to proceed and to establish the apparatus for motivating various levels of the organization to participate in the study. The use of the "key persons" as a research committee is often very effective. In any case, it is important to have a balance of involvement that includes both management, worker representatives, and professional staff. This provides for all viewpoints and for checks and balances by keeping one faction from dominating and coercing the researcher.

Having established the research committee, a written plan should be developed that explicitly specifies how the research will be conducted in terms of the objectives, the employees to be examined, the organizational units involved, the type of management support and involvement, publicity, and resource requirements. At this stage, the document should be reviewed by a researcher(s) outside of your organization for technical adequacy. This "peer review" should be formal and require a written response on adequacy and comments on any shortcomings or problem areas. This input can be used to develop a final research document. This document should then be sent to a medical review committee in order to ensure that the research procedures are not injurious to the health or welfare of the employee participants. This medical review committee can be either within or outside of the organization and should be composed of medical and mental health experts who are knowledgeable of appropriate care and handling of research participants. Once cleared by this medical review group, the research document should be signed by the members of the research committee and forwarded to top management for approval. Written approval from top management should be obtained before proceeding.

SELECTING A METHODOLOGY

Up to this point, the researcher has obtained assistance in setting study objectives and in developing a written plan of how the study will be implemented within the organization. The next step is to select the appropriate methodology to address the objectives, and this responsibility falls exclusively on the researcher. The research committee should not dictate issues of methodology but should only deal with issues of the goals and general scope of the study. The selection of an appropriate methodology depends on many variables that are specific to the study being undertaken and to the questions that are to be answered. Therefore, we can only provide general direction based on our own research experience in examining occupational stress in industrial settings. The following methods of data collection can be used in both quasi-experimental and experimental research designs.

Subjective Approaches

There are two major methods for gathering information that is self-reported by the employee. These are by interview and questionnaires. The methods are referred to as subjective since the employee has a great deal of control over the response and can introduce personal bias into the response. While subjective techniques are many times criticized for this potential bias, 50 years of self-report research has demonstrated the efficacy of these methods in defining the status of groups of individuals. Given that each individual response may contain some bias, when a number of individual responses are pooled, the grouped response is less biased and provides a fairly accurate picture of the group condition. In addition, well anchored self-report measures tend to be stable and consistent over time, while many of the more objective measures of individual response are greatly influenced by situational factors and momentary fluctuations.

Interviews are the oldest technique for collecting opinions and information from individuals. Interviews fall into three basic categories: (1) unstructured, (2) semistructured, and (3) structured. With unstructured interviews, the interviewer approaches a basic line of questioning without any prior developed questions or format. The flow of the interview is based solely on each response of the interviewee. For a semistructured interview general areas to be covered are developed before interviewing, and in some cases a number of specific questions are developed. During the course of the interview if a particular question elicits a response of interest, then an unstructured line of questioning occurs. However, the interviewer always returns to the general areas after the unstructured questioning. With a structured interview all questions are developed before the interview and the interviewer asks each question of each participant in the same order and manner so that all interviewees are asked the same questions in the same way.

Each type of interview has strengths and weaknesses. The unstructured approach allows for flexibility in questioning, particularly if a specific line of questioning can provide important information not addressed by structured questions. However, many times it is difficult to collate and interpret the unstructured responses of a large group of persons. This is not a problem for structured interviews, where each interviewee answers the same questions. However, the structured interview is lacking in flexibility and assumes that all problem areas are known when the interview questions are developed. This is seldom the case, and many times important lines of questioning are missed by the structured format. For most research endeavors, a semistructured interview provides the needed flexibility, the evaluation of all areas of interest, and comparability of responses.

Questionnaires are instruments that allow employees to answer questions of a specific nature in a written format (as opposed to the verbal format of an interview). They come in many dimensions or forms, from standardized psychological tests to homemade question and answer checklists. As with structured interviews, questionnaires provide a structured format for addressing a limited set of questions. Both assume that all areas of interest are known and that employees have little to add in terms of insight. Even more so than structured interviews, questionnaires have very rigid response categories, which "force" employees to answer according to a specific response format. Because of this rigidity, it is extremely important that the questions and answers actually measure the responses of interest. Therefore, much more detail and effort goes into the development of specific areas to be addressed and into the wording of the questions and responses. Also, factors such as the clarity of instructions and the format as well as the layout of questions/responses are critical to obtaining valid responses. Many times questionnaires are pretested on a small group of subjects to determine if they are tapping the areas of interest before they are used on a wider scale.

There are pros and cons when comparing questionnaires to interviews for their usefulness in conducting research. Interviews provide more flexibility in administration and allow for more detailed information to be collected than is possible with questionnaires. Interviews are much more effective when the variables of interest are not well defined and some probing and "fishing" are called for. Under such circumstances the rigidity of the fixed question and response questionnaire is limiting. However, questionnaires, because of their fixed response nature, have results that are much easier to quantify and interpret. Since questionnaires can be given in a concurrent manner to many employees, as opposed to the consecutive manner of interviews, more employees can be included in a research study using the questionnaire and at a much reduced cost. Essentially when problems are well defined and large amounts of data need to be collected, questionnaire surveys are the most efficient approach. When problems are not well defined and therefore more flexibility and detail is needed, then interviews are the preferred method. Interview studies typically are used to define problems to a point where larger questionnaire studies can then be carried out.

Objective Approaches

There are three major methods for gathering objective information about the status of employee mental and physical health; these are records evaluations, physiological measurements, and behavioral observations.

Records evaluations are always retrospective in that they examine an employee's status at a particular point in the past. These evaluations can provide objective measures of employee physical status and behavior over a succession of time (typically years) and allow for trends in these measures to be determined. The types of measures of interest to mental health practitioners are sicknesses and absences; usage pattern of personal benefits such as vacation and insurance benefits; critical incidents in personnel actions such as promotions, demotions, supervisor ratings, and reprimands; physical status (if not confidential); and accidents and injuries. There are a number of sources for these measures, all of which are typically available at the company. Most can be accessed directly; however, some require a signed release for access by the employee.

Some sources of records data are personnel records, insurance claims, absence records, company clinic or dispensary records and accident/injury reports. Besides the direct measurement of interest, for example, the number of sick days per year, these records sources also provide important demographic characteristics that have been shown to influence the direct measures. These include age, sex, race, marital status, education, job tenure, job classification and preemployment history. Since the majority of records of interest are primarily found in personnel files and company clinic files, establishing liaisons with the professionals in these departments is critical to ensuring record access, proper record handling, and follow-up on information included in the records.

There are a number of research strategies that can be employed in evaluating records data. The most effective in examining physical disorders has been to use an epidemiological framework to determine agent-host disease relationships. However, when dealing with mental health issues a traditional epidemiological approach fails to account for the multiplicity of factors that influence the host, the extensive moderating variables present within and outside of the host, and the diverse nature of the etiology of mental health disorders. Therefore, an approach to records evaluation should be undertaken that accounts for these diverse influences. In such a case, the records evaluation needs to include a wide range of variables that can be examined in a "statistical" as opposed to an "experimental" or "epidemiological" way. This approach requires large amounts of data so that appropriate statistical methodologies such as multiple regression and multivariate analyses can be utilized to establish relationships. These approaches require a great deal of statistical expertise, and it is advisable to have a statistical consultant to assist in the analyses.

Physiological measures have been used in many studies to define the type of bodily responses that occur under given conditions and to evaluate the efficacy of intervention approaches for stress reduction. These measures have the advantage of being current and completely objective indicators of employee status. However, they are often hard to measure due to instrumentation inadequacies, are not always stable over time, and can be significantly influenced by situational conditions and events. Given these drawbacks, a great deal of control must be used in applying these measures. That is, the situational conditions in which the measures are taken must be constant (or if not constant then accounted for), and multiple readings of the same measurement must be taken at various times within an experimental setting to determine the variability that is inherent in the measure as opposed to that variability due to the treatment. Finally, the experimenter must take pains to ensure that the instructions to and handling of employees undergoing treatment are the same so that they don't introduce bias into employee responses. Physiological measures that have been used in mental health research include heart rate, blood pressure, skin potentials, internal and external temperature, muscle potentials, eye movements, brain potentials, hormone levels, and biological metabolites other than hormones such as cholesterol and uric acid.

The last type of objective measures is that which examines employee behavior directly through observational techniques. The method of taking and evaluating such measures has been called "applied behavioral analysis" by psychologists and alternatively "time and motion analysis" or "work analysis" by industrial engineers. The approach for both the psychologists and the engineers is the same. First, behaviors that reflect the emotions or motivations of interest are defined and categorized. Next, checklists are made for recording the occurrence of these behaviors. Then, observations are made of a variety of individuals for varying amounts of time to verify that the behaviors do occur and can be quantified once the behaviors are verified, then a program is developed for randomly observing a sample of employees that represent the group of interest. The times of observation must be random and of sufficient quantity and duration to be representative of behavior over the course of a regular working cycle. There are a host of electronic techniques for monitoring employee behavior from activity counters to video-tape systems. The level of sophistication to be used in recording behavior is related to: (1) the need for accuracy in measurement, (2) the amount of data to be collected on each employee, (3) the number of employees to be examined, and (4) the level of employee knowledge of observation. As the need for accuracy increases, and the amount of data on each subject increases, and the number of employees to be measured increases, then the use of electronic monitoring devices enhances the data collection and quality.

Objective methods of data gathering provide an advantage over subjective methods primarily in that they do not rely on the subject to make a cognitive response that could introduce personal bias. There are other advantages. Many objective methods allow for an examination of changes that have taken place in employee status over previous years. This allows for an evaluation of trends in the employee's mental health picture. Also, objective measures are given greater validity by managers and thus are more powerful in decision making. However, objective measures are much more difficult to obtain than subjective measures, and they are more variable than the subjective measures and therefore require more complex research methodologies.

CONDUCTING THE STUDY

In conducting the study, there are a number of common aspects no matter which methodology is chosen. At this point in the study the questions to be answered have been selected and the most appropriate methodology has been chosen. Now the implementation of the methodology begins. This is the point at which many well conceived studies break down. The first step in implementation is to detail the standard operating procedures to be followed in collecting the data. This is necessary so that all persons involved in the research use the exact same procedures and therefore reduce the potential for experimenter bias. Also, this ensures that the study can be replicated. Even if only one person will be collecting all of the data, it is good practice to document how the data will be collected before collection starts to solidify the procedures. This also allows for continuity of data collection over the course of time from day to day or month to month.

After the procedures have been detailed the selection of participants can begin. Strict scientific procedure dictates that participants should be randomly chosen and then randomly assigned to treatment groups. However, in doing research in industry, many times it is not feasible to proceed in this manner. The primary reason for this limitation is that many participants come to the study with select characteristics that are of special interest to us such as hypertension or anxiety. These may be related to the questions of interest to the study, and therefore there can be automatic preselection of participants without the possibility of random sampling. Other participant characteristics such as age or sex may confound our results. Therefore, a certain amount of nonrandom selection has already taken place before we start a study.

There are methods in which personal characteristics can be controlled. One way is to match subjects by the characteristics of interest and then randomly assign each to a treatment. Another is to increase the number of study participants substantially, randomly assign these to treatments and then statistically control for the characteristics. However, a fact of life is that it is not always possible to utilize random selection because of a variety of circumstances such as lack of access, or cost, or not being able to find an unbiased group of participants. Many times in physiological studies only volunteers are used because of liability issues. In such cases, the limiting factor in answering the question(s) of interest will not be the accuracy or validity of the results, but their generalization. When answering many basic questions about mental health, the concern is not for generalizability but for understandability and efficacy. Therefore, the use of volunteers is not a significant concern. Essentially, the problem of not being able to utilize random selection and assignment of study participants is one of the most difficult and limiting areas in conducting "real-life" research in industry.

The logic to use in selecting a sampling procedure should be based on the following: What is the question being answered? If the question is of a general nature and is simple and straightforward such as, "Is anyone in our company under stress?", then the sampling approach should be simple and a "grab sample" may suffice. On the other hand, as the questions become more complex such as, "What percentage of persons in our company are under stress?", then more sophisticated procedures are called for to provide accurate answers.

Another important issue in selecting a sample is the desired accuracy of the answer. The greater the accuracy desired then the greater the need to adhere to random sampling and appropriate sample sizes. Keep in mind that there is always a maximum sample size that will provide the greatest power to answer the question(s). As the selected sample exceeds that maximum, the additional accuracy gained is minimal and money has been wasted collecting too much data. Conversely, if less than the correct sample size is selected, then the ability to make accurate judgments is greatly hampered. You should always have a statistical consultant assist you in determining the best way to select participants and to also help in determining the number of participants needed to accurately answer the question(s) of interest.

Once the participants have been selected then the data collection can start. Promoting the participation of those selected can often be a difficult part in conducting the study. There are ways in which participation can be encouraged. First, be sure that there is adequate information about the study and that its overall objectives are available to the potential participants. This ensures that the potential participants won't develop concerns about participating out of ignorance. Keep the information straightforward and general so that the knowledge obtained does not bias the study. Second, have the organization provide support for the study in the form of written statements of support and verbal statements from company officials. Third, it is often wise to provide incentives to participants such as money, time off, or other special privileges. For the subjective methodologies it is critical that a high percentage of the chosen employees participate so that the power of the data is adequate to answer the questions and to generalize to other employees. Therefore, special monetary incentives are often used with subjective methods.

Once participants have been chosen it is vital that each sign a consent form that states that they are willing to participate in the study and that they are knowledgeable of the study purpose, procedures, and their rights. These rights always include the right to terminate participation at any time and the right to inividual privacy of any responses. The right to privacy will be discussed later under reporting results.

In collecting the data it is always preferable to have a neutral party who hasn't had a role in formulating the questions and methodology carry out the actual collection. This will prevent any experimenter bias due to preconceived notions about what the results should be like. Given that detailed written procedures for data collection have been developed, a neutral party should be able to handle this function easily. The exception may be with the physiological methods where biomedical expertise is necessary to collect the data. In this case, the experimenter has to be extremely careful how treatments are applied so that experimenter bias can be limited.

When conducting surveys, it is generally accepted that not all those selected to participate will respond. The percentage of participation necessary for statistical reliability and generalizability of the data collected will vary with the type and amount of data being collected. Babbie (1973) suggests that a 50 percent response rate is adequate for analysis and reporting of data, while a response rate of 60 percent is good, and 70 percent or more is very good. He goes on to say, "The reader should bear in mind, however, that these are only rough guides, they have no statistical basis, and a demonstrated lack of response bias is far more important than a high response rate." That is, the extent to which the respondents are representative of the target population is more important then the overall rate of response. In general, however, a high rate of response is preferrable to a low rate. For example, Dillman (1978) has demonstrated that a 50 percent response rate can result in an extreme sample of distributional bias of 50 percent, that a 60 percent rate of response will reduce the potential magnitude of distributional bias to 40 percent, and so on. Thus, a higher rate of response reduces the chance of introducing distributional bias.

In some cases, follow-up of nonresponse is necessary to obtain an adequate level of participation. This follow-up can be indirect, as in the case of a second questionnaire survey being sent to the nonrespondents; or it can be direct, such as collecting the desired data in face-to-face interviews. In most surveys, there will be less than 100 percent participation; therefore, it is necessary to collect some basic data on the nonrespondents to assure that those that have responded are representative of the entire population under study. The most reasonable data to collect are demographic characteristics such as age, sex, race, marital status, occupation, and job tenure. The distributions of these demographics for the respondents and nonrespondents can be compared. The more similar the demographic distributions, the less likely that response distributions for respondents and nonrespondents will differ.

A reasonable method for determining response rate has been suggested by Dillman (1978). The response rate is the percentage of contacts with eligible respondents that result in completed interviews or questionnaires. In this method, unmade contacts are excluded from consideration.

After the data have been collected, they must be reduced into a form that will allow analysis. If the data collection instruments are set up properly, it will be simple to translate the participant responses into a format that can be directly entered into a computer. This aspect of questionnaire, interview, records evaluation, and behavioral observation methodologies is often the most costly component, particularly if the data collection instrument requires that the data be transposed to data entry sheets before the information can be processed. The most cost-effective approach is to have responses put on a medium that can be read directly by a computer (e.g., optical scanning). This will also speed up the time for data evaluation, for it can take many weeks to get questionnaires and similar data processed.

The analysis of the data is dictated by the experimental design used. This is another aspect in which a statistical consultant can be very helpful. The type and level of analysis is influenced by the question(s) to be answered, the method of participant selection, the level of participation (quantity of data), the quality of the data, and the rigor needed to convince those who are interested in the answers to your question(s). If a chief executive officer is satisfied with a listing of percentages, then it is overkill and may be confusing to provide more detailed analyses. Conversely, a peer-reviewed journal most likely would not publish a study that didn't have some detailed analyses. Remember who the audience is when carrying out a data analysis and always use a statistical consultant to advise you on the best analytical approach.

DISSEMINATING THE RESULTS OF THE STUDY

The clinical practitioner must give careful thought to how and with whom the results of the study are shared. Recognizing that the type of research that practitioners engage in is mostly applied and highly practical, the reporting of the results of the study should demonstrate this practicality. The results must reflect the original objectives of the research. There are various types of reports that can be developed. A report that is highly technical with numerous statistical analyses may be appropriate for publication in a scientific journal. However, the corporate or department manager may be overwhelmed by such a report and miss the practical implications of the research. Hence, the investigator must take into consideration the needs and sophistication of his or her audience in presenting the results.

The needs of the audience will determine the degree of detail that the report requires. A corporate manager who has only a peripheral interest in the study is unlikely to wade through a long and detailed report. For this individual's needs, a two page executive summary or highlights of the results and their implications would suffice. This type of report enables the corporate manager to obtain a quick thumbnail sketch of the major findings and recommendations. A department manager who will be more directly affected by the results of the study may require more details of the study, particularly the logic that produced the recommendations and some detail about their method of implementation. Essentially, a separate report will have to be written for each audience that is tailored to individual sophistication levels and needs.

Tailoring reports to meet the needs of a particular audience is only the first step in disseminating the results. It is not sufficient to simply write up the results of the research and share them in a written report(s) to concerned parties. It is vital to have an opportunity to present the results in a face-to-face meeting. The results will have greater significance and serve as the basis for further interaction when the investigator has the opportunity to discuss the results with concerned parties. Such meetings will enhance understanding and allow for in-depth discussion of the findings and recommendations. In fact, it is often wise to have preliminary meetings with interested parties to discuss the results of the study before the development of the recommendations. It makes the entire research process more relevant to management and worker groups and facilitates the favorable acceptance of the results and any subsequent recommendations. The parties should be able to identify with and support the research conclusions and develop a sense of control regarding what transpires when specific findings are implemented.

A critical issue in the dissemination of research study results deals with ensuring the confidentiality of individual responses and identifiable small groups (five or fewer persons) of individuals. The Privacy Act of 1974 obliges researchers to keep individual data collected in biomedical research in the strictest confidence so that information on specific persons is not made public (unless the information has already been in the public domain). This requires researchers to handle their data that contain personal identifiers carefully by ensuring access is available only to approved research staff, that records are kept under lock and key with specified access, and that reports do not contain information on individals or small identifiable groups. Data on individuals cannot be reported back to management, medical staff, or other researchers without the written permission of the individual. Therefore, all reports that are developed can report only aggregate data in which no individual can be identified. The Privacy Act calls for staff fines (up to $10,000) and/or prison terms (up to six months) for *each* violation. This requirement should be made clear to management and participants when a study is being conducted, so that misunderstandings do not arise after the research is completed and final reports are being developed.

Case Study

A major corporation was experiencing a high rate of turnover, absenteeism, and medical insurance costs for clerical typists working on computerized word processing systems. Preliminary interviews with a few operators who had gone to the health clinic indicated feelings of emotional distress that the operators associated with work pressure. The vice-president for industrial relations requested that a study be undertaken to determine the extent and causes of the turnover, absenteeism, and health problems.

The objectives of the study were clearly stated by the vice-president requesting the study: that is, to determine the extent and causes of the observed problems. However, the breadth and scope of the study needed to be determined. Since there was little information about the possible causes of the problems, a pilot evaluation of a few work areas was undertaken. This allowed for in-depth evaluations to define critical issues. Using such a focal approach enabled the collection of detailed information on the extent and types of problems as well as specifics about their causes. A large scale study to determine the extent of the problems corporatewide could be conducted later, if necessary, and future studies would be enhanced by the detailed information collected in the pilot study.

After the objectives and scope were determined, liaison with the appropriate management personnel was undertaken. In this case, someone in the office of the vice-president for industrial relations was designated to provide the necessary organization "clout" to access employees and personnel records. Additionally, a top manager in the typing operation was enlisted to assist in this process. The objectives and the scope were reviewed by these persons and put in writing in final form.

Two methods were used to collect data on the following issues: (1) number and type of illnesses of participants in the past two years, (2) frequency and type of specific job activities, (3) type of working conditions and work environmental features, (4) perceived sources of job stress, (5) types and sources of life stress other than the job, (6) health complaints (both physical and psychological), and (7) lifestyle such as alcohol consumption and eating patterns. Health records evaluations using medical insurance forms were the primary source of data on the number and type of illnesses. In addition, absence records, supplemented with structured interviews on absences, were also used to collect this type of data. Semistructured interviews were used to collect the other types of data specified above. These interviews covered basic areas of concern and allowed the participants to freely indicate information they felt to be of importance. This procedure provided for the gathering of detailed data on the issues of interest, but it made for more difficult data reduction and analysis.

The illnesses and absence information was collected on a standardized form that specified date of illness, type of illness, type and severity of symptoms, number of days of absence, and treatment. The interview data were also collected on a second standardized form that outlined the specific areas to be covered in the interview and had spaces for participant responses. The persons who conducted the interviews were clinical psychologists trained in interviewing procedures who were not aware of the purpose of the study. Five percent of the interviews were conducted by two interviewers, whose data were then compared for interinterviewer reliability. The reliability obtained was 93 percent.

Two corporate office facilities (one on the West Coast and one on the East Coast) were selected for examination because both had reported a number of employees with problems. At each facility, medical and absence records were used to group employees into those displaying problems (affected) and those not reporting problems (nonaffected). Within these two groups, employees were stratified by age, sex, race, tenure, and job category. A random sample of 20 employees was selected from each stratum for the records evaluations. This provided a total population of 800 participants at each site. From each population stratum, a 15 percent sample was chosen randomly to participate in the interviews. This provided 120 interviewees at each site.

Interviews were held during working hours in a special area separate from the work premises. The interviews lasted approximately 45 minutes. During the interview, the interviewer asked a broad question in each area of interest and then funneled the employee responses to more specific details based on the content of each response.

The interview data were evaluated and scored by a second group of clinical psychologists trained in interviewing techniques who also were not aware of the purpose of the study. The participant responses were quantified into groupings of areas of interest as specified earlier. Scores on the frequency and quality of particular groups of responses were developed for each participant.

Two types of statistical evaluations were carried out. The first compared the interview data between the affected and nonaffected groups to determine areas of different response. The second evaluations examined associations between the interview data and the type, frequency, and severity of health problems encountered by the affected workers.

The data analyses pinpointed specific job conditions that were more problematic for the affected group. These same conditions were highly correlated to specific types of health complaints, in particular those most responsible for the high rate of clerical employee absences. Based on the data analysis, three reports were prepared. One report of three pages was prepared for the Vice-President of Industrial Relations that summarized the purpose of the study, briefly outlined the methods used, and provided an overview of the findings. In addition, this report made recommendations for further action, including means for dealing with some of the observed problems at the facilities studied, and a suggestion for a corporatewide questionnaire study to determine the extent of problems throughout the corporation.

The second report of five pages was prepared for employees and was similar to that provided to the vice-president, with a few exceptions. First, there was more detail on the results; second, no recommendations were included. A third comprehensive report detailing all aspects of the study methodology, the results, and the recommendations was prepared for the research file as backup for future reference and for study replication.

SUMMARY

Conducting mental health research in industry is a highly complex process and requires a great deal of preparation if the results are to be of practical value. The first step in conducting a study is to set specific objectives that can be met and specify the questions that are to be answered by the research. Both the specific objectives and questions should be put in writing for clarity and so they can be reviewed. The second step is to establish a committee of "key persons" to review the objectives and questions. These "key persons" must represent individuals directly affected by the research and those who can facilitate the research process. Their input will provide "real-life" meaning to the objectives and questions.

The third step is the selection of a methodology that best answers the questions posed given the resources available. Sometimes the most effective methods are not cost-efficient, and therefore other adequate but less expensive methods can be used. The fourth step deals with the selection of potential participants. Industrial research many times limits the use of random sampling and therefore also limits the generalizability of the results. Once potential participants have been identified, it is wise to utilize motivational techniques to gain their cooperation. Messages of management support for the study are mandatory for good response, and the use of incentives to participate are recommended. Data collection should be carried out by a neutral party to enhance unbiased data collection.

The last step is the dissemination of research results to all interested parties. A series of reports should be written, with each specific report aimed at a particular audience in terms of that audience's interests and sophistication. Additionally, oral reports should be given to allow for misinterpretations and misunderstandings to be cleared up. Federal law dictates that such reports must not provide information on individual participants or small identifiable groups of participants.

REFERENCES

Babbie, E. 1973. *Survey Research Methods.* Belmount Calif.: Wadsworth.

Cooper, C.L. and J. Marshall. 1976. "Occupational Sources of Stress: A Review of the Literature Relating to Coronary Heart Disease and Mental Ill Health." *Journal of Occupational Psychology* 49: 11–28.

Dillman, D.A. 1978. *Mail and Telephone Surveys.* New York: John Wiley, 1978.

Manuso, J. 1979. "The Metamorphosis of a Corporate Emotional Health Program." Paper presented at the meeting of the American Psychological Association, September.

Murphy, L.R. 1981. *Stress Reduction in Nursing Personnel: Efficacy of Biofeedback and Progressive Muscle Relaxation.* National Institute for Occupational Safety and Health. Manuscript submitted for publication.

Peters, R.K., H. Benson, and J.M. Peters. 1977. "Daily Relaxation Breaks in a Working Population." *American Journal of Public Health* 67: 946–959.

Privacy Act of 1974. Public Law 93–579, 93rd Congress, 5.3418. Government Printing Office, Washington, D.C. December 31, 1974.

Schleifer, L.M. 1981. *Cue-Controlled Relaxation: An Innovative Method for Reducing Job Stress in a Hypertensive Working Population.* National Institute for Occupational Safety and Health. Manuscript submitted for publication.

Smith, M.J. 1981. "Occupational Stress: An Overview of Psychosocial Factors." In *Machine Pacing and Occupational Stress,* edited by G. Salvendy and M.J. Smith. London: Taylor & Francis.

24 Contemporary Psychological Assessment in Organizational Settings

**Robert B. Most, Ph.D., and
Howard I. Glazer, Ph.D.**

HISTORY OF PSYCHOLOGICAL TESTING

Psychological testing in organizations dates back to the roots of civilization. The Chinese empire (2200 B.C.) utilized civil service examinations (DuBois, 1966) for psychological screening. "In 1115 B.C.... job sample tests were used requiring proficiency in the five basic arts: music, archery, horsemanship, writing, and arithmetic.... Knowledge of a sixth art was also required–skill in the rites and ceremonies of public and social life" (pp. 30-31). The Western roots of psychological evaluation dates back to the Greeks (McReynolds, 1975), who used tests to assess physical and intellectual skills. The Socratic method of teaching utilized testing of students and precursed the European universities' formal examination for awarding of degrees and honors (Anastasi, 1976).

The modern philosophy of psychological testing has its roots in the work of Esquirol and Seguin, who experimented with physiological predictors of mental retardation. Both Esquirol and Seguin (Anastasi, 1976) concluded that verbal ability plays a critical role in mental retardation and the subsequent concept of intelligence. Alfred Binet's work on diagnosing mental retardation led to the first criterion referenced tests. Performance on Binet's tests were predictive of success in school and thus valuable in assessing which children were likely to profit from special schooling. Binet was the first to establish a graded series of tests and a way of norm referencing the tests (Edwards, 1971).

Many of the modern methods and philosophies of psychological testing were developed by Francis Galton. He developed norms for psychological traits, as well as pioneering rating scales and questionnaires. Galton made important contributions to statistical methods for analyzing individual difference data; work that was continued by Karl Pearson, who developed many of the statistical techniques in current use.

During World War I the United States Armed Forces developed the Army Alpha and Army Beta group administered intelligence tests. These were the first example of group testing and were developed from the work of Arthur S. Otis. Following World War I the Army Alpha and Beta tests were released and acted as an impetus for the civilian use of such tests, which became very popular in the 1920s (Anastasi, 1976). Unfortunately, the early crude tests were used indiscriminately and failed to live up to expectations. This failure and lack of early understanding for the limitations of psychological tests probably hindered the progress of psychological testing.

During World War II the air force developed batteries of tests that were predictive of performance in basic flight training school. Later batteries were developed for other air force personnel, and finally, batteries were developed for all the services. The air force batteries were a model of criterion validity. A large number of sensorimotor, perceptual, and spatial factors predictive of performance were identified and utilized in the test construction (Anastasi, 1976). The utility of predicting successful pilots and screening potentially unsuccessful pilots from expensive training was a powerful model for companies developing and using psychological tests for employee screening.

Psychological testing has matured, and the current selection and number of tests and inventories is remarkable (see Buros, 1978). Some inventories such as the Minnesota Multiphasic Personality Inventory (MMPI) have proven to be broadly useful for clinical assessment, corporate screening, counseling, and a number of predictive purposes (e.g., ulcer personality, alcoholism, drug addictive personality). Other psychological tests have specific targeted purposes (e.g., state-trait anxiety measures, leadership surveys).

COMPUTERIZATION

In the past 25 years, computers have had an increasingly strong impact on psychological testing. The computer allows fast, inexpensive, and reliable scoring and interpretation of tests as well as providing powerful statistical techniques for test development.

Computer narrative was first developed for the MMPI. The MMPI code typology was easily transformed into algorithms that point to narrative statements. Extensive narrative, computer-generated reports can be garnered from the MMPI or the California Psychological Inventory (CPI). For example, Behaviordyne's narrative is based on 166 scales and 12 clinical factors. The computer program was developed over a period of 15 years at the University of Kentucky and was verified on a population of over 2,000 men and women (Finney and

Auvenshine, 1970). The computer algorithms for this program can be quite complex. There are over 23,000 independently addressable statements, some of which are flagged after a search of more than 25 scales and factors. Basically, the model is one of a psychologist gathering and interpreting data from researched scales and writing a report based on that data (Finney, et al., 1972). The computer does the same thing as the psychologist, but it utilizes algorithms that point to narrative statements that interpret the research data.

The computer is a valuable tool for utilizing and interpreting pyschological tests; however, there are problems with computerized scoring and interpretation. A computer program is only as good as what goes into it. Thus, the computerized system needs to be examined in terms of the validity of the instrument and research data and the proven utility of the reports. For an explanation of validity and reliability in narrative psychodiagnostic reports see Most (1982). One problem is that many people have the idea that because a report comes from a computer it automatically is accurate and valid. There are others who take the opposite position that a computer cannot be interpretive. Meehl's (1973) tabulation of studies comparing computer "cookbook" algorithms to clinical interpretation of profiles found that out of 35 studies, 23 were in favor of the statistical method, 12 showed no difference between the methods, and not one fell in favor of the clinician's judgment. Of course, any computerized report no matter how good will not be 100 percent accurate. There is statistical variance in the reliability of each scale as well as the variance in the predictive accuracy of the scales. This is not to say that computerized reports are not great tools with great utility and remarkable ability for characterizing the individual.

In terms of the validity of the inventory and the interpretive service, the MMPI is evaluated as the best measure of pathology and has had over 4,000 published studies to its credit. "The CPI is one of the best personality inventories currently available. Its technical development is of a high order and it has been subjected to extensive research and continuous improvement" (Anastasi, 1982, p. 508). The Behaviordyne narrative interpretation of the MMPI and CPI is consistently evaluated as containing about 80 to 85 percent statements that are accurately and discriminantly descriptive of the individual (Most, 1982). The Behaviordyne comprehensive clinical narrative psychodiagnostic report has been judged in court assessments as being equivalent to about three hours of psychodiagnostic interviewing.

Another example is the Sixteen Personality Factors (16PF). The 16PF is a computerized inventory that has become popular and had a number of computerized reports developed from it; yet, there are many outstanding questions about the validity of the instrument (Anastasi, 1976) and about the generalizability of validity across forms (Bouchard, 1978). Many validity questions remain for the 16PF, and yet there is much computerization of this instrument.

Computers are getting smaller and smaller for equal computing power. Already there are several companies that offer tests on in-house minicomputers.

The current systems offer computers that can also be used for standard small business functions such as billing or word processing. The psychological tests are handled via interchangeable floppy disk. Each disk has a number of tests of a particular type (e.g., 50 MMPIs) on it and a counter. When the number of tests on the disk are used up, the customer must buy a new floppy disk. This allows the test publisher to get royalties on the test and for the company to offer more tests and to get continuing funds for tests that are developed. A variation of this procedure is publishers that offer cassettes that are readable on home computer systems.

There are several problems with the minicomputer system. One is that the initial cost of the computer is still high compared to the small cost of scoring and interpreting the tests. Another problem is with test security. The publisher of a test has no control over who utilizes and interprets the test. One problem with on-line testing is that the testee must sit in front of the terminal for the whole testing session. When long inventories such as the 566 item MMPI are administered, this can be a substantial amount of time in which the equipment is tied up.

Several future directions for computer on-line testing are becoming evident. One is that as more and more professionals buy computer systems for office or personal use, floppy disk cassettes will be developed to provide inventories for their computers. Software companies will put inventories onto existing computer systems with ways to count the number of inventories that are scored. Hand-held computer terminals are being developed so that a terminal is not tied up during inventory administration. Card readers will allow the inventory to be administered on computer cards and then quickly read into the terminal.

Another direction is for inexpensive intelligent terminals that can call up the test publisher for scoring and narrative interpretation. The publisher's larger computer can offer a wide variety of tests with greater flexibility and complexity in the interpretation. New services can be offered and promoted very rapidly via direct publisher to professional computer communication.

SELECTION

The value of psychological screening is in discriminating good employees from problem employees. Well designed selection procedures can be a great asset to an organization both in terms of personnel cost savings and in corporate climate.

In developing a selection system via a job analysis, a multistep approach is followed. This system proceeds as follows:

1. A job analysis is conducted in which the needed skills, knowledge, and worker traits are evaluated for the job.

2. Tests are selected or developed to measure these characteristics.
3. The tests are given to current employees (in concurrent validity designs) or to applicants (in predictive validity designs), and the test results are correlated with job performance criteria.
4. Based on the correlations between the tests and the criteria, tests are selected or refined, and cutting scores are developed. These are combined to best predict the criteria, namely, job performance.

Selection system development can be divided into concurrent or predictive validity designs. If the study is done with current employees and the test battery is developed from predicting current employees' work behaviors and qualities, then the study is concurrent. If the tests are given to applicants and then after a period of time the tests are evaluated for how well they predict the job performance of the applicants hired (and discriminating those hired from those not hired), then the study is predictive.

The concurrent validity paradigm is the less expensive of the two, and it allows more rapid completion of the validation study. The predictive design is logically the most accurate since it matches the prediction of future behavior. The arguments for the predictive design (Dunnette, 1966) are that the concurrent design: (1) does not include the applicants who were not hired, thus (2) there is a restriction of range due to measuring only hired employees, (3) there may have been differences between the applicants and the present employees, and (4) there may be effects on the psychological tests of job experience and training.

Besides the cost and time savings of the concurrent validity design, some psychologists (e.g., Barrett, Phillips, & Alexander, 1981) have argued that there is not sufficient empirical evidence for the above concerns or they have proven not to be worse for concurrent than for predictive designs. Empirical comparisons of the two designs have yielded virtually identical validity coefficients (Bemis, 1968). In summary, when choosing a validation design there are sampling considerations that must be considered, but the concurrent validity design has great utility.

Criterion Issues

There are a number of criterion issues that should be considered when evaluating a selection test battery. The quality of the predictive system is partly determined by the quality of the tests (i.e., underlying validity and reliability) but is also greatly (and ultimately) determined by the quality of the criteria against which the test has been validated (Smith, 1976). The criteria should be as objective as possible, and there should be specifications about how the crtieria were derived. Usually conflict criteria consist of some of the following: job measurement such as productivity or work rate; personnel data such as absenteeism, accidents, or infractions; and ratings of performance by supervisors. Supervisors ratings can vary from the global, "How good a worker is the employee?" to specific behaviorally anchored items, "The employee takes too-long coffee breaks."

Often it is difficult to get good criteria. There are many sources of criterion confounding. Job changes, different shifts working on the same project, supervisor bias, and the biases in rating scales are examples of sources of criterion problems. A good set of criteria should be reliable and cover many aspects of the job.

When selecting an already validated test battery the evaluation of the criteria is a very important consideration. The job behaviors predicted in the battery need to be examined for similarity to the behaviors in your work force. There should be an adequate sample size in the test validation study. Sample size is an important consideration even though the large number of varied jobs makes this a difficult requirement. Optimally, the test battery should be cross-validated; that is, the predictive equations developed in the validation study should be verified on a similar population to check their generality. Often this is accomplished by splitting the sample in half, developing the equations on one half, then using those equations on the other half and seeing how well they predict. Such evaluation of shrinkage, or decrease in predictability, can also be accomplished via statistical formula and small sample techniques such as jackknifing.

One promising area in the field of selection test batteries is synthetic validity. The idea behind synthetic validity is that jobs can be broken down into component parts. There are combinations of skills needed for any particular job. If valid predictors can be found for each job component then predictors can be synthetically assembled to make predictions for specific jobs. For example, logical reasoning may be one skill needed for a computer programmer and also for a production scheduler. There are other skills that are part of each job but a valid predictor of logical reasoning could be added to both the programmer's and scheduler's selection batteries. Where the jobs differ they would have other predictive measures selected for their batteries that are not shared. The goal of synthetic validity is to solve the problem of trying to develop selection measures for a large number of different jobs with a host of different skills. In synthetic validity the predictors can be sorted to match the pattern of the particular job's required skills. Synthetic validity is a promising approach where adequate criterion-referenced validation studies are impractical. For further discussion of synthetic validity see Primoff (1975) or Guion (1965).

Selection via Personality Inventories

Increasingly, personality inventories are being used for personnel selection. The value of personality instruments is that they tap dimensions that are related to productivity such as responsibility and self-control, on the one hand, and pathology, on the other. A small proportion of employees account for the majority of problem behaviors (absenteeism, grievances, infractions), and personality measures can be effective predictors of these individuals. For example, Dow Chemical has been using the MMPI as part of their selection test battery since 1952 (Bollinger, 1981). Dow also uses several job analysis developed predictors in their batteries, resulting in a well-rounded approach to selection.

Most, Schultz, and Tondow (1980) have conducted a large scale study with a major manufacturing company that can be used as an example of a validation study with a personality inventory. The study utilized a predictive validity design because the MMPI had previously been used for an employee assistance program screening of alcoholic and drug addictive personalities and for screening psychotics. Besides these three measures, the analysis of the MMPI item pool yielded 161 scales and 12 clinical factors used in developing predictive equations of job behaviors.

The Most, Schultz, and Tondow study utilized MMPI measures in regression analysis of 12 worker behaviors. The regressions were developed on a sample of 864 workers and cross-validated to a sample of 863 workers. Eight of the regression equations provided to have adequate generality on cross-validation. The work behaviors and correlations with the MMPI measures varied from +.53 for Written Warnings, Days Off Due to OSHA Infractions, Accidents, and Number of Insurance Claims, to +.43 for Absenteeism. These behaviors are productivity decreasing, but the same approach is applicable to productive behaviors, such as production rate accuracy or ratings of supervisors.

Discriminant function analysis of the Most, Schultz, and Tondow study yielded approximately 20 percent correct prediction (hits) with an incorrect prediction rate of less than 1 percent (false positives). A similar study was conducted by Most (1981) using the CPI and carefully controlled criteria. One problem with the Most, Schultz, and Tondow study was that the criteria were taken from personnel records. The Most (1981) study carefully controlled criterion confounding and made greater use of supervisor and executive committee ratings. This study, predictive of department store buyer performance, yielded discriminant functions after cross-validation with correct predictions (hits) of 75 percent and incorrect predictions (false positives) of 4 percent. The comparison of these two studies is proof of the value in carefully controlling criterion measurement.

One advantage to predicting productivity that is related to job behaviors is that the dollar cost of the behavior can be related to job behaviors of the selection tool, thus permitting a cost-effectiveness analysis. This is particularly true when discriminant functions are used as the predictive equations.

Taking the Most, Schultz, and Tondow (1980) study as an example, in that manufacturing company absenteeism costs $2,000 per employee per year averaged across employees. Actually, a minority of employees account for the majority of the absenteeism. The equation for absenteeism was set for a cutoff value that would screen the worst 15 percent of the employees. However, the predictive accuracy of the equation (hit ratio) is such that it is only able to correctly target approximately 20 percent of these problem employees. The power of the equation comes from the fact that the 3 percent of the work force that is screened (15 percent of the employees times 20 percent hit ratio) are heavy absenteeism problems and thus disproportionately costly for the company. To calculate the dollar savings via screening with the discriminant equation it is only necessary to relate the frequency of problem behaviors of the individuals that are screened to the corporate cost of those behaviors. In this example, the validation study was conducted on 1,727 employees. These employees as a whole cost $3,464,000 in absenteeism per year ($2,000 per employee). An analysis of the days absent for the 15 percent of the employees that the equation was designed to screen shows that these 15 percent accounted for 40 percent of the absenteeism. This would cost the company approximately $1,385,600 per year (40 percent of the total cost). But the discriminant function is only able to screen 20 percent of these problem employees. Yet, 20 percent of the 40 percent absenteeism cost is still a cost to the company of $277,120 per year. The advantage to psychological screening comes from the fact that the cost to screen the total 1,727 employees is $34,540 ($20 per employee), which shows a net savings for the company of $242,580 per year; and yet, the cost of screening is only in the first year, while the savings are repeated annually over the potential work life of the employee. This example is for only one statistical system, the actual utility of the system to the company is much greater. In addition, the above analysis was for a study with poorly controlled criteria and thus fairly low correct prediction ratios. For more carefully controlled studies the utility is much greater.

The main point of the above analysis is that with corporate data on the cost of productive employee (e.g., work rate) and unproductive employee (e.g., absenteeism, infractions) behaviors, the analysis yielded by a discriminant function can give data for relating the predicted success of psychological testing to the dollar savings that are a function of the testing.

One effect of computers has been to decrease the cost of validation studies. The ability to score inventories and scales from computer readable response sheets has cut the cost of the predictor data. Computers have also cut the cost of the statistical analysis relating the tests to the criterion data. The main costs are for developing the criterion and putting the data into the computer. Given the trend toward computerized human resource systems within companies, if psychologists participate in the structuring of these systems it may one day be possible to retrieve criterion data that is automatically stored in human resource files. Unfortunately, these computerized systems are not currently structured for facilitating selection research.

Equal Employment Opportunity Commission/Act

Since the Equal Employment Opportunity Commission (EEOC) was created by federal statute in 1964, psychological testing has come under public scrutiny.

Through the late 1960s and early 1970s the various requirements of federal law were a focus for psychologists developing personnel selection tests. The string of often conflicting federal guidelines and acts combined with conflicting decisions in the courts not only made it difficult to develop selection tests, but it gave psychological testing a bad name with many employers (for a discussion see Fincher, 1973).

In an effort to end the conflict and develop a set of guidelines that are in agreement with court decisions, the *Uniform Guidelines on Employee Selection Procedures* went into effect in September of 1978. The *Uniform Guidelines* has made a major clarification of federal law in regards to equal employment opportunity and psychological testing. The *Uniform Guidelines* not only apply to psychological testing but to any method of employee selection including interviewing.

Basically the *Uniform Guidelines* state that a psychological test can be used for selection if *either* there is a validation study evidencing the relationship between the tests and the work behaviors *or* there is no adverse impact upon race, sex, or ethnic heritage. These two conditions are independent, so either can be met to conform to the *Uniform Guidelines*.

The *Uniform Guidelines* discuss the criteria for validating selection tests. It permits studies based on criterion related validity, content validity, or construct validity as established in the *Standards for Educational and Psychological Tests* (American Psychological Association, 1974).

In assessing adverse impact, the *Uniform Guidelines* adopt a "rule of thumb" that is a practical means for determining adverse impact. Adverse impact is determined by a four-step process:

> 1. Calculate the rate of selection for each group (divide the number of persons from a group by the number of applicants from the group).
>
> 2. Observe which group has the highest selection rate.
>
> 3. Calculate the impact ratios, by comparing the selection rate for each group with that of the highest group (divide the selection rate for a group by the selection rate for the highest group).
>
> 4. Observe whether the selection rate for any group is substantially less (i.e., usually less than four-fifths or 80 percent) than the selection rate for the highest group. If it is, adverse impact is indicated in most circumstances. (*Questions and Answers on the Uniform Guidelines on Employee Selection Procedures*, 1979, question 12)

For example, if 90 percent of the women applicants are hired but only 60 percent of the male applicants, then there would be adverse impact of men because 60 percent is less than four-fifths of 90 percent.

A few points should be made about "adverse impact." First, where "statistical and practical" differences can be found in selection rates that do not violate the four-fifths rule, adverse impact can still be proven. Second, even though it is convenient to calculate adverse impact for a psychological selection test, the adverse impact determination applies to the overall selection process. Third, where two equally predictive selection procedures exist, the one with the least adverse impact should be utilized. Fourth, data on hiring in relation to race, sex, and ethnic heritage must be maintained.

When psychologists start discussing adverse impact it is easy to forget that any test used for selection should be validated. If the test has been validated then it meets the requirements of the *Uniform Guidelines* and adverse impact is much less of an issue. Most EEOC difficulties arise from informal, nonvalidated selection procedures. Fortunately, it is not necessary to do a validation study for every job in every company; validated selection instruments can be taken from other studies where there is similarity of jobs or work behaviors.

Screening with Regard to Employee Assistance Programs and Litigation

One of the underutilized areas in psychological preemployment screening is the prediction of individuals who could be costly to the corporation either through disability or litigation.

One example of such screening is a program Behaviordyne has conducted for many years with a large manufacturing corporation. This screening system utilizes an analysis of the MMPI that predicts three personality classes: alcoholic personality, drug addictive personality, and psychosis. The correct prediction rates for these three classes are, respectively, 83 percent, 88 percent, and 73 percent, based on empirical studies (Finney, 1973). In this system, when individuals are flagged on one of the three measures, a comprehensive clinical report is automatically generated. The flagged individual is then interviewed by a mental and/or medical health professional. If the alcoholism or drug addiction is confirmed, the individual can be offered participation in an employee assistance program (EAP). If the individual enrolls in the program, countless potentially nonproductive hours are saved. Often without such screening, it takes years to act on an addiction problem with great loss to the company. If the individual elects not to participate in the EAP program, the company is on record as having offered assistance to the individual. When an employee participates in the EAP program all participants gain: the company for avoiding or turning around a potential problem and the individual for getting needed assistance. In the case of the psychotic applicant, the company need not hire the individual, again with the savings of a potential problem.

Tondow (1979) tested the utility of the screening system by checking a sample of alcoholic employees who had been screened by the system and given employee assistance. In the study, two periods of six months were compared: one before the screening and one after. In the postscreening period, absenteeism was reduced by 89 percent and the health insurance utilization was reduced by 75 percent. In a further verification of this result, Most, Schultz, and Tondow (1980) found significant correlations between alcoholic, drug addictive, and psychosis scores and absenteeism and job infractions.

Another potentially valuable area for psychological screening is in the identification of Type A, heart attack prone, personality individuals. The Jenkins Activity Survey (JAS) is a current measure of Type A personality, but it only correlates with the Type A interview, the best predictor, about +.25 (Chesney et al., 1981). A better measure of Type A personality is a special subset of the Adjective Check List, which was found to correlate with the Type A interview +.31 (Chesney et al., 1981). A number of researchers are working on better measures of Type A personality, so a more efficient measure may be available in the near future.

There would be great value in a predictor of Type A personality. DeHart (1980) estimated that coronary heart disease costs the air force about 50 million dollars annually. A measure that could predict even 10 percent of these pilots could have a significant cost savings value. In this example, the high cost of aerospace weapons systems makes the value of such a predictor apparent, but psychological treatment of Type A disposition executives also has great corporate savings potential.

Another aspect of Type A prediction and coronary heart disease is the high cost of litigation when an employee blames the heart attack on job stress. There is some evidence (Most, 1980) that a psychological instrument could be predictive of post-heart-attack individuals who subsequently file litigation. If such individuals could be identified at hire or even post-heart-attack, then a company could minimize the high litigation costs.

Blum (1980) in an analysis of worker's compensation concludes, "It should be pointed out that open-ended liability in Workmen's Compensation for mental impairment could well lead employers to require extensive psychiatric screening prior to employment" (p. 195). Such screening is available with systems such as the alcoholism, drug addiction, and psychosis screening system mentioned above. One model is to give the psychological instrument at hire and then again at the time an employee problem develops. Psychological change can be compared longitudinally to see if there was significant change over the time the individual was employed. If the psychological problem was apparent in the measurement at hire, then it would be more difficult to argue that the problem was work related. Behaviordyne has such a system called a "differential" report, which flags significant personality changes longitudinally.

Screening Where Public Safety Is Involved

With the publication of ANSI (American National Standards Institute) standard N18.17 (1973) it became necessary for the nuclear industry to screen all employees for emotional stability who are allowed unescorted access to nuclear facilities. This standard opened a field for clinically screening industrial employees. The ANSI standard is vague as to what constitutes emotional stability, so the industry has adopted various models for the certification requirement. These range from an interview by a physician, to a decision based entirely on a psychological test, to a decision made only after a psychological inventory report and a clinical interview.

One model for emotional stability certification followed by the Behaviordyne Psychological Corporation, which has conducted over 7,000 of these interviews, is a thorough and efficient approach that can be used as a model for various types of emotional stability evaluation, including police, security guards, and others where the public welfare and safety is involved. The process starts when the company personnel department administers the MMPI to relevant employees. A comprehensive narrative report is generated from these MMPIs. Based on the nature of the narrative report, a licensed psychologist classifies the individual into one of three categories: (1) "OK," which indicates that the report looks like that of an emotionally stable individual: the company can allow the individual immediate access to the facility pending a confirmatory (or disconfirmatory) clinical interview, which must be arranged within 90 days; (2) "hold," which indicates uncertainty about the individual's emotional stability as measured by the report: the individual is not given unescorted access in the facility without a clinical interview to confirm or disconfirm the report; and (3) "no," which indicates that there is sufficient pathology in the report to recommend against the individual unless a subsequent interview evidences otherwise.

The utility company is not given any clinical information. The only data the company receives following the clinical interview is a form indicating certification or noncertification of the individual's emotional stability.

One of the powerful aspects of the clinical interview coupled with the narrative personality report is that the report contains information that would take hours to derive by other means. For example, pathology, substance abuse personality, sociopathology, ethical beliefs, hostility, cyclothymia, and hysteria are all traits that are measured and reported when relevant. These cues about the individual's personality strengths and weaknesses allow the clinician to direct the interview in the most productive manner. The clinician has a focus for investigating. Otherwise, the clinician needs to differentiate the individual and discover weaknesses from scratch.

Perhaps the greatest utility of inventories such as the MMPI over the interview is the ability to screen sociopathic individuals. Most and Schultz (1982) compared two sets of employees rated "no" based on their MMPI narrative reports. One set was never interviewed and thus also considered poor candidates by the utility. The other set was interviewed and thus consisted of employees that the utility would have liked to have at the nuclear facility. The main difference between the groups was that the individuals who were interviewed were higher in sociopathology and lower in general pathology as measured by the

MMPI than were the individuals the utility dropped from consideration after only the MMPI report judgment. The study indicates that the MMPI functioned to screen for sociopathology, that is, for individuals with lower ethical and responsibility standards. These are the individuals most likely to characterize what is known as the "insider threat." One cannot help but consider that without the psychological screening there would be a higher ratio of sociopaths working in the nuclear facility.

The emotional stability certification covers the person only during the time of his or her evaluation. To assess stability during employment, a system of behavioral observation has been developed. The system relies on supervisors who are trained in behavioral observation and who periodically fill out a behavioral observation questionnaire. The questionnaire is then assessed by a psychologist for emotional changes in the employee. Any employee flagged by this system can be reassessed for emotional stability.

In the above screening system the utility receives minimal clinical information about the employee. This preserves the clinical, confidential nature of this assessment system. It should be mentioned that when the employee is interviewed, he or she can receive a "self report," which provides feedback based on the narrative analysis of the MMPI. It is a special report that is designed to provide relevant information to the individual completing the inventory.

As the clinical decision affects the individual vocationally, a review procedure was developed to allow the applicant a way of appealing the decision. When an individual disagrees with the judgment, he or she gets a second opinion by a licensed psychologist or psychiatrist of his or her choice. The clinical file on the individual is sent to this practitioner. If the second opinion is in agreement with the original decision the matter is ended. If the second opinion is in conflict then a third more extensive evaluation is carried out by a practitioner who is mutually agreeable to the individual and the utility. This third decision is binding.

The model developed for nuclear facility employee screening is also applicable for police screening. Several court decisions (e.g., *McKenna* v. *Fargo,* 1978) have ruled that psychological instruments can be used clinically where public safety is involved. Police screening is usually a thorough assessment; the exact model depends on the psychologist. For example, Spielberger (1979), following the extensive Florida Police Standards Research Project, recommends the California Psychological Inventory, the Strong-Campbell Interest Inventory (SCII), the State-Trait Anxiety Inventory, and the Nelson-Denny Reading Test.

Executive Selection

When a psychologist chooses a battery of tests for executive selection that choice is often a function of which tests are familiar and comfortable to the psychologist. For a general overview of tests that can be utilized to garner psychological information see Buros (1978). What follows will be a discussion of tests and data that many psychologists use in executive selection.

A good beginning is to gather information about the applicant. A health history and job history are useful to determine the background, health, and accomplishments of the individual as they relate to the job. A relevant measure to this type of data is a life-stress measure such as the Holmes (Holmes & Rahe, 1967).

Intelligence is a valuable attribute for an executive, but it is not a primary requirement for being a successful executive. The Wechsler Adult Intelligence Scale (WAIS) is a good measure for assessing the current intelligence of the individual. The person's balance between numerical and verbal abilities should be considered and related to the type of job he or she will be performing. For example, an advertising executive would need more verbal skills than an engineering executive. Intelligence is relevant but should not be a primary consideration. For example, creativity does not seem to be related to intelligence (MacKinnon & Hall, 1972).

Another measure yielding information related to intelligence but not requiring the intensive testing is the Watson-Glaser Critical Thinking Appraisal (Watson & Glaser, 1964). The Watson-Glaser measures inference, recognition of assumptions, deduction, interpretation, and evaluation of arguments. The Watson-Glaser was validated on a college population, but the assessment of thinking is quite appropriate for executive selection assessment.

It is important to measure the executive's personality. Narrative interpretations can be of value for the same reasons as were mentioned in the screening for emotional stability. A narrative report gives information that would take hours of interviewing, and it provides leads that can be followed during the interview. The CPI is a good tool for executive selection. Rawls and Rawls (1968) have found that the CPI discriminated successful from less successful executives. Several scales for measuring managerial effectiveness have been derived for the CPI (e.g., Goodstein & Schrader, 1963). Consulting Psychologists Press scores a profile for the CPI that contains Managerial Interests and Work Orientation scales. Other scales on this profile that are relevant to executive selection are Empathy, Independence, Leadership Index, and the Social Maturity Index. The standard scales of the CPI are also quite relevant to measuring important traits in the executive. For example, Dominance, Capacity for Status, Sociability, Social Presence, Responsibility, Self-Control, Achievement via Independence, and Intellectual Efficiency are attributes that are valuable for executive assessment. The CPI was developed to measure coping behavior and normal personality functioning (Gough, 1975).

Achievement urge is measured by the CPI, but a more thorough assessment can be made by the Thematic Apperception Test (TAT). Four pictures measure achievement need (n-Ach), two of which are taken from the original TAT (see McClelland et al., 1953). These pictures are valuable for getting a projective clinical assessment of the individual's achievement orientation.

Leadership can be assessed by a number of instruments (see Pfeiffer, Heslin, & Jones, 1976). For example, the Leadership Ability Evaluation (Cassel & Stancik, 1961) is relevant to corporate leadership style, that is, whether the individual is democratic, autocratic, laissez-faire, etc. When leadership style is being assessed, it should be considered in light of the company's need for a leader with a particular style (Vroom, 1976). For example, an executive in a trucking company may need to be more autocratic than one in a research institution.

The interview of the potential executive should function to validate or invalidate the psychological tests. It should verify the accuracy of the testing and determine whether the test data were unbiased. If taken alone, the interview is not a very predictive measure of job success (McCormick & Tiffin, 1974). The value of the interview, like psychotherapy, seems to be largely a function of the skill of the interviewer. All psychologists have their own interview styles, goals, and procedures. One system for interviewing is to go over the test results, following up on leads developed from the results. Ambiguities and unusual aspects can be explored. Basically, the psychologist is getting a feel for the individual and can tie the report together into a comprehensive balanced assessment with a feeling for how the person functions and what are his or her abilities. The balance and overview is important when comparing the applicants and when evaluating the fit of the applicant to the requirements of the job.

The psychological evaluation report should include a full description of the reasons for the evaluation or referral, a brief history of the individual, the presenting and behavioral observations, and the results of the testing and interview. The results of the testing should be described, but each interpretation should be put into the perspective of the level of psychological understanding of the individual reading the report (American Psychological Association, 1974). The scores should be interpreted as an estimate given the circumstances and not as absolute characteristics. The validity and reliability of the instruments need to be considered, and the test scores need to be referenced to the norms and populations utilized in validating the tests. The current life stress and life situation of the individual can be discussed. Finally, a summary and conclusion should be included.

The individual tested has the right to know his or her scores and the interpretations made of these scores (American Psychological Association, 1974). One tool for accomplishing this is a "self report" or computer generated narrative based on the MMPI or CPI but designed to give feedback to the individual taking the inventories. This is one option for these personality inventories; other instruments have simplified interpretations or need to have the interpretations of the scores explained in a manner the client can understand. When feedback is provided to the individual, this fact should be mentioned in the report to the company.

Some Current Reasons for Psychological Screening

Since the 1978 *Uniform Guidelines on Employee Selection Procedures*, there has been a renewed interest in psychological screening. As mentioned in the section on the EEOC, the conflicting guidelines and court decisions between 1964 and 1978 led employers to believe that using psychological tests for selection was not in favor with the federal government. The 1978 *Uniform Guidelines* have put psychological testing back onto a logical and functional basis.

The utility of psychological screening is the greatest motivation for its use. Since Vitales (1932) developed predictors of error rate for utility switching operators, the dollar advantage to screening has become evident. For example, a current ruling of job discrimination might eliminate the federal PACE (Professional and Administrative Career Examination). The Internal Revenue Service has estimated that the use of a less valid selection measure for agents would cost the IRS a yearly revenue loss of 115 million dollars (Holden, 1981).

Because of computers, psychological tests are getting easier to use, score, and interpret. It usually takes a week total turnaround to get test results by mail, and corporations are establishing computer-to-computer linkages with scoring services. There are more tests and more validation studies available.

The companies that are most interested in psychological testing are those that have well developed personnel policies. New industries are less interested in psychological screening until they mature. For example, the American Telephone and Telegraph Company (AT & T) has been a leader in selection and placement assessment and has been known for its excellent treatment of employees.

Unions are often initially opposed to psychological selection until they understand the benefits. Applicants are not union members, so the union does not represent them. Applicants are not colleagues who need to be protected. However, the same small proportion of employees that cause the majority of problems for the company are also the proportion that cause most of the union problems. Since screening decreases employee problems it also decreases union problems. Knowledgeable unions become allies of psychological screening. When union officials are given adequate explanations as to the role and function of the psychological testing, any negative attitudes can be ameliorated.

PLACEMENT/CAREER DEVELOPMENT

The placement of employees can be considered as a multichoice selection procedure. A good selection device can be considered one that predicts whether the applicant is suited for the particular job. Optimally, the validation of selection tools for a number of jobs that are then interrelated would place an applicant into a job that he or she most closely matches. This approach is the logic behind the Strong-Campbell Interest Inventory (SCII) (Campbell & Hansen, 1981), with regards to matching the individual to the interest patterns of people in various vocations. The SCII has been tremendously popular for placement and career development.

The SCII and the Self-Directed Search (Holland, 1979) have also been successful because they classify individuals into broad, personality related, occupational categories (Holland, 1976). These categories and their related occupational fields (in parenthesis) are: Intellectual (science); Artistic (arts and entertainment); Social (service); Enterprising (business); Conventional (organizations); and Realistic (technology, outdoors).

The main function of placement is to match the applicant to the job that best meets his or her abilities, personality, and goals. If this can be accomplished, then the organization is most likely to gain a productive employee. The vocational counseling to accomplish this function can be the job of corporate psychologists who understand the corporate job structure and are able to relate this to the employee's specific characteristics.

Placement is not necessarily only a function during hiring; it is also important when employees want to change their jobs or move up the corporate ladder. It is not necessary for employees to only expect to reach their boss' position; much can be gained by moving employees to related positions within the company or to complementary (e.g., from marketing to manufacture) positions, which round out their work experience. Especially when selecting management talent, physiological testing can be of value in finding employees who meet the necessary criteria of flexibility and management potential.

A number of different types of information are needed for optimal placement of employees. These include:

1. The current abilities of the individual. Such information can be taken from a current job description, work history, and abilities testing.

2. Personality testing to match the individual's personality to the job. For example, an extrovert rather than an introvert is more likely to enjoy a job in sales. A compulsive, meticulous individual is more likely to enjoy a job requiring detail.

3. The current goals of the individual should be considered in whether to give the person a job with growth potential or whether the person wants a static job. Goals and aspirations can be taken from standardized forms or via an interview.

One example of an extensive placement system is one employed by a major airline (Schwartz, 1981). This system starts with the gathering of extensive information on the employee when the employee requests a job change or a review for management. The information on the employee includes: current job duties and skills, education, training, and ratings by a supervisor on a number of dimensions such as job performance, creativity, customer relations, etc. These data go into a computer and are stored or matched to current job openings. When filling a management vacancy, a supervisor fills out forms stating the attributes of an employee who might fit the job, namely, skills, training, and personality (e.g. creativity). The computer matches the employee data to the job requirement data and generates a list of likely candidates, which are then evaluated. Finally, several candidates are flown to meet with the supervisor and be interviewed. The system is also designed to aid in EEOC compliance and to allow employees with management potential to round out their work experience by taking positions in various aspects of the company (sales, financial, operations, etc.).

Dow Chemical Corporation (Bollinger, 1981) has a different approach to placement. Their engineering staff, for example, is administered the MMPI. A psychologist reviews the inventory and relates the scores to the engineer's strong and weak personality traits. This assessment is then discussed with the engineer. They discuss the individual's personality and consider which characteristics need strengthening and whether the engineer shows management potential. The model is one of feedback to the individual to aid the person's corporate and personal development.

As mentioned before, Dow Chemical has a selection system that is oriented toward placement. It includes several Dow-developed, job-related tests and the MMPI. A psychologist evaluates the battery and looks at the characteristics in terms of placement but also in terms of how well the person would function as a Dow employee. It should be mentioned that Bollinger has found that one of the best predictors of a problem employee is a high MMPI sociopathic score. The same correlation has also been found in other selection systems that utilize the MMPI, such as for police selection and the emotional stability certification program (Most and Schultz, 1982).

CAREER DEVELOPMENT

Increasingly, there is an awareness that employees need to be able to grow within the organization. If employees feel blocked in their career development, then they are more likely to leave the organization. Such a circumstance is expensive for the organization because it loses the best employees and because it sustains the large costs for training new employees. There is one advantage to turnover: the cross-fertilization of ideas and procedures that occurs because of movement of employees across companies of the same type. This appears to be true for the electronics industry. But as a whole (even for the electronics industry), the cost and instability of turnover far outweighs its benefits.

Affirmative action goals can be furthered by a good career development program. For example the airline (Schwartz, 1981) that computer matched the job requirements to the employee characteristics also built in biases to aid minorities and women. Any focus on developing the careers of minorities and women via psychological evaluation, guidance, and training also serves to aid the company's affirmative action program.

Career development should be considered in light of the needs, characteristics, and abilities of the individual employee. Toward this characterization, the theories of Richard Hoffman (1978a, 1978b) are useful. Hoffman discusses four career concepts that characterize the individual's method of career development. Hoffman also describes four styles that individuals may follow in the development of their careers. These are: transient, steady state, linear, and spiral.

People who move from job to job with no particular pattern are called transient by Hoffman. There is no upward mobility in their careers and usually there are yearly job changes. These are individuals who fear commitment or are searching for independence.

Steady state people choose a career in their youth and stick with it at the same level, often in the same company, through their entire life. They do not change to a higher or lower status job. Usually these are individuals who are very security minded. They need a clear-cut, recognized, and valued role in society.

Linear career individuals are those who choose their vocation in youth and constantly perfect and move upward in the same vocation. Linear career people have strong achievement motivation and are most happy when working for a company in which they can climb a socially defined hierarchy or organizational pyramid.

Spiral career individuals are those who change careers on a five to seven year cycle. In the spiral career the individual moves to new fields and develops new expertise. Such people are motivated by personal growth needs and achievement needs within the field.

An interesting aspect of Hoffman's theories is that if an individual's style can be determined, allowances can be made for the style to keep the person within the organization, especially if he or she is a productive employee.

Employee career development is optimally a function for a psychologist who can utilize information about the individual's personality, interests, competencies, concerns, and goals as well as considerations for the corporate job structure. Counseling can help the individual find new direction within the organization.

If a psychologist is not available to corporate career counseling, there are tools that an employee can utilize to facilitate career assessment. For example, Behaviordyne offers a career counseling package consisting of the CPI section called the "World of Work," which relates personality to vocational choice, a Strong-Campbell Interest Inventory profile, and a workbook to explain the inventories and relate them to the employee's vocational situation. Other inventories that are used for vocational counseling are the Career Development Inventory (Thompson et al., 1981) and the Self-Directed Search (Holland, 1979).

HUMAN RESOURCE DEVELOPMENT

There are a number of psychological instruments that can be used for developing corporate human resources, namely, the personal and vocational development of employees. There are assessment instruments available for many human resource goals. Instruments are available for management development, leadership training, team building, and work environment appraisal (Pfeiffer, Heslin, & Jones, 1976). A few of these inventories are described below.

The Meyers Briggs Type Indicator (MBTI) (Meyers, 1980) is a broadly useful instrument for assessing group interaction, team building, and the individual's Jungian style. It can be used to give employees an understanding of their behavior and the behavior of their colleagues.

Basically, the MBTI is based on the bipolar personality theory of C.G. Jung. It gives scores along four dimensions (yielding 16 combinations): Introvert-Extrovert, Feeling vs. Thinking, Intuitive vs. Sensing, and Perceptive vs. Judging. The appraisal of an individual into these domains allows that individual to understand his or her ways of dealing with his or her job situation. Appraisal of colleagues allows an understanding of conflicts and the fact that people have different ways of dealing with the world. In this sense, the MBTI can be used for team building when the job-team requires a particular combination of different attributes. For example, a broad-based, problem-solving team should be made up of a number of types of personality to perform the required job effectively. In problem solving all four MBTI types are needed for the best solution (Myers, 1980): "sensing to establish all the facts, intuition to suggest all possible solutions, thinking to determine the probable consequences of each course of action, feeling to weight the desirability of each outcome in human terms" (p. 173).

A similar instrument to the MBTI is the FIRO-B (Fundamental Interpersonal Relation Orientation-Behavior) (Ryan, 1977). The FIRO-B is a 54 item questionnaire that measures three dimensions of interpersonal relationships. "Inclusion" assesses the degree to which a person associates with others. "Control" measures the extent to which a person makes decisions, assumes responsibility, or dominates people. "Affection" reflects the degree to which a person becomes emotionally involved with others. The FIRO-B can be used to assess groups, assemble balanced work groups, and give group members an understanding for group interactions and stresses.

There are a number of instruments that measure organizational climate. The Work Environment Scale (WES) (Insel & Moos, 1981) assesses three major dimensions and ten subscales. The WES measures:

- Relationship Dimensions: Involvement, Peer Cohesion, Staff Support
- Personal-Growth Dimensions: Autonomy and Task Orientation
- System Maintenance and System Change Dimensions: Work Pressure, Clarity (the extent to which workers know rules and daily routine), Control (management use of rules and policies), Innovation, and Physical Comfort.

The WES measures interpersonal relationships among employees and between managers and employees. It is valuable in giving information about why some work groups are productive while other work groups are not productive or are under stress. The WES is also a tool for comparing employee-supervisor environment perceptions.

There are several leadership and management style instruments. One example, the Leader Effectiveness and Adaptability Description (LEAD) (Pfeiffer & Jones, 1976) gives feedback on leadership style, which is evaluated in terms of task oriented versus relationship oriented leadership behavior. It also considers the individual's leadership style range and adaptability, as well as the degree to which the leadership behavior is appropriate to the demands of a given situation. The LEAD can be used for self-assessing leadership style, team building, or as an outcome measure in evaluating leadership training.

REFERENCES

American National Standards Institute. 1973. *ANSI N18.17, "Industrial Security for Nuclear Power Plants."* Hinsdale, Ill.: American Nuclear Society.

American Psychological Association. 1974. *Standards for Educational and Psychological Tests.* Washington, D.C.: American Psychological Association.

Anastasi, A. 1976. *Psychological Testing*, 4th Ed. New York: Macmillan.

———. 1982. *Psychological Testing*, 5th Ed. New York: Macmillan.

Barrett, G.V., J.S. Phillips, and R.A. Alexander, 1981. "Concurrent and Predictive Validity Designs: A Critical Reanalysis." *Journal of Applied Psychology* 66: 1–6.

Bemis, S.E. 1968. "Occupational Validity of the General Aptitude Test Battery." *Journal of Applied Psychology* 52: 240–49.

Blum, J.D. 1980. "Compensating the Mentally Impaired Worker." In *Mental Wellness Programs for Employees,* edited by R.H. Egdahl, D.C. Walsh, and W.B. Goldbeck. New York: Springer-Verlag.

Bollinger, L. 1981. Personal communication.

Bouchard, T.J. 1978. "The Sixteen Personality Factor Questionnaire." In *Seventh Mental Measurement Yearbook*, edited by O.K. Buros. Highland Park, N.J.: Gryphon Press.

Buros, O.K., Ed. 1978. *The Eighth Mental Measurements Yearbook.* Highland Park, N.J.: Gryphon Press.

Campbell, D.P. and J.C. Hansen. 1981. *Manual for the SVIB-SCII.* Stanford, Calif.: Stanford University Press.

Cassel, R. and E. Stancik. 1961. *Leadership Ability Evaluation Manual.* Los Angeles: Western Psychological Service.

Chesney, M.A., G.W. Black, J.H. Chadwick, and R.H. Rosenman. 1981. "Psychological Correlates of the Coronary-prone Behavior Pattern." *Journal of Behavioral Medicine* 4: 217–30.

DeHart, R.M. 1980. "Coronary Heart Disease: An Expensive Air Force Problem." *Aviation Space and Environmental Medicine* 51: 1057–63.

DuBois, P.H. 1966. "A Test Dominated Society: China 1115 B.C.–1905 A.D."

In *Testing Problems in Perspective*, edited by A. Anastasi, pp. 29–36. Washington, D.C.: American Council on Education.

Dunnette, M.S. 1966. *Personnel Selection and Placement*. Belmont, Calif.: Brooks/Cole.

Edwards, A.J. 1971. *Individual Mental Testing: Part I, History and Theories*. Scranton, Penn.: Intext Educational.

Fincher, C. 1973. "Personnel Testing and Public Policy." *American Psychologist* 28: 489–97.

Finney, J.C. 1973. "Automated Psychodiagnostic Testing for General Physicians and for Psychiatrists." In *Automation in Medicine*. Mount Kisco, N.Y.: Futura.

Finney, J.C. and C.D. Auvenshine. 1970. "Programmed Interpretation of Psychological Tests by Computer." Final Report RD 2465-P, Social and Rehabilitation Services, Department of Health, Education and Welfare.

Finney, J.C., G. LeMaistre, D.F. Smith, R. Sward, C.D. Auvenshine, M. Tondow, and D. Skeeters. 1972. "Computer Simulation of Psychologists' Decision-making." Published in the *Proceedings of the Association for Computing Machinery Annual Conference, 1972*. Boston: Association for Computing Machinery.

Goodstein, L.D. and W.J. Schrader. 1963. "An Empirically-derived Managerial Key for the California Psychological Inventory." *Journal of Applied Psychology* 47: 42–45.

Gough, H.G. 1975. *Manual for the California Psychological Inventory*. Palo Alto, Calif.: Consulting Psychologists Press.

Guion, R.M. 1965. "Synthetic Validity in a Small Company: A Demonstration." *Personnel Psychology* 18: 49–63.

Hoffman, R.A. 1978a. "Career Concept Congruence: A Model for Organizational Development." Paper given to the thirty-eighth annual meeting of the Academy of Management, San Francisco, August 11, 1978.

———. 1978b. "Career Concepts–A New Approach to Career Research." Technical report, Ernst & Ernst.

Holden, C. 1981. "Federal Job Exam to Be Retired." *Science* 211.

Holland, J.L. 1976. "Vocational Preference." In *Handbook of Industrial and Organizational Psychology*, edited by M.S. Dunnette. Chicago: Rand McNally.

———. 1979. *The Self-Directed Search Professional Manual*. Palo Alto, Calif.: Consulting Psychologists Press.

Holmes, T.H. and R.H. Rahe. 1967. "The Social Readjustment Rating Scale." *Journal of Psychosomatic Research* 11: 213–18.

Insel, P.M. and R.H. Moos. 1981. *Work Environment Scale Manual*. Palo Alto, Calif.: Consulting Psychologists Press.

MacKinnon, D.W. and W.B. Hall. 1972. "Intelligence and Creativity." Presented at "Colloquium 17: The Measurement of Creativity." *Proceedings, XVIIth International Congress of Applied Psychology, Liege, Belgium, 25th–30th July 1971*. Brussels: EDITEST, Vol. II, pp. 1883–888.

McClelland, D.C., J.W. Atkinson, R.A. Clark, and E.L. Lowell. 1953. *The Achievement Motive*. New York: Appleton-Century-Crofts.

McCormick, E.J. and J. Tiffin. 1974. *Industrial Psychology*. Englewood Cliffs, N.J.: Prentice-Hall.

McKenna v. *Fargo*, 1978. 451 F Supp 1355 (U.S.D.C., N.J.).

McReynolds, P. 1975. "Historical Antecedents of Personality Assessment." In *Advances in Psychological Assessment*, edited by P. McReynolds. San Francisco: Jossey-Bass.

Meehl, P.E. 1973. *Psychodiagnosis: Selected Papers*. New York: W.W. Norton

Most, R.B. 1980. "An MMPI Profile of Type A Individuals." Paper given to the California State Psychological Association, Pasadena.

———. 1981. *The Development and Validation of Department Store Buyer Performance and Type Predictive Equations*. Behaviordyne Technical Report, November.

———. 1982. *Validity and Reliability in Computer-Generated Narrative Personality Reports*. Behaviordyne Technical Report, January.

Most, R.B. and S.D. Schultz, 1982. *Psychological Screening of Nuclear Plant Employees: Some Statistical Evidence of Utility*. Behaviordyne Technical Report, January.

Most, R.B., S.D. Schultz, and M. Tondow. 1980. *The Development and Validation of Pre-Employment Screening Indices.* Behaviordyne Technical Report, July.

Myers, I.B. 1980. *Gifts Differing*. Palo Alto, Calif.: Consulting Psychologists Press.

Pfeiffer, J.W., R. Heslin, and J.E. Jones. 1976. *Instrumentation in Human Relations Training.* La Jolla, Calif.: University Associates.

Pfeiffer, J.W. and J.E. Jones, Eds. 1976. *The 1976 Annual Handbook for Group Facilitators.* La Jolla, Calif.: University Associates.

Primoff, E.S. 1975. *Job Element Methods. Volume 3: The J-Coefficient.* Washington, D.C.: Personnel Research and Development Center, U.S. Civil Service Commission.

Questions and Answers on the Uniform Guidelines on Employee Selection Procedures. 1979. *Federal Register* 44: 11996–12009.

Rawls, D.J. and J.R. Rawls. 1968. "Personality Characteristics and Personal History Data of Successful and Less Successful Executives." *Psychological Reports* 23: 1032–34.

Ryan, L.R. 1977. *Clinical Interpretation of the FIRO-B.* Palo Alto, Calif.: Consulting Psychologists Press.

Schwartz, D. 1981. "Human Resources: One Company's Approach." Paper given to the San Francisco State University Industrial/Organizational Psychology Colloquium Conference '81, April 10, 1981.

Smith, P.C. 1976. "Behaviors, Results, and Organizational Effectiveness: The Problem of Criteria." In *Handbook of Industrial and Organizational Psychology*, edited by M.S. Dunnette. Chicago: Rand McNally.

Spielberger, C.D. 1979. *Police Selection and Evaluation: Issues and Techniques.* New York: Praeger/Holt, Reinhart and Winston.

Thompson, A.S., R.H. Lindeman, D.E. Super, J.P. Jordaan, and R.A. Myer. 1981. *Career Development Inventory, Volume 1: User's Manual.* Palo Alto, Calif.: Consulting Psychologists Press.

Tondow, M. 1979. "Mental Health in the World of Work: A Description and a Proposal." Presented at the 1979 Convention, California State Psychological Association, Monterey.

Uniform Guidelines on Employee Selection Procedures (1978). 1978. FEP 401:2231. *Federal Register*, August 25, 1978.

Vitales, M.S. 1932. *Industrial Psychology*. New York: W.W. Norton.

Vroom, V.H. 1976. "Leadership." In *Handbook of Industrial and Organizational Psychology*, edited by M.S. Dunnette. Chicago: Rand McNally.

Watson, G. and E.M. Glaser. 1964. *Watson-Glaser Critical Thinking Appraisal.* New York: Harcourt, Brace and World.

Conclusion

The organization and selections of this book were intended to give the reader a state-of-the-art explication of what occupational clinical psychology is and what it is doing. It should be clear that occupational clinical psychology is certainly in its infancy. It remains a malleable, adaptable, flexible, and pragmatic branch of clinical psychology. The selections in this book by no means exhaust the field. There are a number of important applications of occupational clinical psychology missing: (1) occupational crisis intervention, for crises such as that at Three Mile Island and at various bank branches following a robbery; (2) the use of nonmediated audiovisual training programs for employed people aimed at health enhancement, leadership, etc.; (3) the types of counseling programs aimed at assisting women and minorities in their occupational development; (4) the use of corporate simulation models for training better leaders; (5) marketing and cost-benefit questions—and many more. Although occupational clinical psychology is in its infancy, it is a loud and gregarious infant!

Although occupational clinical psychology is different from clinical psychological interventions as practiced in other settings, it should be clear that its roots are unquestionably in clinical psychology. There certainly will be opportunities for interested, able, and adequately trained psychologists in the future, given that the field is slow in developing. Business is tentative in its judgments, and occupational clinical psychology is still being tested in our nation's organizations. It is certain, too, that occupational clinical psychology has much to learn from industrial organizational psychology, worksite social work programs, and occupational psychiatry and medicine. These disciplines have been involved at the worksite for a much longer period of time, yet there remain major contributions to be made. As clinical psychology's interventions become more behavioral and immediately visible in their impacts, organizations will eagerly embrace the field.

The easiest route for one to take into occupational clinical psychology is first and foremost, through a sufficient grounding in clinical psychology, preferably at the doctoral level. Some business experience, regardless at what level, is always helpful as a precursor—it assists the psychologist in experiencing, firsthand, the joys and dilemmas of organizational life. Following completion of the doctorate, an occupational clinical psychology internship would be ideal; however, there are only two such programs known to the author. It is also critical that aspiring occupational clinical psychologists supplement their training by learning more about alcoholism and career counseling, behavioral interventions, the administrative process, and the business as an organization.

Certainly, one of the easiest ways to "bring psychology to the people" is through their workplace. It is here where we may have the most profound and enduring influence. Occupational clinical psychology can and has made major contributions to corporate health, organizational research, leadership development, productivity, quality of work life, and public relations. This can only continue with the attention and dedication of interested psychologists. In the future, I would hope that clinical psychology programs will begin to offer courses and/or advanced tracks in occupational clinical psychology. When this occurs, liaisons will be developed with our nation's organizations, and a genuine partnership may be embarked upon benefiting both psychologists and organizations.

Index

About the Editor and Contributors

JAMES S. J. MANUSO, Ph.D.

In his position as assistant vice-president and director of program planning and development in the medical and personal concerns department of the Equitable Life Assurance Society of the United States, Dr. Manuso is responsible for conceptualizing and operationalizing health systems, programs, and policies for the Equitable. One recently developed pilot program is the wellness project in Charlotte, North Carolina, aimed at helping employees reduce their cardio-vascular risk factors by taking more responsibility for their health and its management. In his former role as chief psychologist and director of the emotional health program at Equitable, Dr. Manuso supervised a staff of professionals in the delivery of comprehensive occupational psychology services. He is the founder of industry's first in-house biofeedback laboratory and is a past president of the New York Biofeedback Society. He is a cofounder and secretary-treasurer of the Board of the American Institute of Stress.

Holding the doctorate in psychology from the Graduate Faculty of the New School for Social Research, Dr. Manuso has taught health professionals in the clinical applications of stress management utilizing biofeedback. He is presently completing a masters degree in business at the Columbia University Graduate School of Business.

MARK J. CARSMAN, Ph.D., is a career counselor and director of Career Information Services at Mainstream Access, a New York City based career consulting firm.

MITCHELL I. CLIONSKY, Ph.D., is a senior in-patient psychologist at Baystate Medical Center in Springfield, Massachusetts, where he is also codirector of the hospital's neuropsychology laboratory. He is an assistant clinical professor of psychiatry at Tuft's University Medical School and also practices privately.

JUDITH A. DeSIMONE, M.B.A., is a consultant to the private and public sectors, specializing in the areas of employee mobility, relocation, and executive development.

G. LAWRENCE FISHER, Ph.D., is an employee health consultant presently serving as coordinator of the employee assistance program of the National Bureau of Standards and on the faculty of the department of psychiatry at Johns Hopkins University School of Medicine.

HOWARD I. GLAZER, Ph.D., is president of Corporate Stress Control Services, Inc., a stress management service organization based in New York City.

ROBERT S. GRAHAM, M.D., is vice-president and principal medical officer of the Equitable Life Assurance Society of the United States.

RONALD M. KADDEN, Ph.D., is an associate professor of psychiatry (psychology) at the University of Connecticut School of Medicine.

HARRY LEVINSON, Ph.D., is the "grandfather premier" of occupational clinical psychology and president of the Levinson Institute in Cambridge, Mass.

DONALD M. MICHAEL was director of NEXUS during the period described in Chapter 21 and is emeritus professor of planning and public policy at the University of Michigan.

DONALD A. MONACO, Ed.D., is a senior vice-president specializing in outplacement counseling with Drake Beam Morin, Inc. in New York.

HENRY MORGAN, Ph.D., is an industrial organizational psychologist and principal in the New York based consulting firm, McCabe Morgan Associates.

ROBERT B. MOST, Ph.D., is director of research and marketing for Behaviordyne, Inc. in San Francisco, where he is on the faculty of the Pacific Graduate School of Psychology.

MURRAY P. NADITCH, Ph.D., is director of design and evaluation in the health care services division of the Control Data Corporation in Minneapolis.

STEVEN C. NAHRWOLD, Ph.D., is director of the employee counseling service at Chicago's Continental Bank.

ALINA NOVAK, B.A., is a financial analyst with the Equitable Life Assurance Society of the United States and the founder of "Networks," a self-formed group of Equitable women and men.

JOHN O'NEIL is president of the San Francisco based California School of Professional Psychology.

KENNETH R. PELLETIER, Ph.D., is a director of the Psychosomatic Medicine Clinic in Berkeley and an assistant clinical professor in the department of psychiatry at the University of California's Langley Porter Psychiatric Institute in San Francisco.

OVIDE F. POMERLEAU, Ph.D., is a professor of psychiatry (psychology) at the University of Connecticut School of Medicine and chief of psychology and behavioral medicine at the Veteran's Administration Medical Center in Newington, Connecticut.

MARILYN PUDER, Ph.D., is assistant vice-president in charge of the staff advisory service, the employee counseling program for Citicorp, based in New York.

JEROME M. ROSOW is president of the Scarsdale based Work in America Institute, Inc.

LAWRENCE M. SCHLEIFER, Ed.D., is a research fellow in the motivation and stress research section of the National Institute for Occupational Safety and Health in Cincinnati.

HAROLD V. SCHMITZ, Ph.D., is director of personnel research and development at Con Edison in New York.

GARY E. SCHWARTZ, Ph.D., is a professor of psychology and psychiatry at Yale University where he is also director of the Psychophysiology Center.

PAUL A. SHERMAN, Ph.D., heads his own consulting firm in Rye, New York. Dr. Sherman is a past president of the Association of Labor-Management Administrators and Consultants on Alcoholism and was formerly director of IT & T's alcoholism and behavioral medical programs.

MARTHA B. SHERWOOD, Ph.D., is in the medical department of the Equitable Life Assurance Society of the United States.

MICHAEL J. SMITH, Ph.D., is chief of the motivation and stress research section of the National Institute for Occupational Safety and Health and assistant clinical professor of environmental health at the University of Cincinnati.

JOSEPH YEAGER, Ph.D., is a psychology consultant in New York. He serves as the chief psychologist for Pfizer, Inc.